Western Marxism and the Soviet Union

First published in 2007 by Brill Academic Publishers
© 2007 Koninklijke Brill NV, Leiden, The Netherlands

Published in paperback in 2009 by Haymarket Books
P.O. Box 180165
Chicago, IL 60618
773-583-7884
www.haymarketbooks.org
ISBN 978-1-931859-69-1

Trade distribution:
In the U.S. through Consortium Book Sales, www.cbsd.com
In the UK, Turnaround Publisher Services, www.turnaround-psl.com
In Australia, Palgrave MacMillan, www.palgravemacmillan.com.au
In all other countries, Publishers Group Worldwide
www.pgw.com/home/worldwide.aspx

Cover image of a painting by Kazimir Malevich, *Morning in the Village after Snowstorm* in 1912, oil on canvas, courtesy Solomon R. Guggenheim Museum, New York.

This book was published with the generous support of the Wallace Global Fund.

Printed in Canada on recycled paper containing 100 percent post-consumer waste in accordance with the guidelines of the Green Press Initiative, www.greenpressinitiative.org.

Special discounts are available for bulk purchases by organizations and institutions. Please contact Haymarket Books for more information at 773-583-7884 or info@haymarketbooks.org.

10 9 8 7 6 5 4 3 2 1

The hardcover edition was catalogued by Library of Congress as follows:
van der Linden, Marcel
    Western marxism and the Soviet Union / by Marcel van der Linden.
        p. cm. -- (Historical materialism)
    Includes bibliographical references and index.

HX314.L57 2008
335.430947--dc22

                                        2008010318

Recycle logo

Western Marxism
and the Soviet Union

A Survey of Critical Theories
and Debates Since 1917

by

Marcel van der Linden

Translated by

Jurriaan Bendien

Haymarket Books
Chicago, IL

Historical Materialism
Book Series

More than ten years after the collapse of the Berlin Wall and the disappearance of Marxism as a (supposed) state ideology, a need for a serious and long-term Marxist book publishing program has risen. Subjected to the whims of fashion, most contemporary publishers have abandoned any of the systematic production of Marxist theoretical work that they may have indulged in during the 1970s and early 1980s. The Historical Materialism book series addresses this great gap with original monographs, translated texts and reprints of "classics." At least three titles will be published every year. For more details, see http://www.brill.nl/download/HiMaBookseries.pdf.

Editorial board: Paul Blackledge, Leeds; Sebastian Budgen, London; Jim Kincaid, Leeds; Stathis Kouvelakis, Paris; Marcel van der Linden, Amsterdam; China Miéville, London; Paul Reynolds, Lancashire.

Haymarket Books is proud to be working with Brill Academic Publishers (http://www.brill.nl) and the journal *Historical Materialism* on the new Historical Materialism Book Series. This is Haymarket's fifth paperback edition of a title initiated in hardcover by Brill.

Other titles in the series from Haymarket Books include:
The Theory of Revolution in the Young Marx • Michael Löwy
Between Equal Rights: A Marxist Theory of International Law • China Miéville
The German Revolution 1917–1923 • Pierre Broué
Lenin Rediscovered: What Is to be Done? *in Context* • Lars T. Lih

Haymarket Books will republish the following titles in Brill's Historical Materialism series in paperback in 2009:
Witnesses to Permanent Revolution: The Documentary Record, Edited and translated by Richard B. Day and Daniel Gaido • *Following Marx: Method, Critique and Crisis*, Michael A. Lebowitz • *Alasdair MacIntyre's Engagement with Marxism*, Edited by Paul Blackledge and Neil Davidson • *Criticism of Heaven*, Roland Boer • *Critical Companion to Contemporary Marxism*, Edited by Jacques Bidet and Stathis Kouvelakis • *Impersonal Power*, Heide Gerstenberger • *Exploring Marx's Capital*, Jacques Bidet • *Althusser: The Detour of Theory*, Gregory Elliott • *A Marxist Philosophy of Language*, Jean-Jacques Lecercle • *Marxism and Ecological Economics*, Paul Burkett • *Globalisation: A Systematic Marxian Account*, Tony Smith • *The Clash of Globalisations*, Ray Kiely • *Utopia Ltd.*, Matthew Beaumont • *Pavel V. Maksakovsky: The Capitalist Cycle*, Translated with introduction and commentary by Robert B. Day • *Making History*, Alex Callinicos • *The New Dialectic and Marx's* Capital, Christopher J. Arthur

Contents

Chapter 4
From the 'Great Patriotic War' to the Structural Assimilation of Eastern Europe (1941–56)

Preface

A large part of this book was first published in Dutch in 1989; a German edition appeared in 1992. This revised, corrected and expanded English edition was realised thanks to the initiative and enthusiasm of Sebastian Budgen.

In writing and revising the manuscript, I was fortunate to be able to discuss and correspond with many scholars and activists whose comments proved invaluable. My special thanks go to Jürgen Baumgarten, Ray Challinor, Paresh Chattopadhyay, the late Tony Cliff, Peter Drucker, Neil Fernandez, Helmut Fleischer, the late Duncan Hallas, Mike Haynes, Idar Helle, Joost Kircz, Knut Kjeldstadli, Bernd Klemm, Peter Kulemann, Per-Åke Lindblom, the late Ernest Mandel, the late Gottfried Mergner, Wilbert van Miert, Alice Mul, Pierre Rousset, Jørgen Sandemose, Jan Willem Stutje, Kariin Sundsback, Fritjof Tichelman, Hillel Ticktin, the late Paul Verbraeken, Els Wagenaar, Hermann Weber, the late Adam Westoby, and the late Pierre Frank.

However, my gratitude goes most of all to Jurriaan Bendien; I could not have wished myself a more able and dedicated translator.

Chapter One

Introduction

> Where there is much desire to learn, there of
> necessity will be much arguing, much writing,
> many opinions; for opinion in good men is
> but knowledge in the making [...]. What some
> lament of, we should rather rejoice at. [...]
> Yet these are the men cried out against for
> schismatics and sectaries.
>
> John Milton, 1644

The 'Russian Question'[1] was an absolutely central
problem for Marxism in the twentieth century.
It was, as Castoriadis put it, 'the touchstone of
theoretical and practical attitudes which lay claim
to revolution'.[2] For that reason, it is all the more
astonishing that, until this very day, not one scholar
has tried to portray the historical development of
Marxist thought about the Soviet Union since 1917
in a coherent, comprehensive appraisal.[3] Quite
possibly, this lacuna in the literature has less to do with
the specific topic area than with the underdeveloped

---

[1] The terms 'Russia' and 'the Soviet Union' are here and there used interchangeably
in this study for stylistic reasons.

[2] 'Introduction', in Castoriadis 1973, p. 18.

[3] Beyerstedt 1987 is a useful attempt for the period 1924–53. However, the author
mistakenly assumes that in countries like Britain 'no noteworthy contributions to the
characterization of the Soviet Union were made' (p. 21).

historiography of Marxist theories generally. Anderson concluded years ago in his *Considerations on Western Marxism* that 'the causes and forms of [Marxism's] successive metamorphoses and transferences remain largely unexplored'.[4] Likewise, in the history of ideas Marxist theories have not received the attention they deserve.[5]

Nevertheless, not only the primary literature, but also the secondary literature about 'Western Marxism and the Soviet Union' is quite extensive, as can be easily verified from the bibliography at the end of this study. Taken as a whole, the relevant contributions fall into four different categories. Firstly, studies concerned with the genealogy of one particular theory. Special attention is usually devoted to the theory of state capitalism.[6] Secondly, studies which – often with a polemical purpose – concentrate on the comparison of some theories considered important.[7] Thirdly, a proportionally large number of studies concerned with the theory of one particular Marxist author. Most works of this type focus on early critics of Russia or the Soviet Union, such as Luxemburg, Pannekoek, or Trotsky. But much has also been written about contemporary authors such as Bahro. Fourthly, there are sparse attempts to make an objective inventory of diverse theories. The qualitatively best example of this genre is Gerd Meyer's textbook, which seeks to provide an overview of 'the most important models of interpretation for the socialist system'; in Meyer's work, various views are first presented by means of fragments of texts, then criticised, and finally included or abandoned in the author's own theory.[8]

From the many contributions which counterpose different theories, it is evident that there has been a strong temptation in the literature to press the available material into an *a priori* schema. David McLellan for example is guilty of this approach, when he distinguishes only two main currents in 'Marxist critiques of the Soviet Union' which 'lean to one side or the other of the capitalist/socialist divide'. As a result, a label is inappropriately forced on

---

[4] Anderson 1976, p. 1.

[5] Thus Hansen (1985, p. 143) writes that Marxist theories of capitalist collapse, 'like the broader Marxist perspective of which they are a part, have led a marginal life in the history of ideas'.

[6] Jerome and Buick 1967; Farl 1973; Olle 1974; Ambrosius 1981.

[7] Bellis 1979; Binns and Haynes 1980.

[8] Meyer 1979.

authors who in truth regarded themselves as being outside the two camps.[9] The same trend appears in the work by René Ahlberg, who distinguishes three currents (transitional society, state capitalism and bureaucratic collectivism) and is thereby forced to label Hillel Ticktin's analysis as 'Trotskyist'.[10]

In this study, I have tried to avoid such Procrustian methods; and, as the amount of material I investigated accumulated, this task also became increasingly easier. By giving primacy to the *genetic* aspect, continuities and turning points in traditions could be traced more accurately, with the result that the question of classification criteria in part resolved itself quite 'naturally'. Gradually, it dawned on me that the division into three types of theories, found not only in Ahlberg but also among numerous other authors – and which I initially believed to be correct – simplified the developments too much; at any rate, it does not enable us to understand the developments since World War II very well. Be that as it may, in preparing this study I have obviously benefited greatly from earlier contributions with a similar aim, however variable their quality may be judged to be.

My own inquiry diverges from earlier research. It aims to present the development of the Western-Marxist critique of the Soviet Union across a rather long period in history (from 1917 to the present) and in a large region (Western Europe and North America). Within this demarcation of limits in time and space, an effort has been made to ensure completeness, by paying attention to all Marxist analyses which in some way significantly deviated from or added to the older contributions.[11] It is not my primary aim to appraise earlier contributions with regard to their utility for my own theory, although, as the reconstruction advances, it becomes increasingly clear that some approaches withstand the test of criticism better than others.

The concept of 'Western Marxism' is used in different ways. It is commonly taken to refer to a group of Western authors who applied themselves to the study and critique of cultural and ideological developments. This interpretation would exclude authors who analysed questions of economics, politics and social power.[12] Sometimes, however, the accent is placed instead on political

---

[9] Bruno Rizzi, for example. See McLellan 1983, pp. 173–6.
[10] Ahlberg 1979, p. 87.
[11] Publications which repeat older ideas without providing new arguments are not discussed, but are often mentioned in the bibliography.
[12] See Anderson 1976; Russell Jacoby 1981.

geography, and 'Western Marxism' is then understood as 'non-Soviet, or non-Soviet-like Marxist thought' in the West.[13] This second definition is the one followed here. It provides the problematic of 'Western Marxism and the Soviet Union' with its symmetry: my inquiry in this study concerns how Marxists who were politically independent of the Soviet Union theoretically interpreted developments in the Soviet Union.

But the category 'non-Soviet, or non-Soviet-like, Marxist thought' itself requires more precise definition. In the first instance, one might well ask what the terms 'non-Soviet' and 'non-Soviet-like' really refer to. In the context of this study, I have defined them operationally as (a) not conforming to the official Soviet ideology, and (b) not regarding the social structure of the Soviet Union either as socialist, or as developing towards socialism. More difficult is, secondly, the question of what 'Marxist' means, in particular because it often happened in the past that one author accused another of failing to argue in a 'Marxist' way.[14] I have circumvented this whole problem in part by regarding all those writers as 'Marxist' who considered themselves as such. Still, some authors never *explicitly* claimed to be Marxists. In those cases, I have followed the interpretation of Howard Bernstein, who distinguishes five 'core concepts' which in combination imply a Marxist approach to historical questions:

1. Material factors and economic and social forces determine the direction and tempo of historical developments.
2. History consists of a specific series of successive social formations.
3. The transition from one social formation to another is a dialectical process.
4. The transition from one social formation to another involves class struggle.
5. Equilibrium and stasis are illusory; change and transformation of the essence of reality are the social norm.[15]

In cases of doubt, I have consistently applied these five notions as criteria; in one case, I have, on these grounds, included an author among the Marxists

---

[13] Merquior 1986, p. 1.

[14] In this study, I distinguish between 'Marxian' thought (which literally corresponds to Marx's own) and 'Marxist' thought which pretends to follow Marx's general approach, although in particular cases it may deviate greatly from Marx's own views.

[15] Bernstein 1981, p. 445.

who himself regarded his work as a final reckoning with Marxism (James Burnham).

I discuss only 'Western-Marxist' authors from North America and Western Europe, and authors from other regions (in particular, Eastern Europe and the Soviet Union) whose work was published in North America and/or Western Europe, or made accessible through translations.[16]

Essential for this study is a long-term perspective. By following the developments of Western-Marxist thought from 1917 to 2005, I aim to identify continuities and changes that would remain obscured if a shorter time-frame was adopted.

The analysis of Western-Marxist thought about the Soviet Union offered here is primarily an analysis of texts. Like all texts, they evolve within many different contexts, varying from their relationship to the intentions, the life and the other works by the author to the culture and society surrounding the author.[17] Although a complete examination of 'the' context of a text is therefore virtually impossible, it remains important for an historical-critical assessment to reveal contextual relationships which, at least to some extent (in a non-deterministic sense), explain why a given text acquired its specific content. In the case of a topic such as the political and economic nature of the Soviet Union, it is obvious that the most relevant contextual relationships are very likely to be political and economic in the first instance. In this study I have therefore adopted as working hypothesis that *three* contextual clusters strongly influenced 'Western-Marxist' theorising about the Soviet Union.

a) *The general theory of the forms of society (modes of production) and their succession.* This cluster involves many aspects, but as will become evident in what follows, in the debate about the Soviet Union the question of the sequence of types of society was especially important. Marxist thought in this respect showed three phases since about 1917. (i) Until the beginning of the 1930s, different interpretations co-existed; some, including politically diverging personalities like Kautsky and Lenin, believed that development occurred in a unilinear way – namely, through the sequence slave society

---

[16] I have made an effort to obtain an overview of the relevant literature in Swedish, Norwegian, Danish, German, Dutch, English, French, German, Spanish and Italian. I have neither attempted to survey the recent Russian discussions, nor older dissident texts which since the 1920s were circulated in the Soviet Union on a small scale, and which are now gradually becoming known.

[17] Lacapra 1983.

feudalism capitalism socialism; others (the *Aziatchiki*) identified a second possible line of development with the 'Asiatic mode of production' as its pivot; a few (e.g. Wittfogel) took this idea further and assumed three possible historical paths of development. (ii) From the 1930s until the second half of the 1950s, unilinear thinking dominated almost completely although, here and there, some Marxists continued to maintain the existence of an 'Asiatic mode of production'. (iii) At the end of the 1950s, the disintegration of the conception of a uniform sequence of development (unilinearism) began. After an initial phase, in which the 'Asiatic mode of production' was rediscovered and treated by many as a panacea for the analytical difficulties, a stormy period of theoretical development followed which resulted in the 'discovery' of more and more modes of production, culminating in the questioning of the validity of the old theory of modes of production itself. The reason why this course of events is so important for the subject of this study is that the general theory of the (consecutive) modes of production can be considered a priori to have determined how Soviet society as mode of production was assigned its place in history. If unilinear thinking was consistently applied, then Soviet society could only be feudal, capitalist or socialist. But, if the Soviet Union was defined as a form of society of a new type, this simultaneously meant abandoning unilinearism.

b) *The perception of stability and dynamism of Western capitalism.* Broadly speaking, this perception went through four stages since 1917. (i) In the first stage, which only ended in the beginning of the 1950s, a pattern of perceptions dominated emphasising the decay, decline and disintegration of a system ruled by generalised commodity production. The brief economic recovery after Word War I was succeeded by a serious crisis, which reached its deepest point in 1929. The 'Great Crash' that followed was overcome only in the second half of the 1930s. But shortly thereafter, World War II broke out. The immediate postwar years did not at all suggest that a general and long-term recovery was in the making; economic growth remained weak, and threatened at the beginning of the 1950s to lapse into a rather serious recession in the United States. It is therefore unsurprising to find that the vitality of capitalism was considered minimal through this whole period.[18] In the Marxist camp, the period from the October Revolution until about 1952

---

[18] This applied not only to orthodox Marxists. See Cannadine 1984, pp. 142–3.

was dominated by thinking in terms of the 'death agony' and 'collapse' of capitalism. A well-known and extreme example was Henryk Grossman, who, at the end of the 1920s, devised a formula with which he believed he could compute the time of the final collapse of capitalism, if numerical values for the variables ('elements') in his model could be established.[19] Very typical also was the assessment by Trotsky, who, in his *Transitional Programme* of 1938, portrayed the world situation as follows: 'Mankind's productive forces stagnate. Already new inventions and improvements fail to raise the level of material wealth. [...]. The bourgeoisie itself sees no way out.'[20]

(ii) The second stage began at the start of the 1950s, and lasted approximately until the end of the 1960s. This period of historically unprecedented economic growth, growing prosperity and low unemployment in the developed capitalist countries caused the consensus to change somewhat. Apart from Marxists who, despite appearances to the contrary, continued to adhere to the previous conception of the epoch, more and more new theoreticians emerged who increasingly doubted the validity of the old classical crisis theory.[21] In a much commented-on empirical study of the rate of profit, Gillman, for example, postulated in 1957 that: 'whereas for the years before about World War I the historical statistics seem fully to support these theories of Marx, after that war the series studied appear generally to behave in contradiction to the Marxist expectations'.[22] A few years later, Baran and Sweezy took this argument further, concluding that, in monopoly capitalism, 'the surplus tends to rise both absolutely and relatively as the system develops'.[23]

(iii) During the third phase from the end of the 1960s, there was again a widespread belief that capitalism is inextricably bound up with economic

---

[19] Grossmann 1929, pp. 198–225.

[20] Trotsky 1938c, p. 1; English translation, p. 111.

[21] 'Most striking, perhaps, were the intellectual reversals by two men who in the 1930s had been immensely influential in persuading the thinking public of the inevitable collapse of capitalism and the necessity of socialism. One was John Strachey, whose book *The Coming Struggle for Power* (1933) became a best-seller in the Depression, and Lewis Corey, whose *Decline of American Capitalism* (1932) argued that an irreversible crisis had set in because of the falling rate of profit. Twenty years later, both men had become proponents of the mixed economy and of economic planning, but, as Corey put it, "without statism".' – Bell 1988, pp. 137–8.

[22] Gillman 1957, p. vii.

[23] Baran and Sweezy 1966, p. 72. By 'surplus' Baran and Sweezy understood not surplus-value in the Marxian sense, but 'the difference between what a society produces and the costs of producing it' (p. 9).

crises. (iv) Although this belief has not disappeared since then, many concluded during the 1990s that capitalism would continue to dominate the world for some time to come.

c) *The way in which the stability and dynamism of Soviet society was perceived.* This cluster can also be divided into four phases. Because each phase is discussed in detail in the course of this study, I will limit myself here to given only a brief indication. (i) The first period lasted until the beginning of the 1930s; society in these years seemed rather chaotic and badly organised. (ii) The second period runs to 1956, the year of Khruschev's revelations at the Twentieth Congress of the CPSU; in this phase, Stalinism seemed to have consolidated its power, and Soviet society seemed to be transformed into a 'planned' totality. (iii) The third phase starting in the 1950s, showed social ruptures, gradually more and more clear political and economic problems of regulation, as well as attempts at reform which constantly failed in important ways. (iv) The last phase, since the mid-1980s, clarified that a very deep crisis was occurring, which culminated in a total collapse. Most probably, each of these phases influenced Marxist theorising, as I will try to substantiate in the course of this study.

These three contextual clusters taken together influenced the authors who produced Marxist theoretical texts about the nature of Soviet society. It is important to note here, however, that these authors generally did not operate in isolation, but were part of a broader community of Western Marxists who thought about these kinds of political problems.[24]

---

[24] The question then suggests itself as to whether it would be pertinent to apply Kuhn's model of a 'paradigm' in this study. In brief, I do not think so. The concept of a 'paradigm' has been used to denote all kinds of aspects of theory-formation. But this wide application of the concept meant that it ceased to refer to anything in particular. The confusion surrounding the term can be partly blamed on Kuhn himself, who, in his *The Structure of Scientific Revolutions* (1962), used the concept in no less than twenty-one different meanings (Masterman 1977, pp. 61–5). Acknowledging the problems created by this vagueness, Kuhn later tried to provide a more adequate definition. In a 1969 postscript to the new edition of his book, he wrote: 'A paradigm is what members of a scientific community share, *and*, conversely, a scientific community consists of men who share a paradigm.' ('Postscript' [1969], in Kuhn 1970, p. 176.) A paradigm is defined here as a scientific practice, in which, according to the description given in the original work 'law, theory, application, and instrumentation together' form a strict cohesive totality (Kuhn 1970, p. 10). In Kuhn's 1969 postscript, the 'scientific community' itself is defined as: 'the members of a scientific community see themselves and are seen by others as the men uniquely responsible for the pursuit of a set of shared goals, including the training of their successors. Within such groups

The further architecture of this study is as follows: Chapters 2 to 7 provide the substance of the text, reconstructing the Western-Marxist debate about the Soviet Union. Chapter 8 draws out the main lines in this reconstruction, and an appendix provides an initial meta-theoretical model of the developments described. The study is completed with a bibliography, as complete as possible, of Western-Marxist theoretical writings about the nature of the Soviet Union published since 1917.

Finally, a few technical comments. As I am quite aware that there exist no universally accepted rules for the analysis of texts – beyond the need to represent the writings studied as accurately as possible – I tried with each author to find an answer to a small number of questions essential for the subject of my inquiry, namely: (i) what is the place given to the Soviet Union in the pattern of the successive modes of production; (ii) are essential class antagonisms seen to exist in Soviet society, and if so, which; (iii) what did the author believe to be the dynamic (the 'motor') of Soviet society?[25] In some cases, I was unable to identify any explicit answer to all these questions by a given author. In reconstructing the different interpretations, I have not hesitated to quote succinct passages, in order to provide the reader with a direct impression of the style of discourse being examined.

Authors who permanently used a pseudonym (Laurat, Trotsky, Dunayevskaya, Cliff) are indicated with that pseudonym. Quotations from texts originally

communication is relatively full and professional judgement relatively autonomous.' (Ibid., p. 177) Although these descriptions still cannot be considered totally free from ambiguity, they do at least clarify that the concept of a paradigm is best avoided here. Firstly, the critiques of the Soviet Union I discuss were in no way comparable to the theories in natural science that Kuhn had in mind, even just because these critiques did not enable a logical transition to empirical research; if anything, a significant gap existed between critical theorising and empirical research. Moreover, Kuhn's 'scientific community' did not exist in the case of Western Marxism; involved was neither an *academic* community, nor a *community* in the sense of mutually shared aims and criteria. Instead, mainly political activists were involved, more or less organised in small political groups or belonging to a circle around a journal, who quarrelled with each other about many issues, and, in some cases, did not communicate with each other at all. So, using the concept of a 'paradigm' would be misleading in this study, rather than helping the inquiry. Instead, I have preferred to use concepts like (political) *theory*, *discourse* and *argumentation*. In my opinion, these concepts create fewer misleading associations than the notion of a paradigm.

[25] Given that Marxism is first and foremost a political theory, a number of authors referred to here not only analysed the Soviet Union, but also formulated ideas about the socialist strategy to be followed. In representing the various standpoints, I have nevertheless focused on the analysis made, and not the strategic proposals.

published in French, German, Italian, Norwegian and Dutch have been translated into English, with a reference to the original text. Where it seemed pertinent, published English translations have been substituted. In cases of linguistic difficulty or where the original text of an author was not available, I have cited from a translation and indicated as much in the notes.

Chapter Two

From the October Revolution to the Stalin Era (1917–29)

The years 1917–29 marked an era in which the social situation in the Soviet Union was uncertain and unstable in every respect. Initially, the new régime expected to be freed rapidly from its political isolation by a revolution in Western Europe. But this revolution failed to occur. Threats of foreign intervention were a constant factor. When the chaotic years of 'war communism' had passed, the period of the New Economic Policy followed, with its intense conflict between the state and market sectors. There was no 'planned development' at that time.

If the Soviet Union differed from Western capitalist countries, the difference seemed to consist especially in a proportionally large state sector in the economy, and in the fact that the new leaders of the state apparatus had conquered power through an uprising of workers and peasants, appealing to Marxism (and later Leninism). Social organisational forms which, in the 1930s, were to give the Soviet Union a new appearance (collectivised farming, five year plans) were at that stage still unknown, and could not be foreseen by anyone. The very idea of another type of society that would be *neither* capitalist *nor* socialist therefore also did not emerge. Thus, the Marxist debate remained locked in the unilinear schema: oppositionist critiques of developments in the Soviet Union focused mainly on whether the October Revolution had been either bourgeois or socialist, or whether a potentially proletarian revolution was degenerating into a bourgeois one, due to various possible factors (such as the absence of a West-European revolution, and political mistakes by the Bolshevik leaders). The idea that the unilinear schema itself might in reality be inapplicable, was not admitted as a possibility in this discussion; but that idea itself could hardly have been conceived of, given the reality of social relations in the Soviet Union at that time.

2.i. Kautsky and the Bolsheviks: three controversies

From 1918, Karl Kautsky carried on a persistent 'ideological crusade against bolshevism', as Salvadori put it.[1] In an impressive series of pamphlets, several books and numerous articles published in among others *Der Kampf* and *Die Gesellschaft*, he showed increasing concern about the issue. Some attention had already been devoted to these writings by Kautsky in the existing literature.[2] I will concentrate here on the aspect essential in the context of my inquiry, which, in a way, expresses the 'special charm' of the old Kautsky: the consistent application of the unilinear schema to all social change.

Kautsky's reasoning was, precisely because of its strongly schematic character, very predictable:

a) Socialism can only be established in a highly developed capitalist society.
b) Russia in 1917 was not a highly developed capitalist society.
c) *Ergo*, the Bolshevik attempt to force the establishment of socialism through a *coup d'état* promulgated as a 'revolution' could only result in an historically impossible bastardised formation.[3]

---

[1] Karl Kautsky (1854–1938) was for a long time regarded as the 'pope' of international Social Democracy. He was in 1883 the founder, and until 1917 the chief editor of *Die Neue Zeit*, the journal which functioned as the theoretical organ of the German Social Democracy. When the SPD split in 1917, Kautsky joined the left wing (the Independent Social-Democratic Party of Germany, the USPD) and in 1922 he followed a part of the USPD which reunified with the right wing. See for biographical information among others Gilcher-Holtey 1987; Panaccione 1987.

[2] The most in-depth discussion is Salvadori 1978, pp. 218–25, 251–312. Less extensive are Waldschmidt 1966, pp. 81–99, 101–24, and Steenson 1978, pp. 201–11, 229–31.

[3] Summarising, Salvadori refers, to a 'régime "*monstrum*"': it was ideologically managed by a radical socialist party, but it was socially impossible to establish

d) This bastardised formation would necessarily be unstable, and would, after a short time, disintegrate.[4]

Kautsky's linear reasoning was elaborated especially in his polemical confrontations with Bolshevik authors. I will briefly discuss three of these debates: successively, those with Lenin, with Trotsky and with Bukharin. The last-mentioned polemical exchange has hitherto been almost unnoticed in the historical literature.

Kautsky versus Lenin

Contrary to accusations by the Bolsheviks – namely that Kautsky had discarded his revolutionary past, and had become a 'renegade' – his analyses after 1917 were actually remarkably consistent with those he made before 1917. Obviously, his ideas did evolve to some extent, but there was no evidence of any genuine new departure in his thinking:

> It is of course indisputable [...] that Kautsky's positions did gradually shift in a moderate direction. But it is also undeniable that this shift occurred within a framework of a general conception of socialism, democracy, and the state which was, from the very outset (taking the Erfurt Programme as its fundamental starting point) of such a character as to be irreconcilable with 1917. Kautsky could be accused of immobility, but not of having abandoned the fundamental lines of his conception of the revolutionary process, the dictatorship of the proletariat, and the socialist state.[5]

---

relationships of production in the socialist sense, and it was organized politically as an absolutist-despotic system.' Salvadori 1973, p. 77.

[4] Again and again, Kautsky, who once confessed he felt himself to be a lone Marxist Cassandra, predicted the rapid collapse of the Bolshevik system. Some quotations by way of illustration: 'We have to reckon with the collapse of the communist dictatorship in the foreseeable future. Just exactly when, we don't know. It could happen sooner or take longer than anticipated. But one thing is clear: since Bolshevism has gone over its limits and finds itself on the rise, the tempo of its demise must naturally also accelerate', Kautsky 1921, p. 77. '[...] [T]he Bolshevik regime [...] is a giant with clay feet, which cannot survive a serious crisis, yet is also unable to regenerate itself. The first major crisis that it experiences must lead it to catastrophe.' Kautsky 1925a, p. 380. 'Bolshevism is heading towards its end. [...] Neither white-guard Bonapartism nor legitimism will replace Soviet rule. Elections will however lead to chaos for the state, as soon as the red sovereigns of the Kremlin lose the power to hold the state together and lead it.' Kautsky 1930, p. 258.

[5] Salvadori 1978, p. 253.

Even prior to 1905, Kautsky had postulated the necessity for a bourgeois and, broadly speaking, democratising revolution in Russia, and, in 1917 and afterwards, he had maintained this viewpoint with rigid consistency. Initially, in April 1917, when the political outcome was still uncertain, he had emphasised that the Russian peasantry was the 'wild card' in the whole process, 'variable X, the unknown magnitude, for which we cannot yet allocate a definite number'. Although the revolution could therefore still yield many surprises, Kautsky did not doubt that it was in essence a process of democratisation, and that, from its completion,

> the essential rights and freedoms of democracy, and therewith the most secure basis for the proletarian mass movement and mass organisations, as well as the proletarian rising to the conquest of political power in Eastern Europe, would be at least as solidly grounded as in the West.[6]

Nearly five months later, he repeated this belief in a different context: the Russian revolution would be primarily political in nature; it would open a new phase of democratic rights and freedoms, which would enable the proletariat to develop, to organise, and thus become 'ripe for the conquest of political power'.[7]

The seizure of power of the Bolsheviks as well as the measures that followed it (such as the dissolution of the Constituent Assembly) consequently shocked him greatly. The Bolsheviks had, Kautsky believed, made a gigantic error. In his pamphlet titled *The Dictatorship of the Proletariat*, he wrote:

> The Bolshevik revolution was based on the assumption, that it would be the point of departure for a general European revolution; that the daring initiative of Russia would rouse proletarians throughout Europe to rise up.[8]

But that idea was incorrect, he argued, specifically because it was not 'Marxist':

> There is an old Marxist axiom, that revolutions cannot be made, that they emerge from the social relations. The West European relations, however,

---

[6] Kautsky 1917a, p. 20.
[7] Kautsky 1917b, p. 507.
[8] Kautsky 1918, p. 28.

are so different from those in Russia, that a revolution there does not of necessity have to cause a revolution here. When in 1848 the revolution broke out in France, it did spread to parts of Eastern Europe. But it stopped at the Russian border. And conversely, when in 1905 the revolution was unchained [in Russia], it caused some strong movements for voting rights in the West, but nothing resembling a revolution.[9]

The Bolsheviks had therefore extended the frontlines too far. And, when their hope for a revolution in the West of Europe proved in vain, they were saddled with impossible tasks. The consequence was that they were forced to replace democracy with dictatorship – a dictatorship which had nothing to do anymore with the 'dictatorship of the proletariat' postulated by Marx. In order to substantiate his viewpoint, Kautsky distinguished between dictatorship as a *situation*, and dictatorship as a *form of government*. The first-mentioned variant referred to the dictatorship of the proletariat proper. The second variant, which was synonymous with the 'disenfranchisement of the opposition' meant something completely different. For Kautsky, the dictatorship of the proletariat was equivalent to a parliamentary democracy with a proletarian majority.[10] That Marx took the same view was proved, according to Kautsky, by Marx's stated opinion that in England and America a transition to socialism might well occur peacefully and democratically.[11]

---

[9] Kautsky 1918, pp. 28–9.

[10] Marx used the term 'dictatorship of the proletariat' in different ways. Kautsky however justifiably appeals to Marx, insofar as Marx did not envisage a one-party system. Mautner explains that 'Insofar as Marx refers to a dictatorship of the national assembly, he does not mean a left dictatorship which is exercised by its participants through abrogation of the rights of all, but much more the exclusive rule of a group (national assembly) in its own interests, of a class (bourgeoisie, proletariat) comprising the great majority of the population ("the people" or real majority).' Mautner 1926, pp. 281–2. In this context, it is also important to note that the concept of 'dictatorship' in the nineteenth century also meant more an energetic government than a despotism, and thus had a less pejorative connotation than it has today. See Draper 1962.

[11] Kautsky's reference was to the following Marx quote: 'You know that the institutions, mores, and traditions of different countries must be taken into consideration, and we do not deny that there are countries – such as America, England, and if I were more familiar with your institutions, I would perhaps also add Holland – where the workers can attain their goal by peaceful means. This being the case, we must also recognize the fact that in most countries on the Continent the lever of our revolution must be force; it is force to which we must some day appeal in order to erect the rule of labor.' Marx 1872, p. 160. Marx's speech was reported in the Brussels newspaper *La Liberté*, and in the Amsterdam newspaper *Algemeen Handelsblad*.

In his pamphlet *The Proletarian Revolution and the Renegade Kautsky*, Lenin replied angrily to the various arguments by Kautsky. Countering the accusation that the Bolsheviks had politically gone too far, Lenin argued that there had been no other possibility, given the existing social relations:

> Yes, our revolution is a bourgeois revolution, *as long as we march* with the peasantry *as a whole*. This has been as clear as clear can be to us, we have said it hundreds and thousands of times since 1905, and we have never attempted to skip this necessary stage of the historical process or abolish it by decrees. [...] But beginning with April 1917, long before the October Revolution, that is, long before we assumed power, we publicly declared and explained to the people: the revolution cannot now stop at this stage, for the country has marched forward, capitalism has advanced, ruin has reached unprecedented dimensions, which (whether one likes it or not) *will demand* steps forward, *to socialism*. For there is *no* other way of advancing, of saving the country which is exhausted by war, and of alleviating the sufferings of the toilers and exploited.[12]

Countering the accusation that the Russian post-revolutionary society was undemocratic, Lenin contended that, to the contrary, there was an unprecedented expansion and development of democracy. This was proved, he said, by the fact that foreign policy was being conducted in public, and also by the structure of the state, which involved the working masses directly in decision-making.[13] In this context, Lenin finally considered that references to Marx's statement about America and England were ahistorical, and falsely reduced the founder of scientific socialism to a 'common liberal'. The situation in both countries in the 1870s could, after all, hardly be equated with the situation that existed at the end of the World War I:

> pre-monopoly capitalism – which actually reached its zenith in the 1870s – was by virtue of its fundamental *economic* traits, which found most typical expression in Britain and in America, distinguished by a – relatively speaking – maximum fondness for peace and freedom. Imperialism, on the other hand, i.e., monopoly capitalism, which finally matured only in the twentieth century, is, by virtue of its fundamental *economic* traits,

---

[12] Lenin 1974, p. 299.
[13] Lenin 1974, pp. 246ff.

distinguished by a minimum fondness for peace and freedom, and by a maximum and universal development of militarism.[14]

In general, Lenin took Kautsky's critique of the Bolsheviks to be proof that the erstwhile leader of international Marxism had betrayed the socialist cause, and was now hardly distinguishable from 'a common liberal bureaucrat'.[15] With this damning conclusion, the polemics between Kautsky and the Bolsheviks were, however, by no means over yet. In the second round, more arguments were raised.

Kautsky versus Trotsky

In his pamphlet *Terrorism and Communism* (1919), Kautsky developed his case further. Referring to the French Revolution and the Paris Commune, he claimed that the Russian proletariat strove for goals which were objectively not (yet) possible. Characteristic of each proletariat was, he argued, that it sought impulsively to be freed as quickly as possible from its predicament, and thus longed for nothing short of the immediate overthrow of capitalism:

> The masses instinctively do not seek out a doctrine which points them on the road to development, but rather one which provides any formula or a plan, the implementation of which, whatever the circumstances may be, brings an end to their suffering.[16]

A socialist party guided by the true Marxist spirit would therefore have to try to prevent such a development, even if it thereby risked the danger of losing its leadership of the masses. If the proletariat seized power at a moment that was 'too early' in an historical sense, then the resulting problems would be immense. After all, the expropriation of capitalists was a simple question of power, and therefore not particularly difficult. But the organisation of production after expropriation – that would be an almost impossible task, for a relatively inexperienced and uneducated proletariat:

> The capitalist enterprise is a complex organization, which finds its head in the capitalist himself, or in his representatives. If one wants to abolish

---

[14] Lenin 1974, p. 239.
[15] Lenin 1974, p. 317.
[16] Kautsky 1919, p. 12.

capitalism, a form of organization must be created, which could function as well, if not better, without that capitalist head. This is not such a simple matter, as in the case of Philip IV or of Stenka Razin in the past; because it demands a certain set of conditions of a material as well as of a psychological kind, a high development of capitalist organization, not only of production but also of output and supply of raw materials. Moreover, it also demands a proletariat conscious of its obligations, not only towards its own neighbours and comrades, but also towards society as a whole – a proletariat, moreover, which has become accustomed to voluntary discipline and self-administration through long years of mass organization; and which, finally, is intelligent enough to distinguish the possible from the impossible, and the scientifically educated leader with the character of an unscrupulous, ignorant demagogue.[17]

Since the Russian proletariat was not yet ready for this gigantic task, a descent into chaos was the necessary result. To substantiate this thesis further, Kautsky – referring to a comment by Trotsky that the Russian working class could, despite lack of experience, nevertheless 'in time learn and arrange everything' – offered the following analogy:

But would Trotsky dare to get on a locomotive and set it going, convinced that he would, during the journey, 'learn and arrange everything'? No doubt he would be quite capable of doing this, but would he have the necessary time? Would not the train be very likely soon to be derailed, or explode? One must have acquired something of the skills necessary to drive an engine, before one tries to set it going. In the same way, the proletariat must have acquired those qualities, which are indispensable for organisation of production, if it wishes to undertake this task.[18]

To save industry, a new class of public servants, a new 'managerial class [Herrenklasse]' would have to be recruited, which would then assume the reigns of power. Thus there would emerge 'the most oppressive of all despotisms, which Russia ever had'.[19] With the old capitalism destroyed, a new capitalism would gradually emerge, which – because the time was not yet ripe for socialism – would be even worse for the proletariat than the old one.

---

[17] Kautsky 1919, p. 112.
[18] Kautsky 1919, p. 117.
[19] Kautsky 1919, pp. 134–5.

Because this new capitalism would not be a highly developed industrial one; instead, it would be characterised by despicable horse-trading and monetary speculation. In that event, 'Industrial capitalism has been transformed from a private to a state capitalism'.[20]

These passages make it clear that Kautsky did not really know how he should define the new 'bastard formation'. The bureaucracy was a new ruling class, there was state capitalism, but whether the bureaucracy was actually a *capitalist* class, remained unclear. But, whatever the case, he was certain that the Bolshevik experiment was necessarily doomed to failure. Either the Bolsheviks restored democracy on their own initiative (which Kautsky thought an unlikely prospect), or else there would be a counter-revolution: 'It would not have to be a 9th Thermidor, but I feel that it will not be far from that'.[21]

In his pamphlet *Terrorism and Communism* (1920), Trotsky sought to parry Kautsky's attack. Specifically, Trotsky rejected any idea that that the Bolsheviks had seized power too early. He offered three main points. Firstly, he claimed that one could not blame Bolshevik policy for the collapse of Russian industry, because the real cause was the Civil War, the blockades against the country, etc.[22] Secondly, he argued against the idea that the proletariat had to have learnt the skills for socialist economic management already *before* the socialist revolution. And, thirdly, he noted that the Bolsheviks had no other option than to seize power. The last two arguments Trotsky combined in a rebuttal of Kautsky's locomotive analogy, which he considered too simplistic:

> With infinitely more foundation one could say 'Will Kautsky dare to mount a horse before he has learned to sit firmly in the saddle, and to guide the animal in all its steps?' We have foundations for believing that Kautsky would not make up his mind to such a dangerous, purely Bolshevik experiment. On the other hand, we fear that, through not risking to mount the horse, Kautsky would have considerable difficulty in learning the secrets of riding on horse-back. For the fundamental Bolshevik prejudice is precisely this: that one learns to ride on horse-back, only when sitting on the horse.[23]

---

[20] Kautsky 1919, p. 134.
[21] Kautsky 1919, p. 146.
[22] Trotsky 1920, p. 105.
[23] Trotsky 1920, p. 82; English edition, p. 101.

Moreover, the Russian working class *had* to mount this horse, if it did not want to be thrown off the historical stage for a whole epoch. And, once it had seized power, and had taken up the reins, all the rest followed of its own accord. The disorganisation of production by the bourgeoisie had to be fought through socialisation, regardless of whether socialisation at that moment was advantageous or not: 'Having mounted the saddle, the rider is obliged to guide the horse – on the peril of breaking his neck.'[24]

Kautsky's reply was not slow in coming. In *From Democracy to State Slavery* (1921), he retorted that, although he was not a Bolshevik, he had nevertheless learnt to ride a horse:

> It is true I did not learn to ride a horse before I mounted one, but the horse had learnt to carry a rider before I mounted it. And I did not ride alone, but with friends, who had learnt to ride, and gave me advice and directions. In the end, however, the challenge became easier because I exercized my body with gymnastics beforehand.[25]

The equine controversy between Kautsky and Trotsky showed with the greatest possible clarity the difference in interpretations: while Trotsky claimed that the Bolsheviks were forced by circumstances to mount the horse first, and then to master riding it, Kautsky argued that an inexperienced rider would in all probability be thrown off the horse. The possibility that both positions could have some validity, and that they could quite conceivably express an essential tragedy of the October Revolution, was, however, not envisaged by either of the polemicists.

Kautsky versus Bukharin

In the course of the following years, Kautsky's critiques of the Bolshevik régime became increasingly aggressive in tone. In 1925, he published his pamphlet *The International and Soviet Russia*, in which he pronounced the Soviet régime the most dangerous enemy of the international working class. The Soviet government, he wrote,

---

[24] Trotsky 1920, p. 83; English edition, p. 102.
[25] Kautsky 1921, p. 12.

is the strongest direct obstacle [of the proletariat's] ascendancy in the world – worse even than the infamous Horthy régime in Hungary or Mussolini's in Italy, the latter which however do not make every oppositional movement so totally impossible as the Soviet Union does.[26]

The Bolsheviks, Kautsky contended,

are today in the position, where they live from the domination and exploitation of the proletariat. But they do not desire to act in this position as a capitalist class. Therefore they stand today above the proletariat and capital, in order to use them as a tool.[27]

Nikolai Bukharin answered Kautsky in a pamphlet that was nearly three times as long as his opponent's: *Karl Kautsky and Soviet Russia*.[28] His response is very important in the context of this study, because Bukharin pursued some of the consequences of the unilinear schema to their logical conclusion, and thus – although this was not his explicit intention – made a contribution to exploring the limits of unilinear thinking about the topic. He tried, as it were, to stand in Kautsky's shoes, be it only for the purpose of revealing the contradictions in the latter's argument.

On the one hand, Kautsky had, in numerous publications, denied that the October Revolution was a genuine proletarian revolution; on the other hand, he had admitted that, since 1917, important changes had occurred, such as the abolition of large-scale landownership. Bukharin then asked himself what the conclusion had to be, if these two claims were put together. If the Soviet state represented neither the rule of the big landowners, nor the rule of the working class, what then could be the real class basis of Bolshevik power? Although Kautsky had failed to answer this question explicitly, Bukharin hypothesised what the logical solution of the problem would have to be in that case. The most obvious possibility was that the Bolsheviks constituted a new bourgeoisie:

---

[26] Kautsky 1925b, p. 11.
[27] Kautsky 1925b, p. 25.
[28] Bucharin 1925. This pamphlet appears to have escaped the notice of Bukharin's biographer Stephen F. Cohen, see Cohen 1975. A.G. Löwy does mention the pamphlet; he does not however regard it primarily as a polemic with Kautsky, but argues that Bukharin intervened in the discussion with Kautsky in order to carry on a debate with someone else, namely Stalin. See Löwy 1969, pp. 259–61.

like some American millionaires, who ascended from the depths of the working class. But they got there, thanks to their personal enrichment; here, however, everything is the other way round: self-enrichment is the result of the conquest of political power.[29]

But such a view, Bukharin argued, led to 'most peculiar conclusions'. Because it was, after all, the 'NEP-men' who most closely resembled the American-type bourgeois – yet it was precisely they who had been divested of their political rights by the Bolsheviks. If the Bolsheviks were bourgeois, then this would be completely inexplicable. The Bolsheviks therefore could not justifiably be called a capitalist class. This view of things also cohered better with Kautsky's allegation that the Bolsheviks were a new ruling class which stood 'above' labour and capital. The question however remained, what did the theory of a 'new ruling class' logically entail? What kind of class would it have to be? A large proportion of the party members were themselves workers and peasants. It was therefore impossible for them to be 'the exploiters'. Only a small group of functionaries were candidates for membership of a 'new class'. But to what extent could these really be said to constitute a ruling class at all?

> A ruling class is always characterised by the fact that it possesses a monopoly over the means of production, or at least of the most important means of production within a definite class order. If any kind of group of people is that class, then this would mean, that this group owns the 'nationalised' means of production as property. In other words, from Kautsky's view it follows, that e.g. the members of the Politburo, among others myself – wretched soul that I am! – are owners and exploiters of the total of large-scale industry, i.e. a financial-capitalist oligarchy, which appropriates its profits, in short, new 'millionaires'.[30]

This whole idea seemed absurd to Bukharin – indeed a 'hoary lie'. If, on the other hand, the Bolsheviks were therefore not a new ruling class, and if Kautsky's use of the concept of 'class' was only therefore only metaphorical, then what did this imply?

> If the Bolsheviks are not a class, then this means that they represent the interests of some class. This class is not the big landowners (they are, as

[29] Bucharin 1925, p. 28.
[30] Bucharin 1925, pp. 34–5.

Kautsky himself admits, expropriated). This class is also not the capitalist class (this too, is admitted by Kautsky). This class is not the peasantry, nor the intelligentsia (the latter which in any case cannot be called a class in its own right). So what remains? The proletariat.[31]

Through this reduction of Kautsky's argument to absurdity, Bukharin considered he had provided definite proof, *ex negativo*, that the Soviet-bureaucracy was proletarian in nature. But his reasoning nevertheless contained two hidden assumptions, namely:

a) That, if the Bolsheviks constituted a new ruling class, then they necessarily had to be a *bourgeoisie*, or more accurately a 'financial-capitalist oligarchy', and not any other class, i.e. he assumed that either capitalism or a workers' state existed, and that there were no other possibilities.

b) That, if the Bolsheviks did not constitute a ruling class, they were a group which necessarily *represented* the interests of a particular class.

These two hidden assumptions would be contested at length in the later Marxist debates about the Soviet Union; even so, Bukharin's theoretical achievement was that he had already thought through the implications of the argument to a great extent.

2.ii. Levi, Luxemburg and the Bolsheviks: criticism and counter-criticism

In 1922, Paul Levi published the main text of Rosa Luxemburg's pamphlet *The Russian Revolution*. Luxemburg had started to write it in the autumn of 1918, but the outbreak of the German uprising prevented her from finishing it.[32] The authenticity of this pamphlet is surrounded by quite a few myths. Among other things, Levi claimed in his preface to the text that, from certain quarters (namely, Leo Jogiches), there had been attempts to burn the original manuscript. Although there is no evidence to substantiate this allegation, it is true that Jogiches did try to prevent its publication, asserting that Luxemburg had revised her opinion in essential respects subsequent to writing it, and had, instead, intended to devote a whole book to the Russian Revolution.

---

[31] Bucharin 1925, p. 35.
[32] Frölich 1967, p. 286.

The version published by Levi was based on an incomplete, and not always accurate, copy. The original manuscript, expedited to safety in the turbulent month of January 1919 and then forgotten, was rediscovered only some years later. In 1928, Felix Weil published the necessary corrections to Levi's version.[33] While the document edited by Levi is therefore not fully authentic, I will nevertheless discuss it, because it was this edition which influenced the Marxist controversies in 1922 and 1923.

Levi

In his extensive introduction to the pamphlet, Levi[34] explained why he had decided to publish it. After a promising beginning, he noted, the Russian council republic had changed in character rapidly. Since February 1921, Bolshevik policy had experienced a complete turnaround. While the Communist leadership in 1918 had striven for the elimination of capitalism, three years later it sought to resurrect capitalism. In the countryside, redistribution of land ownership had transformed the rural class contradictions; in the place of the previous counterposition of *muzhiks* and *kulaks*, an 'intermediate peasantry' had emerged *grosso modo*.[35] Whereas, at an earlier stage, the industrial workers had found their natural ally in the lower strata of the agrarian sector, they were now faced in the countryside with a broad stratum of relatively well-off peasants, who felt little affinity with them. The balance of power had therefore changed to the disadvantage of the proletariat.

In line with the debate between Kautsky and Lenin, Levi remarked that Kautsky was definitely wrong in his interpretations of democracy and dictatorship. But Lenin's standpoint was not fully correct either, because Lenin reduced the form of government to a more or less external appearance of the form of the state. Levi claimed Lenin's position was correct, as far as the definition of the bourgeois state was concerned. He doubted, however, whether

---

[33] Weil 1928.

[34] After the murder of Rosa Luxemburg and Karl Liebknecht in January 1919, the lawyer Paul Levi (1883–1930) was the most important leader of the still very weak German Communist Party. Levi – who had a clear aversion for left-radical adventurism – quickly forced a split with the left wing of the party, which in 1920 founded the Kommunistische Arbeiter-Partei Deutschlands (KAPD). Shortly thereafter, he resigned as chairman and was expelled for his open criticism of the failed 'March offensive' of the KPD (1921). He subsequently joined the left wing of the Social Democrats. See, among others, Beradt 1969.

[35] Levi 1922, p. 16.

the distinction drawn between 'form of state' and 'form of government' made any sense as far as a proletarian state was concerned:

> in this [proletarian] 'state form' different 'forms of government' are possible, just as in the state form of the bourgeoisie the most variegated governmental forms (republic, monarchy, parliamentarism) are conceivable. That (as seems obvious to us) Lenin had studied this question and answered it, is shown by his various statements, in which he affirms it.[36]

According to Levi, Lenin had believed that a state of whatever type is proletarian, if the replacing polity, or the vanguard of the working class, exercised state power *in the name* of the working class. This dubious idea would mean that

> Like a true mother, the vanguard has fashioned a shirt in [creating] the Soviet system, and waits – patiently or impatiently – until the child can wear the shirt. So long as it cannot, the mother stays the mother, and the shirt a shirt, the vanguard stays the vanguard, and the Soviet system the Soviet system.[37]

Levi rejected the validity of this idea of replacement by the vanguard (a 'substitutionist' error).[38] The proletariat, he felt, would have to grow strong in battle, and conquer its own future.[39] By their disastrous policy, the Bolsheviks had effectively lost their class basis after 1917, and had isolated themselves in Russian society. Only their organisational power still kept them going. In search of a new class basis, they had opted for the peasantry.[40] In this way, an essential transformation of political content had occurred under the guise of a 'proletarian' state form; or, to put it differently, through a change in the form of government, the essence of the state apparatus was also altered. 'What has remained of the "dictatorship of the proletariat"? Nothing. None of the objective moments, none of the subjective.'[41]

The central question posed by Levi – whether a workers' state could be defined by one specific type of government (for example a conciliar

---

[36] Levi 1922, p. 35.
[37] Levi 1922, p. 29.
[38] The term is Trotsky's. See Cliff 1960.
[39] Levi 1922, pp. 50–1.
[40] Levi 1922, p. 47.
[41] Levi 1922, p. 51.

democracy) or by several different kinds – would also be debated again and again in later years.

Luxemburg

It is not at all certain that, if Rosa Luxemburg had lived longer, she would have reached the same conclusions as Levi.[42] Her writings provide no indications in that regard; how she would have judged the New Economic Policy is difficult to say. Her publications of 1917 and 1918 nevertheless suggest an attitude of critical solidarity with the Bolsheviks. Her first articles were definitely very enthusiastic.[43] Similarly, the manuscript of *The Russian Revolution* also did not begin with a critique of the Bolsheviks, but, rather, with a critique of Kautsky. Luxemburg resisted Kautsky's interpretation that Russia, because of its economic backwardness, was not 'ripe' for the dictatorship of the proletariat. Her objections were both of a theoretical and practical-political nature. Theoretically, the Kautskyian position would lead to the conclusion 'that the socialist revolution is a national and, so to speak, a domestic affair in each modern country taken by itself'.[44] Practically, this approach would imply a tendency to minimise the responsibility of the international workers' movement, especially the German labour movement, for the Russian events.

> It is not Russia's unripeness which has been proved by the events of the war and the Russian Revolution, but the unripeness of the German proletariat for the fulfillment of its historic tasks. And to make this fully clear is the first task of a critical examination of the Russian Revolution.[45]

---

[42] Rosa Luxemburg (1870–1919), an economist, was prior to World War I a member of the left wing of the German Social Democracy. After the SPD fraction in the *Reichstag* voted on 4 August 1914 for the war credits, she worked with Karl Liebknecht and Franz Mehring among others to develop a left opposition, which from 1916 became known as the Spartakusbund and, around the turn of 1918–19, became the German Communist Party. Luxemburg, who because of her illegal activities had been in prison almost uninterruptedly from February 1915 until October 1918 (first because of high treason, then as a kind of protective custody), was murdered in 1919 by members of the Freikorps. The standard biographies are Nettl 1966 and Laschitza 1996.

[43] See, for example, Luxemburg 1917a and Luxemburg 1917b. Both articles are anonymous, but are attributed to Luxemburg. See Nettl 1966, pp. 680–1.

[44] Luxemburg 1922, p. 69; English translation, p. 368.

[45] Luxemburg 1922, p. 70; English translation, p. 368.

It is perhaps pertinent to note here that, with this critique of Kautsky, Luxemburg took one more step away from the traditional Marxist unilinearism. If a combined German-Russian revolution would take place, then, in her view, it should be possible to establish a proletarian dictatorship in backward Russia immediately. Luxemburg was, however, also conscious of the antithesis contained in this position: if the Russian Revolution did not spread internationally, then the Bolshevik experiment would result in a crippled socio-economic structure. In that case, there would be not only no democracy, but no socialism either – only 'feeble, distorted initiatives' towards it.[46] The situation in which the Bolsheviks found themselves was exceptionally difficult, and the possibilities of making mistakes were immense. No one was served by 'uncritical admiration' in her eyes, yet the only responsible attitude consisted in criticism based on fundamental solidarity.

The first point of criticism advanced by Luxemburg concerned the rural policy of the Bolsheviks. By redistributing land and allowing the peasants to divide up the large estates, she felt a dangerous step had been taken. The reason was that through this policy, social property had not been strengthened, but, instead, a new form of private property had been created. The relatively advanced large farming enterprises were destroyed, and in their place small, primitive farms had appeared which, technically speaking, still operated with 'technical means from the time of the Pharaohs'.[47] The land policy had, in this way, strengthened bourgeois influences in the countryside, and changed the balance of power to the disadvantage of the working class. The new, enormously enlarged, class of property-owning peasants would defend their newly won assets tooth and nail, and thus seriously obstruct the socialisation of agriculture: 'The Leninist agrarian reform has created a new and powerful layer of popular enemies of socialism on the countryside, enemies whose resistance will be much more dangerous and stubborn than that of the noble large landowners.'[48]

---

[46] Luxemburg 1922, p. 71.
[47] Luxemburg 1922, p. 85; English translation, p. 377.
[48] Luxemburg 1922, p. 87; English translation, p. 378.

Her second point of criticism concerned the nationalities question, which for a long time had been a source of political conflict with Lenin, and between the Polish and Russian Social Democrats. Luxemburg had consistently agitated against the demand for the self-determination of nations, setting out from the idea that – if the workers have no country (as proclaimed by the Communist Manifesto) – a nationalities question did not exist. The 'fatherland of the workers', she wrote once, was the socialist international.[49] With this general approach in mind, Luxemburg went on to express her apprehension that Bolshevik policy would lead to the disintegration of the new state. As soon as independence had been won, one nationality after the other would use their new freedom to make connections with German imperialism and promote counter-revolution.[50]

Both through their land policy and through their nationalities policy, the Bolsheviks had created powerful opponents for themselves in their own country. This led Luxemburg to the essence of her criticism – the question of dictatorship and democracy. The dissolution of the Constituent Assembly (in November 1917) was unacceptable to her. Trotsky had theorised that institutions such as the Constituent Assembly could begin to lead 'a life of their own', and that, as soon as that was the case, and an institution no longer mirrored part of life in society, it should be destroyed. Luxemburg objected that historical experience had shown how a continual reciprocal interaction occurred between the elected and the voters. The 'lively fluid of the popular mood [*lebendige Fluidum der Volksstimmung*]' continually washed over the representative bodies, suffused them, and directed them.

> It is precisely the revolution which creates by its glowing heat that delicate, vibrant, sensitive political atmosphere in which the waves of popular feeling, the pulse of popular life, work for the moment on the representative bodies in a most wonderful fashion.[51]

Naturally, the Constituent Assembly was not the most ideal institution. Lenin and Trotsky's alternative was however even less ideal. It destroyed democracy as such, and therefore broke up the political life of the masses.

---

[49] Luxemburg 1916, p. 47.
[50] Luxemburg 1922, p. 90.
[51] Luxemburg 1922, p. 102; English translation, p. 386.

The Bolshevik measure to grant voting rights only to those who lived by their own work, was criticised by Luxemburg from this perspective. She referred to 'a quite incomprehensible measure'[52] which robbed broad layers of the petty bourgeoisie and the working class from their political rights, just because they had been pauperised through lack of employment. More generally, Luxemburg pointed to the need for the broadest expansion of democracy, not as an abstract principle, but as the indispensable prerequisite for political learning processes. It was in this context, that she presented her famous thesis about freedom:

> Freedom only for the supporters of the government, only for the members of one party – however numerous they may be – is no freedom at all. Freedom is always and exclusively freedom for the one who thinks differently. Not because of any fanatical concept of 'justice' but because all that is instructive, wholesome and purifying in political freedom depends on this essential characteristic, and its effectiveness vanishes when 'freedom' becomes a special privilege.[53]

The abolition of democracy, Luxemburg predicted, would lead to a complete petrification of public life. The bureaucracy would become ever more powerful, and the dynamics of mass movements would disappear. In a visionary passage, she sketched a sinister scenario for the future:

> a few dozen party leaders of inexhaustible energy and boundless idealism direct and rule. Among them, in reality only a dozen outstanding heads do the leading and an élite of the working class is invited from time to time to meetings where they are to applaud the speeches of the leaders, and to approve proposed resolutions unanimously – at bottom, then, a clique affair – a dictatorship, to be sure, not the dictatorship of the proletariat, however, but only the dictatorship of a handful of politicians, that is a dictatorship in the bourgeois sense, in the sense of the rule of the Jacobins. [...] Yes, we could go even further: such conditions must inevitably cause a brutalisation of public life – assassinations, shooting of hostages, etc.[54]

---

[52] Luxemburg 1922, p. 105; English translation, p. 388.
[53] Luxemburg 1922, p. 109; English translation, pp. 389–90.
[54] Luxemburg 1922, pp. 113–14; English translation, p. 391, adapted.

If one scrutinises Luxemburg's discourse as a whole, however, it still remains unclear what the precise implications were. On the one hand, she signalled the danger that the strengthening of bourgeois forces in the countryside, and in nations gaining independence, could lead to a bourgeois counter-revolution aiming at the overthrow of Bolshevik rule. On the other hand, she also envisaged the possibility that the Bolshevik system could degenerate into a bourgeois dictatorship. But the latter prospect had the status of only a vague reference. When she spoke of a 'dictatorship in the bourgeois sense', did she really mean the form (i.e. the few deciding for the many) or did she mean a substantive social transformation into a bourgeois system?[55] Whatever one's interpretation, it is clear that Luxemburg believed she could identify many factors, both endogenous and exogenous, which pointed towards capitalist restoration. Nevertheless, she did not conceive of the possibility of an historically unique and unprecedented social system.

Interpretations

There was much discussion about the question of whether, after abandoning work on her pamphlet, Luxemburg had continued to adhere to her original critique or had instead changed her views. In 1922, Adolf Warzawski quoted from memory a letter dated late November or early December 1918, allegedly sent by Luxemburg:

> I shared all your qualifications and reservations, but I have abandoned them in the most important questions, and in some I have not gone so far as you. [...] To be sure, the newly created agricultural relations are the most dangerous, most wounded point of the Russian revolution. But here too the truth applies that even the greatest revolution can only accomplish what has ripened through development. This wounded point can only be healed by the European revolution. And it will come![56]

Clara Zetkin also claimed that Luxemburg subsequently changed her opinion about the Bolsheviks:

---

[55] In his 'Introduction' Levi clearly opts for the second variant.
[56] Warski 1922, p. 7. Gilbert Badia's (1974, p. 204) claim that Warski had remembered this passage 'thirty years later' is completely without foundation, as is evident from the dating of the pamphlet.

Although she wrote me twice in the summer of 1918, I wanted to work through a scientifically-critical position about the Bolshevik politics with Franz Mehring, and although she mentioned to me about her own intended major work, she referred in her subsequent correspondence to this question as 'settled'. The reason is obvious to anyone, since Rosa Luxemburg's stance after the outbreak of the German revolution is well-known. This stance was characterised by a position on the problems of the Constituent Assembly, democracy and dictatorship etc. which contradicts her earlier critique of Bolshevik policy. Rosa Luxemburg had assimilated a changed evaluation of history.[57]

Badia appears to be correct when he states that no proof exists that Rosa Luxemburg definitely abandoned her critique with respect to the nationalities question and the agrarian question.[58] Implicitly, Zetkin confirmed the same when she linked Luxemburg's supposed change of mind only to the question of the Constituent Assembly. But it does seem as though Luxemburg did begin to think differently about the problem of democracy. Under the influence of the German Revolution, her attitude about the importance of parliaments evidently changed. While she had appealed at the founding congress of the KPD for participation in the elections, to give a victorious 'sign' in the national assembly,[59] some time later she endorsed a change in this stance to 'all power to the workers' and soldiers' councils'. With justification, it has been argued that this change in position was hardly of principled significance for Luxemburg. She had simply responded to actual political developments in Germany, and adjusted her views about tactics accordingly. A genuine rapprochment with Lenin need not necessarily have been part of it at all.[60]

Zetkin, Lukács, and Kautsky

Western sympathisers of the Bolsheviks formulated different answers to the criticisms made by Luxemburg (as well as Levi). Clara Zetkin even dedicated a whole book to the issue, titled *Rosa Luxemburg's Position on the Russian Revolution*. She reproached Levi in this work for having 'abused'

---

[57] Zetkin 1922, p. 7.
[58] Badia 1974, p. 205.
[59] Luxemburg 1918–19, p. 484.
[60] Amodio 1973, p. 324 and Jost 1977.

Luxemburg's text, partly because, as previously mentioned, she thought that Luxemburg had later revised her opinion, and partly because Levi had allegedly interpreted Luxemburg's manuscript incorrectly.[61]

Zetkin examined the various arguments which Levi and Luxemburg had offered in detail. The general line of her argument was simply that the maligned Bolshevik policies had been inevitable.[62] Consistent with the Bolshevik line, she also defended the dissolution of the Constituent Assembly as well as other measures aiming to avoid the 'dangers of revolutionary proletarian democracy'.[63] Needless to say, Zetkin definitely rejected Levi's thesis that the youthful Soviet republic had already degenerated, and that the party apparatus, isolated from and towering above the working class, exercised a dictatorial régime. Admittedly, she felt obliged to recognise the social isolation of the party, but she considered it only a political-conjunctural matter of episodic significance. Reasoning by analogy, she clarified her opinion: 'The Bolshevik policy was so daring, stormed towards its goal so unexpectedly, that only the élite of the proletarian vanguard troops have kept their breath, and keep pace with it totally.'[64] Through the use of the trade unions as a communication channel between the party and the working masses, the political bonds would, however, be restored.[65] The Soviet organs would also play a major role in this: they were only the beginning of a rising movement, of a progressive democratisation of society.[66]

While Zetkin tried to rebut individual statements, György Lukács endeavoured in the same year to write a text which submitted Luxemburg's *method* to criticism. Lukács claimed there was a direct connection between the earlier writings by Luxemburg – which had made explicit her differences with

---

[61] Zetkin 1922, pp. 132–44. Zetkin's book is to a certain extent a sequel of her previous articles opposing Kautsky's critique of Bolshevism. See Haferkorn and Schmalfuss 1988.

[62] Zetkin 1922, p. 146.

[63] Zetkin 1922, p. 38.

[64] Zetkin 1922, p. 199.

[65] Zetkin 1922, pp. 202–3. It is remarkable that Zetkin, just like Kautsky and Trotsky had done earlier, reasoned by analogy. The quick forward march of the vanguard, the driver of a locomotive, the rider on the horse: all images of impetuous rapidity which were intended to convey the inevitability of the process.

[66] Zetkin 1922, pp. 204–13. Although she consistently identified with the Soviet Union, it looks like Zetkin's sympathy in later years was with Bukharin, rather than with Stalin. She never adopted an oppositional anti-bureaucratic position. See Hermann 1971, especially pp. 418–21.

Lenin – and the later pamphlet about the October Revolution.[67] He reproached Luxemburg for an 'organic' approach to the problem of revolution, whereas, in his opinion, a 'dialectically-revolutionary' approach was needed. By an 'organic' approach, Lukács meant that Luxemburg had theorised the proletarian revolution according to the model of *bourgeois* revolutions.[68] Luxemburg, he claimed, had failed to recognise that bourgeois and proletarian revolutions were qualitatively different. It was characteristic for a bourgeois revolution, that capitalism had already emerged within the feudal order, causing social and economic dislocations; the revolution was then merely the political and juridical adjustment of a society to changes which, on the economic terrain, had already occurred incrementally to a large extent. That was the reason why bourgeois revolutions proceeded relatively 'organically' and rapidly ('storm[ing] ahead with such brilliant *élan*')[69] to completion. The proletarian revolution, however, had a completely different character. A socialist economy could only be built *after* the proletariat had seized power, which explained why proletarian revolutions were much more radical and extensive than bourgeois revolutions, and were not completed 'at one stroke'[70] but, to the contrary, involved a long and painful process. This process developed consciously, and the revolutionary vanguard party played an important role in it. What was necessarily of central importance, was the imperative

> for *the proletariat to use all the means at its disposal to keep the power of the state in its own hands under all circumstances*. The victorious proletariat must not make the mistake of dogmatically determining its policy in advance either economically or ideologically. It must be able to manoeuvre freely in its economic policy (socialisation, concessions, etc.) depending on the way the classes are restratified and also upon how possible and necessary it is to win over certain groups of workers for the dictatorship or at least to induce them to preserve their neutrality. Similarly, it must not allow itself to be pinned down on the whole complex issue of freedom. [...] Freedom cannot

---

[67] Lukács 1923. Lukács shared the interpretation that Luxemburg was badly informed in writing her pamphlet, but in principle thought it of little importance. 'For – seen abstractly – it might well be the case [...] that the revision of her position noted by Comrades Warski and Zetkin could mean she had taken the wrong turning.' (p. 276; English translation, p. 272).

[68] Lukács 1923, p. 288.

[69] Lukács 1923, p. 286; English translation, p. 282.

[70] Lukács 1923, p. 287; English translation, p. 283.

represent a value in itself (any more than socialisation). *Freedom must serve the rule of the proletariat, not the other way round.*[71]

On the strength of this general-methodological anti-critique, Lukács arrived at the conclusion that all the objections Luxemburg had advanced against Bolshevik policy were misplaced. Just like Zetkin, he considered that no other course of action than the one followed by the Bolsheviks had been possible. Luxemburg had not recognised this, because she had presented the process of the proletarian revolution too simplistically, and had thus over-estimated the organic character of the developments. 'She constantly opposes to the exigencies of the moment the principles of future stages of the revolution.'[72]

Karl Kautsky's response to the pamphlet by Luxemburg was a remarkable mirror-image of those by Zetkin and Lukács. Just like the last-mentioned Marxists, Kautsky held the view that the Bolsheviks had, in several respects, been unable to act differently. Thus he noted about the redistribution of land:

> There is no doubt, that this raised a gigantic obstacle for the progress of socialism in Russia. But this course of events could not be prevented, it could at best have transpired in a more rational way than was realised by the Bolsheviks. It signifies at all events, that Russia in essence finds itself in the stage of the bourgeois revolution.[73]

Similarly, with regard to the nationalities policy, Kautsky disagreed with Luxemburg; national independence for him formed an essential component of democracy. Instead, he reproached the Bolsheviks because in realising the right to self-determination, they had not gone far enough, forcing foreign peoples under the Russian yoke.[74]

By contrast, Kautsky was much more positive about Luxemburg's enthusiastic defence of democracy, even although he considered that Luxemburg had fallen into illusions by believing that Bolshevism and democracy were compatible. According to Kautsky, the one would forever be the mortal enemy of the other.[75]

---

[71] Lukács 1923, p. 296; English translation, p. 292.
[72] Lukács 1923, p. 280; English translation, pp. 276–7.
[73] Kautsky 1922, p. 35.
[74] Ibid.
[75] Kautsky 1922, p. 44.

By means of a schema, we can clearly summarise the three main points of Luxemburg's critique and the reactions to it by Kautsky and the pro-Bolshevik Western-Marxist camp (Zetkin, Lukács) as follows:

Western-Marxist interpretations	Rosa Luxemburg	Clara Zetkin, György Lukács	Karl Kautsky
Land redistribution	Negative: The bourgeois elements are strengthened	Positive: It is a necessary concession	Positive: It shows the bourgeois character of the revolution
The self-determination of nationalities	Negative: The bourgeois elements are strengthened	Positive: It is a necessary component of socialist policy	Positive: It is democratic, but Bolshevism does not implement it consistently
The abolition of the Constituent Assembly, restricting voting rights, etc.	Negative: Bolshevism threatens to become an isolated dictatorship	Positive: Proletarian democracy must be defended	Negative: Bolshevism has turned into a dictatorial régime

If we now compare the different positions in this schema, the special nature of Luxemburg's position is clear. Because, while Zetkin and Lukács, as defenders of Bolshevik policy, had approved all measures taken – believing that only in this way the 'proletarian state power' could be maintained – Kautsky regarded Bolshevism as a dictatorial attempt to deny the bourgeois character of the Russian Revolution, a project doomed to failure. Zetkin, Lukács and Kautsky all assumed that the policy in regard to land distribution etc. was inevitable. But precisely this premise was *not* accepted by Luxemburg. From a more or less voluntarist perspective, she made demands of the Russian Revolution that were deduced from her theory about the proletarian revolution in highly developed capitalist countries. Bolshevism and general democracy (voting rights for all, etc.) were compatible in her view. This is the 'organic' approach for which she was criticised by Lukács, which led her to characterise the social relations created by the October Revolution in a way which emphasised the 'uncompleted' nature of the situation: both a road going forward towards socialist relations, as well as a road going back to a capitalist restoration were among the possibilities.

Although in this way she recognised that, on the one hand, a process was occurring in revolutionary Russia which so far could not be easily fitted into ready-made schemata, on the other hand her thinking remained within the theoretical framework of unilinearism.

2.iii. Left-communist criticisms

Gorter, Pannekoek, Rühle

Initially, the future 'left communists' Gorter, Pannekoek and Rühle were mostly enthusiastic supporters of the events in Russia. But, just like Luxemburg, they quickly developed reservations. Herman Gorter for example[76] dedicated his pamphlet of 1918 titled *The World Revolution* to Lenin, as the revolutionary who 'raised himself above all the other leaders of the proletariat' and who 'ranks equal only with Marx'.[77] What Gorter admired especially about the Russian revolution were two things, namely its 'maximalism' and the workers' councils. But he also referred to four fundamental differences between the situation in Western Europe and Russia:

a) The working class in Russia was small, while in Western Europe it was very large.

b) The poor, propertyless peasants were exceptionally numerous in Russia; their revolutionary behaviour followed from their resistance against the big landownership of the church, the nobility and the state. The peasants in Western Europe, by contrast, were predominantly based in medium-sized and small-sized enterprises, and embodied no revolutionary potential.

c) The revolutionary state apparatus (government and bureaucracy) was 'rotten' in Russia, but strong in Western Europe.

d) The employing class in Eastern Europe was weak, but in Western Europe it was strong.

---

[76] Herman Gorter (1864–1927), classicist, was from 1897 a member of the Dutch Social-Democratic Labour Party (SDAP); as a prominent representative of the left wing, he founded the Social-Democratic Party in 1909 with Wijnkoop and others, which, from 1918, became the Communist Party of Holland. Because of his criticism of Bolshevism, Gorter also resigned from this party, and in 1920 joined the German KAPD; subsequently he founded a Dutch section of this party, the Communist Workers' Party of the Netherlands (KAPN) which, however, remained marginal during its brief existence (until 1932). For a biography of Gorter, see De Liagre Böhl 1996.

[77] Gorter 1920b, p. 77.

In combination, these factors meant that the working class in Russia, 'together with a numerous ally, the poor peasants', confronted a 'weak capitalism', while the proletariat in Western Europe was 'alone' facing a 'very strong capitalism'.[78] Gorter drew two conclusions from this. On the one hand, a revolutionary victory in Western Europe would be much more difficult to realise than in Russia, but, on the other hand, it would be much easier in Western Europe to build socialism after the revolution:

> In Western Europe, the working class finds a stronger foundation to build socialism than in Russia because, firstly, the banks, the main branches of large-scale industry, transport, and trade were already prior to the war (especially in England and Germany) ripe for a socialist society, and secondly, during the war imperialism has organised and centralised production and distribution in Western Europe and America totally. And this organisation is technically very strong, and can be immediately taken over by the proletariat as basis for socialist institutions. This organisation was lacking in Russia, or very deficient. Russian society was not ripe for socialism prior to the war, and its organisation was weakened during the war, whereas West-European society was already ripe for socialism before the war, and its organisation and concentration has been strengthened during the war.[79]

In passing, let us notice here how Gorter implicitly permits the Russian Revolution to skip a stage, contrary to the mechanical unilinear way of thinking that was otherwise characteristic of him: Russia, after all, was said to be 'unripe' for socialism, yet was building it anyway. Gorter would, as we shall see, soon eliminate this inconsistency in his argument.[80] Pannekoek[81]

---

[78] Gorter 1920b, p. 88.

[79] Gorter 1920b, pp. 88–9.

[80] When he wrote *The World Revolution*, Gorter had already criticised the Bolsheviks, but there are few indications of this in his pamphlet. In his private correspondence, Gorter, however, made no secret of his reservations about the politics of land redistribution and the self-determination of nations. De Liagre Böhl 1973, pp. 195–7. The similarity with Luxemburg's criticism here is remarkable. Whether Gorter and Luxemburg had contact with each other, I do not know; the possibility cannot be excluded that they developed their views independently from each other, especially since they were a logical progression from the views which both had already expressed earlier.

[81] As late as 1919, Pannekoek believed that 'In Russia communism is since nearly two years practised in deed'. Horner 1919, p. 495. Pannekoek (1873–1960), an

and Rühle also endorsed this *grosso modo* positive appraisal of the Russian events.

As the conflicts within the Communist International between 'left' and other communists intensified in 1919 and 1920, the distinction made by Gorter and others between conditions in Russia and Western Europe began to be an important basis for political-tactical differences. In this context, Pannekoek's pamphlet *World Revolution and Communist Tactics* of 1920 should be mentioned. While Gorter had stressed especially the political and economic differences between East and West, Pannekoek placed greater emphasis on the ideological factor. Ideology, Pannekoek claimed – anticipating Gramsci – was the 'hidden power' of the bourgeoisie and the proletariat. Especially in Western Europe, the bourgeois influences on proletarian thinking were very great, in contrast with Russia:

> In England, France, Holland, Italy, Germany, and Scandinavia, lived from the middle ages a strong bourgeoisie with petty-bourgeois and primitive capitalist production methods; when feudalism was defeated, a strong, independent class of farmers likewise emerged, who were also masters in their own little economies. On this foundation bourgeois spiritual life developed a definite national culture.[82]

The situation in Russia and Eastern Europe was very different: 'there were no strong bourgeois classes which traditionally dominated intellectual life'. So, while in the West the bourgeois traditions lived in the proletariat, in the East the masses were much less encapsulated, and thus more receptive to communism.[83] From this distinction, it followed that revolutionaries, if they wanted to conquer the spirit of the masses, had to follow a very different tactic in Western Europe. In the West, it was primarily those bourgeois organs in which the proletariat still had confidence, such as parliaments and trade unions, which had to be attacked. Pannekoek's pamphlet, written in

---

astronomist, joined the SDAP in 1899. From 1906 until 1914, he lived in Germany, where he played a prominent role as theoretician in the left wing of the SPD. After 1918 he joined the Dutch Communist Party, but left this organisation in 1921. He sympathised with the KAPD and later maintained contact with the council-communist Groups of International Communists around Henk Canne Meyer. See Malandrino 1987 and Gerber 1989.
[82] Pannekoek 1920, p. 12.
[83] Pannekoek 1920.

1920 on the eve of the Second Comintern Congress, was published at almost the same moment as Lenin's pamphlet *Left-Wing Communism: An Infantile Disorder*. What is striking is that, while Lenin mentions Pannekoek (alias K. Horner) in his own pamphlet as one of the people who talk 'gibberish' and 'nonsense',[84] and while he discoursed at length about the 'Dutch Left', he hardly even mentioned their most important argument – the differences between the East and the West. All this suggested that the distance between the left communists and other currents was rapidly increasing.

Lenin's pamphlet was an enormous disappointment for the left communists. Already during the Second Comintern Congress, Herman Gorter wrote his *Open Letter to Comrade Lenin*, in which he expressed this disillusionment. Even although this text still breathed a spirit of admiration for Lenin – similarly to *The World Revolution*, to which it was, in a sense, a sequel[85] – Gorter's critique was now visible to all. He began his statement with the remark that he had again learned a lot from Lenin's last publication, and that it had chased away many germs of 'infantile disease' from him. Nevertheless, he considered that the main line of Lenin's pamphlet was incorrect, because it simply equated conditions in Eastern and Western Europe. Consequently, he judged that 'It is your [i.e. Lenin's] first book that is not good. For Western Europe, it is the worst possible.'[86]

In other respects, Gorter's reply did not contain any new arguments. It consisted in large part of repetitions of ideas formulated already earlier by Pannekoek, only this time they were more eloquently phrased on paper. Gorter also pointed to the division of Europe, making the argument very clear:

> As we move from the East to the West, in a certain sense we cross an economic frontier. It runs from the Baltic to the Mediterranean, approximately from Danzig to Venice. This line separates two worlds from each other. West of this line, industrial, commercial and finance capital, united with highly developed bank capital, dominates absolutely. [...] This capital is very

---

[84] Lenin 1964, pp. 28, 31.

[85] 'Gorter's *Open Letter* in composition forms a whole with the pamphlets he wrote during wartime. In *Het Imperialisme* he urged the workers to international unity. In *The World Revolution* he pointed out to them the necessity of a direct social revolution. The purely proletarian character of the international revolutionary struggle was the central theme of his Open Letter' – De Liagre Böhl 1973, p. 251.

[86] Herman Gorter 1920a, p. 213.

highly organised, and finds expression in the most solidly founded state governments of the world. To the East of this line, a rapid development of concentrated industrial, commercial, transport and bank capital also exists, but it lacks both a prehistory of solid absolute rule and its corollary, a solidly founded modern state.[87]

That explained why, East and West of the dividing line, very different tactics were called for.

At approximately the same time that Gorter and Pannekoek distanced themselves from the Bolsheviks, Otto Rühle[88] lost the last remnants of positive appreciation for the Russian Communists. After his return as KAPD delegate to the Second Comintern Congress[89] (a congress which he and his fellow delegate Merges did not actually attend, having departed in irritation before it even started), Rühle ventured to speak from the heart in a few articles. The Bolsheviks had, according to Rühle, tried to skip over a whole historical epoch by directly moving from feudalism to socialism. This attempt had failed, because of the delay of the world revolution. What was the result? 'A political socialism without an economic basis. A theoretical construction. A bureaucratic régime. A collection of paper decrees. An agitation phrase. And a terrible disappointment.'[90]

The Bolsheviks had created an ultra-centralism which fitted completely with the bourgeois character of their revolution:

Centralism is the organisational principle of the bourgeois-capitalist epoch.
It serves to build the bourgeois state and the capitalist economy. But not the proletarian state and the socialist economy. These demand the council system.[91]

---

[87] Herman Gorter 1920a, pp. 178–9.
[88] Otto Rühle (1874–1943), a teacher, belonged to the left wing of the SPD prior to World War I. In 1915 he was the second member of the Reichstag who voted against the war credits. Although a co-founder of the KPD he was in 1920 expelled from the party. He was a co-founder of the KAPD and attended the Second Comintern Congress as its representative. Subsequently he became an opponent of all political parties ('Die Revolution ist keine Parteisache!') and was then also expelled from the KAPD. In 1933 Rühle emigrated via Prague to Mexico. See Herrmann 1973; Mergner 1973; Jacoby and Herbst, 1985.
[89] Bock 1969a, pp. 251–5; Mergner 1973, pp. 154–8.
[90] Rühle 1920a.
[91] Rühle 1920b.

In a later publication, Rühle tried to substantiate some of his points further, utilising the unilinear schema. Whoever believed that the Russian Revolution meant the beginning of a social, proletarian overturn, he claimed, was the victim of an error in historical analysis: 'The Russian revolution could – given its historical circumstances – from the outset only be a bourgeois revolution. It had to clear away Tsarism, pave the way for capitalism, and help the bourgeoisie in the saddle politically.'[92] When Rühle wrote this in 1924, Gorter and Pannekoek had meantime arrived at an identical opinion.[93]

Korsch

In the German Communist Party, left-wing and oppositional groups emerged repeatedly, expressing resistance against the developments in the Soviet Union and the 'Bolshevisation' of their own organisation.[94] Among those expressing their concern was Karl Korsch.[95] Until 1925, he had, aside from minor criticisms, viewed the USSR as the only successful example of a revolution.[96] However, when a letter arrived from Moscow in which the KPD leadership (including Fischer, Maslow etc.) was criticised and a new leadership was urged, Korsch went into action. At a party conference in Frankfurt in September 1925, he lambasted the Soviet leadership for what he called its 'red imperialism'. In January 1926, he and others founded the group Entschiedene Linke, which set itself the task of reforming the party. In March 1926, the group set about publishing an oppositional periodical, *Kommunistische Politik*. A month later, its political platform was published, in which the Comintern was accused of liquidating the revolutionary perspective. It was alleged that opportunism had gained the upper hand in the fraternal Russian party.[97] Internationally,

---

[92] Rühle 1924, p. 17.
[93] For a summary, see Bock 1969b, pp. 31–48.
[94] An overview is provided in Langels 1984.
[95] Karl Korsch (1886–1961), a lawyer, joined the Unabhängige Sozialdemokratische Partei Deutschlands (USPD) in 1917 and followed the left wing of this party when it united in 1921 with the KPD. From 1923 he was member of parliament in Thuringia and for some weeks functioned as Minister of Justice in this German state. After his expulsion in 1926, he was briefly active in the Entschiedene Linke. Korsch's thought developed in these years towards council communism. In 1933, he emigrated to Denmark and from there to the United States in 1936. See Buckmiller 1973b; Buckmiller 1976; Goode 1979.
[96] Buckmiller, 1973a, p. 62; Kellner 1975–6, p. 83.
[97] Entschiedene Linke 1926.

too, Korsch attempted to form an opposition; for this purpose, he maintained contact with, among others, Amadeo Bordiga and the Soviet opposition leader T.V. Sapronov.[98] These initiatives, however, yielded few tangible results in an organisational sense. Of interest here is that, within the framework of his oppositional activities (which cost him his party card at the end of April 1926), Korsch tried to fathom the development of the Soviet republic theoretically.

In an important essay dated October 1927, Korsch had developed his theory of the 'creeping counter-revolution'. In post-revolutionary Russia, he argued, two groups had constantly confronted each other. On the one side were those who did not want to pursue the class struggle anymore, or wanted to curb it (Lenin among others). On the other side were those who consistently wanted to carry on the class struggle further. The first current reasoned primarily from reasons of state, the other from class interests. In the conflict between the two tendencies, the étatists had regularly won victories. Proofs of these victories were among others the Brest-Litovsk peace treaty, the defeat of the Workers' Opposition, the repression of the Kronstadt revolt, and the liquidation of the Trotskyist opposition. It was primarily the *accumulation* of partial defeats that had ultimately resulted in one great defeat – the emergence of a new capitalist society:

> For simple, abstract and un-dialectical thought, it appears an irresolvable contradiction, if we praise the proletarian revolution of Red October, and in the same breath call its historical result, the contemporary Soviet state, a new capitalist class state. [...] And to solve this contradiction, most people look for a source of the Original Sin (some find it in the Brest peace of 1917, others find it in the transition to NEP in 1921, a third group find it in the degeneration of the Russian party 'since Lenin's death' in 1924, the fourth see it first emerging in the transition from NEP to neo-NEP since 1925, and so on), in order to register from a given date the steady 'downfall of proletarian dictatorship' and the 'transformation of a revolutionary workers' state into a bourgeois class state' as accomplished fact. With complete justice the Stalinists could reply to this, that such a 'fall from grace', such

---

[98] 'He met Amadeo Bordiga, the Italian Leader in Moscow. Then he met Sapronov, [...] when the latter came to Berlin on what was probably a clandestine trip. They talked a lot and agreed to co-operate in opposition work'. Korsch 1972, p. 42. More information about this attempt to form an international opposition is provided in Montaldi 1975 and Prat 1984.

an absolutely definite break with the previous economy and politics [...] cannot be found.

In reality, he contended, the bourgeois counterrevolution had begun at the same time as the proletarian revolution. Especially since 1921, when, in the changed economic circumstances, the power-relations between social classes had shifted in favour of bourgeois groupings, the counterrevolutionary influence had grown quickly. Thus, in the space of ten years, capitalist restoration had triumphed slowly and almost surreptitiously.[99] During this same process of decline, Leninism had degenerated into an apparently classless, but, in essence, bourgeois and anti-proletarian 'state ideology', with which one had to break utterly and completely.[100]

2.iv. Summary

During the debates in the 1920s, unilinearism totally dominated Western-Marxist thought; all the leading participants assumed that an inexorable historical sequence of feudalism capitalism socialism would occur. However, while Kautsky interpreted this sequence only within a national framework (in each individual country, each stage had to 'ripen', before it could be replaced by the next stage) others recognised the possibility of building socialism in an underdeveloped capitalism with the aid of developed capitalist countries (among others Luxemburg) and/or with an appropriate national policy (Zetkin, Lukács). For the rest, all discussants were agreed that the Tsarist empire constituted at most an underdeveloped capitalism with feudal remnants. But there were striking differences in the conclusions drawn from that interpretation about the 'Bolshevik experiment':

a) One group of authors considered that the time had not yet come for socialism in Soviet Russia; underdeveloped capitalism had to 'ripen' first. From this perspective, two claims were defended:

---

[99] Korsch 1927a. See also Korsch 1932.
[100] Korsch 1927b. See, on Korsch's theory about Soviet society, Orsoni 1981 and Kornder 1987, pp. 149–59. One of Korsch's pupils, also a member of the Entschiedene Linke, was Kurt Mandelbaum (Kurt Martin), who undertook to give a Marxist interpretation of Leninism. See Mandelbaum 1974 and Martin 1979.

i) according to one position, the October Revolution was a voluntarist attempt, doomed in advance, to extricate a country from historical laws; the bastard formation emerging from this effort would collapse within a short time (Kautsky).

ii) According to the other position, the October Revolution – despite other subjective intentions by the Bolsheviks – was only a bourgeois overturn paving the way for a full-fledged capitalist development (Gorter, Pannekoek, Rühle).

b) Another group of authors believed that the October Revolution was a genuine proletarian revolution and that, even in backward Russia, the construction of socialism *was* possible under certain conditions.

i) According to one position, the construction of socialism was a very precarious process; the possibility of a relapse into capitalism remained a real possibility (Luxemburg).

ii) According to a second position, the transition towards a proto-socialist society had failed politically; through a 'creeping counter-revolution', capitalism had been restored (Korsch).

iii) According to a third position, the proto-socialist society was already, to an important extent, consolidated (Zetkin, Lukács).

In fact, all the different permutations which the unilinear schema logically permitted had now crystallised out among Western-Marxist theoreticians – with one exception: not one of them had defended the thesis that a *violent* counterrevolution (as distinct from a 'creeping' counter-revolution) had occurred.

Chapter Three

From Stalin's 'Great Leap Forwards' to the 'Great Patriotic War' (1929–41)

With the benefit of hindsight, and without postulating historical inevitability, one can say that the years of the New Economic Policy (NEP) were a relatively calm intermezzo in the process of state building that started in 1917 and was completed around 1939. The social revolution 'from above', which began in the late 1920s, marked a second stage of this process. The policies implemented in this phase were historically unique, both in their scale, and in their sheer ruthlessness.

The appearance of the Soviet Union then changed drastically. In the years 1927 to 1930, three parallel structural transformations occurred. First, the régime succeeded in definitely consolidating itself. While it eradicated the political oppositions around Trotsky and Bukharin *internally*, i.e. within the party, and in other ways made the central political apparatus immune to attack as well, it expanded its power *externally* over more and more regions of social life. In particular, the trade unions, whose relative autonomy had been seriously restricted during the NEP-period, were completely transformed into party organs. Second, enormous tensions emerged in 1927 in the agrarian sector, leading to a partial paralysis of the grain market (caused in particular by the 'scissors-crisis' affecting relative prices for agricultural and industrial goods). The new régime then took the bull by the horns and in rapid tempo, the agricultural sector was collectivised with terrorist methods – a process which, both because of the physical liquidation of the *kulaks* involved and the resulting famines, caused an enormous number of deaths. And, third, with the introduction of the five-year plans, decided on in April 1929 (the first five-year plan was actually supposed to have started on 1 October 1928), a forced modernisation programme was instigated. Heavy industry (especially the metals industry, machinery and energy supply) were given absolute priority, without however paying much attention to the effects this had on society as a whole.

While, in the economic sphere, market institutions were strongly reduced by a 'great leap forwards' (Alec Nove's term) and replaced with 'planning', 'collectives' etc., in the political sphere, a centralisation took place which eliminated most remnants of democracy and pluralism. A 'mono-organizational society' (as Rigby put it) had emerged:

> overall coordination of the multifarious discrete organizations operating in the various societal sub-systems is itself achieved organizationally, i.e. through super-ordinated structures of command, much as in war-time the Supreme Command directs and orchestrates the numerous formations, branches, and services operating in a particular theatre of war.[1]

Within the society so constituted, the power of the great leader was, however, still not beyond challenge. The Great Purge following the assassination in 1934 of Stalin's competitor Sergei Kirov, a member of the Politbureau, marked the completion of the process of state formation. The mass terror had two combined effects. The leading élite changed in social composition. Not only the Bolshevik veterans from the Czarist period, but also many who had joined the movement in 1917 or later and had actively contributed to Stalin's 'revolution', were murdered. The new managers replacing them were, in a sense, people without a history and with a technocratic outlook. Simultaneously, Stalin's personal dictatorship became impregnable. With these changes, the army of forced labour (slaves) emerging already at the end of the 1920s, grew explosively. At the same time, the repression against 'ordinary' workers increased significantly (introduction of workbooks, draconian penalties for

---

[1] Rigby 1977, p. 53.

absenteeism, abolition of the right to annul employment contracts unilaterally, etc.), a traditionalist family policy was introduced (prohibition of abortion, proclamation of the family as the cornerstone of society) and the arts, sciences and philosophy were completely subordinated to official politics.

In the space of about ten years, the Soviet Union was thus fundamentally changed. Critical-Marxist observers naturally recognised this quickly, and drew their conclusions. These conclusions were, of course, also influenced by their observation of developments outside the Soviet Union.

Overshadowing everything in the 1930s was the Great Depression. The apparent contrast – partly illusory – between the economic difficulties experienced at home and the rapid strides of modernisation in the Soviet Union led many in the West to tone down their criticism of the Russians. In 1931, Kautsky pointed out in this regard that:

> The economic crisis has in the last year gained such insane dimensions, that many among us think that the collapse of capitalism is already occurring. Corresponding to this is the increased advertising by Soviet Russia of its five-year plan. [...] What one wishes for is easily believed. In that way, a need arises out of the terrible emergency of the times to see in Russia the rock on which the church of the future will be built.[2]

If this temptation was strong, then it not infrequently happened that a previous critic of the Soviet Union would re-adjust his views in an apologetic direction. A striking example of this trend was the most important theoretician of Austro-Marxism, Otto Bauer, whose views had initially been close to Kautsky's.[3] In the 1930s, he revised his opinion, and, in his 1936 book *Between Two World Wars?*, he defended Stalinism as an historical necessity, declaring that 'Yet just as terrible the sacrifices which the great industrialisation and collectivisation process incurred, just so intoxicating are its consequences.'[4]

---

[2] Kautsky 1931, p. 342.

[3] See his positive appreciation of Kautsky's critique of Bolshevism: Bauer 1919.

[4] Bauer 1936, pp. 13 and 37. Croan has explicitly pointed to the connection between Bauer's apologetic inclination and the world situation: 'A deepening economic crisis and the spread of Fascism were darkening the horizons of democratic socialism everywhere in Europe. [...] Only in this context can the psychological and political function of Bauer's optimism [...] be understood. [...] *Ex oriente lux*'. Croan 1962, pp. 292–3. For a monograph on Bauer and Bolshevism, see Löw 1980.

Secondly, after Hitler's coup d'état in 1933, a number of common characteristics between national socialism and the Stalinist régime became visible (for example, the one-party system, economic 'planning', terrorist methods). In addition, it sometimes seemed as though the two systems influenced each other at the policy level.[5] The Molotov-Ribbentrop Pact strengthened this impression. Such observations motivated some critics to postulate identical essences for both societies. As is well-known, non-Marxists were also subject to that temptation, and at that time laid the theoretical groundwork for future theories of totalitarianism.[6] A quote from a council communist in 1939 summarises the trend of thought at this time:

> Russia must be placed first among the new totalitarian states. [...] Adopting all the features of the total state, it [...] became the model for those other countries which were forced to do away with the democratic state system and to change to dictatorial rule. Russia was the example for fascism.
>
> No accident is here involved, nor a bad joke of history. The duplication of systems here is apparent but real. Everything points to the fact that we have to deal here with expressions and consequences of identical principles applied to different levels of historical and political development. Whether party 'communists' like it or not, the fact remains that the state order and rule in Russia are indistinguishable from those in Italy and Germany. Essentially they are alike. One may speak of a red, black, or brown 'soviet state', as well as of red, black or brown fascism.[7]

Similar ideas were raised again by various authors later on, as will be discussed in the following chapters.

Insofar as the structural transformation of Soviet society gaining momentum from 1929 did not tempt Marxist critics to see it as a variant of socialism, as Otto Bauer had, the insight now began to dawn that it would no longer do simply to use the label 'capitalism'. Somehow, critical theory had to express the fact that under Stalin's rule something completely *new* had emerged.

---

[5] Schwarz 1951 for example notes that the workbook was introduced roughly at the same time in Nazi Germany (Reichsgesetz, 26 February 1935) and in the Soviet Union (decree of 20 December 1938). However, '[...] the Soviet work books, while fashioned in the Nazi-German pattern, could not perform the functions they performed in the Third Reich' (p. 101).

[6] See Adler and Paterson 1970.

[7] Rühle 1939, p. 245.

Referring to the omnipotent bureaucratic élite, the Left Oppositionist Christian Rakovsky described it as a 'new social category' which called for a completely new analysis.[8]

Various new theories were mooted in the period 1929–41. I will first discuss their content, and then examine the debates among their supporters during this era.

3.i. State capitalism

The history of the concept of 'state capitalism' dates back to well before the October Revolution. According to the consensus view, the term was first invented in the beginning of the 1890s by German Social Democrats, in response to the reformist views of Georg von Vollmar and others. The latter believed that the bourgeois state should be encouraged to adopt policies (nationalisations) which would be a preparation for a future 'state socialism'. Their opponents (Wilhelm Liebknecht and others), however, contended that an expansion of the bourgeois state could not lead to 'state socialism' but only to 'state capitalism', thereby changing the balance of forces to the disadvantage of the working class.[9] From the outset, state capitalism was therefore never a category with a primarily *analytical* intention; instead, the concept was disconnected from reality in two ways: 'by its counterposition to another *concept* and the *latter's* relationship to a future society'.[10]

In the years 1914–18, the German war economy, with hitherto unprecedented state interventions in the economic process (the use of force to compel enterprises to produce, regulation of the distribution of consumer goods, fixing of minimum prices, etc.), stimulated a detailed elaboration of the concept of state capitalism. Nikolai Bukharin at that time developed an interpretation in which state capitalism represented a new and higher stage of capitalist development, a stage in which competition between enterprises in the domestic economy was tendentially regulated by state intervention, and the rivalry between capitals shifted to the world market.[11] Authors with

---

[8] Rakovsky 1929, p. 131. The Russian original literally states 'a new sociological category'.
[9] Huhn 1952–3, pp. 170–80; Olle 1974a, pp. 103–12; Ambrosius 1981, pp. 9–18.
[10] Olle 1974a, p. 107.
[11] Stehr 1973; Haynes 1985.

other political orientations, such as the Social Democrat Karl Renner and the council communist Otto Rühle, formulated similar ideas.[12]

The question of the extent to which state capitalism could be said to exist in Russia after 1917 quickly began to play a role in the discussions of the Bolsheviks themselves. The left communists, grouped around the magazine *Kommunist*, feared that the industrial policy being followed would undermine workers' power in the enterprises, and thus eradicate the foundation of the revolutionary process. Osinsky formulated this concern as follows:

> If the proletariat itself does not know how to create the necessary prerequisites for the socialist organization of labor – no one can do this for it and no one can compel it to do this. [...] Socialism and socialist organization must be set up by the proletariat itself, or they will not be set up at all; something else will be set up – state capitalism.[13]

Around the same time, Lenin had also used the concept of state capitalism to characterise Russia. He opined, however, that a dictatorship of the proletariat could be reconciled with state capitalism. Between freely competitive capitalism and socialism, there would be a transition period; during this period, the revolutionaries needed to appropriate as many technical-organisational means and insights from state capitalism as possible, especially from state capitalism in Germany.[14] In various contributions by Bukharin, Osinsky, Lenin and others, state capitalism was very broadly interpreted as market economy with major state intervention. In the debates about the Soviet Union in the 1930s, the concept of state capitalism was taken on board by many more authors, but, in the process, gained a somewhat different and narrower meaning: that of an economy in which the state is the only employer. Obviously, this shift in meaning was caused by the structural transformation of the Soviet Union itself, which involved both the disappearance of the traditional market after the NEP period, and the construction of the state as the omnipotent centre of power.

Theories of state capitalism were the most popular among all Western-Marxist interpretations mooted in the 1929–1941 period. What explained

---

[12] Renner 1917; Steuermann 1931.
[13] Cited here according to Daniels 1960, pp. 85–6.
[14] Olle 1974a, pp. 121–31; Ambrosius 1981, pp. 29–33; Borilin 1929.

this popularity? The answer must be essentially that these theories remained very close to the old unilinear schema. Even if state capitalism did not constitute an 'ordinary', but a 'new' or 'higher' form of capitalism, it could be straightforwardly inserted into the old sequence of feudalism – (state-) capitalism – socialism. Beyond the variants discussed below, there were still many more other contributions of a similar type. These are not discussed here however, because they add nothing theoretically to the variants covered.[15]

Miasnikov

At the beginning of 1931, the oppositional Bolshevik Gavril Miasnikov[16] completed a pamphlet about the character of Soviet society, which he published himself under the title *The Current Deception* [*Ocherednoi obman*]. A Dutch version was published in the left-communist journal *De Nieuwe Tijd*.[17]

According to Miasnikov, a violent counter-revolution had taken place in the Soviet Union. After the working class had initially held power through its workers' councils, the 'world bourgeoisie' had in three years' time succeeded in achieving a fundamental shift in the balance of power, through interventions and civil war: 'Industry was petrified, the workers had been atomised and therefore the workers' councils were also destroyed. The proletariat ceased to be the ruling class, which possessed political and economic hegemony [...].'[18]

Because an indigenous bourgeoisie was mostly lacking, power fell in the hands of peasants, the numerous 'petty bourgeoisie'. This situation however could not last for very long:

> The small bourgeoisie triumphed, but this victory would not mean progress
> but regression for it. It can govern industry only by means of a bureaucratic

---

[15] For example Steuermann 1931, pp. 183–212; Mänchen-Helfen 1932.

[16] G.T. Miasnikov (1889–1946?), a metal worker, was a Bolshevik since 1906. From 1918 he took a left-oppositionist position; for some time he was a prominent advocate of the Workers' Opposition. In 1928 he escaped from the Soviet Union to France, where he remained until after the Second World War. In 1946, he returned to the USSR and was presumably executed. See Sinigaglia 1973 and Avrich 1984.

[17] Miasnikoff 1932; see also Miasnikoff 1939.

[18] Miasnikoff 1932, p. 40.

apparatus and because of the typical atomised structure of this class, it cannot exercise sufficient control over the bureaucracy, and thus cannot prevent that the latter develops from a maid-servant into a mistress oppressing her.[19]

In the course of the 1920s, the bureaucracy had thus transformed itself into a ruling class. Its power was based on state ownership of the means of production, and it constantly sought to expand this power:

The bureaucracy, which stands at the head of nationalised industry and which gradually destroys or assimilates the remainders of private capitalist exploitation, possesses the tendency to expand its domination over all industrial areas.[20]

Therewith a 'state capitalism' had emerged, which included exploitation and surplus-value production.[21] '[The] whole of the state economy of the USSR represents as it were one large factory, in which an ordered co-operation and division of labor between different workplaces is present.'[22]

Miasnikov warned against placing this new form of capitalism at the same level as the old private capitalism. The nationalisation of land, mines and industry, as well as its complete control over the state budget, meant that the bureaucracy could operate much more effectively than the classical bourgeoisie. It was able to direct capital flows at will, and arrange means of finance for investments which were not available to 'ordinary' employers, without being obstructed in implementing its plans by landowners or other enterprises. In this sense, Soviet society was at a higher level of development than competitive capitalism:

The bureaucracy may not always manage business well, but always does it better than the bourgeoisie. It functions under completely different circumstances and represents a higher form of production compared to any private production system.[23]

In international conflicts, socialists therefore had to take the side of the Soviet Union.

---

[19] Miasnikoff 1932, p. 44.
[20] Miasnikoff 1932, p. 84.
[21] Miasnikoff 1932, pp. 82–3.
[22] Miasnikoff 1932, p. 111.
[23] Miasnikoff 1932, p. 110.

Adler

In 1932, Friedrich Adler,[24] who, from 1923, was the secretary of the Labour and Socialist International, presented his own theory of the Soviet Union as 'an individual comrade and not in my function as international secretary'.[25] Rejecting both Kautsky's continual Cassandra cries as well as apologetic Marxist tendencies, Adler introduced a comparative historical perspective.

He shared Kautsky's and Marx's opinion that a socialist society could only be built in a situation in which industry and the working class were highly developed. But because such a situation did not exist in post-revolutionary Russia, Stalin's 'experiment' should be judged as an attempt to realise, through the sacrifice of a whole generation of workers, the primitive accumulation process[26] which in developed capitalism had already occurred earlier, and in this way lay the foundations for a socialist Soviet Union.

> If we try to understand the contemporary Soviet Union, we find with growing surprise, that in its industrialisation, even though there are no longer any private capitalists, the characteristic stages of primitive accumulation indicated by Marx again make their appearance. *The Stalinist experiment is industrialisation through primitive accumulation without the co-operation of private capitalists.*[27]

Since the historical bearers of the process – free capitalists – were absent, state power as such necessarily took their place. The social function of the dictatorship was accordingly: 'Subordination of the workers themselves, to carry out primitive accumulation over their heads, and nip in the bud every attempt at resistance by the workers against the sacrifices which were imposed on them.'[28]

---

[24] Adler (1879–1960), from 1911 to 1916 secretary of the Austrian Social-Democratic Party, was in 1917 sentenced to prison after the attempt to assassinate premier Karl Graf Stürgkh. He was freed in 1918 and belonged to the founders of the Labour and Socialist International. See Braunthal 1965 and Ardelt 1984.

[25] Adler 1932, p. 4. A short time afterwards Adler polemicised from the same position against Kautsky and said he spoke for the overwhelming majority of the International: Adler 1933.

[26] About 'the so-called primitive accumulation' see Chapter 24 of the first volume of Marx's *Capital*.

[27] Adler 1932, p. 9.

[28] Adler 1932, p. 10.

On the whole, he believed a form of state capitalism existed which, on the one hand, necessarily developed because of the absence of revolutions in more advanced countries that might have supported the young Soviet republic, and, on the other hand, because of the weakness of the private capitalism existing at the time this revolution occurred.

With this conclusion, the phenomena of planned economy were also cast in a different light:

> For Marx and Engels, the transition to *planned economy* was only possible in the framework of the realisation of a socialist social order. Now we realise, that planned economy does not have socialism as its precondition, but only has the negative criterion of the abolition of private capitalist competition as its precondition and is also quite possible on the basis of *state capitalism*.[29]

That this interpretation had wide support in (left) Social-Democratic circles is demonstrated by the response of Rafail Abramovich Rejn, one of the leaders of the Menshevik emigrants, who remarked that Adler's analysis was essentially the same as that of Russian social democracy.[30]

Wagner

In 1933, Helmut Wagner (1904–89), a left Social-Democratic journalist and teacher who had escaped from Dresden to Switzerland at the end of 1934,[31] wrote a text called 'Theses on Bolshevism'. These theses were partly the result of discussions held since 1932 by the *Rote Kämpfer*, a small illegal group influenced by council communism.[32]

---

[29] Adler 1932, pp. 11–12.
[30] Abramowitsch 1932, p. 145. A more in-depth discussion about Menshevik viewpoints can be found in Wolin 1974; Anon. 1981a, pp. 131–204; and Liebich 1981.
[31] In 1941, Wagner emigrated to the United States, and, a few years later, he broke with Marxism. Röder and Strauss 1980, pp. 787–8; Müller 1977, pp. 66, 155 note 480; Buick 2004.
[32] Ihlau 1969. Ihlau believes that the 'Theses' were distributed exclusively as stencils among illegal German groups and that they were 'never published anywhere' (p. 95). This is not correct however. In 1934 the 'Theses' were both published by the *Rätekorrespondenz*, a German periodical published in Amsterdam, and in an American translation by the *International Council Correspondence* in Chicago. See Wagner 1934. Both versions contain 67 theses; in the German text, the last thesis is numbered 68, but thesis 60 is omitted. In the American version, the numbering is from 1 to 67, such that thesis 60 corresponds to thesis 61 in the German version. The American text states in an

Whereas Gorter, Pannekoek and others had earlier emphasised that Eastern and Western Europe were essentially different, Wagner went a step further by considering Russia as a geographical, political and economic *nexus* between Europe and Asia. Europe, together with North America, formed the 'highly developed capitalist center of active imperialist advance'; East Asia constituted 'the colonial center of passive imperialist plunder'. Both these centres embodied axes of the international class struggle, and together influenced the development of Russia.[33] In the Russian economy, an underdeveloped Asiatic agriculture which involved feudal elements and which had continued until 1917 was combined with modern European industry.[34] This special combination of feudalism and capitalism created combined and complicated tasks for the Russian Revolution.[35]

In fact, it had to shoulder the tasks of the bourgeois revolution without support of the bourgeoisie. It had to execute the *tasks of the bourgeoisie*, because the challenge was primarily one of overthrowing absolutism, liquidating the privileges of the nobility and forming a modern state apparatus.[36] All this had to occur without the support of the bourgeoisie, because this class had tied itself to Tsarism, and had thus already become counterrevolutionary even before its own revolution was completed.[37]

A 'class triangle' had taken over the tasks of the bourgeoisie:[38] the enormous peasant masses formed the 'passive foundation', the numerically smaller but militant workers formed the 'fighting instrument', and a small layer of the intelligentsia 'arose as the master mind of the revolution'.[39] Bolshevism succeeded in uniting the rebellions of the workers and peasants and seizing power. But the new régime which was established in 1917 was therefore, from the beginning, in a precarious position: it had to ensure that the two classes on which it was based, despite their partly contradictory interests, did not

---

editorial preface that the theses were collectively written by 'the Group of International Communists of Holland'. Perhaps this explains why the theses 'repeatedly have been falsely attributed to the GIC'. See Jaap Kloosterman, 'Aantekeningen', in Pannekoek 1972, p. 198. The 'Theses' are cited here according to the American version.
[33] Thesis 5.
[34] Thesis 6.
[35] Thesis 10.
[36] Thesis 9.
[37] Thesis 13.
[38] Thesis 18.
[39] Thesis 17.

openly clash with each other.[40] In order to accomplish this, the autonomisation of the state apparatus vis-à-vis both classes was inevitable:

> Just as the state apparatus of Czarism ruled independently over the two possessing classes, so the new Bolshevik state apparatus began to make itself independent of its double class basis. Russia stepped out of the conditions of Czarist absolutism into those of Bolshevik absolutism.[41]

The end result of this development was a capitalism organised by the state without a bourgeoisie, upon a *dual* class basis. Soviet state policy consequently oscillated between the interests of the workers and peasants. The first five-year plan and forced collectivisation were nothing but attempts to contain these contradictions by violence, but, so far, they had only 'increased the economic difficulties to the danger point of an explosion of the economic contradictions'.[42]

The functioning of the Soviet economy was basically capitalist: the foundation was formed by commodity production, the overarching goal was profitability, bourgeois incentive and reward systems were used, and the workers created surplus-value.[43]

> The Russian State does not, to be sure, reveal any class of people, who individually and directly are the beneficiaries of the surplus-value production, but it pockets this surplus value through the bureaucratic, parasitical apparatus as a whole. In addition to its own quite costly maintenance, the surplus value produced serves for the expansion of production, the support of the peasant class and as a means of settlement for the foreign obligations of the State. [...] The Russian state economy [...] is state capitalism under the historically unique conditions of the bolshevik régime and accordingly represents a different and more advanced type of capitalist production than even the greatest and most advanced countries have to show.[44]

In 1936–7, during his exile in Switzerland, Wagner elaborated his theses into a large but unpublished manuscript titled *Foundations of Bolshevik Power Politics*

---

[40] Theses 30, 31, 35, 36, 37.
[41] Thesis 44.
[42] Thesis 57.
[43] Theses 58, 59.
[44] Thesis 59.

(On the Sociology of Bolshevism).[45] He published some parts of his findings under
the pseudonym of Rudolf Sprenger.[46] Broadly speaking, these publications
were consistent with his 'Theses'.

Worrall

The attachment of the label 'state capitalist' to the Soviet Union was not
substantively argued for by Miasnikov, Adler and Wagner. They had
simply asserted that the USSR featured surplus-value production, capitalist
exploitation etc. but did not provide further arguments to substantiate this
interpretation. Unsurprisingly, this weakness was quickly seized upon by
the apologists.[47] Towards the end of the 1930s, the theory of state capitalism
became gradually more sophisticated in a theoretical sense. In 1939, the
American *Modern Quarterly* published an analysis titled 'U.S.S.R.: Proletarian
or Capitalist State ?'[48] Its author, Ryan Worrall (1903–95), an Australian
Trotskyist,[49] endeavoured to create a Marxist foundation for the theory of
Soviet state capitalism. To emphasise his theoretical orthodoxy, Worrall
referred to three arguments from the founders of 'scientific socialism':

a) In two places in the third volume of *Capital* – 'so neglected by students of
   Karl Marx' – the essence of the capitalist mode of production was defined:
   concentration of the means of production in the hands of a small minority
   of owners, social organisation of the labour process, creation of the world
   market,[50] commodity and surplus-value production.[51] The second thing that

---

[45] This title ('Die Grundlagen der bolschewistischen Machtpolitik (Zur Soziologie
des Bolschewismus)') is mentioned in Ihlau 1969, p. 101, note 232. The dating 1936–7
is based on a Spanish pamphlet, published under a pseudonym. See Sprenger 1947,
p. 3.

[46] Sprenger 1933–4, pp. 314–20; Sprenger 1940.

[47] 'Because one cannot deny, that private capitalism does not exist in the Soviet
Union, but on the other hand one cannot affirm that socialism rules there, the only
thing that remains is to say that it is state capitalist' – Linde 1932, p. 3.

[48] Worrall 1939.

[49] See Worrall Tribute 1996.

[50] The reference is to the following passage from the third volume of Marx's *Capital*
(p. 375): 'three cardinal facts about capitalist production: (1) The concentration of the
means of production in a few hands [...] (2) The organization of labour itself as social
labour [...]. (3) Establishment of the world market.'

[51] The reference is to the following passage: 'Two characteristic traits mark the
capitalist mode of production right from the start. *Firstly*, it produces its products as
commodities. [...]', Marx 1981, p. 1019.

particularly marks the capitalist mode of production is the production of surplus-value as the direct object and decisive motive of production.'[52]

b) In his analysis of share capital, also in Volume 3 of *Capital*, Marx had shown that in joint-stock companies, the managers of enterprises became 'directors' of the capital of others, while those supplying the capital only retained an ownership title. In this way, capital as private property was 'abolished' within the boundaries of the capitalist mode of production itself.[53]

c) In his *Anti-Dühring*, Engels had not only anticipated the growth of share-capital, but also the tendency to leave investments too large for private entrepreneurs (for example, in the railways sector) to the state to organise. Both developments did not imply the disappearance of capitalism, according to Engels; the capital relationship was not abolished by it, but only intensified.[54]

From (a) Worrall concluded that private ownership (especially of means of production) did not have to be an essential feature of capitalism 'in every phase of its development'. From (b) and especially from (c) he deduced that 'the further development of capitalism, in the direction of state ownership of the means of production' could lead to 'the virtual abolition of private property' while the essence of capitalism remained the same. With his appeal to the classics, Worrall appears to have wanted to prove in particular that a society in which state and capital fused in one dominating totality was a *theoretical possibility* within the tradition of scientific socialism. Lenin was also cited in this context as witness.

---

[52] Marx 1981, pp. 1019–20.

[53] The reference is to the following passage: 'III. Formation of joint-stock companies. Through this: [...] 2. [...] It is the abolition of capitals as private property within the confines of the capitalist mode of production itself. 3. Transformation of the actual functioning capitalist into a mere manager, in charge of other people's capital, and of the capital owner into a mere owner, a mere money capitalist.' Marx 1981, p. 567.

[54] The reference is especially to the following passage: 'The modern state, no matter what its form, is essentially a capitalist machine, the state of the capitalists, the ideal personification of the total national capital. The more it proceeds to the taking over of productive forces, the more does it actually become the national capitalist, the more citizens does it exploit. The workers remain wage-workers – proletarians. The capitalist relation is not done away with. It is rather brought to a head.' Engels 1878, p. 266.

The next step in Worrall's argument aimed to make a credible case for the view that the theoretical possibility had become *a reality* in the Soviet Union: that an historically unique fusion of economic and political centres of power had really occurred on a capitalist basis. Worrall's theorems in this regard can be summarised as follows:

i)   The Stalinist bureaucracy was not a bourgeois class. Its *structure*, after all, did not show any similarity with the bourgeoisie based on private property.

ii) Nevertheless, the *function* of the bureaucracy was identical to the function of the bourgeoisie:

> its social aim, objectively speaking, is the accumulation of capital in Russia –
> the production of commodities, the extraction of surplus-value from the
> working class, the realization of this surplus-value as profits of the State
> and the conversion of profits into further State property, especially capital
> in the form of further means of production; more factories, more machinery,
> more mines, etc.[55]

iii) The Soviet Union would be a workers' state, if the bureaucracy was subordinate to the working class, that is to say if the soviets or other forms of workers' democracy governed the policy of the bureaucracy. This, however, was not the case and 'precisely that fact makes the Russian State a capitalist instead of a workers' State'.[56]

iv) The Soviet system did not export capital, and exploited no colonies. It was therefore not imperialist, although it was capitalist.

v)   The Soviet system was closer to socialism than ordinary capitalism. It formed: 'a transition stage in which the principle of private property has been abolished, and the means of production are withheld from proletarian control only by a precariously placed bureaucracy'.[57]

vi) Soviet capitalism was able to develop from the proletarian October Revolution because, from approximately 1923, a violent counterrevolution had occurred, 'spread over a decade'. This counterrevolution was possible, because of a combination of objective factors (economic and cultural

---

[55] Worrall 1939, p. 12.
[56] Ibid.
[57] Worrall 1939, p. 13.

backwardness, the influence of the world market and capitalist ideology) and a subjective factor, namely a level of resistance by Trotsky and others during the crucial years of 1923 to 1929 which had been too weak.[58]

Although Worrall's argumentation, to some extent, recalled the views of Korsch (creeping counterrevolution), his contribution is innovative, insofar as he was apparently the first to use the concept of state capitalism not just as a descriptive label, but also *analytically*. For him, the distinction between a workers' state and an accumulation régime rested only on who held political power. A capitalist accumulation régime, he considered, could also be in the interests of the working class, if the working class *itself* had decided on the capitalist exploitation of itself.

Pollock

In 1941, Friedrich Pollock (1894–1970), the well-known economist of the Frankfurt school[59] published a theory of state capitalism in the *Studies in Philosophy and Social Science* (formerly *Zeitschrift für Sozialforschung*). In this publication, he not only continued his studies of the Soviet Union which he had begun in the 1920s[60] but also his series of essays about capitalist crisis and planned economy. Already in 1932, Pollock had argued that capitalism would be able to find a new equilibrium through using planning technology.[61] And, in his contribution of 1941, Pollock developed that idea into a general theory of state capitalism. The theory was primarily inspired by the experience of Nazi Germany and Italy, and Pollock hesitated about the question of whether the theory as a whole could be validly applied to the Soviet Union, because in that society – in contrast to national socialism and fascism – no fusion had occurred between the old capitalist groups and the state, and the means of production were instead expropriated from the previous propertied classes. Cautiously, Pollock therefore expressed his doubts about 'whether our model of state capitalism fits the Soviet Union in its present phase'.[62] Yet this reservation did not stop him from including the USSR in his considerations

---

[58] Worrall 1939, p. 18.
[59] Jay 1973; Dubiel 1975; Wiggershaus 1994.
[60] Pollock 1929.
[61] Pollock 1932.
[62] Pollock 1941, p. 221, note.

and, for example, to claim that the system of state-capitalist distribution was more developed there than in Germany.[63]

Apart from totalitarian variants of state capitalism, Pollock also envisaged democratic variants as a possibility – these, however, would, for the meantime, remain only hypothetical constructions 'to which our experience gives us few clues'.[64] The term state capitalism referred, in his opinion, not so much to a form of government but to more general conditions: it involved a social formation which was no longer privately capitalist but not yet socialist, in which the profit motive still played an important role and the state had taken over essential functions from private capitalists.

In state capitalism, the autonomy of market activity had been abolished. In its place, state regulation had emerged: a general plan indicated the desired production, consumption, savings and investments; prices are no longer freely moving, but fixed administratively; the profit interests of individuals and groups are subordinated to the general plan; guesswork and improvisation are replaced by scientifically-based management; economic 'laws of motion' play no significant role anymore.[65] In the enterprises, private capitalists were divested of their power. Management became as good as independent from capital; the entrepreneurial function was transferred to the state, or, in any case, was strongly determined by the state; the old capitalist remained – insofar as his abilities were not deployed by the state – only as a rentier.[66] The distribution of goods and labour-power could be realised in different ways: through direct allocation, co-ordination by cartels, associated quota-systems, etc.

Since there were no longer any economic 'laws of motion' in this system, there could not be any economic limits either: 'Economic problems in the old sense no longer exist when the coordination of all economic activities is effected by a conscious plan [...].'[67] The only strictures were of a non-economic nature: for example, the supply of sufficient raw materials, know-how, employees; contradictions within the ruling group, arising from diverging

---

[63] Pollock 1941, p. 211, note.
[64] Pollock 1941, p. 200.
[65] Pollock 1941, pp. 204–7.
[66] Pollock 1941, pp. 209–11.
[67] Pollock 1941, p. 217.

social positions, different power strategies, etc.; and pressure from below.[68] As far as the totalitarian variants were concerned, a distinction could be made between Italy and Germany, where a new ruling class had emerged as 'amalgamation of the key bureaucrats in business, state and party allied with the remaining vested interests', and the Soviet Union, where the bureaucratic élite was not tied to the remnants of private property in the means of production.[69]

At the same time that Pollock elaborated this model, his close friend and colleague Max Horkheimer wrote an essay about the authoritarian state, which was published only many years later.[70] Most probably, this essay was inspired partly by an exchange of views with Pollock[71] and it can help to clarify the implications of the latter's theories. More acutely than Pollock, Horkheimer drew a boundary-line between the fascist régimes which he characterised as a 'mixed form' and the Stalinist 'integral étatism or state socialism'. While, under fascism, private entrepreneurs still existed – even if their field of operation was restricted – and continued to consume great portions of surplus-value, in an integral étatism, socialisation was implemented by decree:

> Private capitalists are eliminated. Henceforth, dividends are only collected from government bonds. As a result of the revolutionary past of the régime, the petty struggles between officials and departments is not, as with fascism, complicated by the differences in the social origin and connections inside the bureaucratic staff. This has led to much friction in fascist régimes. Integral statism is not a retreat but an advance of power. It can exist without racism. However, the producers, to whom capital legally belongs, 'remain wage workers – proletarians', no matter how much is done for them. Factory regimentation is extended to the entire society.[72]

Following Horkheimer's interpretation, two stages can be distinguished within state capitalism: the 'mixed form' of fascism, and the 'integral form' of Stalinism. By relating this distinction back to the theories of Pollock, the

[68] Pollock 1941, pp. 217–19.
[69] Pollock 1941, p. 221.
[70] Horkheimer 1942.
[71] Pollock and Horkheimer were friends from 1911 until Pollock's death in 1970 and maintained close relations. See e.g. Gumnior and Ringguth 1983, p. 13.
[72] Horkheimer 1942, p. 19; English translation p. 102. The formulation 'remain wage-workers – proletarians' is a reference to Friedrich Engels (see note 54).

latter's hesitation about subsuming the USSR and Nazi Germany in one model becomes explicable: the theory had concentrated primarily on Nazism, which did not yet feature a complete fusion of the state and capital, yet simultaneously tried to absolve the Soviet Union in the modelling process. Some vagueness therefore necessarily resulted.

3.ii. Trotsky: the theory of the degenerated workers' state

A completely novel theory was developed by Leon Trotsky.[73] Trotsky's learning process with respect to developments in the Soviet Union was extraordinarily complex. From his numerous writings it is clear that, notwithstanding the many contradictions and ambivalences which can be identified in his ideas,[74] he maintained one unitary form of reasoning throughout the whole period as the core of his thought. This reasoning can be formalised as follows:

a) The achievements of a (necessarily violent) social revolution could only be annulled by a (necessarily violent) counter-revolution;

b) The October Revolution was a violent social (proletarian) revolution, which resulted in a workers' state.

From (a) and (b) it followed that:

c) So long as no violent counterrevolution has occurred, it remained necessary to characterise the Soviet Union as a workers' state.

All the phenomena of bureaucratisation and degeneration were fitted by Trotsky into continually changing theoretical frameworks, which had these assumptions as their unchanging core idea. In order to sustain this interpretation when the dictatorship of the bureaucratic élite became

---

[73] Lev Bronstein (1879–1940) alias Lev D. Trotsky, Russian socialist, played an important role in the revolution of 1905 as leader of the St Petersburg Soviet. He led from 1913 the *mezhraiontsy*, a group of Social Democrats who wanted to re-unite the Bolsheviks and the Mensheviks. He joined the Bolsheviks in July 1917, became Chairman of the Petrograd Soviet and led the Military Revolutionary Committee which co-ordinated the October insurrection. From 1918 until 1925, he was People's Commissar of War. In the 1920s, he played a prominent role in the anti-Stalinist opposition; he was expelled from the Party in 1927 and in 1929 exiled from Russia. In 1938, he founded the Fourth International. In 1940, he was assassinated by an agent of Stalin. The standard biography is Deutscher 1954d, 1959 and 1963.

[74] A number of changes and contradictions in Trotsky's thinking are analysed in McNeal 1977, especially pp. 31–3.

increasingly one of terror, Trotsky had to adapt the content of his political categories to the evolving political circumstances. Given that the 'workers' state,' for him, was primarily another word for 'dictatorship of the proletariat', and the 'dictatorship of the proletariat', for him, ultimately meant the same as 'workers' democracy', Trotsky at first could not conceive of a workers' state which did not – at the very least potentially – hold political power. As late as 1931, he declared:

> In the working class, the tradition of the October overthrow is alive and strong; firmly rooted are the habits of class thought; unforgotten in the older generation are the lessons of the revolutionary struggles and the conclusions of Bolshevik strategy; in the masses of the people and especially in the proletariat lives the hatred against the former ruling classes and their parties. All these tendencies in their entirety constitute not only the reserve of the future, but also the living power of today, which preserves the Soviet Union as a worker's state. [...] *The recognition of the present Soviet State as a workers' state* not only *signifies* that the bourgeoisie can conquer power only by means of an armed uprising but also *that the proletariat of the USSR has not forfeited the possibility of subordinating the bureaucracy to it*, of reviving the party again, and of regenerating the régime of the dictatorship – without a new revolution, *with the methods and on the road of reform.*[75]

With this 'reformist' perspective in mind, Trotsky for many years refused to write off the Communist parties in the Soviet Union and elsewhere. It was also for this reason, that he distanced himself from like-minded spirits who ventured to organise outside of the Comintern.[76]

After Hitler's conquest of power in 1933 – an event which the German Communists watched rather powerlessly – Trotsky gradually abandoned his idea that party and state could still be reformed.[77] But, in so doing, he created

---

[75] Trotsky 1931, pp. 11–12; English edition, pp. 224–5 (italics by MvdL).

[76] One thinks of Trotsky's criticism of his co-thinkers Rosmer and Monatte, who wanted to form their own organisation. See Trotsky 1925. Typical also is the following statement from an interview in 1929: 'The talk of a Fourth International which I am supposed to be founding is utter rubbish. The Social Democratic International and the Communist International both have deep historical roots. No intermediate (Two-and-a-Half) or additional (Fourth) Internationals are required'. Trotsky 1929, p. 108.

[77] Trotsky justified these changes in his position by reasoning by analogy: just as in the French revolution a 'Thermidor' would have occurred which resulted in a 'Bonapartist' régime. See on this analogy: Law 1982; Bergman 1987, especially pp. 83–98; Caillosse 1989.

a problem for himself. On the one hand, he had argued that the absence of a violent counterrevolution 'proved' that the Soviet Union was still a workers' state, but, on the other hand, reform of the régime was now no longer possible, and therefore a *new* revolution was on the historical agenda. To clear away this obvious inconsistency, Trotsky seems to have resorted to Kautsky's old distinction between a political and an economic revolution:[78] Trotsky reasoned that, because a workers' state had already been established in the USSR, only a *political* revolution was necessary in the future, which had to clear away obstacles restricting the free functioning and further development of the planned economy.

In 1936, Trotsky completed the manuscript for his book *What Is the Soviet Union and Where Is It Going?* which, in the following years, appeared in several countries in translations such as *La Révolution trahie*, *The Revolution Betrayed*, and *Verratene Revolution*.[79] In this work, which since that time has remained an important – sometimes negative, sometimes positive – point of reference, Trotsky adhered to the concept of a workers' state; at the same time, he sought to integrate the phenomenon of bureaucratisation into his theory. Just like before, his point of departure was that the Soviet régime with its contradictions could not be defined as socialist, but was 'a *preparatory* régime *transitional* from capitalism to socialism'.[80] This then explained why the Soviet state possessed a dual character: 'socialistic, in so far as it defends social property in the means of production; bourgeois, in so far as the distribution of life's goods is carried out with a capitalistic measure of value and all consequences ensuing therefrom'.[81]

Because socialist characteristics dominated in the sphere of production (state monopoly of foreign trade, nationalisation of industry, planned economy), and because that was the only reason why it still made sense to speak of a workers' state, the roots of bureaucracy could, by definition, not be located within this productive sphere. They had to be found in the sphere of distribution, where scarcity and thus bourgeois norms of distribution prevailed:

---

[78] 'Essentially in Russia it is in the first instance not a question of social revolution, not about the conquest of political power by one of the subordinate classes of society to clear the way for a new mode of production, but about a political revolution, about clearing away the political obstacles, which hinder the free functioning of an already existing mode of production.' Kautsky 1904–5, p. 675.

[79] The original manuscript in Russian is held in the Trotsky Archives at Harvard.

[80] Trotsky 1937b, p. 52.

[81] Trotsky 1937b, p. 58.

The basis for bureaucratic rule is the poverty of society in objects of consumption, with the resulting struggle of each against all. When there is enough goods in a store the purchasers can come whenever they want to. When there [are few] goods the purchasers are compelled to stand in line. When the lines are very long, it is necessary to appoint a policeman to keep order. Such is the starting point of the Soviet bureaucracy. It 'knows' who is to get something and who has to wait.[82]

To the extent that the productive forces were less developed in a postrevolutionary country, the social weight of the bureaucracy would, naturally, be greater there. It stood to reason that the bureaucracy would therefore appropriate special privileges:

Nobody who has wealth to distribute ever omits himself. Thus out of a social necessity there has developed an organ which has far outgrown its socially necessary function, and become an independent factor and therewith the source of great danger for the whole organism.[83]

In no other historical situation did the bureaucracy – which Trotsky sometimes refers to as a 'caste' and, at other times, as a '(social) stratum' – acquire such a degree of independence from the ruling class (the proletariat). Even Lenin would, if he had lived longer, only have been able to brake that degeneration, but no more. In brief, 'The leaden rump of the bureaucracy outweighed the head of the revolution'.[84]

Possibly, Trotsky himself sensed that there was something artificial about his argument. It had always been axiomatic for him, that planned economy and workers' democracy necessarily had to go hand in hand. The one could not be maintained without the other, because only in a democracy would trustworthy information and optimal effort from all concerned be guaranteed. This explains why he built a temporal perspective into his theory. A degenerated workers' state, such as described in *The Revolution Betrayed*, could not possibly last for a long time. In 1938, he noted:

Democracy [...] is the one and only conceivable mechanism for preparing the socialist system of economy and realizing it in life. [...]. What the

---

[82] Trotsky 1937b, p. 110.
[83] Trotsky 1937b, p. 111.
[84] Trotsky 1937b, p. 94.

lexicon of Stalin's justice designates as 'sabotage' is in reality one of the evil consequences of bureaucratic methods of domineering. The manifestations of disproportion, wastefulness and entanglement, constantly increasing, threaten to undermine the very foundations of planned economy.[85]

Not long before writing this, he had already warned:

That which was a 'bureaucratic deformation' is at the present moment preparing to devour the workers' state, without leaving any remains [...]. If the proletariat drives out the Soviet bureaucracy *in time*, then it will still find the nationalized means of production and the basic elements of the planned economy after its victory.[86]

The bureaucratic degeneration was, for Trotsky, fundamentally a phenomenon of short duration. 'For Trotsky', as Pierre Frank correctly noted, 'Stalinism was an accident, not a durable creation of history'.[87] Hence Trotsky's use of imagery referring to the bureaucracy as a 'stillborn child', or as a 'cancerous growth' that could and should be surgically removed, or his comparison of the USSR with a car that, although it had crashed, would be able to drive away again after being fixed by a mechanic.[88]

This perception of historical time is almost always overlooked in commentaries on Trotsky. It is doubtful whether the temporal limit can be explained mainly as the product of the personal psychology of Trotsky himself – as Fritz Sternberg suggested.[89] A more plausible interpretation is that it was a direct result of Trotsky's conviction that planned economy and bureaucratic dictatorship were fundamentally incompatible.

In this context, it is also important to consider Trotsky's overall assessment of the international situation. For Trotsky, capitalism had entered its final phase; when he founded the Fourth International in 1938 and bequeathed this organisation with a 'transitional programme for socialist revolution',

---

[85] Trotsky 1938d, p. 19, cited according to the English edition, p. 127.
[86] Trotsky 1938a, p. 18, cited according to the English edition, pp. 67, 69.
[87] Frank 1977c, p. 21.
[88] Trotsky 1939.
[89] 'For Trotsky, recent events in Russia were no longer to be analyzed objectively, but had become components in a personal equation designed to answer the question: shall I, Trotsky, return to Russia as I did in 1905 and 1917, and shall I become the leader of a new anti-Stalinist revolution? This personal equation underlay everything he said, even though he never, of course, expressed it in so many words.' Sternberg 1963, p. 156.

this political document was titled *The Death Agony of Capitalism and the Tasks of the Fourth International*. The long phase of economic downturn affecting the capitalist system meant, for Trotsky, that the productive forces could no longer grow. The system as a whole had stagnated, and had begun to show more and more barbaric and primitive characteristics:

> Mankind's productive forces stagnate. Already new inventions and improvements fail to raise the level of material wealth. [...] The bourgeoisie itself sees no way out. [...] The decay of capitalism continues under the sign of the Phrygian cap in France as under the sign of the swastika in Germany. Nothing short of the overthrow of the bourgeoisie can open a road out.[90]

The Soviet Union, which showed rapid economic development despite Stalinist dictatorship, appeared in a clear positive contrast with this picture of general social decay. The distinction between a developing and a decaying society was, for Trotsky, also the ultimate foundation for his appeal to defend the Soviet Union unconditionally, in the event of armed conflicts with capitalist countries.

The world situation was, in Trotsky's eyes, so unstable at the end of the 1930s that, with a new world war looming ahead, the existence of both capitalism and the Stalinist bureaucracy would be challenged by a forward-storming proletarian revolution. Only workers' power still had a future, in the short term. In 1938, he expressed his prognosis accordingly in the following way:

> If this war provokes, as we firmly believe, a proletarian revolution, it must inevitably lead to the overthrow of the bureaucracy in the USSR and regeneration of Soviet democracy on a far higher economic and cultural basis than in 1918. [...] If, however, it is conceded that the present war will provoke not revolution but a decline of the proletariat, then there remains another alternative: the further decay of monopoly capitalism, its further fusion with the state and the replacement of democracy wherever it still remained by a totalitarian régime.

The Soviet bureaucracy would, in that case, be able to transform itself into a new exploiting class, which would reflect 'the eclipse of civilization'.[91] In

---

[90] Trotsky 1938c, pp. 1–2; English translation, pp. 111, 113.
[91] Trotsky 1939, p. 4; English translation, pp. 8–9.

this way, Trotsky translated the old adage 'socialism or barbarism' as though it concerned two short-term alternatives. A third, intermediate route, along which the proletariat would not achieve world revolution, and in which both the structures of the Soviet Union and those of capitalism would remain intact in their essentials, was a prospect he could not envisage.

3.iii. Theories of a new mode of production

The first attempt at a theory according to which the Soviet Union had become a wholly new kind of society is usually credited to Bruno Rizzi, who published an interpretation of this type in 1939.[92] Further research, however, reveals that, already in the first years after the beginning of Stalin's 'great leap forwards', similar ideas were presented by among others Laurat and Weil.[93]

Laurat

Lucian Laurat (1898–1973) was born in Vienna as Otto Maschl. In 1918, he was one of the founders of the German-Austrian Communist Party. After teaching for some time as university lecturer in Moscow, he left the communist movement around 1927 and settled in France. There he soon joined the social democrats, and became from the beginning of the 1930s a prominent advocate of Henri de Man's 'planism'.[94]

In his 1931 book, titled *The Soviet Economy*, Laurat presented an all too often ignored and wrongly interpreted analysis of Soviet society.[95] In fact, he was the first to create an elaborate theoretical foundation for the view that

---

[92] One example will suffice: '[...] the main idea which Rizzi could claim to have fathered was the neo-marxist notion of communist society as a distinct social form (in his terminology "bureaucratic collectivism") – a fact which turned upon its being ruled by its own "new class"'. – Westoby 1985, p. 2. An exception to the rule was the 1977 Portuguese anthology *A Natureza da USSR*, in which Simone Weil is featured.

[93] Most probably, the theory of the new class society emerged already in the first half of the 1930s among broader circles of critical Marxists. Thus Domanevskaja wrote in 1935 about 'some critics of the Soviet system', who claimed that 'in the place of the capitalist class a new ruling class has appeared. The state, they say, owns the means of production, and the state bureaucracy, which manages the means of production only in its own interests, exploits the working class.' Domanevskaja 1934–5, p. 272.

[94] Hautmann 1971, pp. 80, 105, 125, 256; Lefranc 1966, pp. 72–3. Partly autobiographical is Laurat 1965. See also Harmel 1973 in the theme issue about Laurat of the magazine *Est & Ouest*.

[95] Totally unjustifiably, Gras states that: 'Laurat himself defends both the theory of the USSR as imperialist power and state capitalism'. Gras 1971, p. 385, note.

the Soviet Union had developed into a new type of society.[96] According to Laurat, the October Revolution had definitely been socialist. To claim that Russia had not been 'ripe' for socialism in 1917 (as Kautsky, Gorter, Rühle and others had done) did not make sense in his view, because, in principle, no single isolated country, however highly developed, could be called 'ripe'. After all, socialism demanded the rational use of all the resources which the planet had to offer. Hence, Laurat believed that a more correct view of the matter was that Russia had been ready for socialism, if its revolution had been part of an international revolution.[97]

That, in the course of the 1920s, an élite of bureaucrats unchecked by democratic norms had managed to consolidate themselves was, apart from the absence of a revolution in Western Europe, also attributable to a lack of proletarian cadres. The constitutionally established right to recall functionaries therefore remained a dead letter. The bureaucratic cancer could, precisely because functionaries could not be replaced, nestle in all the state institutions. The bureaucracy:

> more and more lost its connections with the proletarian masses. It erected itself as unmovable curator of the assets of the expropriated bourgeoisie, and as tutor of workers who were still insufficiently capable of management themselves. Thanks to a fortuitous omnipotence bestowed on it due to an historically exceptional situation, converted by means of the Bolshevik theory of the dictatorship into a party *over* the class, it wound up erecting itself as tutor in perpetuity.[98]

The social system that emerged in this way had many things in common with a capitalist society. *Prima facie* one could even justifiably regard the Soviet state as the greatest capitalist in the world; after all, it owned all the industries and banks, and bought labour-power from workers and employees. Nevertheless, Laurat did not believe that this captured the essence of the system. Talk of capitalism presupposed, among other things, a class antagonism, in the

---

[96] Trotsky suggested, in an attempt to downgrade the creativity of Laurat, that Laurat had committed plagiarism: 'In all probability, Laurat borrowed his theory, directly or indirectly, from Myasnikov, investing it only with a pedantically "learned" air'. Trotsky 1933, English edition, p. 112. Trotsky's accusation seems misplaced for two reasons: (i) Miasnikov's contribution misses the theoretical depth of Laurat (only a small text is involved) and (ii) Miasnikov defends a state capitalism theory.

[97] Laurat 1931, pp. 15–23.

[98] Laurat 1931, p. 162.

sense that one class owned the means of production and the others just their labour-power. But that was not the case in the Soviet Union, at least not in the non-privatised part of it (the state sector and co-operatives).

> The Soviet workers and employees work [...] in *their own* enterprises. The sums appropriated as profit in the balance sheets of those enterprises cannot be regarded as a capitalist surplus-value; they do not return to a class possessing the means of production, but to the collective [...].[99]

The bureaucratic oligarchy, therefore, did not actually own the means of production as its own property: 'It distributes the product as curator of the capitalist inheritance and as tutor of the workers. It sells its labour-power, just as its minions.'[100]

Notwithstanding his rejection of the capitalism theory, Laurat nevertheless felt obliged in his further economic analysis of the Soviet Union to use terminology which Marx had devised for his analysis of capitalism. Thus, he claimed the bureaucracy did appropriate 'surplus-value', but not in the same way as the bourgeoisie did under capitalism. Likewise, he thought the law of value still operated 'within the socialist sector',[101] even though he had previously concluded – consistent with Marx – that the law of value was 'practically inoperable'[102] under conditions of complete monopolisation of capital, i.e. when competition had disappeared.

Laurat also attacked the problem of the social position of the bureaucratic oligarchy (which he referred to alternately as a caste and a class) with concepts drawn from Marx's analysis of capital. The point of departure here was the category of productive labour, i.e. labour which creates surplus-value. As is known, Marx argued that, under capitalism, agents of circulation are excluded from this category, and performed unproductive labour.[103] But Laurat argued productive and unproductive labour nevertheless shared the common characteristic of being useful for the functioning of society. The labour of the bureaucratic élite contrasted with this, because it mostly had no use at all:

---

[99] Laurat 1931, p. 81.
[100] Laurat 1931, pp. 168–9.
[101] Laurat 1931, p. 167.
[102] Laurat 1931, p. 78.
[103] A wage-earning agent of circulation 'works as well as the next man, but the content of his labour creates neither value nor products. He is himself part of the *faux frais* [overhead costs] of production'. Marx 1978, p. 209.

When there are three people doing one job when one could do it without trouble, two of them cease to be useful. Under these conditions, the work of two workers is not only unproductive, but useless, not only a 'costly expense, although necessary' but a waste of time. [...] The bureaucrats, however useful they might be in proportionate numbers, become parasites when their numbers are disproportionately large [...]. The *faux frais* of circulation are thus more strongly increased in Russia than in Western countries.[104]

The useless character of the major part of bureaucratic work activities is then seen to result in a qualitative difference between workers' wages and bureaucrats' salaries. The latter are parasitic in nature:

[The bureaucrats] are obliged, in order to safeguard their income [...] to encroach on other categories of the national income; they withhold a part of the individual salary of the workers; they appropriate more and more the part of profit which ought to constitute the accumulation fund of industry [...].[105]

Because both competition and democratic control from below were absent – i.e. both the capitalist and socialist correctives – this parasitism could fester without restrictions.

On balance, one could say that, for Laurat, the Soviet Union was a kind of 'bastard formation' – not completely, in Kautsky's sense, but distantly related to it – in which the workers own the means of production *de jure*, but where the leadership of enterprises and the state is in the hands of a predominantly parasitic bureaucratic class. Against this background, it is no surprise that Laurat completely rejected Korsch's idea that a restoration of bourgeois relations had taken place. After all, nothing had been restored, and something completely new had come into existence:

That which distinguishes the Russian revolution from previous revolutions, and which defies every comparison, is *the appearance of a new ruling caste and the formation of an economic position of this caste in the course of the revolutionary process itself, after the conquest of power.*[106]

---

[104] Laurat 1931, pp. 171–2.
[105] Laurat 1931, p. 175.
[106] Laurat 1931, p. 155.

In a subsequent pamphlet, a sequel to his book, Laurat again explicitly posed the question whether or not 'another form of exploitation of man by man is in train of substituting itself for capitalist exploitation?'[107] A condition for characterising a society as socialist was, after all, not only that the economy was consciously and centrally led, but also that exploitation was absent and decision-making occurred democratically. Both conditions were not met in the Soviet Union. The bureaucratic élite formed 'a new exploiting class, a consumer of surplus-value'.[108]

In a later publication, titled *Is Marxism Going Bankrupt?*, Laurat – implicitly referring to Marx's portrayal of the Luddites – compared modern planning techniques with a machine which, under different social circumstances, could be operated in divergent ways. The 'intermediate régimes', in which he had meanwhile included not only the Soviet Union, but also Italy and Germany, utilised this machine in a politically abhorrent way. This, however, would not prevent democratic socialists from studying the 'new facts' that had become visible, in order to use them for their own purposes. Although the nature of fascist and Stalinist régimes differed somewhat – 'In Germany and in Italy, the ruling class is *pluto*-technocratic; in Russia it is *bureau*-technocratic'[109] – they nevertheless had in common that there was no immediate connection anymore between the leadership of the economic apparatus on the one hand, and property rights on the other; in that sense they embodied 'the decay of the capitalist class'.[110] At the same time, they completed in other ways and on a greater scale, the historical mission of capitalism, namely the preparation of socialism. Through centralisation, accumulation and planning techniques, they definitely created the possibility that the workers would seize power by means of a 'new overturn' and build a new democratically planned society.

---

[107] Laurat 1931, p. 4.
[108] Laurat 1931, p. 8. Ostensibly this passage conflicts with the thesis in *L'économie soviétique* that the bureaucratic caste sells its labour-power just like the working class. This inconsistency disappears when one considers that Laurat coupled his initial thesis to the view that the bureaucracy through its partially parasitic character appropriates 'surplus-value'.
[109] Laurat 1939, p. 210.
[110] Ibid.

Weil

The writer and philosopher Simone Weil (1909–43), a revolutionary syndicalist at the beginning of the 1930s, and famous, among other things, for working in a Renault factory in 1934–5,[111] explicitly followed up the earlier work by Laurat in her 1933 essay 'Are We Going towards Proletarian Revolution?'. She combined Laurat's analysis of 'the mechanism of exploitation exercised by the bureaucracy'[112] with other opinions which were increasingly popular at that time, about the growing power of managers and technocrats.[113] The result was a 'simple hypothesis, for the perusal of the comrades'.[114]

The point of departure of Weil's analysis was the growing division of labour and specialisation, which manifested itself on many terrains in capitalism; this tendency had as consequence that individuals lost the capacity to comprehend society in its totality. They had become imprisoned in a social constellation of which they could no longer fathom either the logic or the history. As a parallel development, a new specialism emerged: the co-ordination of numerous fragmented activities. The consequence of this was an extraordinarily rapid growth of the 'administrative function' and of bureaucratic apparati.

It was a process that could also be witnessed in the enterprises, where mental and manual labour were increasingly separated. A second contradiction was thereby created, next to the old capitalist contradiction between those who buy and those who sell labour-power, resulting in a threefold division of society, which replaced the division between capital and labour:

> Nowadays there are, around the enterprise, three very distinct social layers: the workers, the passive instruments of the enterprise, the capitalists who retain the dominant position in an economic system on the road to decomposition, and the administrators who are on the contrary supported by a technology whose evolution can only increase their power.[115]

If capitalists were removed from this system, she argued, a system of workers' power did not automatically replace it. Much more likely was that such

---

[111] Davy 1956; Cabaud 1960, pp. 11–42; Rees 1966; Krogmann 1970; Accornero et al. 1985.
[112] Weil 1933, p. 314.
[113] A well-known sign of the times was Berle and Means 1932, a work which highlighted the growing power of managers.
[114] Weil 1933, p. 314.
[115] Weil 1933, p. 315.

an 'expropriation of the expropriators' – which, after all, did not affect the new contradiction between executive and co-ordinating functions – would transform the administrative forces into a dictatorial bureaucratic caste. And a social stratum which possessed a definite monopoly would not voluntarily give up that monopoly:

> the social layer defined by the exercise of administrative functions will never accept that the legal régime of property opens access to these functions by the working masses [...]. Expropriation of whatever kind cannot resolve this problem, confronted by which the heroism of the Russian workers is broken.[116]

Once the rule of the bureaucracy was established, then an immanent tendency of subordinating all spheres of life to its power began to manifest itself. Where capitalism and even feudalism still contained certain freedoms, the bureaucratic régime had the unstoppable tendency to penetrate social life in all its facets – differences of opinion were transformed into a carefully cultivated fanaticism, and individual values made way for a state religion.

Weil also believed that tendencies in this direction were apparent outside the Soviet Union as well. After all, everywhere the 'tripartite bureaucracies' were growing: in the trade unions, in the enterprises and in the state. Roosevelt's New Deal had intensified bureaucratic intervention in the economic process significantly, and, in Germany, a definite fusion of enterprise and state bureaucracies seemed to be happening. Weil thus forecast a gloomy future, all the more because all political mass movements – regardless of whether they called themselves fascist, socialist or communist – operated in the same direction. But however discouraging all of that might seem, acquiescence to the inevitable was misplaced: 'If, this being the most likely possibility, we should perish, let us make sure that we do not perish without having lived.'[117]

Rizzi

In 1939, the Italian Bruno Rizzi (1901–85), a shoe seller and student drop-out wandering about in the political peripheries of Bordigism and Trotskyism,[118] privately published *The Bureaucratisation of the World*, a book which, for a

---

[116] Weil 1933, pp. 315–16.
[117] Weil 1933, p. 318.
[118] Westoby 1985.

long time afterwards influenced the debate about the Soviet Union, especially through hearsay. This work spirited like a mystery around critical-Marxist circles for some time. Not only was the author himself shrouded in mystery – he signed himself only as 'Bruno R.' – but, in addition, copies of the book were confiscated by the French police shortly after being published, on the ground of antisemitic passages in the text.[119] *The Bureaucratisation of the World* initially became known only because, just prior to his assassination, Trotsky had attacked it in a polemic.[120] Although Pierre Naville in 1947 revealed Rizzi's identity,[121] it was only at the end of the 1950s that this became known in broader circles.[122] We now know that, prior to the publication of his book, Rizzi had already reflected for several years on the nature of the Soviet Union. In 1937, he had written *Where Is the USSR Going?*, a work of which he later said that, while it did pose the real questions, it had not arrived at a good answer to them.[123]

In Rizzi's work, Simone Weil's theme returned: he too perceived the forward march of bureaucratic power everywhere; similarly, he described the Soviet Union as a society in which the bureaucracy had become a ruling class. But his argument lacked the socio-historical derivation of the bureaucratic phenomenon presented by Weil, and Rizzi identified a consolidated bureaucratic class not only in the USSR, but also in places where Weil detected only 'tendencies' in that direction: in Italy, Germany and Japan.

Just like most Marxists in his time, Rizzi considered the bourgeoisie 'a spent social force', which politically had been completely forced into a defensive position. But this did not mean, as Trotsky and others had believed, that the socialist revolution was on the agenda, but, rather, 'bureaucratic collectivism'.

---

[119] Westoby 1985, pp. 16–17. See Rizzi 1939, Part III, Chapter IV: 'La Question Juive', where one can read: 'Hitler is right and we are wrong. We should correct ourselves and become anti-Jewish because we are anti-capitalist' (p. 296). See also Adler 1985–6, who provides an English translation of Rizzi's antisemitic fragment (pp. 109–13).

[120] Trotsky 1973, pp. 1, 4, 10, 11, 52.

[121] Naville 1947.

[122] See also Chapter 5 in this study.

[123] Rizzi 1937. About the immediate prehistory of his most well-known book Rizzi wrote: 'Always far from our comrades and Marxist propaganda, we received only in the month of November 1938 the 9th issue of *Quatrième Internationale* and we found there the article by Trotsky "Not a Workers' and not a Bourgeois State?". A month later we obtained a special issue dated June 1938 of *Quatrième Internationale* with contributions by Naville, Trotsky and Craipeau. Since then we wanted to write this work, since the ideas being raised had been advanced by us three years earlier, in contrast to the thoughts of these comrades.' R[izzi] 1939, p. 334.

To analyse this new social formation, Rizzi conceptualised his book in three parts: the Soviet Union, fascism and the American New Deal. Only the first and the third part were finally included in *The Bureaucratisation of the World*. The middle part was never published.[124]

As regards the Soviet Union, Rizzi postulated that a ruling class, the bureaucracy, had established itself there as a result of the demise of the October Revolution: 'Possession of the state gives the bureaucracy possession of all those mobile and fixed goods which, despite being socialized, do not belong any the less *in toto* to the new ruling class.'[125] With this new, collective way of appropriation of society's wealth, bureaucratic collectivism transcended the irresolvable contradiction which paralysed capitalism (socialized production versus private appropriation), in order to raise this contradiction to a higher plane: 'Exploitation remains, but instead of being exploitation of man by man it is of class by class.'[126]

In the transition from private to collective exploitation, Rizzi diagnosed a repetition in the reverse direction of the transition from a classless to a class society.

> Property, after belonging to everybody, and consequently, for ancient man, being non-existent, first passed collectively to communities, and then later became private property. Now it seems that it is taking on a collective form again, but as the property of a class.[127]

In bureaucratic collectivism, exploitation – that is to say, the appropriation of surplus-value[128] – occurs via the state apparatus, which simultaneously also organises oppression. Political power and economic power were, therefore, fused together. The demand for labour was no longer determined by capitalists, but by the monopsonic state. Wages were fixed by the plan. The same applied to the prices of goods. It was, therefore, incorrect to call workers 'free' anymore (in the double meaning of 'freed' from means of production and 'free' from personal dependence): 'The Soviet worker has but

---

124 Westoby 1985, p. 13.
125 R[izzi] 1939, pp. 25–6; English edition, p. 50 (translation amended).
126 R[izzi] 1939, p. 47; English edition, p. 63.
127 R[izzi] 1939, p. 46; English edition, p. 63.
128 R[izzi] 1939, pp. 48, 64; English edition, pp. 64, 75. The term 'surplus-value' is used by Rizzi, in contrast to 'surplus-product' although he denied that the Soviet Union was capitalist. It is probable that this is terminological carelessness, to which no great significance should be attached.

one master, he can no longer offer his labour-commodity, he is a prisoner with no possibility of choice.'[129] Rizzi therefore perceives a definite similarity with slave labour:

> Exploitation takes place exactly as in a slave society. The subject of the state works for the master who has bought him, he becomes a capital good, he is livestock which has to be cared for, housed, and whose reproduction is of great concern to the master.[130]

There was only one important difference from the slaves in ancient times: the Russian workers were allowed to perform military service, a 'privilege which the old slaves did not have'.

Rizzi's approach to the USSR was primarily descriptive. A causal analysis, or even a modest attempt in that direction, was absent. It seems he was mostly concerned to project a number of static images, which could be used in polemics with other interpretations. In his discourse about the USSR, a lot of space is accordingly reserved for criticism of Trotsky and his 'lieutenant' Naville.[131]

The part devoted to the American New Deal also offers little in the way of analysis. Rizzi's thesis that the New Deal signified the rise of a new ruling class is only asserted, but not substantiated. Nevertheless, this thesis fits into his general theory that capitalism on a world scale was being succeeded by bureaucratic collectivism, which as such formed the last historical stage prior to socialism:

> Nationalization, statification of the large means of production, economic planning and production for a purpose other than that of individual speculation, represent the great drawing cards of bureaucratic collectivism. [...] From the historical point of view this society has as its task to raise the total global production in an orderly manner.[132]

---

[129] R[izzi] 1939, p. 71; English edition, p. 80.

[130] R[izzi] 1939, pp. 72–3; English edition, p. 80.

[131] Naville owed this 'title' probably to the circumstance that in the French Trotskyist movement he was the most prominent defender of Trotsky's standpoint. In 1937–8, Naville had protected orthodoxy against Yvan Craipeau, who called the Soviet bureaucracy a new ruling class. See Naville 1938 and Craipeau 1938. Rizzi indicated himself that he was influenced by this discussion (see note 123).

[132] R[izzi] 1939, p. 253.

This bureaucratic state was historically necessary, but: 'The last ruling class of history is so close to a society without classes that it denies its status as a class and as owner!'.[133]

The bureaucratic-collectivist rulers were closer to the working class than the bourgeoisie. All feelings of bitterness or hate towards Hitler, Stalin and others should therefore be put aside. These leaders performed a progressive task, since they rationalised industrial production. They too were but instruments of history, 'great prisoners, arrived at a golden cage' who privately yearned for liberation.[134]

> We do not believe that Stalin, Hitler and Mussolini, in the bottom their hearts and as men, delight in their régimes, nor that they are in their life reduced to being detached from humanity by some kind of isolated and watchful subject, expressed through the medium of their personal police and their admirers. They have accepted the fact, both for the sake of political necessities and out of social necessities [...].[135]

Burnham

In the same year in which Bruno Rizzi penned *The Bureaucratisation of the World*, the debate about the Soviet Union was rapidly evolving in the American Trotskyist movement. Already in 1937, there had been an internal conflict when two leaders of the Socialist Workers' Party, James Burnham and Joseph Carter (Joseph Friedman) had adopted a somewhat dissident stance by claiming that the USSR could no longer be regarded as a workers' state 'in the traditional sense given to this term by Marxism'.[136] One of them, the philosopher Burnham,[137] played a key role in the subsequent conflict. The occasion for the second round in the controversy was the invasion of the Red Army in Finland. The orthodox Trotskyists wanted to support the

[133] R[izzi] 1939, p. 254.
[134] R[izzi] 1939, p. 345.
[135] R[izzi] 1939, p. 343.
[136] Burnham and Carter 1937. Trotsky replied with his 'Not a Workers' and Not a Bourgeois State?' (Trotsky 1938a). Rizzi refers to this discussion in R[izzi] 1939, pp. 33–5; English translation, pp. 55–7. See also Bubis 1988.
[137] James Burnham (1905–87) had joined the American Trotskyist movement in 1933 and rapidly rose to a leadership position. See Nash 1976, pp. 87–91, Borgognone 2000, Kelly 2002.

Soviet Union, given that they stood for the unconditional defence of this 'degenerated workers' state'; their opponents instead considered the invasion as an aggressive action, which should be strongly criticised.[138] Burnham supplied a theoretical rationale for the latter position, arguing that the Soviet Union was a new kind of class society. His co-thinkers included, apart from the mentioned Joseph Carter, also Max Shachtman, C.L.R. James, Irving Howe and Saul Bellow. A fierce polemical debate ensued, in which Trotsky, exiled in Mexico, intervened with several articles.[139] It was also Trotsky who pointed to the similarity of Burnham's ideas and those of 'Bruno R.'. In 1940, the SWP split, and the group around Burnham and his associate Shachtman founded the Workers' Party.[140] That same year, however, Burnham withdrew from the new organisation as well, stating in his letter of resignation that:

> The faction fight in the Socialist Workers Party, its conclusion, and the recent formation of the Workers Party have been in my own case, the unavoidable occasion for the review of my own theoretical and political beliefs. This review has shown me that by no stretching of terminology can I regard myself, or permit others to regard me, as a Marxist.[141]

In the following year, 1941, Burnham's famous book *The Managerial Revolution* was published. Although it was not considered 'Marxist' by its author, I will discuss it here because it was not only still very strongly influenced by Marxist thinking,[142] but also played an important role in later Marxist debates.[143]

In *The Managerial Revolution*, Burnham brought together different interests. On the one hand, it represented a further elaboration and substantiation of his analysis of the Soviet Union which he had already defended in the last year of his membership of the Trotskyist movement. On the other hand, it was also a continuation of earlier analyses which he had published about the American New Deal. Since 1935, he had surveyed the development of the New Deal, the increasing influence of the state and the expansion of

---

[138] Macdonald 1958, pp. 17–18.

[139] Trotsky's contributions are collected in Trotsky 1973.

[140] An extensive account of the crisis and split in the Socialist Workers' Party in 1939–40 is given by Myers 1977, pp. 143–71.

[141] The resignation letter is published in Trotsky 1973, p. 207.

[142] See the criteria used by Bernstein mentioned in Chapter 1.

[143] Even in 1947 a Menshevik author mentioned that: 'Burnham has travelled a long way from his past socialist beliefs. Yet to a certain degree he has maintained the Marxian method [...]'. Sapir 1947, p. 366.

bureaucracy in government and private enterprise, writing in the Trotskyist theoretical journal *The New International* under the pseudonym of 'John West'.[144] In terms of its initial assumptions, *The Managerial Revolution* shows remarkable similarities with Rizzi's *The Bureaucratisation of the World*. The likeness is so great, that Shachtman and Naville actually accused Burnham of plagiarism.[145] Nevertheless this accusation is unproven and not necessarily pertinent, because the idea was already 'in the air', as it were,[146] as shown by Weil's contribution. In *The Managerial Revolution* – a book which according to its author contained neither a programme nor a moral[147] – Burnham affirmed with certainty that which for Simone Weil had been only a frightening premonition: a new bureaucratic class domination was inexorably establishing itself on a world scale:

> we are now in a period of social transition [...], a period characterized, that is, by an unusually rapid rate of change of the most important economic, social, political, and cultural institutions of society. This transition is from the type of society which we have called capitalist or bourgeois to a type of society which we shall call managerial. This transition period may be expected to be short compared with the transition from feudal to capitalist society. It may be dated, somewhat arbitrarily, from the first world war, and may be expected to close, with the consolidation of the new society, by approximately fifty years from then, perhaps sooner.[148]

More clearly than in Rizzi's case, it becomes evident here how theories of a new class society, which in the first instance seemed to break with unilinearism (after capitalism there are two possibilities: socialism or a new class domination) had the tendency to establish a *new* unilinear schema,

---

[144] Ashton Meyers reports that 'John West' was Burnham's pseudonym. See Myers 1977, p. 104. Articles by Burnham about Roosevelt and the New Deal include: West 1935a, 1935b, 1935c; West 1936; Burnham 1938b, 1939.

[145] Rizzi himself also felt robbed by Burnham, the latter whom he alleged 'used plagiarism when he launched his bestseller of 1941'. Rizzi 1972, p. 92.

[146] Westoby 1985, pp. 24–6. Burnham himself noted that his theory was not in any way 'a startling and personal innovation': 'During the last twenty years many elements of the theory have been included in various articles and books, to which I must acknowledge a general indebtedness without being able to name any particular one by which I have been specially influenced.' Burnham 1941, p. 7. See also Draper 1999, p. 30.

[147] Burnham 1941a, p. 8.

[148] Burnham 1941a, p. 71.

impressed by the advances of fascism and its similarities with Stalinism, in which only the shackles in the chain are partly changed: the sequence is from feudalism to capitalism and then to a new class society that could possibly lead to socialism.

Burnham showed that the decline of capitalism did not automatically lead to socialism, by referring to failed revolutions (Germany, China, the Balkan) and to an overturn which had completely different results than anticipated (Russia). This failure of the socialist perspective, he argued, was connected to an over-estimation of the role of the working class in Marxist theory. Not only did the proletarianisation of the population not occur to the extent that Marxists had anticipated, but, in addition, the structural powerlessness of the workers was increased by their deskilling. On the one hand, the level of schooling of the workers had decreased, on the other a stratum of highly educated engineers and production leaders had emerged between enterprise owners and workers. This meant that the workers were no longer capable of leading the production process themselves, if the enterprise owners were to disappear.

The only ones who were technically speaking really capable of abolishing capitalism, were the managers, the leaders of the production process. The identity of these future rulers was precisely delineated by Burnham. He did not mean the highly skilled workers and the chemists, physicists, engineers etc. but exclusively managers in the strict sense:

> We may often recognize them as 'production managers', operating executives, superintendents, administrative engineers, supervisory technicians; or in government [...] as administrators, commissioners, bureau heads, and so on.[149]

Managerial rule was most advanced in the Soviet Union, but elsewhere was growing rapidly as well (Germany, Italy, etc.). In the construction of their type of society, the national managerial classes confronted three problems, namely the fight against capitalism (in their own country and across the whole world), the subordination of the masses, and fights among themselves along the road to world domination, via national states. The order in which

---

[149] Burnham 1941a, p. 80.

these problems were solved, differed from country to country. The Russian schema appeared as follows:

> (1) Speedy reduction of the capitalist class at home to impotence [...]; (2) the curbing of the masses in a more gradual and piecemeal manner, over a considerable number of years; (3) direct competition, in the days still to come (though the preparations started some while ago) with the other sections of the rising managerial world society.[150]

In Germany, a different schema operated. There, the subordination of the masses preceded the liquidation of capitalist power. The schema for the transformation occurring in the United States resembled the German one more than the Russian, although the process in North America was seen to occur more gradually, capitalism remaining much more powerful there.

What did a realised managerial society look like? In such as society (Burnham thought in this context especially of the Soviet Union), the managerial élite had become the ruling class. This ruling class was recognisable by two essential characteristics, namely 'first, the ability [...] to prevent access by others to the object controlled (owned); and, second, a preferential treatment in the distribution of the products of the object controlled (owned).'[151] The second characteristic was derived from the first. Because only if one owned the means of production one could appropriate its fruits. It was clear to Burnham that, in this sense, managers in the USSR formed a ruling class:

> The Russian revolution was not a socialist revolution [...] but a managerial revolution. [...] Today Russia is the nation which has, in its structural aspects, advanced furthest along the managerial road.[152]

In the managerial economy, money had less significance than in capitalism. It no longer functioned as individual capital, and played a less important role in the exchange process. In areas where the state sector dominated (health care etc.) the role of money was reduced. Theoretically it was not possible to define a limit for this reduction of the role of money. In practice, however, money would remain insofar as differences in incomes could be instituted by it.

---

[150] Burnham 1941a, p. 210.
[151] Burnham 1941a, p. 59.
[152] Burnham 1941a, pp. 220–1.

The workers were – as Burnham concludes, in a passage which strongly recalls Rizzi's argument – no longer workers with a double freedom. The freedom from owning means of production obviously remained, but the freedom to sell, or refuse to sell labour (Burnham does not use the expression labour-power) to a particular capitalist is lacking.

The managerial society functioned in a planned way, and was, in that sense, superior to capitalism. It was able to solve a number of social and economic problems (mass unemployment, declining production), as proved by the Soviet Union and Germany. The masses obtain a somewhat higher living standard, although this was not guaranteed. At the same time, the managerial society would also experience serious tensions, because it remained an antagonistic society.

Burnham made several predictions in his book concerning the course of future developments. In global politics, three centres of power would emerge: the United States, Germany and Japan.[153] The Soviet Union would disintegrate into two parts. The Western part would become part of the German sphere of influence, and the other, Eastern part would fall under Japanese influence. Furthermore, the managerial society – which still featured dictatorial characteristics – would gradually become more democratic. The dictatorial phase was, after all, necessary only to conquer power and consolidate it (Burnham draws an analogy here with the absolutist state). If that phase succeeded, then democratisation became essential for two reasons, namely (a) a planned economy could only function effectively if the masses have the feeling that their interests are not disregarded, and (b) a certain amount of democracy made it possible for oppositional forces to blow off steam.

Shachtman

Max Shachtman, initially Burnham's ally in the faction fight with Trotsky,[154] launched his own contribution to the debate in 1940 with his article 'Is Russia a Workers' State?'. Contrary to Burnham, Shachtman set out from the idea

---

[153] Rizzi predicted in passing 'seven or eight closed autarkies or so'. R[izzi] 1939, p. 343.

[154] Shachtman (1901–72), belonged in the 1920s to the leaders of the Communist Party of the USA. He subsequently joined the Trotskyist opposition and became one of the leading lights of the Socialist Workers' Party. For extensive biographical information, see Drucker 1994.

that the October Revolution had been genuinely proletarian, and that the gains made had been lost only after the Stalinist 'counterrevolution'. Trotsky's opposing argument, that there had been no violent overthrow of the workers' state arising in 1917, was rebutted by Shachtman with the observation that the establishment of Stalinism had cost a lot of lives (contrasting with the seizure of power by the Bolsheviks, which had, so he added, been 'virtually bloodless and non-violent').[155]

Shachtman drew an analytical distinction between property forms and property relations. If the state controlled the majority of means of production, then a specific property form existed, which however could combine with various property relations: 'If we can speak of nationalised property in the Soviet Union, this does not yet establish what the property relations are.'[156] The question then arose of who controlled the state. If the state was in the hands of the proletariat, then it controlled property via the state, and a workers' state existed. If, on the other hand, the proletariat was politically expropriated, then there was no sense in which it could be said that a workers' state existed anymore. And it was the latter situation which he believed to be the case in the Soviet Union. The bureaucratic counterrevolution 'meant the systematic hacking away of every finger of control the working class had over its state'.[157] Bureaucratic property relations with a new ruling class, the bureaucracy, were the result.

While Rizzi and Burnham regarded the bureaucratic class as the future rulers of the whole globe, Shachtman opined that a short-lived and regionally limited phenomenon was involved. In his view, the emergence of Stalinist rule had been possible due to a very specific combination of factors: the failure of an international socialist revolution to materialise, and the underdeveloped forces of production in Russia. In the highly developed capitalist countries, revolutionary resistance would lead to a socialist society, which would mean the end of the Soviet Union in the not too distant future. In the twentieth century, all events and phenomena tended 'to be telescoped in point of time'. The bureaucracy would therefore soon collapse, because it constituted

---

[155] Shachtman 1940b, p. 199. The reprint of Shachtman's article in Shachtman 1962, pp. 37–60, is an edited version, adjusted to fit with political standpoints which Shachtman later adopted.
[156] Shachtman 1940b, p. 197.
[157] Shachtman 1940b, p. 198.

a 'ruling class of an unstable society which is already a fetter on economic development'.[158]

The Soviet Union was a 'reactionary obstacle' for socialism; and a proletarian overturn would maintain the property *form* (nationalisation of the means of production and exchange), but fundamentally change the property *relations*. Nevertheless, it was conceivable that socialists would defend the USSR against capitalism, if capitalism would undermine nationalised property.

> Such a transformation of the Soviet Union as triumphant imperialism would undertake, would have a vastly and durable reactionary effect upon world social development, give capitalism and reaction a new lease on life, retard enormously the revolutionary movement, and postpone for we don't know how long the introduction of the world socialist society. From this standpoint and under these conditions, the defense of the Soviet Union, even under Stalinism, is both possible and necessary.[159]

The 'property form' of the Soviet Union was, therefore, progressive, but the property relations were not.

Carter

Joseph Carter (1910–70)[160] considered the analysis of his comrade Shachtman confusing, because it combined 'the position that Russia is a new, reactionary economic system with the opposite view, that it is a progressive economy established by the Russian workers' revolution but distorted by bureaucratic domination'.[161] In his view, there was nothing to defend about the Soviet Union for socialists, neither in times or war, nor in times of peace. 'From a historical viewpoint, Russia has taken a bastard path backward from the régime established by the Bolshevik Revolution.'[162] By drawing a distinction between property forms and property relations, he alleged, Shachtman had tried to evade that conclusion; but the distinction did not make sense:

---

[158] Shachtman 1940b, p. 201.
[159] Shachtman 1940b, p. 205.
[160] On Carter see Trotzki 1988, p. 1119, note 2.
[161] Carter 1941, p. 220. On the Carter-Shachtman debate, see also Drucker 1994, pp. 131–8; Haberkern and Lipow 1996; Callinicos 1996.
[162] Carter 1941, p. 219.

When Marxists speak of the 'form of property' they invariably mean *social* form of property, that is, property relations; as feudal form of property (and economy), capitalist form of property (and economy), socialistic, transitional form of property (and economy), etc.

If for the sake of greater clarity on the new Russian phenomena Shachtman chooses to introduce a terminological distinction between 'form of property' and 'property relations' he can do so but only on one condition: *By making clear that by 'form of property' he does not mean 'social form of property.'* Otherwise the result is not clarity but confusion; otherwise property forms *are* property relations.[163]

Carter characterised Stalinism as *bureaucratic collectivism*, a concept that afterwards would be used also by other theoreticians of a 'new class society'. In bureaucratic collectivism, the ruling class – i.e. the bureaucracy – attempts to expand the social surplus product by force, to increase its own revenue, power and position. 'Forced labor is thus an inherent feature of present-day Russian productive relations.'[164] In contrast to most other Marxists, Carter considered the Soviet Union a very *inefficient* society, in which the productive forces grew more slowly than would become possible within a system of democratic planning. Even if the USSR had succeeded in raising the industrial level of the country, the annual growth rate declined more and more, and income inequalities increased. Bureaucratic relations and the associated state terrorism were to blame, because these caused 'constant disruptions in production; disproportions in the output of the various industries dependent upon one another and therefore large-scale economic waste; low efficiency of production.'[165]

Internationally, the USSR functioned as 'a huge national trust'[166] which did not admit world capitalism to its domestic market, and strove to overthrow this capitalism, as 'an indispensable condition for the liberation of its own nationally confined productive forces, so that it could benefit fully from advanced Western technique and take its place as an integral part of a progressive world economy'.[167]

---

[163] Ibid.
[164] Carter 1941, p. 218.
[165] Ibid.
[166] Ibid.
[167] Carter 1941, p. 219.

Pedrosa

The extensive discussions about the Soviet Union in and around the US-American Trotskyist party generated a whole stream of articles in 1941, especially in the journal *The New International*.[168] The great majority defended the kinds of opinions which have already been discussed in this chapter. An exception, however, was the contribution of Mário Pedrosa, alias M. Lebrun, a Brazilian art critic living temporarily in the United States.[169] In his essay, titled 'Mass and Class in Soviet Society', Pedrosa emphasised the centrality of the Soviet state as such, rather than social classes, and postulated the following:

> The inherent tendency of every State, if left to itself, to elevate itself above classes, above society, has been able in Russia, thanks to exceptional historical circumstances, and perhaps for the first time in history, to work itself out to this end. This development of the process has been possible because the proletariat, the dominant class, has been too weak to exercise its control over the bureaucracy, the incarnation of the State. The bureaucracy has identified itself with the State. In so identifying itself, it has attained an absolute development, as far as it can go as a bureaucracy.[170]

The bureaucracy, originally the servant of the state, had become its master. The state, having elevated itself above society, turned against that society and tried to atomise all social classes, becoming a 'free state' in the sense that Friedrich Engels used the term.[171] This development was 'extremely

---

[168] Following Shachtman's article, *The New International* published a number of articles in vol. VII (1941) about how the nature of the Soviet Union should be defined: Alvin 1941a and 1941b; J.R. Johnson 1941a and 1941b; Coolidge 1941; Kent 1941a and 1941b; Lund 1941; Carter 1941.

[169] Mário Pedrosa (1905–82) was from the beginning of the 1930s the most important leader of the small group of Brazilian Trotskyists. In 1938, he was, together with C.L.R. James and others, one of the founders of the Fourth International. In 1940, Pedrosa was the only non-American member of the leadership of the Fourth International who joined Shachtman's opposition. A report that Lebrun was Pedrosa's pseudonym can be found in: 'Conférence de fondation de la IVe Internationale' 1979, p. 57. More information in 'Mario Pedrosa (1905–1982)', *Cahiers Léon Trotsky*, no. 10 (1982); Dulles 1973, pp. 421, 457; Dulles 1983, p. 167; and Castilho and Neto 1996. In 1980, Pedrosa became the first member of the Brazilian Workers' Party (PT).

[170] Lebrun 1940, p. 88.

[171] Most probably Pedrosa had in mind the following passage: 'Grammatically speaking, a free state is one in which the state is free vis-à-vis its citizens, a state, that is, with a despotic government'. Engels 1875, pp. 63–4.

transitory' because although the bureaucracy sought to constitute itself as a class, it lacked an independent economic basis as yet. An underproduction crisis, which had manifested itself already for some considerable time, forced the bureaucracy to look for ways of economic expansion; it was

> as restless as a hen that is looking for a safe place to lay her egg. It wants to get itself a proper, stable, economic and social base on which it can spread itself at ease and assure itself a permanent place in history *as a true social class*.[172]

On the one side, this led to longings for adventures in foreign policy; on the other side, it also led the bureaucracy into the temptation to privatise plots of land and light industry.

Hilferding

In 1940, the Menshevik journal *Sotsialisticheskii Vestnik* published a Russian translation of the article in which Worrall had expounded his theory of state capitalism. But also published was a critical response to it, by the famous Social Democrat Rudolf Hilferding, in which he advanced his own theory.[173] Hilferding's contribution (later also published *inter alia* in English and German) represented the conclusion of a series of articles he had published after Hitler came to power, which dealt with developments in Nazi Germany and the Soviet Union.[174]

---

[172] Lebrun 1940, p. 91.

[173] Rudolf Hilferding (1877–1941), originally a medical practitioner, published some important contributions to Marxist economic theory, of which *Das Finanzkapital* (1910) was the most famous. He joined the USPD during World War I and followed its right wing in 1922 back into the SPD. He was Social-Democratic member of the Reichstag in 1924–33 and Minister of Finance in 1923 en 1928–9. He emigrated in 1933 to Switzerland and then to France. In 1941 he was murdered, presumably by the Gestapo. See Gottschalch 1962, pp. 13–31. Bibliographic information is available in Kurata 1974.

[174] For example, Richard Kern 1936a, 1936b. Hilferding seems to have written his article in *Sotsialisticheskii Vestnik* especially after discussions with Boris Nikolaevsky. See Sapir 1979, p. 367. The core idea in his theory of the autonomised state was expressed by Hilferding in a letter to Kautsky: 'Indeed state organisation and its interests are a factor, which gains independence and especially in times of dictatorship strives to subordinate other social interests.' (Hilferding 1937)

Hilferding's theory is distinct, although there are some identifiable similarities with Rizzi, Burnham and Pedrosa. The bureaucracy, in Hilferding's view, could not be a ruling class, because it was too heterogeneous in composition, and did not have consensus-generating mechanisms:

> Bureaucracy everywhere, and particularly in the Soviet Union, is composed of a conglomeration of the most varied elements. To it belong not only government officials in the narrow sense of the word (i.e. from minor employees up to generals and even Stalin himself) but also the directors of all branches of industry and such functionaries as, for example, the postal and railway employees. How could this variegated lot possibly achieve a unified rule? Who are its representatives? How does it adopt decisions? What organs are at its disposal?[175]

The bureaucracy *cannot* be a social class – to that extent, Hilferding agreed with Trotsky. But, in contrast to the latter, Hilferding did not view the bureaucracy as a parasitic organism dependent on the working class and its workers' state, but, rather, as the instrument of the state leader, Stalin. The Georgian despot had subordinated the servants of the state together with the rest of the population completely to himself.

Because of this development, the economy was no longer the factor that determined politics, nor did politics direct the economy and dominate it. The state had uprooted itself from all classes, and had become an 'independent power'. This theory marked a remarkable turnaround in Hilferding's thinking. During the Weimar Republic, he had shown great confidence in the state (according to some, too great); but, evidently, the experience of Stalinism and national socialism prompted a retreat. Whereas originally his belief had been that the state – under Social-Democratic leadership – had to subordinate the economy, now it had become apparent that such subordination resulted in dictatorship.[176] For all that, one constant theme in Hilferding's thought remained visible in his article: the state is, in the last instance, a classless institution, which, under definite relations of power, can be used for good or for evil; whether that occurred by means of a Social-Democratic government or an omnipotent dictator, had little effect on this core idea.

---

[175] Hilferding 1940. This was a response to Uoroll 1940. Cited according to the American translation published in *Modern Review*, p. 268.

[176] Stephan 1974, p. 141. See also Gottschalch 1962, pp. 242–61 and James 1981.

3.iv. Criticism

Criticism of theories of state capitalism

Adler's theory of original capitalist accumulation on a state-capitalist basis was criticised by the German Communist H. Linde from a pro-Stalinist perspective. This author offered two points as counter-arguments. Firstly, the thesis allegedly contained a *contradictio in terminis*. After all, primitive accumulation meant, in Marx's view, 'an accumulation, which is not the result of the capitalist mode of production, but its point of departure'.[177] This was taken to imply a chronological order: first primitive accumulation, then capitalism. The logical conclusion was, according to Linde, inescapable: either state capitalism existed in the Soviet Union, and then there could be no primitive accumulation, or else primitive accumulation occurred, but then it was impossible to maintain the idea that state capitalism existed.[178] In the second place, for Marx, the separation from ownership of the means of production was an essential characteristic of primitive accumulation on a capitalist basis;[179] the collectivisation of farming in the Soviet Union, however, had realised precisely the opposite, the unification of producers and means of production at a higher level:

> What is collectivisation? It is not separating the small producers from their means of production, it is the unification of the means of production of small producers, their socialisation, in which these means of production (exclusively those which the state places at the disposal of the collective economy) remain the property of the collective, but not the private property of individual members of the collective, outside of their common, collective ownership.[180]

---

[177] Marx 1976, p. 873.

[178] Linde 1932, pp. 26–7.

[179] 'So-called primitive accumulation, therefore, is nothing else than the historical process of divorcing the producer from the means of production. It appears as "primitive" because it forms the prehistory of capital, and of the mode of production corresponding to capital.' Marx 1976, pp. 874–5.

[180] Linde 1932, p. 27.

The thesis that the Soviet economy was (state-)capitalist in structure was vehemently denied by several authors. The Menshevik emigrant Olga Domanevskaya pointed out that the central dynamic of capitalism consisted of competition and the quest for profit. In the Soviet Union, by contrast, these factors did not play a dominant role. Essential here was the fact that the economy was centrally led by the state.[181] Hilferding additionally pointed out that wages and prices in the USSR were not formed in the same way as in a market system; they were not established through autonomous processes (supply and demand) but were fixed by the state, and, in that way, a means for directing the economy:

> Formally, prices and wages still exist, but their function is no longer the same; they no longer determine the process of production which is now controlled by a central power that fixes prices and wages. Prices and wages [...] now constitute a technical form of distribution which is simpler than direct individual allotment of products which no longer can be classified as merchandise. Prices have become symbols of distribution and no longer a regulating factor in the economy. While maintaining the form, a complete transformation of function has occurred.[182]

The thesis that the Soviet bureaucracy embodied a new bourgeoisie was rejected by Trotsky also on sociological grounds:

> The bureaucracy has neither stocks nor bonds. It is recruited, supplemented, and renewed in the manner of an administrative hierarchy, independently of any special property relations of its own. The individual bureaucrat cannot transmit to his heirs his rights in the exploitation of the State apparatus. The bureaucracy enjoys its privileges under the form of an abuse of power. It conceals its income; it pretends that as a special group it does not even exist. Its expropriation of a vast share of the national income has the character of social parasitism.[183]

---

[181] Domanewskaja 1934–5, p. 271.
[182] Hilferding 1940, pp. 266–7.
[183] Trotsky 1937b, English edition, p. 236.

The thesis that a 'creeping' restoration of capitalism had taken place – a thought which, as we have seen, originates with Korsch – was contested by Trotsky for reasons of historical asymmetry:

> The Marxist thesis relating to the catastrophic character of the transfer of power from the hands of one class into the hands of another applies not only to revolutionary periods, when history sweeps madly ahead, but also to the periods of counterrevolution, when society rolls backwards. He who asserts that the Soviet government has been *gradually* changed from proletarian to bourgeois is only, so to speak, running backwards the film of reformism.[184]

A counter-argument was, as we have seen, supplied by Shachtman: Stalin's counter-revolution *was* 'catastrophic' and violent.

Criticisms of the theory of the degenerated workers' state

Burnham criticised the thesis that the working class in the Soviet Union, although it was politically 'expropriated', remained economically the ruling class, on the grounds that the means of production were mainly nationalised. He mooted as argument that a *petitio principii* was involved here:

> We ask them [i.e. the defenders of the theory], What kind of state is the Soviet Union? They answer, It is a workers' state. We ask, Why is it a workers' state? They answer, *Because* there is a nationalized property. We ask, Why does nationalized property make it a workers' state? And they answer, *Because* a workers' state is one where there is nationalized property.
>
> This is, in form, exactly the same argument used by those who tell us that the Bible is the Word of God. We ask them, How do you know it is the Word of God? They answer, *Because* the Bible itself says it is the Word of God. We ask, But how does that prove it to be true? And they answer, *Because* nothing that God said could be a lie.
>
> In both instances, the conclusion has been taken for granted in the premises; the argument is entirely circular, and can prove nothing whatever.[185]

---

[184] Trotsky 1933a, p. 2; English edition, pp. 102–3.
[185] Burnham 1938a.

The same thesis by Trotsky was also criticised considering that nationalised property was an insufficient qualifying condition for a workers' state. Rizzi pointed out in this context that bourgeois states as well increasingly resorted to nationalisation and planning, and that the new bureaucratic class in the Soviet Union could most certainly use the 'innovations of the October revolution' for its own purposes.[186] J.R. Johnson (pseudonym of C.L.R. James) made a similar criticism:

> Trotsky and we who followed him failed to distinguish between first, means of production in the hands of the state where the state is merely an economic form like a trust, a bank, or a cartel; second, state ownership as a purely juridical relation, which tells us no more than that it is the duty of the state to organize production and distribute the product; and third, a workers' state, i.e. a state transitional to socialism; this last is not a juridical question at all but a question of economic conditions and social relations of production, which can be summed up in one phrase: is the working class master or not? The third category includes the other two. But neither singly nor together do the first two necessarily include the third. [...] *Within the state property form the working class can be master as in 1921 or enslaved as in 1941.*[187]

Together with the point of criticism just mentioned, another closely related argument was advanced: Trotsky had separated economic and political power in his theory but that was, precisely, impossible in the case of a workers' state. In the words of Joseph Carter:

> The proletariat is a propertyless class. Its control over the economy and its domination in society is possible only through first winning political power. It is through its state power that the working class becomes the ruling class and develops the conditions for the abolition of all classes, the socialist society. Without political power the working class cannot be the ruling class in any sense.[188]

---

[186] R[izzi] 1939, pp. 38–9.
[187] Johnson 1941a, pp. 54–5.
[188] Carter 1941, p. 218.

Criticisms of theories of a new mode of production

Trotsky advanced an argument against every kind of theory that claimed the bureaucracy is a new ruling class:

> A class is defined not by its participation in the distribution of the national income alone, but by its independent role in the general structure of the economy and by its independent roots in the economic foundations of society. Each class (the feudal nobility, the peasantry, the petty bourgeoisie, the capitalist bourgeoisie and the proletariat) works out its own special forms of property. The bureaucracy lacks all these social traits. It has no independent position in the process of production and distribution. It has no independent property roots. Its functions relate basically to the political *technique* of class rule. The existence of a bureaucracy, in all its variety of forms and differences in specific weight, characterizes every class régime. Its power is of a reflected character. The bureaucracy is indissolubly bound up with a ruling economic class, feeding itself upon the social roots of the latter, maintaining itself and falling together with it.[189]

W. Kent advanced a counter-criticism to this objection by Trotsky, which was that Trotsky had unjustifiably declared old social relations universally applicable:

> Granted that, in European history, the bureaucracy was never a ruling class and that it always served other ruling classes. Does that mean that it can never become one itself? Can there never be anything new in history? A clever 'theoretician' could have argued just as well, 200 years ago, before the great bourgeois revolutions: What, the bourgeoisie become a ruling class? Ridiculous! Capitalists, such as we have always known them – merchants and moneylenders – have always only served kings and lords![190]

Domanevskaya criticised the belief that the state had extricated itself from the working class; in her view, the apparatus did not possess such an autonomy:

---

[189] Trotsky 1937b, pp. 112–13. Also Domanewskaja 1934–5, p. 272.
[190] Kent 1941a, p. 179.

If one assumes the possibility of the formation of a new class [...] then some or other publicly established and durable relations between the means of production and the state apparatus [must] be presupposed. One must be able to suppose the state apparatus as their unification to a greater or lesser extent. In reality that is not the case here. The characteristic (negative) feature of the Soviet apparatus is the continual flux in the composition of personnel, the redirection [Hinüberfluten] of state functionaries from one branch of management to another, from the apparatus to production and vice versa. In addition, there is the important circumstance, that the state apparatus in substantial mass is formed from the real working class, that a reciprocal fluctuation takes place between the working class and the apparatus; therein lies the social meaning of shifting overly zealous bureaucrats, who in some way have transgressed to the factories, 'back to the work bench'. The experience of this process is, that the apparatus despite tendencies towards bureaucratisation ultimately cannot separate itself permanently from the surrounding environment, [and] does not become an instrument of forces hostile to the proletariat.[191]

The conclusion by Rizzi and Burnham that national socialism, fascism and Stalinism amounted to the same – already anticipated in outline by Weil – was contested both by Trotsky and Shachtman. Both admitted that the régimes at issue showed many common features (terror, secret police, political structure etc.) but thought that at the level of property relations essential differences could be identified. Both pointed out that Mussolini and Hitler had allowed capitalist private ownership of means of production to continue and thus operated with a different social basis from Stalin.[192]

3.v. Summary

With the consolidation of the Stalinist régime, a qualitative change took place in the Western-Marxist debate. All the critics of the Soviet Union now seemed to be profoundly aware that the events in 'the fatherland of the workers' could no longer be squared with the classical unilinear sequence

---

[191] Domanewskaja 1934–5, pp. 272–3.
[192] Trotsky 1940a; Shachtman 1940, pp. 201–3.

in an unreflected way. Those who stayed closest to the old schema were authors who perceived in the USSR a special variant of either capitalism or a workers' state; theoreticians who believed they could detect a new type of society in the Soviet Union ventured a little further.

The October Revolution was now interpreted in *three* different ways: as a proletarian revolution, a bourgeois revolution, or a revolution which 'brought a new ruling class to power'. Those who adopted the first interpretation saw the revolution as being followed by a bureaucratic degeneration, or, alternatively, a bourgeois or bureaucratic counter-revolution. The schema below summarises these variants and the authors which exemplified them:

Nature of the October Revolution	Later development	Author
	Bureaucratic degeneration	Trotsky
Proletarian revolution	Bourgeois revolution	Worrall
	Bureaucratic counterrevolution	Shachtman
Bourgeois revolution		Wagner
Bureaucratic revolution		Burnham

While, in the 1920s, not one critic had claimed to be able to diagnose an open, violent counterrevolution, the social changes in the USSR around 1930 were apparently perceived as so drastic that various authors now believed that such a development had occurred.

Within each main theoretical current, different versions developed – except in the theory of the degenerated workers' state, which remained unique to Trotsky and his supporters. Both among the adherents of the theory of state capitalism, as well as among those who supported the theory of a new type of society, opinions were divided especially about two problems:

(i) Was the Soviet Union unique, or were there structural similarities with fascist societies? Three different responses were given to this question: some set out from uniqueness (Adler, Shachtman), others saw in the USSR one variant of a form of society of which fascism was another variant (Pollock, Horkheimer) and yet others posited fascism and Stalinism as being in essence identical (Rizzi, Burnham).

(ii) Was the bureaucracy already a new ruling class, or was it not? This question also received three kinds of responses: Hilferding contended that it was structurally impossible that the bureaucracy could become a class, Pedrosa perceived in the bureaucracy a social group straining to transform itself into a class, and Miasnikov, Rizzi et. al. considered that this had already happened.

Chapter Four

From the 'Great Patriotic War' to the Structural Assimilation of Eastern Europe (1941–56)

A sudden offensive by German troops against the Soviet Union on 22 July 1941 unambiguously ended the two-year old pact between the two countries. The rapidly advancing German armies forced the Soviet régime to take drastic action. Apart from the obvious military preparations (mobilisation of recruits, declaration of war in the European part of the USSR, and suchlike) a series of economic measures were implemented, such as the military conversion of farming and industry, and the integral removal of many industrial plants to the East. The legendary efforts which soldiers, workers and technicians displayed in this campaign can only be explained by the fact that, from the beginning, the war was fought as a national, defensive war. Patriotism and hate for the devious enemy were the mainfare of all official propaganda. The German offensive initially seemed unstoppable, but the beginnings of a counter-offensive became apparent during the battle over Moscow (in the winter of 1941–2), which intensified in 1943 (the battles of Stalingrad and Kursk). On the international level, Stalin formed an alliance with Great Britain and the United States. As regards his supposed objective of 'world revolution', he tried to reassure his foreign allies as much as possible, among other things by disbanding the Communist International in 1943.

During its 1944–5 offensive in Eastern Europe, the Red Army met with a lot of resistance. But the Nazi occupying forces were in many cases demoralised, and groups in the local populations rebelled openly against them, liberating large areas on their own strength in some cases. The organised bourgeois forces played a relatively small role in the events; in the former 'Axis' countries (Hungary, Romania, Bulgaria), they had been discredited because of their collaboration with the Third Reich, while, in the Allied countries (Poland, Czechoslovakia), they were seriously weakened by the occupying forces. At the same time, some government apparatuses had more or less disintegrated (especially in Poland).

The arrival of the Red Army was in general greeted with enthusiasm. In Poland, Romania, and Bulgaria, there were uprisings as the Red Army drew nearer, with mass strikes and demonstrations, factory occupations and even embryonic worker's councils. Stalin, it seems, initially did not aim for a social transformation of the newly occupied territories.

> Stalin's European goals in 1944 and 1945 were military and territorial rather than those of social transformation. – in so far as they were social they were socially conservative. Had he then intended to 'sovietise' Poland he would neither have accepted so many pre-war politicians in Warsaw, negotiating for a share of power, nor – more importantly – would he have made central the issue of which territory was to be part of Poland and which part of the Soviet Union. At the close of the war 'socialism in one country' meant to Stalin 'friendly' governments ruling 'friendly' territory on the Soviet Union's Western border, protecting it against a possible resurgent Germany and a capitalist West.[1]

The East-European developments in the period of 1944–5 to 1947–8 can be summarised as follows:

– Under the slogan of 'people's democracy', coalition governments between the Communist Party (or, alternatively, a socialist unity party) and bourgeois parties were formed – the latter were in a few cases (re-)founded at the insistence of the Communists.[2]

---

[1] Westoby 1981, p. 10.

[2] As regards Hungary, Hugh Seton-Watson concluded for example: 'In the first months it is a curious paradox that the reconstitution of these [bourgeois] parties was largely the work of teams of communist agitators who travelled around in Red

– New central state apparatuses were established, which incorporated (and bureaucratised) the organs of self-management created during the uprisings and assimilated as many 'progressives' as possible.

– Parts of the economy were nationalised; in many cases, this did not involve expropriations of employers. Often, they concerned takeovers of enterprises which had been the property of the German occupiers, and/or which had been under workers' self-management. Despite nationalisations, a large part of the economies – notably the farm sector and retail trade – remained in private hands.

Altogether, the East-European *glacis* retained its capitalist character in this first phase, be it under the direct supervision of the Soviet Union. Under pressure of the conflict that meanwhile began to manifest itself between the Soviet Union and its former Western allies, all this changed in 1947–8. The concept of 'people's democracy' then acquired a new meaning.[3] A process of structural assimilation occurred,[4] through which the buffer states strongly began to resemble the USSR, politically and economically. Three interconnected structural transformations were implemented. First, the dismantling of the remaining power-bases of bourgeois forces. In the political sphere, the coalition governments were dissolved, the independent peasant parties liquidated, etc. In the economic sphere, 'command-planning' following the Soviet model was introduced,[5] bilateral trade with the USSR was strengthened, and the development of heavy industry was strongly accentuated. Second, consolidation of monolithic Communist parties. The nature of the Communist parties differed from country to country. Some parties, like the Polish one, had been postwar creations, although a part of the cadre originated from the prewar period. Others, such as in Czechoslovakia and Bulgaria, had already been real political forces before 'liberation'. But,

---

Army vehicles' (Seton-Watson 1956, p. 191). Compare also the following comment by Klement Gottwald, made in a speech for Communist party functionaries in May 1945: 'We must continually remind ourselves that in the present phase, we are following the line of the national and democratic [...] and not the line of social revolution.' Cited in Brzezinski 1961, p. 27.

[3] Heiter 1986.

[4] This concept is used by Tim Wohlforth, 'The Theory of Structural Assimilation', in Westoby and Wolforth 1978, especially pp. 20–34.

[5] The introduction of five year plans provides an indication of the moment at which economic assimilation had been completed: Bulgaria and Czechoslovakia in 1949, Poland and Hungary in 1950, Romania and East Germany in 1951.

regardless of their diverse pre-histories, all Communist parties from 1944 experienced a very rapid growth. The consolidation of these parties was achieved in two ways: through large-scale purges,[6] and through forced mergers with social-democratic parties. Third, fusion of the monolithic parties with the state apparatuses. Parallel with the 'monolithisation' of the Communist parties, trade unions lost their autonomy once and for all, and state apparatuses were 'purged'. The consequence was that the Communist parties now dominated all the power-bases in society.

These three great changes combined with the founding in September 1947 of the Cominform, an 'information bureau of the Communist parties' which served as means to co-ordinate the politics of Moscow with the Communist parties abroad (especially in the *glacis*).[7] Soon however a split occurred in the East-European *cordon sanitaire*. From March 1948, tension between the leaderships in Belgrade and Moscow increased rapidly. After some terse exchanges of correspondence between the Central Committees of the Yugoslav and Soviet Parties, the Communist Party of Yugoslavia was summarily expelled from the Cominform on 28 June 1948. The leadership of the excommunicated party was accused of 'animosity in its policy towards the Soviet Union and the CPSU', spreading slanders 'from the arsenal of counter-revolutionary Trotskyism', and internally pursuing an anti-Leninist policy because, among other things, it failed to nationalise land.[8]

The background of this political secession is complex. In the literature, the deeper cause suggested is that the Yugoslav Communists were the only ones who, already during the World War II, had wrested control of large parts of their own country from the German occupiers. This meant that the Yugoslav leadership – like the Chinese Communist Party, which would also break with Moscow, in 1963 – commanded an autonomous power base, and was less inclined than other East-European leaderships to accept a political yoke from

---

[6] Fejtö estimates that 2.5 million people, about a quarter of the total membership, were purged from the East-European Communist parties, and that between 125,000 and 250,000 people were imprisoned. Fejtö, n.d., p. 246.

[7] When the Cominform was founded in the Polish town Szklarska Poręba, delegations were present of the Communist parties from Eastern Europe and the two largest Communist parties in Western Europe (Italy and France).

[8] The relevant documents from the period 20 March to 28 June 1948 are reproduced in Bass and Marbury 1959, pp. 4–46.

the CPSU. Since Yugoslavia had also suffered the most from Stalin's policy in neighbouring Greece (which had been sacrificed to the Western powers), grounds for conflict were already present at an early stage.

In the wake of the breach between Yugoslavia and the Soviet Union, 'Titoist' currents and sometimes (small) sympathising parties emerged in many Western countries. The criticisms of the USSR formulated by Yugoslav ideologists such as Kardelj and Djilas found a receptive audience in those circles, and, in some cases, those criticisms were extended further.

Compared to the 1930s, the structural problematic appeared differently from 1944–5 onwards: 'Whereas previously the inner structure of the Soviet Union experienced a profound transformation, even although its external situation remained broadly the same, now its inner continuity faced a significant change in its external position.'[9]

4.i. The theory of the degenerated workers' state

In the 1920s and 1930s, left-wing social democrats had made essential contributions to the Western debate about the Soviet Union. But, during and after World War II, the political spectrum of discussants narrowed significantly. More strongly than previously, the debate was now concentrated in left-communist and radical-socialist circles. The majority of contributions came from the Trotskyist side, although Bordiga and his co-thinkers, left socialists and others also actively participated. Gilles Martinet, who can be included among the apologists for the USSR in these years, pointed out in 1947 that the Fourth International and its political periphery was responsible for the most far-reaching and coherent criticisms of Stalinism; by contrast, he called social-democratic thinking on this topic 'dead'.[10]

This predominance of critics from the Trotskyist milieu did not mean however that the theory of the degenerated workers' state was able to sustain itself without problems, or even to develop. To the contrary, the Fourth International found itself confronted with major conceptual problems, which occasioned fiery controversies in its ranks. Trotsky, as noted previously,

[9] Beyerstedt 1987, p. 232.
[10] Martinet 1947, p. 14.

had assumed that the Soviet bureaucracy would either be overthrown by a proletarian revolution, or else that its unstable grip on power would stabilise itself through a counterrevolution explicitly aimed at capitalist restoration. In the background, his overall assessment of international developments played a very important role in his forecasts. He had, after all, assumed – fully in the tradition of the Communist International – that capitalism had reached its final phase. After Nazi troops invaded Belgium and the Netherlands, he stated:

> The capitalist world has no way out, unless a prolonged death agony is so considered. It is necessary to prepare for long years, if not decades, of war, uprisings, brief interludes of truce, new wars, and new uprisings.[11]

More and more frequently, the bourgeoisies would be forced to resort to authoritarian political forms (Bonapartism, fascism). At the same time, the workers would be shaken out of their lethargy, and rise up in revolt. War violence in particular was destined to accelerate political developments across the board: 'Those great tasks which only yesterday seemed long years, if not decades away, can loom up directly before us in the next two or three years, and even sooner.'[12] The epoch was thus one of the final struggle, and precisely for that reason, the situation in the Soviet Union would no longer stay the same.

After the Fourth International had recovered somewhat from the consequences of the War (and Trotsky's death), it sought to adhere strictly to Trotsky's prognosis, even although it soon turned out to be in conflict with reality. In 1946, the organisation declared that the failure of the predicted events to occur should be explained in the following way:

> If the war did not immediately create in Europe a revolutionary upsurge of the scope and tempo we anticipated, it is *nonetheless undeniable that it destroyed capitalist equilibrium on a world scale, thus opening up a long revolutionary period.* All self-criticism [...] limits itself essentially to the tempo and not to the *fundamental character* of the period which follows the imperialist war.[13]

---

[11] Trotsky 1940b, p. 218.
[12] Trotsky 1940b, p. 220.
[13] The 1946 resolution 'The New Imperialist Peace and the Building of the Parties of the Fourth International' was drafted by Ernest Mandel.

Completely consistent with this perspective, the possibility of capitalist restoration in the Soviet Union was denied, and an imminent political overturn was predicted.

Here and there, empirical arguments were mounted against this 'catastrophism',[14] but without success. When, after a few years, international capitalism did definitely show renewed dynamism, and Stalinism proved to be more stable than ever, the mood among Trotskyists changed to one of acceptance. But Michel Raptis, the most important leader of the movement, subsequently went further in revising world perspectives. He published an essay in 1951 in which he forecast – influenced also by the Korean conflict – the inevitability of a third world war, which could result in an historical phase of 'Stalinoid' workers' states that could last for centuries.[15] Thus, whereas previously it had been believed that Stalinism would be unable to survive World War II, now it was being claimed that it would emerge victoriously from a third world war, which would occur in the near future and result in Soviet-type régimes enduring for an indefinite time. This partial 'revisionism' could conceivably have sparked a reappraisal of the whole theory of the degenerated workers' state, but that did not happen.[16]

The continued rigid adherence to orthodoxy – albeit with the suspension of the time factor considered essential by Trotsky – caused great difficulties in dealing with the events in Eastern Europe. How should the nature of the new societies be understood? If they were defined as bureaucratised workers' states, on the ground of their increasing structural resemblance to the Soviet Union, then this interpretation ran into two theoretical objections, the first more principled than the second:

a) Workers' states could, if one took an orthodox approach (following Marx's thesis that the workers can only emancipate themselves) result *only* from an autonomous, proletarian process of emancipation, under the leadership of a revolutionary mass organisation. How then could workers' states be

---

[14] See especially Cliff 1947. Cliff's contribution was a response to Germain 1947a. Mandel claimed in this article among other things that 'in the period of capitalist decadence British industry *can no longer* overgrow the stage of revival and attain one of a real boom'. Cliff denied this in his reply.

[15] Pablo 1951. On Raptis (1911–96) see Richardson 1996.

[16] This was pointed out by Bleibtreu-Favre 1951, p. 60.

established from above, and under the leadership of Stalinists who had been deemed 'counter-revolutionary through and through'?

b) Previous cases of assimilation of other states to the first workers' state had consistently been combined with their incorporation into the Soviet Union (Georgia, the Baltic republics, East Poland, etc.). Trotsky himself had accordingly believed that a 'structural assimilation' of other states would be combined with the abolition of their national boundaries.[17]

In the years 1947–51, three positions were articulated on this question. Ernest Mandel initially considered that *all* East-European buffer states, from Yugoslavia to Poland, were still capitalist. Michel Raptis agreed with this view, *except* as far as Yugoslavia was concerned; that country was, in his opinion, a workers' state, because of the civil war it had experienced. Lastly, Joseph Hansen and Bert Cochran defined all the occupied East-European countries as workers' states, but *bureaucratically deformed* from their foundation. In 1951, the debate ended with the victory of the last-mentioned position.[18]

If we survey the successive official texts of the Fourth International, we can see how difficult and protracted the process of forming a definite opinion must have been. In 1947 the buffer states were described as capitalist countries in a transitional situation:

> the bureaucracy [of the USSR] will, in the long run, prove incapable of successfully carrying out the veritable structural assimilation which demands the destruction of capitalism. This can be achieved on so large a scale only by the proletarian revolution.[19]

In 1949, this interpretation was revised:

> The social differences between the USSR and the buffer zone [...] are of a qualitative nature even though the quantitative point of view society in the buffer zone approaches more closely Soviet society rather than that of the 'normal' capitalist countries, in the same sense in which the USSR itself is quantitatively closer to capitalism than to socialism.[20]

---

[17] See for example Leon Trotsky's 'Balance Sheet of the Finnish Events' (1940), republished in Trotsky 1973.
[18] Conner 1973, p. 6.
[19] Fourth International 1947.
[20] Fourth International 1949.

And, finally, in 1951, the conclusion was reached that:

> The structural assimilation of these countries to the USSR must be considered
> as having now been essentially accomplished and these countries as having
> ceased to be basically capitalist countries.[21]

The theoretical consequence of this development was that the Soviet Union
was now no longer viewed as the *prototype* of a workers' state, but rather
as a *special case*. Nevertheless, the theory of the degenerated workers' state
itself remained unrevised. In that sense, the 'official' Trotskyist movement
continued to adhere to the old assumptions.

4.ii. Theories of state capitalism

The theoretical difficulties of the supporters of the theory of the degenerated
workers' state gave rise to oppositional currents within the Trotskyist
movement in various parts of the world. Most of the oppositionists adopted
a theory of state capitalism. They drew support in this from the guardian
par excellence of Trotsky's political heritage, his own widow Natalia Sedova.
From about 1946, Sedova believed that the Soviet Union definitely could not
be regarded as a workers' state anymore, and, in 1951, she broke with the
Fourth International. In an open letter to the most influential section of the
organisation, the American Socialist Workers' Party, she argued her case for
taking this step:

> Time and again, he [i.e. Leon Trotsky] pointed out how the consolidation
> of Stalinism in Russia led to the worsening of the economic, political and
> social positions of the working class, and the triumph of a tyrannical and
> privileged aristocracy. If this trend continues, he said, the revolution will
> be at an end and the restoration of capitalism will be achieved.
>
> That, unfortunately, is what happened even if in new and unexpected
> forms. There is hardly a country in the world where the authentic ideas
> and bearers of socialism are so barbarously hounded. It should be clear to
> everyone that the revolution has been completely destroyed by Stalinism.

---

[21] Fourth International 1951. To distinguish them from the USSR, the *glacis* countries
were not called 'degenerated workers' states', but workers' states 'deformed' from
the beginning.

Yet you continue to say that under this unspeakable régime, Russia is still a workers' state. I consider this a blow at socialism.[22]

Grandizo/Péret

In Mexico, a small group of Spanish Trotskyists had established itself around 1940, after 'the fight against General Franco ended in defeat. The animating spirit among these exiles was Manuel Fernandez Grandizo (1911–89; writing under the *nom de guerre* of 'G. Munis'),[23] who, in 1936, had founded the Spanish section of Trotsky's movement for the Fourth International.[24] In 1938, he was imprisoned by the Stalinists, but, in the following year, he managed to escape. Grandizo's close collaborator was the French surrealist poet Benjamin Péret (1899–1959), who likewise lived for some time in Mexico, and had also published on political topics under the pseudonym of 'Peralta'.[25]

In 1946, Grandizo and Péret went public with their criticism of the official Trotskyist line about the class nature of the Soviet Union. An important stimulus was the 'Manifesto' adopted in April that year by a conference of the Fourth International. The most important thesis in this manifesto was that the International's analysis – including of the Soviet Union – had been proved completely correct by all recent events.[26] Péret wrote a very critical pamphlet about the manifesto, which he slated as a complacent document, unworthy of the Fourth International and permeated by self-righteous vanity [*vanité béate*]. Since the signing of the Molotov-Ribbentrop Pact at the latest, Péret argued, it should have been clear that *nothing* was left in the USSR of the gains made by the October Revolution. The bureaucratic counterrevolution had triumphed, and state capitalism had been established.

---

[22] See the letter to the SWP from Natalia Trotsky (Trotsky 1951). Together with this letter, an 'Answer of SWP to Natalia Trotsky's Letter' was published. Commentary is provided by Max Shachtman in Shachtman 1951b.

[23] Sinclair (no date), p. 338; Prager 1978, p. 432.

[24] Grandizo was a child of Spanish emigrants Mexico. In 1930, he returned to Spain and became politically active there. See Broué 1982a, p. 16, note; Gramonte 1977, pp. 513–17; Guillamón Iborra 1993.

[25] Evidence that Peralta was a pseudonym of Péret (1899–1959) is found in handwriting on the IISH copy of Peralta 1946. The note states: 'Peralta: Pseudonimo empleado en Mexico y como militante de Fomento Obrero Revolucionario, por el poeta frances surrealista Benjamin Peret. G. Munis'. About Péret, see Goutier 1982.

[26] *Quatrième Internationale* 1946.

As such, this idea by Péret could hardly claim originality, yet his characterisation of the bureaucratic élite showed some novel features. While abandoning Trotsky's theory of the degenerated workers' state, he also maintained, to a certain degree, Trotsky's conception that the élite was not a ruling class, but another kind of social group. A ruling class, he reasoned along traditional Marxian lines, had the historic task to develop the social formation ('system of property') which gave rise to it. It therefore fulfilled, at least at the beginning of an historical epoch, a progressive function. The bureaucratic élite in the Soviet Union, however, did not embody any progress, only decadence and decay; it therefore had to be characterised in a different way. Péret offered two possibilities here:

i) On the one hand, the bureaucracy could be defined as 'a de facto class whose final structure is still in the process of formation'. If this class were at some time to crystallise itself out, it would be able to fulfill a progressive function comparable to that of the bourgeoisie.

ii) On the other hand, the bureaucracy could be defined as a caste, comparable with the Brahmins during the decline of antique-Indian culture. Péret believed that evidence of the religious character of such a social group, developing within a civilisation in decline, could also be seen in the Soviet Union, where Stalin was gaining the status of some kind of prophet.[27]

Grandizo elaborated on this idea of a 'state capitalism without a mature ruling class' in his pamphlet *The Revolutionaries in the Face of Russia and World Stalinism*.[28]

In the first instance, he tried to show with economic arguments that state capitalism existed in the USSR. His lengthy argument was essentially as follows: in capitalism, wage costs are kept as low as possible, and the surplus-product (embodied in surplus-value) is used by capitalists either for new investments or for unproductive consumption; by contrast, in the transitional society from capitalism to socialism, the distribution of the surplus-product would be decided on democratically by the whole population, and the standard of living of the masses would rise. In the development of the Soviet

---

[27] Peralta 1946, pp. 3–9.
[28] Munis 1946.

Union (featuring declining buying power of the workers, use of the surplus-product for a forced investment policy and bureaucratic consumption) there was no evidence of the characteristics of a transitional society, but, rather, of capitalism.

Secondly, like Péret, Grandizo tried to clarify the class position of the bureaucracy with an historical analogy. He compared contemporary international capitalism with the decline of the Roman Empire. When the old empire had entered its phase of downfall, and the transition to feudalism had not yet been completed, a shift in power occurred within the ruling circles: the patricians – the old, previously triumphant class – had to make way for new, energetic elements lacking a genealogy or history. Caesar and Octavianus were the protagonists of this stratum. They extended the power of the state, and thus formed a final bulwark against social disintegration. In the same way as those patricians, Grandizo argued, the international bourgeoisie now also experienced difficulties. Just like the Romans, it was also forced in its declining phase to transfer power to elements which ruled in its place, and thus prolonged the existence of the system: social democrats and Stalinists.

State capitalism in the Soviet Union was, viewed from this perspective, a sign of degeneration: the bourgeoisie had been able to strangle the proletarian revolution, but had not succeeded in enthroning a dynamic ruling class. In a much later publication, Grandizo elaborated this thesis further and, as it were, inverted Burnham's theory of 'managerial revolution': the managers in the Soviet Union were just like their Western colleagues not a ruling class, but, rather, a symptom of the fact that the old bourgeoisie had lost its grip on events, and therefore had created room for reactionary helpers.[29]

James/Dunayevskaya

Cyril Lionel Robert (C.L.R.) James, a revolutionary originating from Trinidad, who in 1938 had been one of the founders of the Fourth International,[30] and

---

[29] Munis 1975, especially pp. 48–62.

[30] James (1901–89) moved in 1932 from Trinidad to Great Britain, where he worked as cricket journalist. In 1936 he co-founded the Trotskyist Revolutionary Socialist League and in 1938 participated in the founding conference of the Fourth International. From the end of 1938, James lived in the United States. In 1952, he was interned, and, in 1953, banned from the United States. Subsequently, he lived for five years in Great Britain and returned to Trinidad in 1958, where he was secretary for some years

Raya Dunayevskaya (pseudonym of Rae Spiegel), an American woman who had been one of Trotsky's collaborators for some time,[31] led the 'state-capitalist' opposition in the American Trotskyist movement.

In 1941, the group around James and Dunayevskaya – also known as the 'Johnson-Forest Tendency' after the respective cryptonyms of each – had left the Socialist Workers' Party together with Shachtman and his supporters, and founded the Workers' Party. But the debate of this group with the majority in this new organisation, which adhered to the theory of bureaucratic collectivism, more and more involved basic principles. Thus, in 1948, the Johnson-Forest Tendency left the Workers' Party – peculiarly enough in order to rejoin the Socialist Workers' Party, until a final break with Trotskyism occurred in 1951. The group then continued its activities independently under the name 'Facing Reality'.[32]

The overall theoretical development of James and Dunayevskaya in this period can be summarised as follows. Around 1940, both had reached the

---

of the West Indies' Federal Labour Party. James became famous as theoretician of black emancipation, and wrote *The Black Jacobins. Toussaint L'Ouverture and the San Domingo Revolution* (1938). See Buhle 1986 and 1988; Boggs 1993, Worcester 1995, Dhondy 2001.

[31] Biographical data in Anon. 1987; Anderson 1988, Marković 1988.

[32] To my knowledge, there is not yet any substantive scholarly study about the history of the Johnson-Forest Tendency. The information given in various relevant publications is not always consistent, especially where the renewed affiliation with the Fourth International is concerned. Jerome and Buick 1967 write: 'In 1947, this group Johnson-Forest rejoined the SWP, but left again in 1951' (p. 68); Ashton Myers 1977 writes: 'C.L.R. James, having left with Shachtman came back to the Socialist Workers Party for two years, 1948 and 1949, only to be expelled' (p. 200); Robinson 1983 claims: 'Then, in 1942, [...] a group centering around James and Raya Dunayevskaya, the Johnson-Forest Tendency, had left the "Shachtmanites". Later, in 1949 or so [sic], the Johnson-Forest Tendency would rejoin the SWP only to become resolutely independent again two years later' (p. 389). I base my own interpretation on statements by James himself. In a foreword to the second edition of *The Invading Socialist Society*, he wrote: 'The Johnson-Forest Tendency was a grouping in the Trotskyist movement which split off from the Socialist Workers Party in 1940 and went with what became the Workers Party. However, inside the Workers Party, the movement found it necessary to clarify its positions, not only against the eclectic jumps of Max Shachtman; we found it imperative to clarify our positions against those of Trotsky, positions which the Socialist Workers Party was repeating with ritual emphasis. It was in the course of doing this that in 1947 we published *The Invading Socialist Society*. But precisely our serious attitude to the fundamentals of Marxism led us to leave the happy-go-lucky improvisations of the Workers Party, and in 1948, to return to the Socialist Workers Party.' James, 1972, p. 1. And in an article dating from 1967 entitled 'Black Power', he states: '[...] in 1951 my friends and I broke irrevocably and fundamentally with the premises of Trotskyism' (James, 1980a, p. 235).

conclusion that Trotsky's theory of the degenerated workers' state was
completely incorrect, because it turned state ownership of the means of
production into a 'fetish' in the Marxian sense.[33] This partial break with
Trotsky was the beginning of a growing divergence. James and Dunayevskaya
undertook a comprehensive reappraisal of Marxism, its methods and
philosophical foundations, in which they returned – in contrast to the
conventions of the Anglo-Saxon tradition at that time – specifically to one
of the important sources of Marx's thought: Hegel.[34]

At the same time, the rejection of Trotsky's 'state fetishism' was combined
with a strong emphasis on the relations of production, such as they influenced
the life of the modern worker. The group published reports by workers about
their daily work[35] and tried in general to link a totalising Hegelian-Marxist
vision with an approach 'from below'.

This resulted in a theory of state capitalism which was, to some extent, unique,
but which also did not develop without difficulties. The first contribution was
by James. Subsequently, Dunayevskaya, who was well-versed in economics
and able to consult Russian sources,[36] refined the analysis.

In his first article on the topic, James advanced as his most important
argument for the existence of state capitalism in the Soviet Union that the
workers and peasants were dependent on wages:

> The predominance of wage-labor makes the means of production capital.
> The means of production, monopolized by a section of society, in their role
> of capital, have an independent life and movement of their own.[37]

At the same time, however, James realised that wage-labour had also
dominated during the first years after the October Revolution, at which

---

[33] 'In order, therefore, to find an analogy we must take flight into the misty realm
of religion. There the products of the human brain appear as autonomous figures
endowed with a life of their own, which enter into relations both with each other
and with the human race. So it is in the world of commodities with the products of
men's hands. I call this the fetishism which attaches itself to the products of labour
as soon as they are produced as commodities, and it is therefore inseparable from
the production of commodities.' Marx, 1976, p. 165.
[34] See, in particular, James 1980b, originally published in 1948. In this book, James
uses Hegel's *Wissenschaft der Logik* as guide for a dialectical critique of Trotskyism.
[35] The most famous became an 'egodocument' by the worker 'Paul Romano' (Phil
Singer). See Romano and Stone 1946.
[36] See Dunayevskaya 1944, 1945.
[37] Johnson 1941a, p. 55.

time – in his stated opinion – a workers' state had still existed. He solved this obvious inconsistency in the following way:

> Was there wage-labor in Leninist Russia? In form only; or yes and no, as is inevitable in a transitional state, but more no than yes. [...] Whereas in a capitalist society the basic relationship is on the one hand wage-labor and on the other hand means of production in the hands of the capitalist class, in Leninist Russia the relationship was: the form of wage-labor only on the one hand because on the other were the means of production in the hands of the laborer who owned the property through the state.[38]

In fact, we might conclude from this passage that it is not wage-labour as such which makes a society (state-) capitalist – as implied by the first quote I cited – but, rather, the combination of wage-labour and the absence of proletarian sovereignty.

After arguing his case for a state-capitalist characterisation, James took a second step: if economic and political power was concentrated on one point (the central state), and the workers and peasants were dependent on wages in the capitalist sense, then, logically speaking, a 'national capitalist' existed, a capitalist who commanded a whole country from which surplus-value could be extorted. The latter, however, did not take the form of profit as in competitive capitalism, but the form of capitalist (bureaucratic) 'wages'.

This thesis, however, created a theoretical problem. A capital which no longer competes with other capitals is not a capital in the Marxian sense. If the Soviet Union did not consist of many capitals, but only of one, how then could there still be market competition? In a second article, James tried to answer this question. He sought the solution in a new area: the world market. Competition of the Soviet Union in the world market with other national capitals would mean that the law of value continued to apply in the USSR.

> [The] Stalinist economy is regulated by wages and those wages are governed by the law of value. For owing to the enormous expenses of a class society in the modern world; the need to keep up with other states in the constant technical revolutions of production and the competition on the world market; the choice between autarky (with enormous increase in cost of production) or penetration into the world market (and being thereby subjected to all its

---

[38] Johnson 1941a, p. 56.

fluctuations); the imperialist struggle and a backward economy; all these compel Stalin to treat labor exactly as in Germany, to treat it as a commodity, paid for at the cost of its production and reproduction.[39]

Three conclusions in any case seem to be implied by this not altogether clear passage, namely:

i) The USSR tried to produce its own goods as cheaply as possible so as not to have to buy these on the world market and/or to sell them in the world market ('the need to keep up').

ii) The USSR tried to acquire specific goods abroad because their production domestically would make these goods too expensive ('autarky (with enormous increase in cost of production)').

iii) Labour-power in the USSR was a commodity, because wages were kept as low as possible ('paid for at the cost of its production and reproduction').

Dunayevskaya elaborated the arguments advanced by James further. After she had in three articles assembled a considerable amount of information about socio-economic relations in the USSR, using Russian sources, and, among other things, had tried to show that the new ruling class – statistically defined by her as the 'most advanced' part of the intelligentsia – comprised 2.05 percent of the total population,[40] she developed a more systematic theory in a three-part essay, written at the end of 1946 and early 1947. Just as Worrall had done previously, Dunayevskaya also set out with a 'proof' that Marx had recognised the possibility of state capitalism. She appealed to another passage in Marx's *Capital* than the Australian had done, namely the paragraph in which the extreme limit of all capitalist centralisation was mentioned: the fusion of all capital into one big capitalist corporation.[41]

Next, Dunayevskaya – again just like Worrall – tried to show that this theoretical possibility had become a reality in the USSR. In an orthodox-Marxist way, she established that, in state capitalism, the fundamental law of

---

[39] Johnson 1941b, p. 214.

[40] Forest 1942–3. I refer to the third article, p. 57.

[41] 'In any given branch of industry centralization would reach its extreme limit if all the individual capitals invested there were fused into a single capital. In a given society this limit would be reached only when the entire social capital was united in the hands of either a single capitalist or a single capitalist company.' Marx 1976, p. 779.

capitalism had to apply (i.e. the law of value), but the way in which capital appropriated surplus-value had to be different from in 'normal' capitalism. Both features were, in her view, applicable to the USSR. On the one side, appropriation of the surplus took place in a new way (via a central plan), and, on the other side, the law of value asserted itself in numerous different ways: the contradiction between rich and poor had grown; the workers *had* to sell their labour-power at its value to prevent loss of their livelihood; production of means of production was more important than that of consumer goods; there existed (hidden) unemployment; there was a continual battle with other capitals in the world market; and there were constant crises, caused by problems of economic co-ordination.

The new system had, according to Dunayevskaya, been established in the middle of the 1930s. The counterrevolution had occurred in a different way than Marxists had expected: not violently, but in a creeping way. Gradually, workers' rights had been eroded. Then Stakhanovism and piece-wages had separated the workers from the means of production. Finally, in 1936, the power of the bureaucracy as a ruling class had been legitimated by means of a new constitution, and the old guard of the Bolsheviks had been exterminated during the Great Purges.

The still more-or-less incidental references to Stakhanovism and to complete separation of workers from means of production received greater emphasis in subsequent publications by James and Dunayevskaya – parallel to an increasing interest, as previously noted, for the everyday life of modern workers. In his pamphlet *State Capitalism and World Revolution*, written in 1950, James constructed a complete analogy between highly developed American corporations on the one hand, and Soviet state capitalism since 1936, on the other hand. Both types of organisation forced workers to mind-numbing drudgery in similar ways (production lines, piece-wages) while the knowledge of the production process was concentrated elsewhere, in the bureaucratic apparatuses, being applied in a planned way to promote the accumulation process and discipline the workers.[42]

If we bring together the various relevant publications by James and Dunayevskaya, we obtain a picture of the Soviet Union as a gigantic capitalist corporation, which, through state planning, oppressed and exploited its own

---

[42] James 1969, pp. 39–46.

workers, and competed in the world market with foreign corporations and countries.

Castoriadis/Lefort

From 1946, the economist Cornelius Castoriadis, of Greek origin, formed an opposition in the French section of the Fourth International in collaboration with Claude Lefort, a philosopher from the circle around Merleau-Ponty.[43] Because of the names of their respective organisations, the group was known as the Tendance Chaulieu-Montal. They presented their heterodox ideas in two documents, dated 1946 and 1947 respectively. Rejecting the Trotskyist theory that the Soviet Union, despite its many shortcomings, nevertheless had to be defended as a workers' state against capitalism, they argued that, in the Soviet Union, a new élite, the bureaucracy, had conquered all power, and that this élite exclusively followed its own interests, and not those of the workers. The Soviet Union was said to be a new type of society, which just like Western capitalism strove for expansion.[44]

Initially, the theory of Castoriadis and Lefort went in the direction of a 'third historical solution' (a kind of bureaucratic collectivism), but, from 1948–9 onwards, they referred to the society ruled by Stalin as 'bureaucratic capitalism', apparently without seeing any need for justifying this theoretical change.[45] Why they remained relatively indifferent about the precise 'label' to be applied to the USSR became clearer when, in 1949, the first issues appeared of the journal *Socialisme ou Barbarie* – a periodical which Castoriadis, Lefort

---

[43] The Greek economist Castoriadis (1922–97) had joined the Trotskyist group of Spiros Stinas after a brief stint in a Communist youth organisation. In 1945, he emigrated to Paris, where he worked for a long time for the OECD while being simultaneously active in revolutionary-socialist circles under a pseudonym. Lefort (b. 1924) had, as student, already in 1943 formed an underground group tending towards Trotskyism. He studied philosophy with Maurice Merleau-Ponty as his main teacher. From 1946, he and Castoriadis collaborated politically. See Castoriadis 1975; Lefort 1976–7; Liebich 1977; Ciaramelli 1987; Busino 1989; Gottraux 1997; van der Linden 1998; David 2000.

[44] Chaulieu and Montal 1946.

[45] Note that Castoriadis/Lefort did not refer to 'state capitalism'. Castoriadis later explained, that he regarded 'state capitalism' as 'an almost completely meaningless expression' creating 'a disastrous confusion […], for it makes one think that capitalism's economic laws continue to hold after the disappearance of private property, of the market, and of competition, which is absurd.' Castoriadis 1973, pp. 20–1; English translation, pp. 9–10.

and their supporters published after they had left the Fourth International in 1948. The dissidents wanted to emphasise specifically the fact that, in the Soviet Union, *exploitation and oppression had persisted despite the elimination of classical private property.*

Exploitation was defined by Castoriadis as the social relationship in which a social group, due to its special relationship with the production apparatus, is able to appropriate a part of the social product, of which the magnitude is not equal to its contribution to the production process. The Soviet bureaucracy, in his eyes, constituted such an exploiting group. The bureaucracy, after all, controlled the means of production and distribution system, and ruled the social consumption fund. It thus embodied the supremacy of dead labour over living labour. That it ruled and exploited as a collectivity – unlike the traditional bourgeoisie – made the Soviet Union no less capitalist, because capitalist exploitation meant

> that the producers do not have means of production at their disposal, either individually (artisans) or collectively (socialism), and that living labour, instead of dominating dead labour, is dominated by it through the intermediary of the individuals who personify it (the capitalists).[46]

The fact that, in the USSR, there was only one all-powerful employer obviously changed the position of the workers. Because, while the wage-earners in competitive capitalism could change their employer, the freedom of the Russian worker was restricted: in general, they could neither leave their place of residence, never mind their country. In that sense, their position somewhat resembled that of serfs.

These limited possibilities for mobility by the workers were connected to an almost total lack of limits to exploitation. While, in competitive capitalism, the level of wages and other employment conditions resulted from negotiations between capital and labour, the Soviet bureaucracy unilaterally imposed those conditions. It was admittedly restricted to certain limits (e.g. the physiological minimum which kept workers alive), but its ability to manoeuvre remained exceptionally great. For their part, the workers – robbed of autonomous organisations and reduced to a subsistence minimum – had only two possibilities of resistance – theft (of finished and semi-finished goods, tools,

----

[46] Chaulieu 1949, p. 34; English translation, p. 131.

etc.) and indifference, expressed, among other ways, in producing goods of inferior quality.

This whole situation – which could be characterised as a contradictory unity of total concentration of power in a small social group and a 'terrible crisis in the productivity of human labour'[47] – was, Castoriadis suggested, in one sense the fault of the Russian workers themselves. Namely, they had not understood that the expropriation of the capitalists after 1917 signified only the 'negative motivation' of a proletarian revolution. The positive half, after all, would consist of the transfer of all management to the working class. The Russian workers had not been thoroughly aware of this, and thus had, by their own actions (or rather their inaction), brought the bureaucracy to power:

> Having overthrown the bourgeois government, having expropriated the capitalists (often against the wishes of the Bolsheviks), having occupied the factories, the workers thought that all that was necessary was to hand over management to the government, to the Bolshevik party, and to the trade union leaders. By doing so, the proletariat was abdicating its own essential role in the new society it was striving to create.[48]

With this approach, Castoriadis and Lefort came close to the views of James and Dunayevskaya. Admittedly, they did not pose a number of questions which the Americans had considered very important (e.g. the question of the world market), but their stress on power relations at enterprise level strongly resembled the Johnson-Forest Tendency. It is, therefore, no great surprise that Chaulieu-Montal and Johnson-Forest maintained contact with each other, and that the journal *Socialisme ou Barbarie* published writings by the Americans.[49]

---

[47] Chaulieu 1949, p. 47; English translation, p. 141.
[48] Chaulieu 1949, p. 35; English translation, p. 97.
[49] The pamphlet by Paul Romano (Phil Singer) and Ria Stone (Grace Lee) was serialised as 'L'ouvrier Americain' in *Socialisme ou Barbarie* in 1949–50 (issues 1–7). In 1958, the group around James and Socialisme ou Barbarie published a joint pamphlet. See Lee, Chaulieu and Johnson 1958. Background information in Boggs 1998, p. 62.

Cliff

Ygael Gluckstein (1917–2000), a Trotskyist from Palestine writing under the pseudonym of Tony Cliff,[50] carried on a 'state-capitalist' opposition in the British section of the Fourth International from about 1947. After he had initially criticised both the theories of the degenerated workers' state and bureaucratic collectivism in 1947, he published an extensive account of his own views in 1948, under the title *The Nature of Stalinist Russia* – a work which, in revised and expanded editions, was reprinted several times. Cliff was set thinking by the events in Eastern Europe after 1944. If, as some claimed, the buffer states were workers' states, then – so he concluded – Stalin was the man who had realised proletarian revolutions there. But, if that was so, then it would be possible to establish proletarian states without proletarian self-activity. Cliff saw himself faced with two mutually exclusive logical possibilities: either the East European *glacis* comprised real workers' states, and then the emancipation of the working class could also be accomplished by others, or else only the working class could emancipate itself, and then the theory of the degenerated workers' state could not be sustained. His own choice in this dilemma was clear:

> When I came to the theory of state capitalism, I didn't come to it by a long analysis of the law of value in Russia, the economic statistics in Russia. Nothing of the sort. I came to it by the simple statement that if the emancipation of the working class is the act of the working class, then you cannot have a workers' state without the workers having power to dictate what happens in society. So I had to choose between what Trotsky said – the heart of Trotsky is the self-activity of the workers – or the form of property. I decided to push away the form of property as determining the question.[51]

---

[50] Gluckstein/Cliff was born in 1917 in Palestine. From about 1938, he was a Trotskyist, and he emigrated to Britain in 1946. In 1947, he was extradited, and settled in Ireland. But he visited Britain regularly, because his family lived there, and joined in the discussions of the British Trotskyists. In 1952, he returned to Britain, where he became the leader of the small Socialist Review Group within the Labour Party, out of which the International Socialists and still later the Socialist Workers' Party emerged (not to be confused with the US-American party of the same name). This information is based on an interview with the author in London, 9 July 1979. See further Cliff 1979 and 2000, and Sarney 2000.

[51] Cliff 1979, p. 21.

Cliff returned to the standpoint defended by Trotsky before 1933, namely that it only made sense to talk of a workers' state, if indeed the working class exercised political power and possessed direct control over the means of production. As soon as this was no longer the case, one could also no longer say a workers' state existed, whether one called it 'degenerated' or not. In that sense, one could still apply the concept of a workers' state to the period 1917–28 – be it with a socially autonomised bureaucracy – but not to the period since then. The first five-year plan constituted a revolutionary qualitative change: the bureaucracy began at that point to execute in high tempo the historic task of the bourgeoisie (the creation of a large proletariat, and the accumulation of capital).[52]

Cliff characterised the state capitalism consolidated under Stalin as 'the extreme theoretical limit which capitalism can reach'.[53] Just as a workers' state embodied the transitional phase to socialism after the proletarian revolution, Soviet state capitalism was the last transitional phase of capitalism prior to the socialist revolution. Schematically, one could represent this idea in the following way:

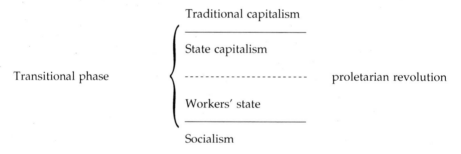

While the transition from state capitalism to workers' state was necessarily violent in nature, since a bourgeois army could not be wrested from the ruling class in a gradual way, Cliff believed that the inverse transition, said to have occurred in the USSR around 1928, was also possible without violence. The only requirement here was that internal democracy in the army was gradually broken down, and replaced by a command structure uncontrolled from below.[54]

---

[52] Cliff 1948, pp. 59–60, 81; reprint 2003, pp. 56, 75.
[53] Cliff 1948, p. 62; reprint 2003, p. 58.
[54] Cliff 1948, p. 82.

What, then, were the characteristics of this state capitalism? Cliff, who showed he had studied the relevant contemporary literature relatively well,[55] combined elements of various earlier Marxist contributions in a distinctive synthesis which, at first sight, appears very consistent. With Hilferding, he agreed that the price mechanism in the Soviet Union did not express autonomous economic activity, but only a (not entirely arbitrarily determined) transmission belt, with which the state apparatus regulated the production and division of labour of the whole society. With Dunayevskaya and James, he shared the belief that the individual enterprises in the USSR were not autonomous economic units, but just subordinate cogs in a greater whole.[56] If one saw the Soviet Union in isolation, without taking into account the international context, then it would strikingly resemble 'one big factory', which was led from a central point. The capitalist character of this big state enterprise became visible if one included world relations in the analysis; then it transpired that the Soviet Union as a nation was comparable to any individual capitalist enterprise which sought to survive within competitive relations.

Cliff, however, did not leave the analysis at that. While James and Dunayevskaya had left the precise nature of the competition between the USSR and foreign rivals out of consideration, he developed his own theory about the subject. His point of departure was the following observation:

> Hitherto, Russia's backwardness has ruled out any question of flooding foreign markets with Russian goods. On the other hand, Russian markets are kept from being flooded with foreign goods by the monopoly of foreign trade which only military might can smash.[57]

This circumstance could, however, be taken to imply that the Soviet Union as a national capitalist enterprise did *not* compete with other foreign capitals.

---

[55] See, for example the references to Laurat's *Marxism and Democracy* (p. 16; reprint 2003, p. 15), Burnham's *Managerial Revolution* (p. 61; reprint 2003, p. 57) and Hilferding's critique of state capitalism (p. 97; reprint 2003, pp. 128–9).

[56] For a brief period, Cliff maintained comradely relations with Dunayevskaya. Ray Challinor reports that the two had agreed on a 'division of labour' in theorising about the USSR: 'I had a letter from Raya [Dunayevskaya] saying she met Cliff in 1946 at the Fourth World Congress [of the Fourth International]. They agreed she would devote her time to study the philosophical implications and that Cliff would look at the economic issues.' (Challinor 1995, p. 27.)

[57] Cliff 1948, p. 99; reprint 2003, p. 91.

And if that was the case, would it then still make sense to talk about 'capital' at all? Cliff thought he could neutralise the obvious objection by postulating that international competition did not take place by means of commodities, but by means of use-values in the form of armaments. This 'innovation' with regard to the Marxist law of value – which, after all, only involved competition by means of realised values (effective sale of commodities) – was defended by Cliff in the following way:

> Value expresses the existence of competitive relations between independent producers. The result[s] of Russia's standing in competition is expressed by the elevation of use values to an end, the end being victory in this competition. Use values, therefore, while being an end, still remain a means.[58]

Bordiga

Amadeo Bordiga (1889–1970), a former leader of the Italian Communist Party who had been expelled from the organisation in 1930, had remained completely silent about political topics until the definite downfall of Mussolini.[59] However, immediately after the World War II, when his influence had been reduced to a few marginalised political groups in France, Italy and some other countries, he began to mount an extensive publication campaign. Strongly emphasising Marxist 'invariance' (the unchangeable nature of historical-materialist principles, as he interpreted them), Bordiga saw it as his most important task to draw the lessons from recent historical events.

---

[58] Cliff 1948, p. 100; reprint 2003, p. 92. Various authors claimed that Cliff's theory strongly resembled the theory of bureaucratic collectivism, because both assumed that the law of value did *not* apply within the Soviet Union (see e.g. Hobson and Tabor 1988, p. 369). Obviously, there are striking parallels between Cliff and Joseph Carter especially, who had defined the USSR as a 'huge national trust' (Carter 1941, p. 218; see Chapter 3 above), but this interpretation overlooks the most important reason why Cliff devised his own theory, namely because the theory of bureaucratic collectivism, in his opinion, could not explain economic growth in the USSR. Cliff called bureaucratic collectivism a theory which was 'only negative' and 'thus empty, abstract, and therefore arbitrary' (Cliff 1948b, p. 156).

[59] There are two political biographies of Bordiga: de Clementi 1971 and Livorsi 1976. Both studies understandably devote special attention to Bordiga's earlier 'glory days'. See also Camatte 1974 and 1975; Grilli 1982; Goldner 1991; Peregalli and Saggioro 1995 and 1998; Bresciani 2001.

In this process of critical historical reconstruction, the analysis of the society emerging from the October Revolution occupied a central place. From 1946 until his death in 1970, Bordiga published an impressive number of articles about the Soviet Union, which were later bundled into books. The high point of this *œuvre* lies, as Riechers remarks, between Stalin's death in 1953 and the launch of the Sputnik in 1957.[60] Bordiga distinguished himself from most other Marxists in this period by striving to obtain a detailed empirical insight into the USSR.

Apart from an early essay, published under the pseudonym of 'Alfa',[61] Bordiga's most important (mostly anonymously published) contributions can be divided into two categories. Firstly, there are lectures given at meetings of his political organisation, the Internationalist Communist Party. These prolonged speeches were serialised in parts in the party organ *Il Programma Comunista*. Noteworthy are especially the speech at a meeting in Bologna, 31 October and 1 November 1954, published under the title 'Russia and Revolution in Marxist Theory';[62] and speeches at meetings in Naples, 24 and 25 April 1955, and in Genoa, 6 and 7 August 1955, published as 'Economic and Social Structure of Russia Today'.[63]

Secondly, there are the imaginary dialogues. Each of these dialogues (which really seem more like monologues) was divided into three 'days', and expounded the standpoint of the author about a text issued from the Soviet side. The relevant publications are 'Dialogue with Stalin' (1952), a critique of Stalin's essay about 'Economic Problems of Socialism in the USSR' in the same year,[64] and 'Dialogue with the Dead' (1956), a response to Khruschev's secret speech at the Twentieth Party Congress of the CPSU.[65] In addition, Bordiga discoursed about all kinds of other topics, where he made more or

---

[60] Riechers 1977, p. 157. See also Camatte 1975, p. 8: 'As far as what he [Bordiga] called the "Russian question" is concerned, he wrote a lot [...]. Especially in the period 1954–57 when he was very preoccupied with it'.

[61] Alfa 1946.

[62] Bordiga 1954–5. A short report on the meeting in Bologna in Anon. 1954.

[63] Bordiga 1955a, 1955b, 1955–7. Information about the meetings in Naples and Genoa is provided in Anon. 1955a and 1955b. The series of articles at 'Naples' en 'Genoa' were later republished with additions in Bordiga 1976.

[64] Bordiga 1952a. Republished as a book titled *Dialogato con Stalin*. See Bordiga 1953.

[65] Bordiga 1956a and 1956b.

less incidental references to Stalinism and Soviet society.[66] The enormous interest for the Soviet Union, evident in Bordiga's later *œuvre*, was shared by the whole 'Bordigist' current. This preoccupation in fact went so far that a profound disagreement about Stalinism caused a split in 1952.[67]

Bordiga considered the revolution of 1917 primarily as an anti-feudal, i.e. a bourgeois revolution, in which the bourgeoisie (to which the peasantry is also said to be allied) and the proletariat formed a temporary alliance. Such a revolution, with an important proletarian contribution, could lead to three outcomes:

i)   Victory – implying a blessing primarily for the bourgeoisie – is transformed by the movement into a proletarian revolution; this was the model of Marx's 'revolution in permanence'.
ii) Victory is followed by a consolidation of bourgeois rule.
iii) Defeat, which brings the restoration of the old absolutist order.[68]

The Bolsheviks strove for the first-mentioned outcome, but were not successful. The international bourgeoisie was able – due to the ebbing away of a radical élan during the 1920s, especially in Western and Central Europe – to realise the second variant. This occurred apparently without much bloodshed, and without formal replacement of the power élite, during a 'lengthy period of involution'.[69] Thus the feudal chains in short order made way for a violently unfolding capitalism.

Whereas Trotsky and others had regarded the Soviet Union as a *post-*capitalist complex, and Cliff and others thought they could detect a *developed* capitalism, Bordiga believed only a very *incipient* capitalism existed, in his own words 'a transition not from, but towards capitalism'.[70] Even in 1952, Bordiga compared the developmental level of the Stalinist society with Germany, Austria and Italy after 1848.[71]

---

[66] For example, Orso 1948–52.
[67] Vega 1952; Damen 1977; Bourrinet 1981, p. 180. Damen equated Soviet 'capitalism' with that of the United States, while Bordiga expressly rejected that idea.
[68] Bordiga 1951.
[69] Alfa 1946, p. 35.
[70] Bordiga 1953, p. 29.
[71] Bordiga 1952b.

In his characterisation of the Soviet Union as 'early-capitalist', Bordiga adopted a very idiosyncratic concept of capitalism. Sociological factors, such as the existence of a ruling class or lack of it, or political factors such as the nature of state intervention, played no role at all in his definition; capitalism existed, if an economy consisted of enterprises which calculated revenues and expenditures in terms of a general quantitative equivalent (money) and strove to maximise the difference between outputs and inputs ('profit'). This definition was asserted in separation from the question of who appropriated this 'profit':

> Capitalism always exists when products are sold in the market or in any case are 'accounted for' as assets of the enterprise, understood as a distinct, but very large economic island, while the compensations of labour are placed on the side of liabilities. Bourgeois economics is economics with double-entry bookkeeping. The bourgeois individual is not a human being, but a company.[72]

> For us every system of production of commodities in the modern world, in the world of associated *labour*, i.e. of the grouping of workers in productive companies, is defined as capitalist economy.[73]

Based on this catch-all definition, it was obviously not difficult for Bordiga to 'prove' in a logically consistent way that the nature of the Soviet economy was capitalist. The fact that the Soviet state was qualitatively different from the states in 'normal capitalism' was, as noted previously, of little importance to Bordiga. The state, after all, belonged to the superstructure, and therefore could not play a significant role in the characterisation of production relations. The state in the USSR, moreover, did not embody the power of an independent class – at most, it could be regarded as the *representative* of such a power.

In reaction to Burnham, Bordiga claimed that, throughout the whole of history, the state bureaucracy had only ever formed *instruments* of ruling classes, but never *incorporated* ruling classes themselves. Beyond that, talk of a ruling bureaucracy in the Soviet Union did not make any sense for yet

---

[72] Orso 1948–52 (November–December 1948), p. 497.
[73] Bordiga 1953, p. 17.

another reason: the majority of the population was employed by the state.[74] Although capitalism had triumphed, a new capitalist class had therefore not arisen. The state was only an intermediary, an 'emulating channel' through which the working class was exploited and oppressed. The real agents profiting from this situation were the Russian peasants as well as the international bourgeoisies.[75]

4.iii. Theories of a new mode of production

Guttmann

Josef Guttmann (1902–58) was for some time regarded as the most promising young Communist leader in Czechoslovakia. He had been active in the ranks of the Communist Party of Czechoslovakia since its foundation in 1921, when he was 19. Eight years later, he was elected to the Politbureau, and appointed chief editor of the party organ *Rudé Právo*. In 1931 followed his appointment to the political secretariat of the Communist International. This dazzling political career came to an abrupt end however when, in 1932, Guttmann started criticising the tactics pursued by the German Communists against Hitler. Accused of 'Trotskyism' – a current with which he did indeed began to feel an affinity – he was removed in 1933 from all leading party organs.[76]

After leaving Czechoslovakia in 1938, Guttmann travelled via Copenhagen and London to the United States; arriving there, he participated actively in the political discussions among socialist emigrants from Europe, and developed his own theory of the Soviet Union, first presented at a famous meeting in the house of fellow emigrant Karl Wittfogel, and subsequently published in 1944 under the pseudonym of 'Peter Meyer'.[77] Guttmann rejected the *tertium-*

---

[74] '[…] [I]n state capitalism all are bureaucrats'. Bordiga 1952c. This statement must be regarded as a rhetorical exaggeration; in other places in the *œuvre* one finds passages which relativise the generalised public service.

[75] Bordiga 1976, p. 507.

[76] Lazitch and Drachkovitch 1973, pp. 137–8; Rupnik 1976; and Broué 1982b.

[77] Wittfogel said during an interview in the 1970s that: 'My first contact, which I had [as immigrant in the USA – MvdL] here in this house, was with […] radical splitters, early Trotskyists, Communists and left social democrats. But in the chair sat the man, who made an analysis – which so impressed Koestler – about the Soviet Union "as a class society". For us with our doomed Trotskyist, Leninist and half-Leninist ideas this inquiry was taken extraordinarily seriously.' Greffrath 1979, p. 328. Henry Jacoby

non-datur that was implicitly or explicitly the fundamental premise of both the theoreticians of state capitalism and those of the (degenerated) workers' state. They had pointed to the absence of particular defining characteristics of capitalism or socialism in the Soviet Union, and inferred that *for that reason* a different social system existed. Guttmann, by contrast, wanted to recognise a third possibility, namely that *both* interpretations were correct with regard to the *negative* propositions they formulated about the Soviet Union. In the USSR, a bourgeoisie and the rule of the law of value were absent, as the 'socialists' and the proponents of a 'workers' state' correctly claimed, but social equality, freedom and democracy were also absent, as the 'state-capitalist' theoreticians had correctly said. Only the combination of these two perspectives could, he believed, provide real insight into the Stalinist formation:

> It begins to appear then that both sides are right in their negative propositions, and that both are wrong when from these they make a breakneck leap [...] to their conclusions. Perhaps there is neither capitalism nor socialism in Russia, but a third thing, something that is quite new in history.[78]

After referring to the dominant role of the state in the economy, famine and the decline of real wages, income disparities, the powerlessness of the workers and the absence of political rights, Guttmann concluded that there were exploiters and exploited, rulers and ruled in the Soviet Union. Nevertheless, the dominant class was of a different kind than the bourgeoisie. Schematically, Guttmann's interpretation can be presented as follows:

---

wrote in his memoirs: 'Günther Reimann took me to meet with Karl Wittfogel. Arriving there, we encountered Josef Guttmann, nicknamed Pepik, the erstwhile leader of the Prague Communists with Kalandra.' 'As soon as he began to speak, one admired his clarity and acuity. He expounded an interpretation of the Soviet Union as class state. Management and control were private property in the hands of the ruling class. Later he wrote extensively about it under the pseudonym of Peter Meyer in *Politics*.' Jacoby 1983, p. 120. More information is available in Ulmen 1978, pp. 266, 566. This author however claims incorrectly Guttmann later changed his name to 'Gordon'. Meyer [Josef Guttmann] 1944, p. 49 and Greffrath 1979, p. 328.

[78] Meyer 1944, p. 49.

	Capitalism	**Soviet Union**
Means of production	Control through right to private property	Control through right to social administration
	Management by private employers	Management by hierarchical collectivity
Labour-power	Worker can choose to whom he will sell his labour-power (for a limited time)	Labour-power of the worker belongs for an indefinite time to the collective exploiter
Wage level	Boundary between value and surplus-value is determined by competitive labour markets and spontaneous operation of economic laws	Boundary between total product and surplus-product determined by bureaucratic striving for exploitation. The wage level is depressed to a lower limit, below which the working class is in danger of dying out.

Guttmann also identifies intermediate classes in the Soviet Union, comparable to simple commodity producers and the petty-bourgeoisie in capitalism (the *kolkhoz* farmers, labour aristocrats – *Stakhanovtsy* – etc.). Their existence could not, however, prevent that the class boundary between rulers and workers was closing with surprising speed. Through nepotism, a monopoly of higher education, and inherited wealth, the bureaucracy would, in future, comprise mainly children of the bureaucracy.

In contrast to earlier theoreticians, Guttmann had an eye for structural contradictions and disproportions in the bureaucratic system. Firstly, he identified a vicious circle in the accumulation process: because the social position of each member of the ruling class – his status, salary etc. and occasionally even life and limb itself – depended on the realisation of the Plan, and because the input and output prices of goods were determined from above, every bureaucrat felt compelled to lower wages and raise the work tempo.[79] But the undernourishment of the workers, due to low wages, reduced labour productivity, and thereby also reduced the social product, so that the bureaucrats again had to reduce the living standard of the workers to realise the planned output volume.

---

[79] The logically necessary link, namely that the realisation of the Plan is impossible if the prices and wages existing at the beginning of the plan are maintained, is not argued for by Guttmann.

Secondly, the absence of capitalist and socialist correctives (prices and profits on the one side, and democratic control on the other side) meant that the whole planning process became chaotic:

> Regulation and criticism 'only from above' are no substitute for public control. If orders from above may not be criticized even when they are senseless and impossible to carry out, then their carrying out has to be faked. The despotic system forces everybody to lie. [...] Errors of planning are inevitable even with the best statistics. But under conditions such as these they become the rule.[80]

That the bureaucracy had been able to maintain itself internally as well as in the fight against Nazi Germany, was explained by Guttmann by the advantage which planned economy nevertheless offered: in an emergency situation, all people and materials could be concentrated on one task, without any social obstacles getting in the way.

If a genuine transition of Soviet society to socialism was to occur, then a political revolution such as Trotsky proposed did not suffice; a total social revolution was required, that would change the production relations qualitatively.

4.iv. Interpretations 'without labels'

In the beginning of the 1950s, an interesting theoretical development occurred. Several independent Marxists, all from West Germany, abandoned the labels used from the 1930s onwards to describe the Soviet Union. They regarded these labels as too hasty, and tried to formulate new theories which were more 'open' than the old approaches. These authors were not so much searching for a correct description, but for a theory that was as consistent as possible with the observable facts. Even those among them who still cherished older theories admitted their reluctance in ascribing any traditional 'label' to the Soviet Union. Thus, for example, Helmut Fleischer – who considered that a bourgeois degeneration had occurred in the Soviet Union – remarked:

---

[80] Meyer 1944, p. 83.

An unambiguous definition of Stalinist Russia can only be given, if the historical origin of this régime and its place in history is appropriately taken into account. Both these points are much more essential than the name which one might select.

He accordingly refused to use labels like 'state capitalism', 'degenerated workers' state' or 'bureaucratic collectivism'.[81]

Probably this (temporary) anti-dogmatism was related to the split between Yugoslavia and the Soviet Union in 1949, and the emergence of a Titoist movement in the Federal Republic of Germany under the name of 'Independent Workers' Party' (UAP).[82] While the UAP was a phenomenon of short duration – the party existed only from 1950 to 1951 – and while Tito's most important ideologist, Milovan Djilas, defended a variant of the theory of state capitalism in this period,[83] it seems that the corrosion of Communist orthodoxy which it evinced also stimulated other, more daring interpretations. The new heterodoxy became visible both in the left wing of the German social democracy as well as in the circles around the UAP.

Sternberg

The economist Fritz Sternberg (1895–1963),[84] who was known internationally since 1926 when he published his main work *Imperialismus* – made some contributions to the analysis of the Soviet Union at the beginning of the 1950s. From these writings, it is clear that Sternberg was no longer close to Trotskyism, as he had been twenty years earlier, but had meantime developed his own variant of 'democratic socialism'.

In his wide-ranging book *Capitalism and Socialism on Trial*, published in 1951, Sternberg tried, among other things, to analyse in outline the development of Russian society since 1917, with due regard for the changing world situation. Significant in the first instance was that he resisted, unlike many others, any inclination to labelling. Russia – Sternberg almost never referred

---

[81] Lenz 1950. That 'Lenz' was a pseudonym of Helmut Fleischer was revealed in a letter by Fleischer to the author dated 3 February 1987.
[82] See on this topic Kulemann 1978. This party should not be confused with the right-wing extremist Unabhängige Arbeiter-Partei founded in 1962.
[83] Djilas 1951.
[84] More biographical data in Grebing 1981, pp. 582–92.

to 'the Soviet Union' – had, on the one hand, put to an end the feudal relationships at home, and had also eradicated capitalism. On the other hand, neither socialism nor anything resembling it had been established. Instead, a repressive party dictatorship had emerged, which continued some Czarist traditions. Politically considered, the result of this ambivalent situation (which, according to Sternberg, had been historically inevitable) was a *hybrid* form of society, which mixed progressive and reactionary tendencies: 'It is useless, to attempt to cover it [i.e. the new state form] with a name; it is misleading, to mistake one side of the Russian development for the other.'[85]

In his reconstruction of developments since the October Revolution, Sternberg noted many aspects which had already been identified by others as well: the shrinking social basis of the party dictatorship, as shown by the statification of the trade unions, the tendency to autarchy in the world market, etc. In so doing, he pointed out that the party dictatorship had initially (under Lenin) been directed primarily at the old exploiters, but had gradually more and more evolved into a dictatorship which, through a drastic intervention in the standard of living of the workers and peasants, had forced an industrialisation process.

To these already well-known ideas, Sternberg added two new elements. Firstly, he believed that the collectivisation of agriculture could be correctly understood only if one recognised in its results a parallel with the Asiatic mode of production. Namely, the fact that the state owned the machinery of the agrarian collectives (tractors and suchlike) meant that these collectives were just as dependent on the state as the village communities were in the old China. It is unclear whether or not this judgement was influenced by Wittfogel's work. But, if so, then Sternberg certainly approached the theory of oriental despotism in a very modern way, by interpreting the water-economy only as an analogy.

Secondly, Sternberg was prepared to call the postwar expansion of the Soviet Union into Eastern Europe 'red imperialism', with the proviso that a quite different imperialism was involved from capitalist imperialism. While capitalism implemented a coalition with the big landowners in its colonies, the USSR promoted agrarian revolutions; while capitalism braked the industrialisation of its colonies, the USSR, to the contrary, stimulated it;

---

[85] Sternberg 1951, p. 172.

and, while capitalism expanded in order to sell its surplus of commodities for high profits, the Soviet Union experienced a shortage of goods, and had no need to sell them elsewhere. In short, the social content of 'red imperialism' was completely different from the content of Western imperialism. This also meant, according to Sternberg, that, for the Soviet Union, no inherent necessity for expansionism existed, although such an expansion might have a certain utility for the maintenance of the régime.

In the same year in which his book was published, Sternberg also published a pamphlet about the Soviet Union, titled *So It Ends...* In this work, he advanced broadly the same ideas, with one important difference: no longer did he refer to a society which combined progressive and reactionary tendencies, but, rather, to the 'most reactionary state in the world', which globally needed to be fought on every level (political, militarily and ideologically).[86]

Cycon

In 1952–3, the journalist Dieter Cycon (b. 1923)[87] published some remarkable articles initialised 'D.C.' in *Funken*, the independent left-socialist monthly of Fritz Lamm and others. In response to replies (by Henry Jacoby, alias Sebastian Franck, and the Dutch socialist Frits Kief) Cycon later expanded his analysis somewhat.

Cycon, who knew Sternberg's work,[88] was at least as cautious as the latter. In answer to his critics, he argued as follows:

> Most observers take the view, that we know too little about progress in the Soviet Union, and that the little we do know is incomplete, and is always seen from a special point of view. In the end we are dealing with a historically unique experiment and there are no possibilities of comparison. We can from various points of reference carefully draw some conclusions with the awareness that in time they could be proved false.[89]

---

[86] Sternberg 1952.

[87] Cycon was from 1948 editor of *Stuttgarter Zeitung*. From 1951 to 1953 he published in *Funken*. From 1957, he evolved politically to the right. In 1969, he became chief of the foreign affairs desk of the conservative daily *Die Welt*. This information is based on a letter by Bernd Klemm (Hannover) to the author, dated 22 October 1986 and on Kreter 1986, pp. 94–6, 190.

[88] See the reference to Sternberg 1951 in Cycon 1952b, p. 6.

[89] Cycon 1953b, p. 9.

In the development of the Soviet Union since the beginning of the first five-year plan in 1928, Cycon perceived three key factors operating: the dictatorial power of a small leading group in the Communist Party; the forced industrialisation; and, in the wake of this industrialisation, the emergence of a broad layer of technical and economic functionaries, which he labelled the 'new intelligentsia'.

This new intelligentsia occupied a socially very important role, given that significant private ownership of means of production no longer existed, and knowledge therefore became a greater source of power than property. It was a stratum encompassing a broad range of occupational groups that differed greatly in income and social power. Although, on average, they were all materially better off than the workers and peasants, they were internally so strongly differentiated that the living standard of the lowest levels approached that of the workers. The mutual social boundaries were therefore rather fluid.

The most important way in which members of the new intelligentsia could conquer and retain their position was their professional knowledge. To the degree that this knowledge became socially more and more monopolised (because higher education was made impossible for anyone other than the children of the new intelligentsia), the 'knowledge élite' could isolate itself increasingly from the rest of society, and transform itself into a true ruling class. A tendency in that direction was, according to Cycon, already clearly visible, but the process was by no means complete: 'the supervisors of millions of small and greater functionaries have in no way succeeded in stabilising this class formation'.[90]

Cycon did not explicitly answer the question of whether the process of class formation would ever reach the point of stabilisation. His argument indeed seemed to point in another direction. He noted that the 'phenomenal growth' of the Soviet economy since about 1930 was made possible by a combination of three elements: the prioritising of the production of investment goods; a very low living standard, due to the relatively modest scope of the production of consumer goods; and extensive terror, necessary to force the population to accept the sacrifices that had to be made.[91]

---

[90] Cycon 1952a, p. 4.
[91] Cycon 1953a, p. 8. Cycon's articles stimulated considerable discussion. I refer

At the beginning of the 1950s, Cycon claimed that this policy had achieved results: heavy industry had reached a high level, and the military power of the country had become considerable. Therefore, the time had come to pay more attention to the consumer-goods sector, as suggested also by the objectives of the latest five-year plan. Now it became possible either to raise the living standard of the new intelligentsia, so that its consolidation as a ruling class would occur, or to raise the living standards of the working class, in order to promote equality (which could also enable a reduction of terror).

Which of these options would be chosen by the Soviet leadership would depend on the power relations at the top of the social hierarchy. Cycon perceived a contradiction between the party leadership on the one hand, and the bureaucracy in the economy and the state on the other. The last-mentioned force, which had gained more power during World War II, operated in the direction of a class state; the first-mentioned force by contrast braked this development. The party leadership – standing *above* the emerging new class – resisted bureaucratic expansionism, and tried via purges to make the social system more dynamic. By seeking support among broad layers of the population, it tried to bring the bureaucracy under control. Cycon seemed to have had faith in the success of this project. One of his articles, at any rate, hypothesises that the general standard of living would rise very significantly from 1960 onwards.[92]

Frölich

Paul Frölich (1884–1953) was a veteran of the German labour movement, who in the Weimar Republic had represented the KPD as parliamentarian in the Reichstag, and who later (in 1932) had joined the German Socialist Workers'

---

especially to Franck 1953a; Kief 1953; Cycon 1953b; Hellmann 1953; Weinberg 1953; and Leonhard 1953. Of these contributions, the article by Susanne Leonhard is the most interesting from the point of view of my study. Leonhard was – in contrast to Cycon – of the opinion that the Soviet bureaucracy was increasingly a closed and self-reproducing élite, but saw no reason to designate it as a class, because it was too heterogenous and internally divided. She thought that the Soviet workers also did not form a class, because there was no free labour market anymore with multiple buyers, nor a possibility for free organisation. Globally, she characterises the Soviet Union as a (not further specified) development dictatorship. See Weber 1984 about the life of Leonhard (1895–1984), who spent many years in Stalin's 'Gulag Archipelago'.

[92] Cycon 1953a.

Party. He lived the life of an exile from 1934 to 1950, first in France and later in the United States. Upon his return to the Federal Republic of Germany, he joined the SPD and published among others in *Funken*, a journal to which Cycon also contributed.[93]

During the last years of his life, Frölich worked on a book about the nature of the Stalin régime. Fragments of this incomplete study were published only much later,[94] but important elements of Frölich's theory became known already at the beginning of the 1950s, through small contributions in the West-German political press and his correspondence with other left-wing socialists. Frölich – who, in a letter to Rosdolsky, called the Soviet Union 'a *new* historical phenomenon!' and added 'The name for it will be found. Meantime it suffices, if one frames the question'[95] – explained the origins of Stalinist dictatorship, like most authors, to an important extent with reference to the absence of socialist revolution in the West. But, in contrast to most, Frölich deduced this absence from objective causes: not just in Russia, but also elsewhere the preconditions for socialism as yet did not exist. The Russian Revolution therefore *had* to fail in its attempt to establish socialism. The result was:

> an economic order, which strives towards capitalist development, a statised planned economy. But it is one which has broken through capitalist barriers, a planned economy without capitalists, for which the capitalist laws no longer apply. And this planned economy is realised in a society with the most brute contradictions and barbaric methods of domination, which ultimately are the fruit of the unripeness for socialism.[96]

In the posthumously published fragments (which partly overlap with reflections published during his life), Frölich tries to gain more insight into the Soviet bureaucracy by investigating differences and similarities with 'classical' ruling bureaucracies, such as in imperial China. Setting out from the idea that apparently stable bureaucracies of the 'Chinese' type could only exist in relatively balanced social formations, in which economic and social development remained limited, he drew the conclusion that the Soviet

---

[93] Klemm 1983.
[94] Frölich 1976.
[95] Letter by Frölich to Roman Rosdolsky, 20 June 1950, in the Rosdolsky archive, International Institute for Social History. Wilbert van Miert, the archivist of Rosdolsky's papers, kindly drew my attention to this letter.
[96] Frölich 1952, p. 13.

bureaucracy was a phenomenon of quite a different order. In the society issuing forth from the October Revolution, Frölich perceived a combination of a number of precarious equilibria, which would, in the shorter or longer term, become destabilised.

Firstly, intermediate layers were lacking which could absorb and channel the contradiction between the bureaucratic 'machine' and the majority of the population. While, for example, the absolutist state continued to draw support for a long time from the aristocracy and from significant parts of the bourgeoisie in exploiting the rural population, the 'totalitarian' Soviet bureaucracy formed a unity of state apparatus, exploiter and oppressor. This forced the ruling stratum to a very brute and repressive régime, the position of which would be challenged as soon as the masses of the people began to mobilise.

Secondly, the ruling bureaucratic layer was becoming more and more a closed élite, which reserved a monopoly of education for itself, and began to show the characteristics of a tightly-knit caste. This had, in time, great consequences for the élite's capacity for action and resoluteness in policy:

> Where the ability to rule becomes a secure privilege, the morality of its bearers inevitably dissipates. Willpower, the preparedness for great sacrifices, the reckless engagement of one's own personality, and certainly also an inflexibility in attitude as the ruling layer must become paralysed. Governing becomes a routine. If however the machine becomes routinised, it becomes incapable of adapting to new conditions.[97]

Thirdly, the ossification of the élite led to a progressive bureaucratisation. Not just the workers, but also various layers within the bureaucracy were deprived of their freedom of movement and possibilities for free initiative. Intrigue and servility then began to determine the code of conduct.

Fourthly, the emergence of a powerful bureaucracy stifled every form of independent thought. Criticism became impossible; rubber-stamped doctrinairism began to take over. The party, which in the old days had been a forum for profoundly searching discussions, degenerated to a mere collection of yes-men giving or taking orders.

All these factors together meant that the non-socialist 'totalitarian' bureaucratic dictatorship in the non-capitalist planned economy was

---

[97] Frölich 1976, p. 152.

exceptionally vulnerable. Although the possibility could not be excluded that the régime would remain 'unshakeable' for quite some time, its downfall was deemed inevitable.

Kofler

Leo Kofler (1907–95), a pupil of the Austro-Marxist Max Adler who regarded himself a *'Marxist socialist*, who admits to being a member of the Social-Democratic Party, to which he has belonged since his youth',[98] had worked from 1947 to 1950 in East Germany, and had subsequently shifted to West Germany.[99] After his resettlement, he wrote in quick tempo several pamphlets about Stalinism. In 1951, he published *Marxist or Stalinist Marxism?* using the pseudonym of Jules Dévérité. In this tract, he polemicised, among other things, against those who claimed a causal connection between the existence of a planned economy and the rise of an all-pervasive bureaucracy. In 1952, Kofler's *The Case of Lukács* appeared, an essay about the Hungarian philosopher who, in his opinion, was at the same time both the greatest critic and the greatest theoretician of Stalinist 'bureaucratism'.[100] Immediately afterwards followed the publication of *The Essence and Role of the Stalinist Bureaucracy*.

In this last-mentioned work, the author – occasionally leaning towards Titoism – attempted to penetrate to the essence of Soviet society. Although Kofler referred, just like the Trotskyists, to the Stalinist bureaucracy as a privileged social layer[101] which operated within a planned economy largely based on socialist principles,[102] he nevertheless resisted the idea that this bureaucracy was essentially parasitic in nature. The fact that it strove for and defended privileges after all explained little; the real question concerned the circumstances which allowed the bureaucracy to acquire so much power, enabling it not just to accumulate privileges, but also to retain them for decades.[103]

Kofler's argued that even a post-revolutionary society emerging from a highly developed capitalist country with a lengthy democratic tradition would

[98] Dévérité 1951, p. 5. Emphasis in the original.
[99] Biographical data in: Garstka and Seppmann 1980, pp. 11–26; Jünke 2006.
[100] Kofler 1952a.
[101] Kofler 1952b, p. 25.
[102] Kofler 1952b, p. 73.
[103] Kofler 1952b, p. 24.

have to contend with severe internal difficulties. Consistent with Marx's remarks in the *Critique of the Gotha Programme* (1875), Kofler postulated that, in such circumstances, a contradiction would continue to exist between the new mode of production and the surviving old mode of distribution (money, bourgeois justice) as well as bureaucracy. However, in the case of a democratic transitional society, decision-making would occur from below, and thus the possibility of a bureaucratic degeneration of the planned economy would be precluded thereby.[104]

In the case of the Soviet Union, however, other big problems complicated the situation. Firstly, democratic traditions were lacking almost completely. Those few forces which could have prevented a development towards a new dictatorship were decimated during the Civil War. Secondly, Russia around 1917 did not have an advanced level of industrial development. In a highly developed country, accumulation of capital and production of consumer goods grew towards each other – a concept which Kofler does not elaborate further – and accumulation did not occur at the expense of consumption. In an underdeveloped society like the Soviet Union, however, a gap between both sectors of the economy was visible. Primitive accumulation, consisting of the production of means of production, took place at the expense of the production of consumer goods. The bureaucracy thus shouldered the contradictory task of bridging the gap, or, at any rate, of ensuring that it did not become explosive. Ostensibly, it acted as an objective umpire, exclusively interested in the interests of the totality, i.e. the maintenance of a 'balance' between accumulation and consumption. But, in reality, it defended the interests of accumulation against the interests of the masses. Within the framework of this policy, it had no scruples about extending its power over more and more areas of social life, including the cultural and spiritual ones.[105] Most remarkable was that the Stalinist bureaucracy, in contrast to the contemporary capitalist one, consisted of people who were 'idealistic' and subjectively self-sacrificing. Kofler identifies a certain parallel with the early-bourgeois bureaucracy (in the sixteenth and seventeenth centuries). Just like functionaries in that era – embroiled as they were in a stubborn fight against the vestiges of feudalism – the Stalinist élite was also dedicated as well as

[104] Kofler 1952b, pp. 19–22.
[105] Kofler 1952b, pp. 23–4.

optimistic. Both social groups showed those features which Marx and Weber considered typical of the early bourgeoisie:

> Accumulation frenzy, diligence and the grounding of this attitude in morality, with the goal of realising a primarily discipline-oriented educative effect not only in one's own ranks, but above all among the working masses.[106]

It goes without saying that Kofler linked this analogy – which he did not want to extend too far, since the Stalinists lacked ascetic fanaticism and individual striving for frugality – to the fact that both bureaucracies were instrumental in a process of primitive accumulation.[107] On the strength of this analysis, Kofler reached the conclusion that Stalinism, with its bureaucracy and terror, would 'sooner or later' disappear.[108] As soon as the gap between accumulation and consumption has been closed, a planned economy on a democratic foundation could emerge.

4.v. Debates and mutual criticism

The Deutscher debate

Well into the 1940s, the discussions had revolved mainly around the question of how the Soviet system had originated, and how it should, in Marxist terms, be situated in the broad sweep of history. Insofar as participants thought about the end of this social formation, there were two main opinions: either the working class would, in due course, make short shrift of the Stalinist bureaucracy, or else this dictatorship would continue for a long time, and then gradually make itself redundant.

The Polish-Jewish journalist and historian Isaac Deutscher (1907–67), who, until about 1940, had been a member of the Fourth International (under the pseudonym of Josef Bren),[109] developed a different vision about the downfall of the bureaucratic order during the 1940s. This became clear when his biography

---

[106] Kofler 1952b, p. 45.
[107] Ibid.
[108] Kofler 1952b, p. 73.
[109] Bornstein and Richardson, 1986, p. 50, note 97. Although he had resisted the founding of the Fourth International, Deutscher had joined it all the same. See Syré 1984, pp. 56–7.

of Stalin was finally published in 1949. In this monumental work, Deutscher left no doubt that he considered a rapid evolution towards democracy possible, or even probable.[110] He elaborated this forecast in detail in his 1953 book *Russia After Stalin*, written in the first months after Stalin's death. Here, the theory of the degenerated workers' state was both defended and inverted. Deutscher considered Stalinism – in which he perceived both Marxist and 'half-Asiatic' elements – as an historically inevitable industrialisation-dictatorship, which, in rapid tempo, had created a new, highly developed socio-economic structure. Now that the work of forced accumulation had been completed, the political régime became more and more obsolete:

> Stalinism has exhausted its historical function. Like every other great revolution, the Russian revolution has made ruthless use of force and violence to bring into being a new social order and to ensure its survival. An old-established régime relies for its continuance on the force of social custom. A revolutionary order creates new custom by force. Only when its material framework has been firmly set and consolidated can it rely on its own inherent vitality; then it frees itself from the terror that formerly safeguarded it.[111]

The changes following Stalin's death according to Deutscher formed a prelude for far-reaching adjustment of the political-cultural 'superstructure' to the new economic 'base'.

Although he did not exclude the possibility of a relapse to Stalinism, Deutscher believed that such a regression, given its structural redundancy, could only be short-lived in nature. As a second possible scenario, he envisaged the establishment of a military dictatorship, which could emerge if the dismantling of Stalinism led to chaos and weakened social discipline. Such a 'Napoleonic' régime would leave the economic order intact, but transform the superstructure in an authoritarian way, and quite possibly adopt an aggressive stance in foreign policy. This variant would, however, only have a realistic chance of being realised if the third alternative went out of control. The third alternative was, for Deutscher, the most probable: the reformers, led by Malenkov, would implement a gradual evolution in a democratic direction:

---

[110] Deutscher 1949.
[111] Deutscher 1953, pp. 96–7.

In the 1930s Trotsky advocated a 'limited political revolution' against Stalinism. He saw it not as a fully fledged social upheaval but as an 'administrative operation' directed against the chiefs of the political police and a small clique terrorizing the nation. As so often, Trotsky was tragically ahead of his time and prophetic in his vision of the future, although he could not imagine that Stalin's close associates would act in accordance with his scheme. What Malenkov's government is carrying out now is precisely the 'limited revolution' envisaged by Trotsky.[112]

Deutscher repeated this theory of 'democratization from above' in numerous contexts, and maintained it until his death.[113]

There can be no doubt that Deutscher's interpretation diverged from Trotsky's perspective. While Trotsky could imagine a 'political revolution' only as an overturn wrought by the *working class* from below – on the assumption that no élite would voluntarily cede its power to others – Deutscher declared (part of) the *bureaucracy* as a revolutionary subject. Unsurprisingly, this revisionism prompted furious criticism from the orthodox Trotskyists. The journal *Fourth International* compared Deutscher to Eduard Bernstein, and accused him of fantasising:

> Malenkov's 'limited revolution' has so far remained a product of Deutscher's imagination. The ink was hardly dry on his new book when the new bloody purge started in the Soviet Union and Malenkov's army answered the revolting East German workers with tanks and machine guns and wholesale arrests of strikers.[114]

This criticism did not, however, prevent some Trotskyists from giving credence to aspects of Deutscher's heterodox theory. Most of those – including people like Bert Cochran and Harry Braverman – soon left the Trotskyist movement.[115]

---

[112] Deutscher 1953, p. 164.

[113] For example, Deutscher 1955b, especially pp. 113–30 and 173–228; Deutscher 1967.

[114] Cannon 1954, p. 13. A little later, strong criticism was also voiced by ex-Trotskyists who had opted for a theory of state capitalism or bureaucratic collectivism. See Cliff [Ygael Gluckstein] 1964–5 and Jacobson (from the Shachtman school) 1964–6.

[115] The opposition around Cochran (1915–84) began to organise independently from 1953, founding the Socialist Union of America. From 1954 until and including 1959, they published a journal, *The American Socialist*. An early (implicit) defence of Deutscher was Clarke 1953. A later implicit defence is Braverman 1954.

Deutscher also provoked intense controversies outside the Trotskyist milieu. The French sociologist Raymond Aron sharply attacked him in the anti-Communist journal *Preuves*. Rejecting Deutscher's prognosis, Aron disqualified the idea of a 'gradual democratization' as a desparate attempt to rescue Marxism, socialism and 'the dream of 1917'. Much more probable was the advent of a Bonapartist dictatorship, a prospect which Aron welcomed with some optimism, since military leaders would, according to his perspective, seek closer relations with the West.[116]

Deutscher replied to Aron, and *en passant* to his Trotskyist critics, in the left-Catholic magazine *Esprit*. In this reply, he resisted in a principled way all those authors, Marxist or otherwise, who depicted the Soviet Union as an ossified monolithic bloc. More strongly than in *Russia After Stalin*, Deutscher defended his opinion that Stalinism was a non-capitalist industrialisation dictatorship, which had violently forced the development of a socialist economic base, and which subsequently would be able to democratise itself on its own strength, so long as the domestic and international situation remained reasonably stable. Deutscher emphasised the conditionality of his analysis; regarding the connection between industrialisation and the need for democratisation, he remarked that

> All that I have said, is that industrialization tends to raise the democratic aspirations of the masses. These aspirations could, of course, be frustrated or contradicted by other factors.[117]

Likewise, his thesis that the necessity of great socio-economic inequality had waned in the Soviet Union should, so he insisted, be interpreted as a statement referring only to a tendency. The privileged minority would, *in the longer term*, have no interest in maintaining the social antagonisms and political repression. The significant differentiation in incomes (and thus the privileges of the élite) had, during the forced industrialisation process, coincided with the need for strong material incentives, and thus with the 'broader national interest'. Now that the initial social poverty had been overcome, a progressive levelling out of incomes would become desirable. Such a redistribution would not be to the disadvantage of the élite. Political

---

[116] Aron 1953.
[117] Deutscher 1954a.

unfreedom, too, had become dysfunctional for the system (Deutscher did not explicitly argue for this thesis) and would be able to disappear for that reason. If international tensions increased, then this could lead to democratisation being blocked. If that happened, and strong tensions also occurred internally, social instability could bring a Russian Bonaparte to power, which could raise the spectre of war. Because, just as Stalin's terror at home had combined with his relatively 'peaceful' foreign policy, this connection would in the event of a new Bonaparte be reversed: 'he would be forced to find solutions abroad for [the USSR's] internal tensions'.[118]

Within a few months, the independent American socialist journal *Dissent* had published a slightly abridged translation of the *Esprit* article,[119] which sparked off a discussion lasting for more than a year. The Marxist-inspired sociologist Lewis Coser, originally from Germany, contended that industrialisation could lead to democratisation only and exclusively if there were autonomous workers' organisations, which educated the working population in democratic awareness. The fact that the workers had, thanks to Stalinism, become better educated meant nothing in this context; the possibilities for indoctrination were only increased by that education. Deutscher's argument that a more egalitarian income distribution could be achieved was also a target of Coser's criticism:

> If most of the goods in Russia were 'free goods' as, say water is in the Eastern
> part of the United States, no competitive struggle over it would be likely to
> arise, but does one seriously need to discuss this alternative?[120]

As long as the Soviet Union had not changed into a workers' paradise yet, the élite – which Coser referred to as a class – would seek to retain its power. A ruling class, he noted, had never voluntarily given up its privileges, except in situations of actual or acutely threatening revolutionary developments.

Henri Rabassière (Heinz Pächter) made his critique from another angle. Without denying the possibility of a certain democratisation of the USSR, he believed there were potential structural limits. Contrary to Deutscher and his earlier critics, Rabassière thought he could identify a cyclical pattern of

---

[118] A commentary on the Deutscher-Aron controversy (sympathetic to Deutscher) is Pouillon 1954.
[119] Deutscher 1954b.
[120] Coser 1954, p. 240.

reform. Within the élite, different sectors allegedly existed which were all linked to specific groups in the population, industrial sectors or cultural interests. Whenever a part of the bureaucracy made its case for special favours to such a sub-group, the central planners would assess whether the relevant measures were compatible with the rest of the planning. If that was the case, then 'democratisation' would result. If not, then the sub-group of bureaucrats was branded as 'traitors'. Phases of 'relaxation' and 'tension' thus repeated themselves in succession:

> a constant cycle of relaxation and tension creates factions and rejects them, attracts new managerial personnel into the whirlpool of the administration and destroys them. [...] It is very different from either democracy or Bonapartism. – the two alternatives alone Deutscher envisages for the Soviet Union, after a brief 'relapse' into Stalinism.[121]

Since they did not emerge from real social changes, the different cycles did not correspond either to the specific contents of foreign policy.

Pierre Tresse accentuated in his critique the question of the criteria which Deutscher applied in contending that the Soviet system was flexible enough for a gradual transition to democratic socialism. What justified Deutscher's inference that such a peaceful transformation could occur in the USSR and not in capitalism?

> Both contain determinate social groups, which are to different extents antagonistic to each other and thus carry on corresponding social struggles. Can these struggles be disposed of and, as it were, be overcome automatically in the mere course of things? Are the obstacles to be overcome in such a process of transformation greater or smaller in Russia than in the West? Which system is more flexible and more rigid? These are the questions that Mr. Deutscher must answer before he can so blithely pose the possibility of a peaceful emergence from Stalinism.[122]

Finally, Paul Willen considered that Deutscher had generalised too quickly, and therefore ended up with a fallacy. Of course, it was not correct to regard the bureaucratic élite as a monolithic bloc; in times of great social tensions,

---

[121] Rabassière 1954, p. 246.
[122] Tresse 1954, pp. 402–3.

one could indeed not exclude the possibility that individual members of the élite would change sides and join the masses, providing them with the type of leader that a critical situation demanded. But what really followed from such a thought? If one concluded that it was not the whole bureaucracy which was consistently opposed to reforms, one surely could not deduce from this that the bureaucracy would take the lead in the democratisation process? Deutscher, in other words, seemed to identify himself too much with the élite, interpreted as having good intentions, and too little with the oppressed masses.[123]

Deutscher concluded the debate with a rejoinder which gave another systematic exposition of his ideas,[124] without, however, responding to all the arguments made by his critics. Completely in the Trotskyist mould, he characterised the Soviet bureaucracy as a 'giant amoeba' which derived its privileges not from ownership of the means of production, but from the sphere of consumption. The power base of the élite was therefore extraordinarily precarious: and the importance of the privileges – as well as the tenacity with which these would be defended by the élite – was dependent on the general social wealth or poverty. As the Soviet Union was now in transition from the 'primitive socialist accumulation' (a concept Deutscher seems to have borrowed from Preobrazhenskii)[125] to normal socialist accumulation, so that the consumer goods sector could begin to grow strongly, the difference in living standards between the élite and the masses could be reduced. Without making a situation of general abundance a precondition, as Coser had done, Deutscher argued that one ought to recognise such a development would have an egalitarian effect. Obviously, the income distribution would also remain skewed in the future, but *less* skewed than during Stalinism. The struggle over the national income would therefore become less explosive: '[With] the growth of the national loaf the competition for "shares" does tend to become less savage and more civilized; the shares can at last become "fair".'[126]

This factor enabled the reduction of repression, and therewith democratisation. Obviously, there was no automatic connection between industrialisation and democracy, but more wealth meant that social contradictions would become

---

[123] Willen 1955.
[124] Deutscher 1955a.
[125] Preobrazhenskii 1926, pp. 86–152.
[126] Deutscher 1955a, p. 27.

less acute, enabling the powerful to rule on the basis of a certain consensus, and to permit more civil freedoms. It was, all in all, not an historical accident that the most durable bourgeois democracies were found in the USA and Great Britain, countries which were relatively speaking the most wealthy. Whether the Soviet bureaucracy would see sufficient reason in the reduced social contradictions to relinquish its privileges, was something Deutscher could not affirm with certainty. To what degree it would promote reforms he had also deliberately left as an open question. However, the fact that he did consider the bureaucracy capable of certain drastic reforms could not, as Willen had alleged, be interpreted as a capitulation to the élite. Deutscher insisted strongly that, to the contrary, 'my primary allegiance – need I say this ? – is not to the bureaucrats [...], but to the oppressed, the persecuted, and the deceived peoples of the world.'[127]

Responses to Burnham

Burnham's *The Managerial Revolution*, published in New York in 1941, became available in the West-European continent after the end of the World War. The book appeared in 1947 in a French translation as *L'ère des organisateurs* and in German as *Die Revolution der Manager*. The public response was overwhelming, and the number of reviews impressive.[128] I will limit myself here to discussing only some of the more salient comments.

Burnham's work contained two main theses: (i) upon the downfall of capitalism in some countries, a new class society had emerged there, and (ii) the same would inevitably, or in any case most probably, repeat itself in the rest of the world. Critics were generally agreed that the first thesis, if not correct, was at least partly correct. Their objections concerned either the idea that developments in the Soviet Union or elsewhere implied a break with capitalism, or the idea that the new class society would rapidly expand across the rest of the world.[129]

---

[127] Deutscher 1955a, p. 39.
[128] See, for example, Romano 2003.
[129] I leave out of consideration the contribution by Orwell 1946. Orwell's essay focuses more on Burnham's 'power worship' than on his analysis of the Soviet Union.

Die Zukunft, a monthly journal of Austrian Social Democracy, published an essay by Jacques Hannak at the end of 1947, in which Burnham's position was partly supported.[130] Insofar as the American critic described how a new class society had emerged in Russia, Hannak argued, one could hardly disagree with the argument. But Burnham's reasoning became untenable as soon as it came to the supply of proof that the 'revolution of the managers' would triumph everywhere else. Hannak pointed out, that the 'new class' of enterprise directors and technocrats had been able to develop into rulers only in the context of a rather backward society, while its power seemed to be reduced in the measure that capitalism was more highly developed. The fact that, precisely in the United States, the managers had not advanced further than the New Deal was very revealing in this respect. Hannak therefore opined that Burnham's fatalism was not justified, and that he abstracted too much from the social preconditions under which the managers had to expand their power.

The German council communist Willy Huhn devoted a lengthy essay to Burnham's theory. Huhn's thesis was essentially that Burnham had correctly noted the growing power of the managers, but that Burnham had incorrectly deduced the disappearance of capitalism from that power. Huhn took the view that the rise of the managers represented only the expression of what Marx had called 'the abolition of the capitalist mode of production within the capitalist mode of production itself': the growing separation between capital as *property* and capital as *real enterprise management*. If the state usurped the autonomised ownership function (and thus became a 'real total capitalist') and realised a fusion of enterprise directorships at a higher level, this did not mean a *break* with capitalism, but, rather, a further development of it.

One could, Huhn argued, agree with Burnham that 'after bourgeois class rule not a proletarian, but a managerial one follows', but, in that case, one had to recognise that only a new stage of capitalist development was involved. Because Burnham did not recognise this, he was forced to turn Marxist theory on its head. In defining a mode of production, it was, after all, a question of determining the economic structure, and this depended on the relationship between producers and means of production. This relationship was just as alienated in the Soviet Union as in the West. While Burnham did admit this,

---

[130] Hannak 1947.

he had claimed that the *differentia specifica* of the managerial society was the state ownership of the means of production. But, in so doing, a superstructural criterion was declared to be the decisive factor: the juridical relationship between state and means of production was considered more essential than the base, the economic structure. Huhn's conclusion was clear: 'Burnham, who certainly makes a "Marxist" impression on many, does not adopt what is precisely the distinctive perspective of Marx.'[131]

Léon Blum, the well-known French socialist, gave his opinion on Burnham in the journal of the SFIO, *La Revue Socialiste*. Blum also believed that the managerial society was nothing more than a specific form of capitalism: the worker was not liberated in it, the laws of wage-labour still chained him, only the masters were different. The destruction of capitalism occurred only when all relevant aspects of it were eliminated, including the 'moral relations' bound up with private ownership expressed in 'an *inequality* in all forms of human behaviour'. Stalinism did not create a new type of society, but only proved that: 'It is possible to destroy capitalist private property with having destroyed capitalism.'[132]

In the United States, Blum's contribution was published in the *Modern Review*,[133] and Peter Meyer (Guttmann) replied to it, taking the opportunity to criticise all theories of state capitalism. Could one meaningfully talk about capitalism if the state was the owner of the means of production? His answer was negative. As soon as, through an absolute concentration of capital, all competition had disappeared, then the law of value did not apply anymore either; commodity prices were then no longer related to values, the distribution of means of production across economic sectors is no longer regulated by profits, enterprises could survive without making profits, anarchical production made way for planned co-ordination. A labour market no longer existed, because workers could sell their labour-power only to one employer, namely the state. The result was that although – as Blum correctly argued – exploitation and inequality persisted, (state) capitalism could not be said to exist:

---

[131] Huhn 1950a, p. 22.
[132] Blum 1947a, p. 7. Italics in the original.
[133] Blum 1947b.

> Different class societies always differ in the *specific way* in which the ruling
> class forces the producers to yield their surplus product. The specific way
> of capitalist exploitation is the *sale of labor power* by a free worker for its
> value; the specific way of the new class society is the *enslavement* of the
> workers by the state.[134]

The most extensive debate took place in the pages of *La Revue Internationale*, a
remarkable French journal in which, for a rather brief period, representatives
of different left-wing currents all expressed their views. The editors (under
the pen of Pierre Naville) opened the discussion in June 1947, declaring
Burnham a plagiarist, whose work was no more than a copy of Rizzi's *The
Bureaucratisation of the World*.[135]

The economist Charles Bettelheim – whose mature views will be examined
later in this study – took the lead. He dismissed Burnham's analysis of the
declining power of the employers and the growing power of the managers
as exceptionally superficial. Bettelheim considered that the similarity between
Nazi Germany and the Soviet Union which the ex-Trotskyist had postulated
was completely untenable. The state enterprises had a significantly smaller role
under Hitler than Burnham suggested; and, if the theory of the managerial
revolution was adopted, how could one explain that the Germans dissolved
the *kolkhozy* in occupied Russian territories and restored private ownership
of means of production?

More generally, Bettelheim perceived in Burnham's theory an inadmissible
revision of the Marxist interpretation of history. In Burnham's approach,
classes were not defined on the basis of their role in the production process,
but as groups which received different fractions of social revenues (a
distribution criterion). The fact that different social layers existed in the USSR
with distinct levels of remuneration, was, for Burnham, sufficient reason to
talk about 'classes'. Bettelheim, however, did not share this interpretation at
all; he perceived in the better-paid groups only relatively well-remunerated
parts of the working class. The rapid industrialisation of the Soviet Union
and the consequent complexity of social organisation had inexorably led to

---

[134] Meyer 1947, p. 319.
[135] Naville 1947. As I noted in Chapter 3, this was the first time that the real name
of 'Bruno R' was revealed.

'significant sacrifices [of income]' by the majority of workers and 'economic stimuli' for the highly educated. The most privileged functionaries in the Soviet Union were also just executors of the plan, and they could be removed from their position at any moment. What Burnham saw as expressions of a new class society, were just unforeseen aspects of the development of a 'proletarian society': while the phase of revolt had egalitarian features, history taught that a lengthy non-capitalist accumulation process necessitated a degree of inequality.[136] The left socialist Gilles Martinet joined Bettelheim in these apologetic tones.[137]

The former Trotskyist Aimé Patri, who had also voiced his admiration for Burnham elsewhere,[138] defended the theory of the new class society. He began by raising the question of whether a 'ruling class' of managers could in principle exist at all, according to Marxist theory (a problem which Worrall and Dunayevskaya had already formulated explicitly earlier, with reference to state capitalism). His answer was affirmative. In situations where the state was separated from the production apparatus (such as in private capitalism) the state bureaucracy was always a superstructural element, and thus not able to form a class in the Marxist sense. But, in a situation where the state was completely *fused* with the economy, where production and exchange were collectively organised processes, matters were different. Then the public service personnel could change into a political and economic ruling class.

In such a 'régime of economic planning without political democracy' a different accumulation structure ruled from private capitalism or socialism. In capitalism, everything depended on the growth of capital as such, and thus the development of production. The growth process occurred inefficiently because of competition between producers, dependence on the market, and resistance from labour organisations. In socialism, everything revolved around consumption, the alpha and omega of creation. In a society like the Soviet Union, where managers ruled, the growth of the production apparatus was central, just as in capitalism, but without the restrictions which existed in capitalism. In that sense, the managerial economy was 'a "liberated" capitalism'.[139]

[136] Bettelheim 1947.
[137] Martinet 1947.
[138] Patri 1947b.
[139] Patri 1947a, p. 100.

The fact that high-placed functionaries in the USSR could lose their position overnight was not, as Bettelheim claimed, an argument against the class character of the new élite. After all, did not permanent large contradictions also exist between employers under capitalism? Just as a capitalist could go bankrupt, just so it was possible that a manager was ousted by members of his own class.

Pierre Bessaignet directed his fire both at Bettelheim and Martinet. In both, he perceived two essential ideas which had to be rejected: that socialism existed as soon as property is nationalised, and that the state apparatus could serve one fraction of the proletariat against another. Both ideas formed, according to Bessaignet, 'an absolute break' with Marxist theory. As against the first idea, Bessaignet – in a formulation reminiscent of Shachtman – advanced a distinction between *production* relations and *ownership* relations. The fact that means of production were nationalised at most said something about the way in which the social product was appropriated (by the state), but nothing about the relationships between people in society. Socialism meant nothing less than freely associated producers who consciously and purposively govern the social process.

Against the second idea, Bessaignet advanced the following reasoning, which, in his own opinion, was orthodox: within the framework of the socialist revolution, the working class needs the state apparatus to consolidate its dictatorship over the old ruling class. With this consolidation process, socialist production relations were established which, as they became generalised, made the necessity of a separate state increasingly redundant: 'A society without classes, socialism, cannot be created if the state – to be more precise, the workers' state – remains. It must be the case that it disappears.'[140] It was inconceivable that, under socialist relations, the state would instead be strengthened in order to rule over a part of the working class. And, when Bettelheim admitted that the Soviet régime defended the privileges of a part of the working class, then that state was, for that reason, the instrument of the privileged against the non-privileged. On the whole, Bettelheim and Martinet had tried to justify the bureaucratic economy of the USSR by representing the ruling class as a social stratum *within* the working class.

---

[140] Bessaignet 1947, p. 108.

In a collective answer to their critics,[141] Bettelheim and Martinet emphasised the distinction between a *socialist society* and a *society in transition to socialism*. In a transitional society, the division between mental and manual labour, and between leaders and led in the work process, inevitably persisted. But this division of labour now existed totally *within* the working class, and was thus unrelated to class antagonisms. In addition, in a transitional economy, production could not immediately be purely consumer-oriented; first, a further expansion of the productive apparatus was required. Even if such a transitional society did not have to contend with foreign aggression, this would still be necessary. It was therefore incorrect to regard this as 'proof' of a new class society, in the way Patri had done.

The pressures of accumulation and the division of labour also meant that, within the working class of the transitional society, different levels of reward existed. Particular scarce qualifications had to be better paid. Obviously, this created the possibility of abuse and corruption, but, if these phenomena occurred, then this was social parasitism and not systematic exploitation.

Bessaignet's thesis that, in defining the nature of a society, the production relations, and not property relations were relevant, was dismissed by Bettelheim and Martinet as 'utopian'. It was impossible to establish a society of freely associated producers immediately after a socialist revolution. *First*, the property relations had to be changed, and, only when the workers' state had the economy in its grip, could one begin to transform the production relations. Bessaignet's second objection (the state as instrument of a part of the working class) also received rebuttal. It went without saying that the state was, in Marxist theory, a repressive apparatus *par excellence*. But the same theory also stipulated that the state had a second task: the regulation of relations between ruling classes and fractions of those ruling classes among themselves. A society without class oppression could thus have a need for a state apparatus anyway.

Bettelheim and Martinet concluded their anti-critique with a call to renew Marxist theory, so that 'the crisis of contemporary communism' could be overcome. They considered it very remarkable that both Stalinists and Trotskyists allowed their analyses to be determined by one aspect of

---

[141] Beyond the cited contributions in *La Revue Internationale*, see also Martin 1947, an essay which offers little of theoretical importance, however.

history: the international isolation of the post-revolutionary society. Stalin used it as a justification for the hypertrophy of his state; Trotsky regarded it as the cause of degeneration. Of course, the significance of isolation could not be denied. But much more weighty were the *endogenous* laws of motion of a transitional society. It was a question of transcending Trotskyism and Stalinism as theoretical orientations. The contradictions of Soviet society, about which Stalinism remained silent, had to be laid bare; but the analysis of this society could not be satisfied with the 'fixed system' of the Trotskyists. A positive attitude was required:

> In the actual circumstances, it appears to us impossible to proceed with a critical analysis of the Russian system which does not stress the importance of the Soviet achievement and the possibilities for evolution which it contains.[142]

Mandel's critique of 'state capitalism' and 'bureaucratic collectivism'

In the period 1946–51, the well-known Belgian Marxist Ernest Mandel (1923–95), who, already very early on, had emerged as the most important postwar Trotskyist theoretician[143] – developed a series of arguments against the theories of state capitalism and bureaucratic collectivism, which he would later repeat in many contexts and occasionally extend.

His first important contribution in this area was the resolution he drafted for the International Secretariat of the Fourth International entitled 'The Russian Question Today' (1947).[144] In this text, it became clear how Mandel had adopted arguments from some opponents against yet other opponents, when they seemed useful to defend the theory of the degenerated workers'

---

[142] Bettelheim and Martinet 1948, pp. 41–2.
[143] Mandel, active during the World War II in the revolutionary-socialist resistance, developed after 1945 into one of the most important leaders and the most important theoretician of the Trotskyist Fourth International. He worked from 1945 as journalist and correspondent for various newspapers (*Het Parool, L'Observateur, Le Peuple, La Gauche* and others). He was also economic advisor from 1954 to 1963 for the Belgian trade-union federation FGTB. He studied economics during 1963–7 at the Sorbonne, and gained his PhD in 1972 with the book *Der Spätkapitalismus*. See Gorman 1986, pp. 209–11; Stutje 2004.
[144] Note the remarkable similarity between Mandel's draft text and the resolution that was adopted by the Fourth International. See Germain 1947b and Fourth International 1947.

state. Thus we rediscover, to give just one example, the argument of Bettelheim – whom Mandel characterises as representative of the 'most finished "pro-Stalinist" expression' of contemporary 'revisionism' – that Nazi Germany and the Soviet Union differ in structure, since the Hitler régime had felt it necessary to change the ownership and production relations in occupied Russian territories.[145]

Against the theory of state capitalism, Mandel advanced as main objection that the argument was *a priorist*. First, it was assumed that Russia was capitalist, and then analogies between capitalism and a workers' state were used to bolster the correctness of this assumption. Mandel admitted that some important developments had occurred in capitalist countries that resembled the Soviet Union (in particular, the increasing statification of the means of production, the autarchic tendencies of national economies, tendencies towards planning, and 'production for production's sake') but he argued that this did not constitute proof. After all, involved here were analogies between a capitalist society and a 'transitional economy such as will exist in every workers' state until the complete disappearance of classes and the final advent of communism'.[146]

In *every* transitional society, the law of value still operated, because commodities were still being produced. But this law operated in a different way in those societies: prices were no longer determined by the average rate of profit, and money could no longer be transformed into capital. The correctness of this thought was also made evident by the inconsistencies of the theories of state capitalism. For these were unable to explain how the bureaucracy could be a 'state-capitalist' class on the one hand, while, on the other hand, they allowed the ownership relations emerging from the destruction of capitalism to persist, and additionally had suppressed a newly emerged rural bourgeoisie. This theory, furthermore, was unable to explain how ownership relations could be overthrown without an accompanying social revolution. But the most important problem for the 'state capitalists' was the Stalinist parties outside the Soviet Union, which, according to this theory, would instantly change from workers' parties into bourgeois parties

---

[145] Fourth International 1947, p. 272.
[146] Ibid.

as soon as they seized power somewhere. 'This belief is the most striking refutation of the theory'.[147]

Against the theory of bureaucratic collectivism, Mandel objected that it put into question 'a series of fundamental bases of historical materialism in general'. If the Stalinist bureaucracy was a 'class', then it lacked all of the characteristic features of other classes in history:

a) Every class in history is characterized by an independent and fundamental function in the process of production – at a definite stage in the historic process – and by its own roots in the economic structure of society.

b) Every class in history represents a definite stage of historical progress, including the classes that arise in periods of historic recession whose task is to safeguard the technical conquests etc. Each represents a definite stage in the social division of labour, a definite stage in the evolution of the ownership of the means of production.

c) Every class in history is a historically necessary organ fulfilling a necessary function from the standpoint of the development of the productive forces.

d) Every class in history, advancing its candidacy to power – and all the more so, every ruling class! – is conscious of its role, possesses its own specific ideology and features; and attains a minimum of stability in its composition, a stability which it endeavours to transmit to the succeeding generations.

e) Explicitly according to Marx, no social formation can become a class solely on the basis of its higher income, its political privileges or its monopolies (of education and so on).[148]

All these features were not applicable to the Soviet bureaucracy. This bureaucracy was not rooted in the sphere of production, but a parasitic outgrowth of the relations of distribution; it embodied no historical progress, but, to the contrary, retarded it; it represented no new property relations, but maintained those resulting from the October Revolution; it did not have its own ideology and lacked a stable social composition. But, most important of all, in contrast to what was normal in class societies, the special interests

---

[147] Ibid.
[148] Fourth International 1947, pp. 272–3.

of the alleged 'ruling class' – expressed in privileges – were diametrically opposed to the efficient functioning of the economy.

The 'bureaucratic collectivists' – who had never said anything about the laws of motion and contradictions of the type of society they postulated – threatened to undermine Marxism totally, not only theoretically, but also politically. If their interpretation was correct, then this, after all, implied that the socialist revolution was not on the immediate agenda, and that the working class was, in reality, not able to rule itself.

The criticism of the theory of bureaucratic collectivism in this early text appears more systematic than the criticism of 'state capitalism', for which the economic argument was still relatively undeveloped. Four years later, that changed when Mandel published an extensive polemic against the theory of state capitalism.[149] The occasion was a number of publications from Yugoslavia, in which the theory to be opposed was defended.[150] In this article, Mandel advanced the following counter-arguments:

a) Under capitalism, money fulfilled simultaneously three functions: it was a means of circulation, a measure of value and potential capital. Every sum of money in capitalism had the characteristic that, upon being loaned, it increased in value with a part of the social surplus-value (interest). In the Soviet Union, as in any transitional society, money retained the first two functions, but had, for the most part, lost its interest-bearing function (which survived only as illegal usury, or in the conditions for state loans established by the plan).[151]

c) Within capitalism, prices oscillated around commodity values under the influence of blindly operating economic laws (market laws, monopoly

---

[149] Germain 1951a, 1951b, 1951c. The article in German stimulated a discussion. Mandel's opponent was the left socialist Heinz Meyer, the son of the old KPD functionary Ernst Meyer, who wrote under the pseudonym of 'Oeconomicus' or 'Öconomicus': see Öconomicus 1951; Germain 1951d; Öconomicus 1952; Germain 1952, p. 48. Another response to Mandel was by Huhn 1951. Meyer's analysis, reminiscent of Bordiga in many respects, was essentially that a) Mandel's definition of the essential features of capitalism was too broad (Meyer himself, however, believed three criteria were sufficient: labour-power is a commodity; labour is wage-labour; and labour products take the form of commodities); b) the bureaucracy in state capitalism is not a ruling or owning class, but only a trustee of a completely anonymous capital; c) state capitalism only had a chance in those countries which could be regarded as weak links in international capitalism.

[150] Djilas 1951.

[151] Mandel concurs at this point with an earlier remark by Trotsky. See Trotsky 1933b, pp. 222–3.

prices etc.). In the Soviet Union, these fluctuations were determined by the plan, and prices were the most important regulator of accumulation.

d) In capitalism, accumulation was oriented completely towards maximising profits, a condition culminating in the law of the falling tendency of the rate of profit. This law meant that capital tendentially moved to those sectors of the economy where the profit rate was proportionally the highest; it therefore moved historically from basic industries to the periphery. In the Soviet Union, the exact opposite applied. There, the emphasis remained on basic industries.

e) In capitalism, technical innovations were regularly not applied in industry, because these innovations threatened large masses of capital in monopolist sectors with devalorisation (destruction of capital). In the Soviet Union, innovations were implemented in industry as quickly as possible.

f) In capitalism, the export of capital from the industrialised countries occurred as a result of the tendency of the rate of profit to fall. From the Soviet Union, no export of capital occurred; to the contrary, the bureaucratic régime imported (openly, or through robbery) industrial and agrarian capital from its vassal states.

g) In capitalism, cyclical crises occurred as the result of the disproportionalities between production of production and consumption goods dictated by the quest for profits. In the Soviet Union, such a form of motion of the economy did not exist.

All these circumstances, according to Mandel, proved that not a single law of motion of capitalism operated in the Soviet Union. But one could also make the same arguments plausible from yet another angle:

> Just the very fact, that it was possible in the Soviet Union to build the second largest industry in the world over the last 25 years, should be sufficient for every Marxist to prove the non-capitalist character of Russian society. Given the pressure of the capital amassed on a world scale, such a development is impossible for every capitalist country. Only because Russia, thanks to its [state] monopoly over foreign trade, broke with the capitalist world market, could the unprecedented growth of Russian industry occur external to the influences of 'monopoly-capitalist laws of motion'.[152]

---

[152] Germain 1951b, p. 113.

4.vi. Summary

The unforeseen stability of the Soviet Union and structural assimilation of the buffer states forced a difficult choice on the supporters of the theory of the degenerated workers' state: either they had to revise Trotsky's standpoint, or they continued to uphold it, while abandoning the temporal factor. Many chose the first option.

Within the current of supporters of theories of state capitalism – in which 'heretical' Trotskyists began to play a prominent role – a broad range of variants emerged. The differences related not only to the reasons for referring to capitalism, but also the characteristics attributed to capitalism:

i)   While Cliff, James and Dunayevskaya considered the Soviet Union to be one big capital, Bordiga perceived a large number of smaller capitals.

ii) While Bordiga, Grandizo and Péret believed that there was no ruling class in the Soviet Union, Cliff, Castoriadis and Lefort took the opposite view.

iii) While Cliff, Grandizo and Péret regarded the Soviet Union as representative of the final phase of capitalism, Bordiga opined that it represented an early stage of capitalism.

Among theorists of the new mode of production, two relevant developments were apparent. Firstly, there was an attempt by Guttmann to describe the internal contradictions and dynamics of the 'new class society'. And, secondly, there were attempts to analyse the Soviet Union 'without attaching labels' in Germany. As far as the latter was concerned, various authors emphasised different aspects. Both Sternberg and Frölich tried to improve their perspective through analogies with the Asiatic mode of production, or pre-revolutionary China; Cycon devoted attention especially to the intelligentsia as a new ruling class *in statu nascendi*; and Kofler emphasised the bureaucratic 'stratum' as co-ordinator of a process of primitive accumulation.

Chapter Five

From the Twentieth Congress of the CPSU to the Repression of the 'Prague Spring' (1956–68)

The year 1956 marked a turning point in the world of 'actually existing socialism'. The Cominform, not even ten years old yet, was dissolved again. Khruschev made his famous secret speech at the Twentieth Congress of the CPSU, in which he strongly criticised Stalin and Stalinism. In Budapest, a rebellious crowd pulled down the statue of the dictator, dead three years earlier, and, in the Polish city of Poznan, a revolt also broke out. Both in Hungary and in Poland, workers' councils were formed. Order was restored in the Danube republic with Russian tanks.

These developments, unsurprisingly, caused great commotion in Western Communist circles. In many countries, oppositions developed. Thus, for example, the British Communist Party suffered an exodus of a large group of intellectuals, including the likes of Edward P. Thompson and John Saville – a group out of which the well-known journal *New Left Review* would subsequently emerge. In Denmark, the Communist Party split when the former party leader Axel Larsen left the organisation to form a new party. In France, deputy Aimé Césaire left the PCF, together with intellectuals such as Roger Vailland, Claude Roy and Jacques Francis Rolland.

The nuclei of the 'New Left' were thereby created internationally, and, in the course of the 1960s, they grew to maturity. The Sino-Soviet split in 1962–4, Ernesto 'Che' Guevara's attempt to unleash a revolutionary *foco* in Bolivia, the national-liberation war in Vietnam, the black mass movements against 'Jim Crow' in the United States – all of these determined to an important extent the thinking of the new crop of young socialist intellectuals who revolted at the campuses of Berkeley, the Parisian Nanterre, the London School of Economics, and the Free University of Berlin.

The stimuli created by these developments for theorising about the Soviet Union were initially limited however. In the first instance, 'New-Left' thinking mainly fell back on older frames of reference.

5.i. Theories of state capitalism

The current around Cliff

As discussed in the previous chapter, Cliff (Gluckstein) claimed that the USSR should be defined as one big capital, which operated in the world market, and, in so doing, competed with the West, above all through the arms race.

This interpretation received its finishing touches in the 1950s and 1960s with the addition of a theory about the 'permanent arms economy', which argued that the postwar boom of the capitalist West had been caused by the same militarisation dynamic deemed very important for Soviet society. This theoretical supplement – developed notably by Michael Kidron[1] – led in the

---

[1] Although Paul Sweezy (1942, Chapter 17) had argued, elaborating on Rosa Luxemburg's theory, that militarism in declining capitalism develops its own expansionist dynamic, the true founder of the theory of the 'permanent arms economy' was the American Ed Sard, who wrote under the pseudonyms of Frank Demby, Walter S. Oakes and T.N. Vance (Drucker 1994, pp. xv, 218; Hampton 1999, p. 38). In an essay published in 1944 (Oakes 1944), which can be considered brilliant in some respects, Sard predicted – while the World War was still in progress – a postwar arms race. In particular, Sard argued the USA would retain the character of a war economy; even in peacetime, the American arms expenditures would remain considerable, namely between 10 and 20 billion dollars, with the result, among other things, of the drastic reduction of the percentage of unemployed compared to the 1930s. A few years later, Sard expanded this analysis further (Vance 1950). He strongly emphasised the fact that an irreconcilable contradiction existed between capitalism in general and the USA in particular on the one side, and the 'bureaucratic collectivism' of the Soviet

1960s to a greater emphasis on the interdependence of developments within and outside the Soviet Union. A principled alteration of the original theory itself was, of course, not implied thereby.

5.ii. The theory of the degenerated workers' state

The refusal to re-examine or revise any essential aspect of Trotsky's theory of the 'degenerated workers' state' had typified the publications of Trotsky's followers about actually existing socialism. As noted in the previous chapter, the Fourth International had, after World War II, disconnected the time factor that Trotsky built into his theory (the postulate of the limited duration of the Stalinist phenomenon). Subsequently, the Trotskyists considered it their most important theoretical task to discover in all new developments a confirmation of the old theory. At the Fifth World Congress of the Fourth International in 1957, i.e. shortly after the Polish and Hungarian revolts and the Twentieth Congress of the CPSU, it was declared that the dramatic developments in the USSR, the buffer states and the Western Communist Parties, had totally proved the correctness of the Trotskyist analysis. With evident self-satisfaction, it was noted that the Fourth International was the

---

Union on the other: 'Stalinist imperialism [...] is essentially an "import" imperialism whose aggressive policy is based on the economic necessity of acquiring constantly new sources of labor power, both skilled and slave, and of adding to its stock of producer and consumer goods, and which can feel safe politically only when it has integrated the major centers of working population and production into the system of bureaucratic collectivism. [...] American imperialism [...] is an "export" imperialism, inexorably driven by the most rapid accumulation of capital in the history of capitalism to export capital in all its forms in ever-increasing quantities'. (p. 325). In a series of articles, Sard subsequently elaborated the implications, especially with regard to the American economy (Vance 1951). Tony Cliff [Ygael Gluckstein] took up the same idea (Cliff 1957). Michael Kidron, one of Cliff's comrades, then tried to reformulate the theory, which, until that time, had been more Keynesian than Marxist (Kidron 1961). Kidron's article was, like an earlier piece by Alasdair MacIntyre (MacIntyre 1961), an answer to Henry Collins's 'The Case for Left Reformism' (Collins 1961). Subsequently, Kidron expanded his analysis in his book *Western Capitalism Since the War* (Kidron 1968). However, a decade later, Kidron criticised his own theory, reaching the conclusion that 'it is hard to sustain the view that it was the permanent arms economy that fuelled the long boom. On the contrary, such expenditure must have worked towards stagnation'. See Kidron 1977. Interestingly, Kidron's political associates continued to defend the theory which Kidron himself had rejected in the meantime (see Harman 1977). On Kidron (1930–2003), see Birchall 2003.

only tendency in the labour movement which had foreseen the evolution of Stalinism, and correctly interpreted it.[2]

Noteworthy especially is the report which Mandel presented together with the relevant resolution. Referring to Trotsky's old 1939 alternative ('either restoration of capitalism or re-establishment of Soviet democracy') Mandel considered that now, in 1957, this alternative no longer applied in the same way.

> The two terms of this alternative were conceived in close connection with the development of the relationship of forces on the world scale. [...] Two terms of an alternative do not mean two possibilities of *simultaneous* solutions. When Trotsky formulated this perspective for the first time in a precise way, that is, after Hitler's victory in 1933, he was obliged to place a question mark over the future dynamics of the relationship of forces on a world scale. Would revolution advance again, or would it go on being defeated everywhere in the world? No one could seriously answer this question in 1935. But towards the end of the Second World War, with the victory of the Yugoslav revolution, the victory of the Chinese revolution, and the spread of the colonial revolution, with the enormous progress of the Soviet economy, it became clear that the relationship of forces was turning in favour of Revolution on the world scale.

So international capitalism was seriously weakened, which meant that one of Trotsky's alternatives (counter-revolution) did not seem very realistic anymore. The other possibility seemed more realistic:

> The revolutionary opening has come about in the East. [...] The working class has given up its passive attitude. It no longer 'tolerates' the dishonest watchman. On the contrary, it hounds him more and more, waging war on the field of factories and on that of principles, forcing him to put aside his insolence, and preparing to overthrow his power.[3]

This prediction was, in fact, not realised. The pretence of the Trotskyist current, that it was the only one able to see through the crisis of Stalinism totally, turned out to be without justification. This perhaps explains why the Trotskyist theoreticians for a long time afterwards let Trotsky's alternative rest.

---

[2] Fourth International 1958.
[3] Germain 1958.

Having initially positioned himself primarily as a critic of rival theories,[4] Mandel also gained prominence from around 1960 as the most important 'moderniser' of the theory of the degenerated workers' state. From the numerous writings in which he devoted attention to the analysis of Soviet society, I will take one: his monumental *Marxist Economic Theory*, completed in 1960 and first published in 1962, in which an important chapter advanced an 'orthodox' defence of the theory of the 'degenerated workers' state'.[5] In this work, Mandel elaborated on Trotsky's theory: beyond the contradiction of the non-capitalist mode of production and the bourgeois distribution norms, there were also other contradictions. Thus, while the tense relationship between production and distribution was a defining feature of all societies in transition between capitalism and socialism, the Soviet Union featured specific contradictions, arising from the bureaucratic grip on the state and the economy. These additional contradictions fell into three groups.

First, contradictions arising from the malformed relationship between the development of industry and the decline (or stagnation) of agriculture. Their origin lay in the fact that industrialisation had begun too late, while the integral collectivisation of agriculture had occurred too early, so that an insufficient technical and social basis existed for such a revolution in agriculture. Second, contradictions arising from the fact that the material interest of the bureaucracy was the real driving force of the economy:

> The normal vehicle of socialist planning and accumulation is consciousness on the part of the industrial producers that they are defending their own interests, together with their creative initiative. But facts must confirm theory; every increase in productive effort must be immediately reflected in an increase in consumption by the masses. When this driving force is largely absent, because the excessive rate of accumulation imposes excessive sacrifices on the producers, the bureaucracy becomes the regulator and chief director of accumulation. It thereby acquires substantial consumer privileges (in money, housing, luxuries, and other scarce consumer goods, etc.).[6]

---

[4] See the previous chapter.
[5] Mandel 1962, II, Chapter 15, pp. 208–73.
[6] Mandel 1962, p. 240. English edition, p. 584.

The bureaucrats were stimulated to expand production continuously, through fear of being purged and the close correlation between their own position and enterprise profits.

Third, contradictions arising from bureaucratic administration as such:

> The contradiction between the planned character of the Soviet economy and the personal interests of the bureaucrats, considered as the chief driving force for the fulfillment of the plan, is the principal contradiction introduced into the Soviet economy as a result of its specifically bureaucratic management. The effects combine with two other contradictions resulting from this bureaucratic management: the contradiction between the high level of development of the productive forces and the scarcity of consumer goods on the one side, and the contradiction between the needs of integral planning and the harm done by bureaucratic hyper-centralization.[7]

5.iii. Theories of a new mode of production

Djilas

For some time, Milovan Djilas (1911–95) was regarded as the most important theoretician of the Yugoslav Communist Party.[8] After the split between Belgrade and Moscow, he developed into a sharp critic of the Soviet Union. Partly inspired by the relevant writings of Trotsky, Djilas became convinced that the working class in the USSR no longer possessed any political power. In his 1950 pamphlet *On New Roads of Socialism*, he had this to say about the Soviet Union:

---

[7] Mandel 1962, p. 247. English edition, p. 589.

[8] Djilas became a communist during his literary studies at the University of Belgrade. Under the monarchic dictatorship of King Alexander, he had spent a long time in prison. At the end of the 1930s, he supported Tito in the battle for power in the Communist Party; in 1928 he was elected to its Central Committee, and a year later became member of the Politburo. From 1948 to 1953, he was with Edvard Kardelj and Boris Kidrić one of the architects of the Yugoslav system of self-management. In 1953, he became vice-president of Yugoslavia and chairman of the federal assembly. Because of his social criticism, he was divested of all powers during an extraordinary party plenum in 1953–4. In the years 1956–61 and 1962–6, he was again in prison as a dissident. See Reinhartz 1981.

In the Soviet Union, there are no economic bases for the creation of a new class. What is happening there, the outward manifestations of which we see, does not mean and cannot mean a return to capitalism, this is actually a matter of new phenomena which arose on the ground and within the framework of socialism itself.[9]

Although this passage still shows strong associations with Trotsky's *The Revolution Betrayed*, this changed when, in a subsequent text, Djilas accused the Soviet Union of bureaucratic 'imperialism'. Then he argued that the ruling stratum – cornered by the growing contradiction between the productive forces and relations of production – sought a solution for its internal problems by external expansion, through the exploitation and subjugation of other countries.[10]

In his pamphlet, Djilas drew a clear analytical distinction between the Soviet Union and Yugoslavia. Although he noted bureaucratic tendencies in his own country, he thought that they could not gain the upper hand there, since the historical preconditions and the balance of power tended more towards the dismantling of the bureaucracy.[11] Later, however, he changed this assessment, and, in 1953, he began to express principled criticism about Yugoslavia itself. In a series of articles, which caused his expulsion from the party, he pointed to serious deficiencies of the Yugoslav system, and to the danger of a despotism of the Soviet type. Parallel to this development was his far-reaching revision of Trotskyist theory. In the aftermath of the Hungarian popular uprising, he published an article in which he claimed that both in the Soviet Union and in Yugoslavia a new class, the communist bureaucracy, was emerging.[12]

In his book *The New Class*, published in 1957, Djilas elaborated his theory that a new type of ruling class had been established. His analysis, which recalls the ideas of Rizzi, Burnham, Shachtman and others, and did not pretend to be original ('Almost everything in this book has been said somewhere else [...]'),[13] focused centrally on the so-called political bureaucracy. This stratum should not, he argued, be equated with the bureaucracy as such:

---

[9] Djilas 1950, pp. 12–13.
[10] Djilas, pp. 16–18.
[11] Djilas, passim.
[12] Djilas 1956.
[13] Djilas 1957, p. vi.

> Only a special stratum of bureaucrats, those who are not administrative officials, make up the core of the governing bureaucracy, or, in my terminology, of the new class. This is actually a party or political bureaucracy. Other officials are only the apparatus under the control of the new class.[14]

So while, on the one side, the bureaucracy was a fraction of the whole state apparatus, it was, on the other side, only a fraction of the party apparatus. The party formed the heart of the class, but not all party members were part of the political bureaucracy. Only those bureaucrats who possessed special privileges, as a result of their administrative monopoly, belonged to the new class.

In Djilas's view, the ruling 'political bureaucracy' differed from previous ruling classes. He noted three essential deviations from the traditional pattern. First, while earlier ruling classes had seized power by means of revolution after economic changes had already occurred within the old social relations, the political bureaucracy created its own economic system only when the revolution had succeeded: 'It did not come to power to complete a new economic order but to establish its own and, in so doing, to establish its power over society.'[15] Second, while earlier ruling classes had existed as classes already before the revolution, this was not the case in the USSR. There, the new class was formed definitively only after it had seized power. The consciousness of the vanguard of the new class was thus ahead of events; it already possessed the idea of its class power, before it actually acquired power.[16] Third, from this advanced consciousness followed another difference: in contrast with previous classes, the new ruling class could only emerge in an organisation of a special type, the Bolshevik Party.[17]

Related to these 'birth defects' of the political bureaucracy, he noted further differences with other ruling classes. The new élite had an exceptionally weak class consciousness; the average political bureaucrat was not even aware that he belonged to a new possessing class, although he knew that he belonged to a group with specific ideas, goals and attitudes.[18] Moreover, the

---

[14] Djilas 1957, p. 43.
[15] Djilas 1957, p. 38.
[16] Ibid.
[17] Djilas 1957, p. 39.
[18] Djilas 1957, p. 59.

political bureaucracy was more compact and more rigidly organised than any other ruling class, with the consequence that its power was historically unequalled:

> Contemporary communism is that type of totalitarianism which consists
> of three basic factors for controlling people. The first is power; the second
> is ownership; the third, ideology. [...] No totalitarian system in history,
> not even a contemporary one – with the exception of Communism – has
> succeeded in incorporating simultaneously all these factors for controlling
> the people to this degree.

The history of the USSR could, Djilas argued, be divided into three phases: the revolutionary communism of Lenin, the dogmatic communism of Stalin, and the undogmatic communism from the mid-1950s, featuring an ostensibly collective leadership. Schematically the differences between the three periods can be summarised as follows:

Period	Leadership	Relation to power
'Revolutionary period'	Lenin	Power is seized; the foundations for the rule of the new class are established
'Dogmatic period'	Stalin	With the slogan of 'socialism' a massive industrialisation process is initiated. The power of the new class is thereby consolidated
'Undogmatic period'	Collective Leadership	With the slogan of 'legality' the 'calm' maintenance of class society is effectuated without large-scale purges etc.

Djilas emphasised, however, that this threefold division should be seen only as a rough and abstract schema. Clearly delineated phases did not exist, in his opinion; dogmatism also existed under Lenin; Stalin was not a counter-revolutionary; and the undogmatic nature of the collective leadership should, he argued, be relativised. Nevertheless, clear shifts had occurred in the course of history. Power, initially considered only a means to an end, had more and more become an end in itself. In a certain sense, the Soviet system had fulfilled its function; through industrialisation, the new class was now firmly in the saddle, and had thereby reached its goal. Historically, only mediocrity and stagnation could still arise.[19]

Clearly, Djilas added new elements to the theory of bureaucratic collectivism. In contrast to Rizzi, he did not characterise the working population as slaves. In contrast to both Rizzi and Burnham, he believed that the bureaucracy was a purely East-European and Soviet phenomenon. Finally, Djilas – in contrast to both Rizzi, Burnham and Shachtman – paid close attention to the differences between old ruling classes and the political bureaucracy. Precisely the greater nuance of Djilas's theory shows that the theory of the new ruling class was ultimately difficult to reconcile with the Marxist perspective on history. After all, if the party was the nucleus of a new ruling class, was historical materialism (which interpreted political parties as *representatives* of social classes, and not as their *source*) not turned on its head? Djilas recognised the difficulty, referring to an 'unusual' phenomenon, but only stated that: 'In history, it is not important who implements a process, it is only important that the process be implemented.'[20]

Kuroń/Modzelewski

While among earlier theoreticians of the new class society, the laws of motion of the postulated bureaucratic-collectivist society had usually remained unspecified,[21] the Polish dissidents Jacek Kuroń (1935–2004) and Karol

---

[19] Djilas 1957, p. 168.

[20] Djilas 1957, p. 41. Following the great publicity around Djilas, Bruno R(izzi) was also rediscovered in 1958, when *Le Contrat Social*, the journal edited by old-Bolshevik Boris Souvarine (1895–1984), featured a contribution about 'Bruno R et la "nouvelle classe"' (Henein 1958); the title seems to refer to an earlier article in the same journal (Lazitch 1957). Here, the Egyptian surrealist Georges Henein (1914–73) presented 'Bruno R' wrongly as 'Bruno Rossi' and referred to his forgotten work *La Bureaucratisation du Monde*: 'What Djilas discovered and experienced at the end of a disillusioning personal experience, Bruno R. had proclaimed eighteen years earlier, in a duel with the living'. It was the beginning of a veritable Rizzi renaissance, which in the 1960s and 1970s led to new publications and translations of his book (see also Paragraph 6.iii). In his contribution, Henein claimed that 'R' had disappeared without trace after 1942: 'He [...] disappeared forever, probably the victim of one of the razzias by the occupying army.' A false suspicion, as it soon turned out. *Le Contrat Social* shortly thereafter received a personal letter from Rizzi, in which he revealed his true identity. The American Marx scholar and Shachtman supporter Hal Draper (1914–90) published a letter in the journal with biographical details about Rizzi. See also Bell 1959.

[21] The exception being Josef Guttmann (Peter Meyer), discussed in Chapter 4.

Modzelewski (b. 1937) made an attempt in 1964 to focus centrally on this difficult problem.[22] In their *Open Letter to the Party* – which they could not finish because they were arrested – they developed a theory of the dynamics of what they called a 'monopoly bureaucracy'. These authors considered the Soviet Union and their own country as attempts at industrialisation outside of the capitalist world market. Both Russia and Poland had, at the moment that capitalist society disintegrated, been underdeveloped countries. They had only a poorly developed industry, and at the same time a large surplus of workers, in the form of urban unemployed and overpopulation in the countryside. The economy of both countries was dominated by the capital of industrially highly developed imperialist states. Under these circumstances, an industrialisation process was in the interest of society as a whole. The new rulers accordingly accepted this as their primary task. But they could not count on help from the highly developed capitalist countries. To the contrary, if industrialisation was to succeed, then the mechanisms which dominated capitalism had to be abandoned.[23] Given the large reserves of unused labour, industrialisation acquired an extensive character. However, rapidly growing industrial employment could – given the initially low level of accumulation – not combine with a proportional rise in the volume of consumer goods, so that living standards declined. Production for production's sake was the central goal.

> For the new authorities, industrialisation was a 'raison d'être' and a fundamental task. They set about realising that task despite the differing interests of the remaining classes and social strata and, in a sense despite them: against the peasantry, deprived by force of its surpluses and threatened with loss of property through collectivisation, against the working class,

---

[22] Inspired by the Polish anti-Stalinist resistance in 1956, Kuroń and Modzelewski (the son of the second postwar Polish minister of foreign affairs) searched for a democratic–socialist alternative. Thus they maintained contact with the Polish Trotskyist historian Ludwick Hass, and read Trotsky's *The Revolution Betrayed* and the resolution 'The Decline and Fall of Stalinism' adopted by the Fifth World Congress of the Fourth International. Both were until 1964 employed as research assistants at the Historical Institute of the University of Warsaw and active in the Polish socialist youth organisation ZMS. They were punished for their 'Open Letter' with prison sentences of respectively three and three and a half years. See Wagner 1968; Raina 1978, pp. 82–95; Jedlicki 1990; Soltysiak 1992; Lugowska and Grabski 2003, pp. 195–208; Gaudillière et al. 2005.

[23] Kuroń/Modzelewski, English translation, p. 44.

whose wages were held down to the lowest possible level and even reduced; against the intelligentsia and the technocracy. The effective realisation of such a process of industrialisation required that all classes and strata be deprived of the means of defining their differing interests and fighting for their implementation or in their defence.[24]

So, all power had to be concentrated at the top in the monopoly-bureaucracy. The result was a one-party system, conferring the same status on all social institutions (in particular the organisations of the working class), monopolisation of the mass media and propaganda, liquidation of civil freedoms, and a centrally-led economy. The formation of the monopoly-bureaucracy as a ruling class, given the industrialisation process, was, therefore, an historical necessity.

The social surplus-product in Soviet-type societies was divided into three segments: i) a large part of the surplus-product was used for accumulation, i.e. the expansion of production; ii) another part served the maintenance of state power: the army, the political police, the courts, the prisons; iii) finally, a part of the surplus was used for activities which did not directly relate to the existence of a class society, such as science, education, healthcare, culture, etc. The magnitude of that part of the surplus-product wasted on luxury consumption by the élite was rather insignificant.

As soon as the industrialisation process had been more or less completed (at the end of the 1950s), a fundamental imbalance emerged because the monopoly-bureaucracy wanted – even if this was no longer an historical necessity – to continue expanding the capital-goods sector ('heavy industry') more and more, to the disadvantage of living standards.

As a result, a contradiction emerged between the low level of consumption and productive potential, which took the form of an enduring crisis. The problems expressed themselves among other things in reduced economic growth, although the investments in Sector A (means of production) were increased. After all, Sector B (consumer goods) grew more slowly than A, the consequence being a structural disproportionality which became ever more serious:

---

[24] Kuroń/Modzelewski, English translation, p. 36.

Production relations based on bureaucratic ownership have become chains hampering the country's productive forces; with every day this continues, the crisis deepens. Therefore, the solution of the economic crisis requires the overthrow of these production relations, and the elimination of the class rule of the bureaucracy.[25]

5.iv. Theories 'without labels'

Wittfogel and his critics

In 1957, the sinologist Karl Wittfogel (1896–1988)[26] published his magnum opus entitled *Oriental Despotism*. In this book, he invented a *bilinear* schema for world history in which, in an almost Manichean way, the Western 'democratic' tradition was counterposed to an Eastern 'despotic' tradition. To explain this presumed contrast, Wittfogel adduced especially geographical and climatological arguments. In the East, he claimed, agriculture had become possible through the construction of great irrigation systems which subsequently formed the basis for extensive state apparati and absolutist rulers: 'the agromanagerial despot [...] exercises unchecked control over the army, the police, the intelligence service; and he has at his disposal jailers, torturers, executioners, and all the tools that are necessary to catch, incapacitate, and destroy a subject'.[27]

Wittfogel applied his theory also to Russia and the Soviet Union. In order to do so, Wittfogel had to make a plausible argument that 'oriental despotism' could also be exported to non-hydraulic regions.[28] Such a transfer, he argued, had occurred in Russia's case during the Mongolian invasions;[29] from that time, oriental despotism had consolidated itself. The period from Ivan III

---

[25] Kuroń/Modzelewski, English translation, p. 48.

[26] A Communist from 1920 to 1939 and, from 1927, China specialist of the Comintern, Wittfogel had already, during the 1930s, acquired international fame for his publications at the Frankfurt Institute for Social Research. After emigrating to the USA in 1934, Wittfogel evolved in an anti-Communist direction, although he continued to regard himself as Marxist. See Ulmen 1978.

[27] Wittfogel 1957, pp. 420–3.

[28] In outline, Wittfogel had developed this idea already earlier (Wittfogel 1950). After the publication of *Oriental Despotism*, he expounded his interpretation further (Wittfogel 1960 and 1963a).

[29] Wittfogel 1957, p. 174; see also p. 225.

until the February revolution in 1917 was accordingly characterised by an autocratic régime which constantly adapted to new circumstances.[30] Even so, under the influence of industrialisation and modernisation, oppositional forces emerged. In the first months of 1917, when the Czarist army was paralysed as a result of the World War, they finally appeared to be strong enough to form a short-lived, anti-absolutist and democratic government. Thus, 'a genuinely open historical situation' briefly arose.[31] The new democratic leaders, however, committed important errors; they continued the War, even although they lacked the strength for it, and they had postponed land reforms until after the opening of the Constituent Assembly which, however, never met.[32] These shortcomings in democratic policy gave the Bolsheviks their chance; and, so, the Soviet Union was established, a society which raised oriental despotism to a higher plane, and gave birth to a system of general (state-)slavery on an industrial basis.[33]

Wittfogel's interpretation of Russian history continued to have some influence until the 1980s (see Chapter 6). Various experts nevertheless pointed to its doubtful scientific validity. In a debate with Wittfogel in *Slavic Review* in 1963, Riasanovsky denied that there had ever been an oriental despotism in Russia. That form of society, after all, was defined by weakly developed and fragmented private ownership. In Russia, however, different kinds of private property had existed for a long time, which, in addition, had shown remarkable growth and differentiation. And, precisely, the Mongols had tried to reverse the fragmentation of ownership. Fundamentally, Riasanovsky reproached Wittfogel for imposing schemata on history without studying history itself.

---

[30] 'The masters of the despotic state apparatus responded to the changing historical situation with changing attitudes, but until 1917 they did not relinquish their total power.' Wittfogel 1957, p. 179.

[31] Wittfogel 1957, p. 437.

[32] Wittfogel 1957, p. 438.

[33] Wittfogel 1957, p. 441. Wittfogel was inspired in this theory by Plekhanov. Bertram D. Wolfe (1896–1977) had in 1948 referred to Plekhanov's presentation at the second RSDLP Congress (1906); the founder of Russian Marxism had explicitly stated that nationalisation of the land would again bind the peasants to the land and cause the revival of 'Asiatic' traditions. Wolfe himself added: '[...] it was, as Plekhanov had foreseen, the real economic and political foundation for a "Restauration" – of personal absolutism, labor fixity, purges, forced labor, bureaucratic privilege, police rule – a swelling of the state that would make Tsarism seem a limited state by comparison.' (Wolfe 1948, p. 468.) Under the influence of this remark, Wittfogel arrived in the next years at his theory of industrial despotism. Ulmen 1981, pp. vii–viii.

Wittfogel's interpretation therefore remained 'extrinsic throughout'. According to Riasanovsky, the influence of the Mongolian occupying forces on the further development of the Russian empire was relatively insignificant. Admittedly, they had introduced some new institutions, but one ought not to exaggerate:

> For example, Mongolian financial policies often failed in Russia. Thus the invaders replaced the old 'smoke' and 'plow' taxes with the cruder and simpler head tax, which did not at all take into account one's ability to pay. But this innovation disappeared when Russian princes, as intermediaries, took over from the Mongol tax collectors, and even the postal system dated back to Kievan times, although the Mongols enlarged and improved it.

More generally, Riasanovsky questioned how a tribal society such as the Mongolian one could have a lasting influence on a highly developed community like that of Kiev.[34]

Dittrich likewise opined that it was not a credible proposition to claim that the Mongols had brought Chinese despotism to Russia. In his eyes, Wittfogel's theory raised more questions than it answered; he attributed this to its one-sidedness, simplifications and factual errors, associated with a rigid, deterministic way of thinking.[35]

Marcuse

The attitude of the philosopher Herbert Marcuse (1898–1979) towards the Soviet Union showed an ambivalence which regularly caused errors of interpretation in his circles. Characteristic was Karl Korsch's comment made at the end of the 1930s about the members of the (formerly Frankfurt) Institute for Social Research: 'Internally, all of them are without exception anti-Stalinists in varying degrees. *Marcuse* is by nature an orthodox Marxist who, however, could just as well be a Stalinist.'[36] The responses by critics to Marcuse's *Soviet Marxism* (1958), his most important publication about the

---

[34] Riasanovsky 1963. In his response to Riasanovsky, Wittfogel denied that the Mongols were nomads. In his opinion, their society was pastoral in nature and was led from a strong urban centre (Wittfogel, 1963b).

[35] Dittrich 1966.

[36] Letter by Korsch to Paul Mattick dated 20 October 1938, cited here after Buckmiller and Langkau 1974, p. 183.

Soviet Union,[37] exemplified the confusion: while some branded Marcuse an apologist, others saw him as a 'Cold Warrior'.[38]

Marcuse considered that the social preconditions for socialism did not exist in Russia in 1917, and he analysed the Soviet Union as a society dominated by bureaucracy, which under a 'educational dictatorship' laid the foundations for a socialist society.[39] A bureaucratic stratum had developed, which, on the one hand, was *not* a class, since 'the traditional sources of economic power are not available to the Soviet bureaucracy; it does not own the nationalized means of production', but, on the other hand, *was* a class if not ownership but control over the means of production is used as the criterion.[40]

The bureaucratic 'class' was 'not a separate homogeneous group', because the ruling group at the top 'is itself changing and comprises "representatives" of various bureaucracies and branches of the bureaucracies, economic as well as political: management, army, party. Each of them has a special interest and aspires for social control.'[41] Two forces worked against the monopolisation of power:

> On the one side, the Central Plan, in spite of its vagaries, loopholes, and corrections, ultimately supersedes and integrates the special interests; on the other side, the entire bureaucracy, up to the highest level, is subject to the competitive terror, or, after the relaxation of the terror, to the highly incalculable application of political or punitive measures, leading to the loss of power.[42]

The whole of Soviet society, including the bureaucracy, was subordinated to the diktats of accelerated development of the productive forces as 'precondition for the survival and competitive strength of the Soviet state in the circumstances of "coexistence".'[43] For that reason, the bureaucracy lacked a social basis 'for the effective perpetuation of special interests against the overriding general

---

[37] Marcuse 1958. With justification, Schoolman pointed out that '*Soviet Marxism* is near to an exact theoretical counterpart to Marcuse's subsequent *One-Dimensional Man*. In the second work, arguments occasionally are duplicated almost verbatim from the earlier study' – Schoolman 1980, p. 150; see also Söllner 1987–8.

[38] Kellner 1984, pp. 197–8.

[39] See, for this concept Marcuse 1964, p. 40.

[40] Marcuse 1958, pp. 109–10, 116.

[41] Marcuse 1958, p. 111.

[42] Ibid.

[43] Marcuse 1958, p. 118.

requirements of the social system on which it lives'.[44] Namely, from the diktats of developing the productive forces ensued 'principles' belonging to the internal structure of society which worked themselves out in contradiction to the competing powers and manifest interests, including the priority attached to heavy industry, the implementation of socialist property throughout the country, and the effort to create a 'respite' through coexistence with the capitalist world.[45]

On the whole, the Soviet bureaucracy represented the interests of society in a hypostatised form:

> the state becomes, without intermediary factors, the direct political organization of the productive apparatus, the general manager of the nationalized economy, and the hypostatized collective interest. The functional differences between base and superstructure therefore tend to be obliterated: the latter is methodically and systematically assimilated with the base by depriving the superstructure of those functions which are transcendent and antagonistic to the base.[46]

Rosdolsky

The Trotskyist economist and historian Roman Rosdolsky (1898–1967),[47] originating from the Galicia region in the Austro-Hungarian Empire, arrived at heterodox views about the Soviet Union in the 1950s. In his obituary of Rosdolsky, Ernest Mandel stated that:

> His differences with the Fourth International pertained notably to his interpretation of events like the Korean war and the Hungarian revolution of 1956. But in the course of the last years of his life, these differences would crystallize themselves on the correct definition of states where capitalism had

---

[44] Marcuse 1958, p. 116.
[45] Marcuse 1958, pp. 115–16.
[46] Marcuse 1958, p. 124.
[47] Rosdolsky was a founding member of the Communist Party in the Western Ukraine, and, from 1926, a staff member of the Marx-Engels Institute in Moscow for some time. He evolved at the end of the 1920s in a left-oppositional direction. During World War II, he suffered internment in concentration camps at Auschwitz, Ravensbrück and Oranienburg. In 1947, he emigrated to the USA. He became well-known for his publications *Frederick Engels and the Problem of 'Historyless' Peoples* (Rosdolsky 1964) and *The Making of Marx's 'Capital'* (Rosdolsky 1968). See Radziejowski 1978; Melville 1992.

been overthrown, but where the proletariat did not directly exercise political power. He took the view that the formula of a degenerated workers' state [...] no longer corresponded to reality anymore, and that one could not exclude the eventuality that the bureaucracy would become a class, if the socialist revolution continued to be delayed in the advanced imperialist countries. Occasionally, he used the formula of 'state socialism' to characterize these states, but with much reticence and circumlocution.[48]

In 1959, Rosdolsky wrote an essay about the question of 'workers' states' which was published only after his death, in 1978.[49] As Mandel's obituary indicated, the main argument of this essay was already known in limited circles. This is not altogether unsurprising, because Rosdolsky corresponded with all kinds of Marxists, both Trotskyist and non-Trotskyist.

In his 1959 contribution, Rosdolsky set out from the idea that the ultimate results of the Russian Revolution showed almost no resemblance to the intentions of the original bearers of the revolutionary process. This meant, he argued following Frederick Engels, that historical inevitabilities had operated in the background which had not been recognised by the historical actors.

> Given that the Russian Revolution so much resembled a primal event that rolled over the heads of those involved, given that so many actions by its spokesmen in the final analysis had very different results from those that had been wished for – we have to investigate the historical meaning of this revolution after the fact, to track down its hidden inner law of motion.

Implied here was the idea that the post-revolutionary developments had been *inevitable*. This inevitability was, according to Rosdolsky, related to the development of the social productive forces. After all, pre-revolutionary Russia had stood before a choice:

> either to overcome the centuries-old backwardness through a rapid development of its productive forces, or to sink back for a long time to the level of a semi-colony of foreign (above all, American) imperialism.

When the Russian working class triumphed in the Revolution, it became apparent that it could not realise the accelerated industrialisation. Therefore,

---

[48] Mandel 1968b.
[49] Rosdolsky 1959.

this urgent task had to be implemented by another social force: the bureaucracy. This assumption of power completed itself with iron logic, because the Revolution had been internationally isolated. And, so, a social system developed in the 1920s, in which an autocratic bureaucracy decided about the means of production, the tempo of production, distribution relations, etc. According to Rosdolsky, the bureaucracy was 'not yet a class in a historical sense'. In its totality, the USSR was a relatively indeterminate 'transitory construction' between capitalism and socialism, which one could neither define as capitalism, nor as a degenerated workers' state:

> It is obviously nonsensical, to define this new social formation as 'capitalism' (or 'state capitalism'), given that, as we know, not every class stratum must necessarily be capitalist, and on the other hand given that the distinctive defining feature of the capitalist class – the profit motive – is absent. It would be just as inapposite to call this formation a 'workers' state' or a 'degenerated workers' state', because in the Soviet Union the workers themselves have the least say, and because the ruling bureaucracy does everything it can, and must do, to *prevent* the transformation of state property into real popular ownership!

In a footnote, Rosdolsky stated that he was aware that in holding this opinion he distanced himself from the Trotskyist tradition.

Boeuve

In the middle of the 1960s, a *rapprochement* occurred between the French Socialists and Communists. In the context of this development, a (very modest) debate took place about the nature of the Soviet Union within the Socialist Party, the SFIO, which, at the time, was one of the last member parties of the Socialist International still referring to Marxist principles. It was the first significant debate on the topic in France since the 1930s.

The most remarkable position was taken by the French-Romanian Socialist Gaston Boeuve (1894–1969), alias 'Şerban Voinea'.[50] With justification, this

---

[50] The jurist Boeuve was from 1914 active in socialist student circles in Bucharest, and had, in 1921, left the Social-Democratic Party when it sought affiliation with the Comintern. He moved to Paris in 1948, where he was active in the milieu of Romanian socialist exiles. See Haupt et al. 1986, pp. 387–8.

author pointed out that: 'democratic socialism has scarcely endeavoured to analyse the nature of societies dominated by Communist dictatorships'.[51] Boeuve argued that the USSR was neither socialist (because exploitation and oppression continued) nor capitalist (in particular because the state owned all the means of production and thus could escape from market laws), and he therefore described the Soviet Union and its buffer states as 'specific societies' featuring nationalisation, planning and surplus-value production.

When criticising a 'state-capitalist' theorist,[52] Boeuve provided more details about his interpretation. It appeared that he used the concept of 'surplus-value' in a very broad (and, it seems, non-Marxian) sense, namely as 'materialised surplus-product'. But what was more important, Boeuve argued, was that the means of production were no longer commodities; that the bureaucracy was not a ruling class, because it has no class consciousness;[53] and that exploitation nevertheless occurred, because the working population created surplus-value (i.e. a surplus-product) over which it had no control.[54] Boeuve declined to give this new form of society a name, and, in that respect, placed himself explicitly in the tradition of Sternberg and Hilferding.

5.v. Summary

As far as Marxist theorising about the Soviet Union was concerned, the period 1956–68 can be described as lacking significant creativity. The proponents of the theories of the 'degenerated workers' state' and 'state capitalism' for the most part just repeated themselves, which meant that, relatively speaking, the most important developments occurred in the area of theories of a new mode of production. It is remarkable that almost all new contributions in that area, both those made by theoreticians of the 'new class' (Djilas, Kuron and Modzelewski) as well as by supporters of an interpretation 'without a label' (Rosdolsky and Boeuve) originated from Eastern Europe. In that respect, one could say that the period 1956–68 marked an almost complete theoretical stagnation on the Western-Marxist front – a stagnation which would, in due course, turn out to have been a 'silence before the storm'.

---

[51] Voinea 1965a, p. 43.
[52] Le Corre 1965a.
[53] An interpretation already defended in Voinea 1955, pp. 197ff.
[54] Voinea 1965b.

Chapter Six

From the Repression of the 'Prague Spring' to
Perestroika (1968–85)

The repression of the 'Prague Spring' caused
widespread shock in left-wing circles. The American
Marxist Paul Sweezy suspected that Moscow-
oriented Communism had dealt a death-blow to
its own influence in the West: '[T]he Czech crisis
marks the beginning of the end of Moscow's political
and ideological influence in the advanced capitalist
countries.'[1]

The massive upsurge of the student movement,
which had already started earlier and reached its high
point in Paris in May 1968, signified the radicalisation
of broad strata of (future) intellectuals. While they
often considered themselves socialists or communists,
they mainly took an independent position towards
'actually existing socialism' in the Soviet Union
and its buffer states. Within a few years, a Marxist
debate broke out among them about the nature of
the USSR which was unprecedented in its scope.
Just as in the beginning of the 1960s, the participants
initially reached back to older theories, but very
quickly new variants were added. While the existing
theories of 'state capitalism', 'degenerated workers'
state' and 'bureaucratic collectivism' were restated

---

[1] Sweezy 1968, p. 15.

once again, the number of original contributions to the theory of a 'new mode of production' increased dramatically.

6.i. Theories of state capitalism

Cliff's current

Cliff's theory, which had shown little in the way of new developments during the period 1956–68, generally stayed at the level of repetition. The discussion among Cliff's followers concentrated on one point: the social position of Soviet workers.

In 1948, Cliff had stated that the worker in the Soviet Union differed from a worker in competitive capitalist relations, because the former, in contrast to the latter, could not choose his employer; he had only one employer, namely the state: 'a "change of masters" is impossible, and the "periodic sale of himself" becomes a formal thing only.'[2] But, in the 1970s, Cliff's supporters Peter Binns and Duncan Hallas, without much ado, revised this idea. Their position was that the Soviet workers were, in reality, 'ordinary' wage-workers, since it appeared that many different enterprises existed to which they could sell their labour-power. The Soviet worker was, therefore, in the same situation as an employee of the National Coal Board, or British Rail: 'In short, the dominant mode of production includes, as an essential feature, wage-labour; a wages system in the strict Marxian definition of that term […]. But wage-labour implies capital just as slavery implies slave holding.'[3]

In a later contribution by Peter Binns, co-authored with Mike Haynes this time, this idea was however abandoned again. Now it was argued that labour-power in the USSR could not be a commodity, since an authentic labour market was lacking and 'wage-labour in Marx's sense of the word' therefore could not exist. This did not represent a serious theoretical problem however, since other kinds of labour relations were known to be compatible with capitalism, such as the early plantation slavery in the American South.[4]

---

[2] Cliff 1948a, p. 95; reprint 2003, p. 88.
[3] Binns and Hallas 1976, pp. 23–4. This article was a reply to Purdy 1976, an apologetic publication which attacked Cliff's analysis and, in so doing, used arguments formulated by Ernest Mandel. About Purdy, see also Law 1976–7.
[4] Binns and Haynes 1980.

The new thesis met with strong resistance. Duncan Hallas contended that it threatened to undermine the whole of the state-capitalist theory:

> What is at issue here is nothing less than whether there is a proletariat (in Marx's sense) in the USSR or whether there is not. [...] If labour is not a commodity in the USSR, then there is no proletariat. Moreover, if labour power is not a commodity then there can be no wage-labour/capital relationship and therefore no capital either. Therefore there can be no capitalism in any shape or form. [...] No exchange, no capital. Exchange requires wages and therefore money (the generalised commodity) and the production of commodities – goods produced for sale.[5]

In order to sustain the theory of state capitalism, Hallas argued, it was therefore crucial to define work in the Soviet Union as wage-labour (a good example of reasoning which considers the conclusion more important than the route along which the conclusion is obtained).[6] Alex Callinicos also weighed in, offering a similar argument.[7]

The debate about this question in any case clarified that the theoretical connection between wage-labour and state capitalism was regarded as extremely controversial.

Mattick

In the course of the 1960s, the German-American council communist Paul Mattick (1904–81)[8] extended the theory in the tradition of Rühle, Wagner, Huhn and others. In so doing, he arrived at a position which, at least as far as the Soviet Union was concerned, came close to the ideas of Tony Cliff and others. In his book *Marx and Keynes*, published in 1969 – an expanded version of an essay with the same title which he had written seven years

---

[5] In fact, Hallas contradicts Cliff here. Cliff wrote: 'In essence the laws prevailing in the relations between the enterprises and between the labourers and the employe-state would have been *no different* if Russia was one big factory managed directly from one centre, and if all the labourers received the necessary products directly in natura'. Cliff 1948a, p. 97; reprint 2003, p. 89.

[6] Hallas 1980.

[7] Callinicos 1981.

[8] For biographical details, see Dingel 1981; Buckmiller 1981 gives a full bibliography.

earlier[9] – Mattick tried to develop an analysis of the totality of contemporary capitalism in all its different forms of appearance. One of those forms, in his view, was the Soviet formation. State capitalism did differ fundamentally from mixed capitalism, because a market did not exist anymore,[10] but, at the same time, there were essential similarities:

> All the state-capitalist systems resemble the capitalist market economy in their maintenance of capital-labor relations and their use of capitalist business methods. Instead of being owned by capitalists, the means of production are now controlled by governments. The latter set a certain value (in money terms) on productive resources and expect a greater value (in money terms) following the intermediary of production. Money wages are paid to the workers, whose function it is to create a value greater than that represented by their wages. This surplus is allocated in accordance with the decisions of governments. It feeds the non-working population, secures national defense, takes care of public requirements, and is re-invested in additional capital. All economic transactions either are exchange-transactions or appear as such. Labor power is sold to management of some enterprises. There is quasi-trade between the management of some enterprises and the management of other enterprises, like that which is carried on between the various divisions of large corporations in all capitalist nations and which reaches its complete from in the fully centralized state economy. Formally, there is not much difference between private enterprise and state-controlled economies, except for the latter's centralized control over the surplus-product.[11]

The similarity between a capitalist mixed economy and state capitalism should, he argued, not obscure the fact that they were, in reality, separated from each other by a deep cleavage – the one system could most probably not transit peacefully to the other:

> Capitalism will not turn itself into state-capitalism; and it would be just as difficult to make a state-capitalist revolution as it is to make a socialist revolution. Since a conscious organization of social production presupposes the expropriation of private capital, the transformation of the mixed economy

[9] Mattick 1962.
[10] Mattick 1969, p. 283.
[11] Mattick 1969, p. 289.

into state-capitalism can only be a revolutionary, not an evolutionary, process.[12]

Mattick thus extended Marxism with the idea that, not only in the transition from one mode of production to another, but also within a mode of production, a drastic social and economic revolution could be necessary for the internal transformations.

Mattick – in contrast to Cliff – emphasised that state capitalism had the opportunity to develop especially in capital-poor countries, where capital formation was the precondition for the socialisation of production and distribution. State ownership of the means of production was the capitalist form of socialist ownership, the latter being understood as workers' ownership of the means of production. For societies such as the Soviet Union, the rule applied that they were still capitalist 'because they are controlled by government instead of being at the disposal of the whole of society'.[13] Striking here is the very limited definition of capitalism used by Mattick (wage-labour and absence of workers' self-management). While a writer like Cliff still made attempts to render plausible the idea that the USSR was subject to *all* the laws of motion formulated by Marx (the tendency of the rate of profit to fall, profit maximisation, and so on), Mattick no longer believed this was necessary. Consequently, he had no qualms about asserting that the surplus-product in the Soviet Union did not have to be realised as profit.[14]

Maoist variants: Holmberg; Bettelheim and his critics

In October 1961, the Twenty-Second Congress of the CPSU brought the conflict between the Soviet Union and the People's Republic of China into the open. This conflict became more acute in the following years, and led the Chinese leadership from 1967 onwards to defend the position that capitalism had been 'restored' in the Soviet Union. Not without justification, it has been argued that this 'theory' – which was never seriously substantiated by the Chinese themselves – above all had the function of legitimating a changing foreign policy.[15]

---

[12] Mattick 1969, p. 284.
[13] Mattick 1969, p. 290.
[14] Ibid.
[15] In a later phase, the Chinese leadership refined the theory by announcing that the United States was a decaying, declining capitalism, while Russia was a rising,

Among Western Marxists, the political tensions between Moscow and Beijing caused considerable confusion. Typical was the mind-set of the editors of the famous American journal *Monthly Review*. In the editorial of the December 1961 issue, written by Leo Huberman and Paul Sweezy, it was claimed that, while both the Chinese and the Russian standpoints were grounded in Marxist theory, the Russians nevertheless had the correct line:

> The Chinese position seems to us to be a typical example of a kind of dogmatic leftism that has appeared again and again in the history of the international socialist movement. Two of the distinguishing hallmarks by which it can be recognized are underestimation of nationalism and the lumping together of all opposition in an undifferentiated reactionary mass. It always exudes supermilitancy and preaches no compromise. To the extent that it is translated into policy, the results are for the most part the opposite of what is intended.[16]

One and a half years later, the assessment became radically different. The editorial of May 1963, again written by Huberman and Sweezy, contained the announcement that the previously defined position had become untenable. Now, it was claimed that the Chinese had, in the main, the correct line. Nevertheless, Chinese accusations aimed at the Russians, according to which oppression and exploitation existed in the Soviet Union, were dismissed.[17]

But this position, too, would later be revised again. After a few years, *Monthly Review* began to endorse large parts of the Chinese criticism of the USSR.[18] Yet it took quite some time before pro-Chinese intellectuals began to take stock of the theoretical implications of the Chinese critique. Al Szymanski, an American old Maoist, wrote in this regard:

---

powerful capitalism. On that basis, co-operation with the United States was legitimated a few years later (cf. Nixon's visit to the People's Republic of China in 1972 and the hostility towards the Soviet Union). The nadir in Sino-Soviet relations was reached in 1974 with the theory of the three worlds, according to which Muscovite 'hegemonism' was the main enemy of humanity.

[16] Huberman and Sweezy 1961.

[17] Huberman and Sweezy 1963.

[18] Clecak (1973, p. 130) spoke with reference to Sweezy about a 'movement from one paradigm of socialism/communism, largely derived from classical Marxism and Soviet experience, to a second, largely distilled from Maoist and Cuban perspectives. The first paradigm, which he used with considerable confidence until the Hungarian uprising in 1956, fell apart during an interlude of doubt, disillusionment, and revaluation – roughly from 1957 until 1960. After visiting Cuba in the spring of 1960, Sweezy began to develop a second paradigm'.

Although the Chinese had been calling the Soviet Union capitalist since 1967, few of us took them literally at the time. We had not yet come mechanically to accept everything that the Chinese (or Albanian) leadership said as literal truth. It was not until the early 1970s, 1973 being the pivotal year, that the Marxist-Leninist remnants of the New Left seriously confronted the actual Chinese position that capitalism had literally been restored in the Soviet Union.[19]

In Western Europe, an important role was played in the first discussion in Maoist circles by *Peaceful Counter-Revolution*, a Swedish book by Nils Holmberg (1902–81) dating from 1974–5, which was translated into German and Dutch.[20] In the United States, the book by the famous *Grundrisse* translator Martin Nicolaus, *Restoration of Capitalism in the USSR* (1975) performed a similar function.[21] Holmberg's contribution illustrates the Maoist way of thinking in a striking way. It assumed that the Soviet Union under Stalin was still socialist, but argued that even at that time a bureaucratic clique was able to nestle in the party. This clique became increasingly powerful, and could only be prevented from conquering power by Stalin himself. When Stalin died in 1953, this ultimate barrier to the bureaucrats had fallen away, and they then used the state apparatus to restore capitalism in quick tempo. Workers were deprived of the decision-making power over the means of production. They had henceforth to sell their labour-power to the state, and their trade unions became instruments of the new capitalists. The consequence was that the Soviet Union no longer resembled the society that had existed under Stalin in any essential respect:

> The working class was separated from the means of production, was no longer a ruling and leading class comprising only wage-workers. The bureaucratic élite, using the power of the state, appropriated the right to decide and control the means of production and the total quantity of

[19] Szymanski 1979, p. 7.

[20] Holmberg became a member of the Swedish Communist Party (SKP) in 1924. Among other things, he was Comintern emissary in Britain, and founder of the SKP newspaper *Arbetartidningen*. In 1958, he resigned as member at large of the party, and earnt a living writing children's books. After a sojourn in China for two years around 1960, Holmberg became a pioneer of Swedish Maoism. In 1967, he co-founded a Chinese-oriented organisation, and subsequently led the Maoist paper *Gnistan* (The Spark) with his wife. See 'Über den Autor', in the German edition (Holmberg 1974b, pp. 160–1); Anon. 1981b.

[21] Nicolaus 1975. See also Revolutionary Union 1974.

commodities which are created in production. It has since that time used this right to exploit the workers and to appropriate the surplus-value that they create.[22]

According to Holmberg, a capitalist society was defined by two features: a) the means of production are applied to exploit the workers, and b) the workers must sell their labour-power in exchange for a wage. Given that both defining features were said to apply to the Soviet Union, Holmberg uses the term 'restored capitalism'.[23] In brief, we could summarise Holmberg's theoretical construction by saying that Stalin unknowingly tolerated bourgeois bureaucrats in his entourage, who, after his death, seized power in order to restore capitalism. This 'putsch' idea is admittedly a rather vulgar variant of Maoism.[24]

A more intelligent version was the theory of the French economist Charles Bettelheim (1913–2006). The foundations of his interpretation were expounded in his slim but compact 1969 study *Economic Calculation and Forms of Property*.[25] His monumental, multi-volume *Class Struggles in the USSR* was essentially only a further elaboration of his earlier work.[26] Just like Holmberg, Bettelheim postulated that a peaceful counter-revolution (or, rather, a coup) had occurred, but he tried to situate this development within a broader context. Accordingly, he rejected any simplistic putsch theory:

> The central question is the contradiction between a scientific and a non-scientific approach. The latter pretends that one can define a social formation on the basis of a few individual characteristics, or 'explain' an historical process on the ground of a few splits or manipulations occurring at the apex of the state apparatus. The extreme case, which is especially typical, is the theory of a 'coup': it is postulated, that a manœuvre carried out at the top of a small group of people was able to change the character of a whole social formation. In reality, Marxism teaches us that a coup is the last phase, which takes place in the forefront of the political scene on the basis of a revolutionary process in class relations, itself a process which culminated

---

[22] Holmberg 1974b, p. 141.
[23] Holmberg 1974b, pp. 141–2.
[24] See also the critique by Frühling 1976.
[25] Bettelheim 1970a.
[26] Bettelheim 1974, 1977, 1982, 1983.

beforehand. The coup can only appear in the foreground of the political scene, because of those revolutions which already took place beforehand. The attempt to 'explain' the social changes by means of a coup derives from an idealist view of history and not a materialist one.[27]

So Bettelheim did not see it as his task to unmask bourgeois bureaucrats in a subjective manner. Instead, he wanted to reveal the objective roots of the restoration of bourgeois power in the Soviet Union. To accomplish that, it was first of all necessary to delineate the essential difference between a socialist and a capitalist society. Rejecting that which he branded as 'economism' (the one-sided subordination of the transformation of social relations to the development of the productive forces), Bettelheim argued – inspired by the Chinese Cultural Revolution – that the first precondition for the establishment of a socialist society was not raising labour productivity, but the conduct of the class struggle under the leadership of a conscious socialist vanguard. In *Class Struggles in the USSR*, Bettelheim thus defended the thesis that the most important characteristic of capitalism was not that the means of production were in private hands, but, rather, that the bourgeoisie as a class both monopolised the means of production (regardless of the juridical form of the monopoly) and exercised political and ideological hegemony. In that sense, and only in that sense, capitalism constituted the dictatorship of the bourgeoisie over the working class. Socialism, to the contrary, was the dictatorship of the proletariat, which could only be established because the working class conquered state power through a revolution. Socialism therefore had to be defined primarily in *political* and not in *economic* terms. Once the working class finally held state power in its hands, then it could undermine the bourgeois culture and bourgeois education. But insofar as this battle against the bourgeoisie was incomplete, or did not succeed, then a new bourgeoisie would spring up, which would try to re-capture state power.

This new bourgeoisie could quite possibly include old Communist cadres and functionaries, because all those who occupied a position in the system of social production and reproduction which *reflected* a bourgeois position, would form a new bourgeoisie despite the dictatorship of the proletariat. So if, for example, in an enterprise where the old capitalist owner had died, or had been

---

[27] Bettelheim 1979, p. 157.

exiled, the hierarchical structure of the production process was maintained, and if functionaries in higher echelons of the hierarchy could issue commands and enjoy privileged treatment, then the leading persons in that enterprise were members of the bourgeois class. And so it could happen that, in the Soviet Union, the leading role of the Communist Party (originally the voice of the proletariat) was more and more undermined by a group of functionaries who were fundamentally hostile to the dictatorship of the proletariat. This resistance was possible because of the place these functionaries occupied in economic life and at the top of the administrative machine, and because of the bourgeois methods and practices which they propagated.

The Communists had insufficiently diagnosed this bourgeois-restorationist danger, and so they had neglected to mobilise the masses against it (unlike the Chinese during the Cultural Revolution). Gradually, the power of the new bourgeoisie was thus able to extend itself, and with the economic reforms of the end of the 1950s and the middle of the 1960s, capitalist restoration had been completed.[28] Ultimately, the proof of this degeneration was the systematic deviation from the correct Leninist line.

Economic Calculation and Forms of Property contained the underlying economic rationale for the interpretation, which was not unlike Bordiga's position, and can be summarised in three points. Firstly, the core of capitalist production relations is constituted by the enterprises:

> The capitalist character of the 'enterprise' (which, primarily in industry, is the concrete 'unit of production' on which, as a general rule, state property exerts its effects in transitional social formations) is due to the fact that its structure assumes the form of a *double separation: the separation of workers from their means of production* (which has, as its counterpart, the possession of these means by the enterprises, that is, in fact, by their managers), and the *separation of the enterprises from each other*. This double separation forms the central characteristic of the capitalist mode of production [...].[29]

Secondly, so long as the enterprises operated with this double separation, they had to be capitalist, they perpetuated market relations, and formed a counter-pole to the plan. For Bettelheim, it was clear that, since the reforms of September 1965 at the latest – when Soviet enterprises gained greater

[28] Bettelheim 1974, pp. 7–56.
[29] Bettelheim, 1970a, Vol. II, p. 8.

autonomy – the battle between socialism and capitalism was decided in favour of the latter. In 1965, the point was finally reached where the planning organs left enterprises 'free' (formally or in reality, it did not matter) to work out the essentials of their 'plans' by themselves. Investments were therefore no longer decided by the plan, but by the directors of the enterprises. The plan thus was no longer a real plan, but a 'guide' of market relations.

And, finally, because the market ruled rather than the plan, the operation of the law of value was restored. For that reason, power was no longer in the hands of the working class. The plan remained only as a simple deceptive appearance [*simulacre*] of planning. Under the guise of this appearance, there existed a new dominating force alien to the direct producers. While, in the enterprises, the function of the capitalist was assumed by the directors, a 'state bourgeoisie' had grown up within the planning organs: the real class content of state ownership depended on the relations between the working masses and the state apparatus. If the state apparatus was really and totally ruled by the workers themselves (instead of standing above it, and dominating the workers) then state property would be the juridical form of the social ownership of the workers. But if, by contrast, the workers did not rule the state apparatus, and if this apparatus was dominated by a body of functionaries and administrators, escaping from the control and leadership of the working masses, then this body of functionaries and administrators became the real owner (in the sense of a production relation) of the means of production. This body then formed a social class (a state bourgeoisie) because of the relationship which existed with the means of production on the one hand, and the workers on the other hand.[30]

In later publications written during the second half of the 1970s, Bettelheim added some other arguments, assisted by Bernard Chavance (b. 1947).[31] Thus both economists claimed that the fact that the Soviet Union had become a 'state monopoly capitalism of a new type' could be deduced from the following eight criteria:

---

[30] Bettelheim, 1970a, Vol. II, pp. 26–35.

[31] Bettelheim distanced himself from China as well at the end of the 1970s, because, after the 'coup' by Hua Guofeng, socialism had allegedly been replaced by capitalism there as well. See Bettelheim 1978. In 1985, Bettelheim opined that capitalism existed everywhere in the world (Bettelheim 1985, p. 44). This did not affect his analysis of the Soviet Union, at most it meant that the schema developed for this country could now also be applied to other countries, albeit with modifications.

1. Because of the economic reforms of 1965, profit had been introduced as most important objective criterion for industrial productivity.
2. The economic activities were extremely concentrated and in the hands of the state.
3. At the same time, enterprises competed for raw materials, employees etc. Therefore competition existed.
4. Surplus-value was appropriated by the state, which is ruled by the previously mentioned state bourgeoisie.
5. Economic development showed cyclical characteristics and accumulation crises.
6. There were expansionist tendencies.
7. The working class was fully employed etc., but was, apart from that, just as bereft of rights as in Western capitalism.
8. The ruling ideology was revisionist; it masqueraded as Marxist-Leninist, but was in reality bourgeois.[32]

Gradually, Bettelheim changed his position in one important respect. In the third volume of his *Class Struggles in the USSR*, he declared that he no longer viewed the October Revolution as having been a proletarian revolution, but a capitalist one. The Bolsheviks had initiated an 'open process' in 1917 which, from the beginning, showed state-capitalist characteristics, but, until 1929, 'strained to create an opportunity for a peasant revolution that might result in a cooperative solution'.[33]

Criticism. Bettelheim's presentation solicited many responses. The most well-known were the essays by Paul Sweezy, which were part of a very lengthy debate between this American critic and the French author.[34] But many other authors also testified their approval or disapproval.[35]

From many sides, Bettelheim's 'anti-economism' came under fire; not because his critics favoured economism, but because Bettelheim had narrowed

---

[32] The individual arguments were made in several different publications: Chavance 1977 and 1983; Bettelheim 1983 and 1985.

[33] Bettelheim 1982, p. 14.

[34] The debate started with Sweezy 1968, to which Bettelheim replied. The debate continued until the second half of the 1980s.

[35] Some important contributions were: Mandel 1970b; Chattopadhyay 1972; Dallemagne 1972; Miliband 1975; Ticktin 1976; Damkjær 1979a.

the application of the concept of 'social relations' to the superstructure and, in particular, to ideology.[36] Related to this objection was the observation that Bettelheim used the 'deviation from the correct Leninist line' as the ultimate criterion for the restoration of capitalism, and thereby reduced class struggle to a battle of ideologies:

> Bettelheim offers no criterion for judging whether or not the proletariat is in power other than the policies pursued by the government and the party. Is it not essential for the theory to have explanatory value that there should be an independent method of establishing the identity of the class in power? Or [...] what are the modalities and stages in the growth of the new state bourgeoisie? Perhaps most important of all, under what conditions can one expect a victory of the proletariat, and under what conditions a victory of the new state bourgeoisie?[37]

Bettelheim's deduction of the capitalist character of the Soviet Union from the existence of separate enterprises, where wage-labour was performed, received methodological criticism. The French Trotskyist Dallemagne claimed that things were turned on their head here: only if capitalism ruled would enterprises be the 'matrix of capitalist relations'. Under other circumstances, they were not. The existence of separate enterprises therefore proved nothing.[38]

In addition, many objections were made about the thesis of the double separation (wage-labour from the means of production, and enterprises between themselves). Firstly, it could not be validly argued that the enterprises in the Soviet Union were independent: 'the enterprise is not able to determine prices, wages, its source of suppliers or its buyers. For that matter it cannot really determine by itself what it is to produce'.[39] And, secondly, it was argued that labour-power in the Soviet Union was, despite the existence of wages, not a commodity, for several reasons: (i) a real labour market did not exist, (ii) wages were not proportional to performance, and (iii) the money earnt from labour was only one of the ways of acquiring consumer goods.[40]

---

[36] Callinicos 1979.
[37] Sweezy 1970. See also Stuurman 1979, pp. 80–3.
[38] Dallemagne 1972, paragraph II-A-2; Naïr 1972.
[39] Ticktin 1976, p. 23. Mandel 1970b.
[40] Ticktin 1976, pp. 32–4.

In the literature, the eight defining features mentioned by Bettelheim and Chavance were all contested. Two main types of argument were advanced. Firstly, the *factual accuracy* of some of the characteristics was disputed. This happened, for example, with regard to the introduction of enterprise profits after 1965. Sweezy contended that something completely different was happening here than the formulation of the most important criterion for industrial productivity. If profit was indeed the most important variable, then not only production costs but also investments, prices etc. would be determined by it. But that was not the case: 'under the Soviet system [...] the basic definitions concerning the variables above the enterprise level are made by an administrative planning system in which maximization of profit plays at most a secondary and minor role'.[41] As regards the postulated competition between enterprises, it was also noted that it did not occur in a capitalist way, but in the form of rivalry in the appropriation of use-values.[42]

Secondly, it was argued with respect to particular characteristics that they were *irrelevant* for the definition of a society as capitalist. That which was supposed to be proved, was assumed *a priori*. The fact that economic activities were concentrated in the hands of the state did not prove that capitalism existed.[43] The same applied regarding competition between enterprises, or the existence of expansionism and cyclical crises.[44]

Bettelheim (and Chavance) were therefore attacked on several fronts: their method, their definition of capitalism, and their empirical arguments were all subjected to criticism.

The operaïst variant

Maoist influences could also be found in the writings of the so-called 'operaïst' current. Operaïsm originated in Italy at the end of the 1950s, when Marxists from socialist and communist circles sought to analyse a number of strategic questions of the labour movement from 'a worker's point of view', i.e. by looking at the situation from the standpoint of the factory-floor.[45] The operaïsts

[41] Sweezy 1977c, pp. 11–12.
[42] Mandel 1970b.
[43] Mandel 1970b, p. 16.
[44] Sweezy 1985b.
[45] The history of the operaïst current in Italy is described in Rieland 1977 and Wright 2002.

were initially grouped around the journal *Quaderni Rossi*. Only six issues of this journal were published (1961–5), but it was nevertheless influential in Italy, and later also in West Germany. After *Quaderni Rossi* ceased publication, the operaïst current continued to exist. In particular, the economist Rita di Leo (b. 1940) applied an operaïst approach to the Soviet Union, analysing society 'from below'. She too came to the conclusion that (state) capitalism existed there, because the workers and the means of production were separated from each other (one of the two criteria also used by Bettelheim). In her book *Operai e sistema Sovietico* [Workers and the Soviet System], published in 1970, di Leo accordingly wrote that, just as in the West – be it in other forms – surplus-value was produced in the Soviet Union, and that the same relation between living labour, machines and raw materials could be found there.[46]

6.ii. The theory of the degenerated workers' state

Elaborations

Just like the theory proposed by Cliff, the Trotskyist theory stayed mostly the same. In the period from 1968, two relevant elaborations of the theory can however be identified, which could, with justification, be interpreted as corrections. In the first place, the concept of the 'degenerated workers' state' was increasingly abandoned in favour of the term 'transitional society'. Behind this change was the interpretation that – in line with the idea of the Trotskyist philosopher George Novack, who first expounded it in 1968 – there had been many 'transitional formations' in the history of human society who shared certain abstract properties – the transition from hunting and gathering to agrarian production, from villages to cities, from communal property to private property, from Roman slave societies to feudalism, from feudalism to capitalism, and finally from capitalism to socialism.[47]

Secondly, the transitional society in the Soviet Union was gradually interpreted more and more as a specific, self-perpetuating type of society – an understandable conclusion given the continuation of 'temporary degeneration' for more than half a century. Typical of this development is Mandel, who

---

[46] Leo 1970. See also Leo 1977.
[47] Novack 1968.

in 1968 had still referred to the USSR and similar societies as 'countries with a socialist economic base'[48] but, in 1973, claimed that: 'The transitional society is characterized by specific production relations; these are *not simply a combination* of what has been superseded and the gradually unfolding great historic mode of production.'[49] A few years later, he expressed the same thought more precisely:

> a society in transition between capitalism and socialism does not represent any form of socialism, or any 'combination' of capitalism and socialism. It is a society with relations of production which are specific to it, and which are neither those of capitalism nor those of socialism.[50]

These alterations of the theory can, of course, hardly be considered substantive. The supporters of Trotsky in fact devoted most of their energy to critiques of representatives from other political-theoretical currents – critiques which were often pertinent.

Criticisms. After Mandel had established a profile for himself as a sharp critic of the theories of state capitalism and a new ruling class, a no less sharp criticism of the theory of the 'degenerated workers' state' began in 1968. It is true that, before that time, already quite a few objections had been advanced against Trotsky's views about the Soviet Union, but they had mainly revolved around two (not unimportant) arguments: (i) how could a state be a workers' state, if the workers themselves had no control over it? (ii) How could workers' states be formed in 'buffer countries' (the East-European *glacis*) without the leading role of the working class?

From 1968, arguments by critics of the theory became more numerous, although the previously mentioned objections continued to play a role, and surfaced repeatedly in the debates. Controversy centred on Mandel's interpretation of Trotsky's theory. As we saw earlier, the Belgian Marxist had eliminated the time factor from Trotsky's theory, and he had interpreted Soviet society as a 'hybrid' society, in which three elements were combined:

---

[48] Mandel 1968a, p. 276. On p. 283 reference is made to an 'economy with a socialist base'.
[49] Mandel 1973a.
[50] Mandel 1979–80, p. 117.

'non-capitalist' production (planning), bourgeois distribution in the sphere of consumer goods, and a parasitic bureaucracy.

The criticism targeted all these different aspects of the theory. Sweezy questioned the *time factor*:

> [T]he longer the rule of the bureaucracy lasts, the less convincing is the Trotskyist theory of its essential nature. The notion of a ruling class that never gets to rule but must always submit to the mistreatment and exactions of a caretaker regime of bureaucrats makes little sense. Either the second revolution comes and proves the correctness of the theory; or it fails to come, the theory has to be abandoned and another put in its place. [...] We should note, and indeed emphasize, that this conclusion is in full accord with the thinking of Trotsky himself, who never for a moment believed that the bureaucratic regime in the USSR was anything but a strictly temporary phenomenon.[51]

The *parasitic* character of the bureaucracy was doubted by many authors. Chris Arthur considered that

> [t]his metaphor implies that attached to an otherwise whole and healthy body is a separate organism exacting tribute. However it is clear that there is no such distinct separation to be made in Soviet society. The bureaucracy is as much constitutive of the body of Soviet society as is the working class. It does not simply levy a toll on the produce of the economy – it organises production itself, it alone projects the course of the economy. Of course there are sectors of the bureaucracy solely employed on non-economic functions necessary for the general rule of the stratum [...] and this represents an enormous waste of resources. [...] Nevertheless, it is incontestable that the bureaucracy does not simply exact tribute with the mailed fist, but has a basis in production itself right down to the factory level.[52]

As a corollary, Harman argued that, if one saw the bureaucracy as a parasite, it was impossible to understand the dynamics of Soviet society. After all, if the bureaucracy was only motivated by parasitic – and therefore consumptive – motives, then the continued priority given to expenditures in department I

---

[51] Sweezy 1978, pp. 7–8.
[52] Biro 1969, pp. 5–6.

(the sector producing means of production) vis-à-vis department II (the sector producing consumer goods) remained inexplicable:

> Clearly something other than the 'consumption needs of the bureaucracy' is behind the forced development of the economy. It was obviously not the privileges of the bureaucracy that determined the need for hundreds of millions of tons of iron and steel in the thirties and forties. Nor was it these that produced the collectivisation of agriculture and the near stagnation of consumer good production after 1929.[53]

The precise nature of the *'non-capitalist'* element in the USSR formed the third point of criticism. The theory of the degenerated workers' state had, after all, claimed that Soviet society was *not* socialist (i.e. democratically planned by the freely associated producers) but rather a post-capitalist *transitional* society featuring imperfect planning, which was a precursor of socialism. This reasoning contained two difficulties however. In the first place, it violated Marxist principles:

> [W]e have a society whose economy is regulated by a form of planning, but whose production relations represent no form of associated production or socialism. This is nothing more than an impossible contradiction in Marxist terms.[54]

Secondly, it was said to cause a *logical* contradiction. If the sphere of production was indeed non-socialist, yet, at the same time, also non-capitalist, then the sphere of production *itself* was a hybrid form. But, Ticktin objected,

> If production is a hybrid then he [i.e. Mandel] has not indicated the elements which are present in production. Furthermore, if it is such a hybrid then there must be a conflict within production itself between the two logics, of value and planning. If that conflict exists, then the conflict between the relations of production and the bourgeois relations of distribution cannot be the fundamental contradiction. If the conflict does not exist in production

---

[53] Harman 1969–70, p. 38. The quote in the passage is taken from Mandel 1969, p. 14. Cliff's pupil Harman mentioned 'the pressures of rival ruling classes outside Russia' as a factor which could explain the dynamics of Soviet society.

[54] Meikle 1981, p. 110. This critique in fact echoed a comment by Trotsky himself that 'The Soviet economy today is neither a monetary nor a planned one.' (Trotsky 1933b, p. 224.)

then Mandel must be saying that the relations of or production are socialist. He is caught here in an insoluble contradiction – and what is worse, in a simple logical contradiction.[55]

Finally, doubts also arose about the existence of *bourgeois norms of distribution*. Money was, after all, only one of the means by which consumers could acquire consumer goods in the Soviet Union:

> In the first place distribution which some people see as being under the law of value is to a large extent direct. Housing being allocated by the local factory or town society is to a large extent direct. Housing being allocated by the local factory or town society with a rent which is so close to zero as to make no difference is effectively outside its operation with certain exceptions. In regard to food those who have money and can use it are the fortunate. For most of the population outside the biggest towns two things are more important than money: time (to stand in queues) and the right contact to obtain the food. [...] In the second place since the prices fixed by the state have no relation to the cost and in the case of many consumer durables in so far as they exist are so great as to exclude purchase by the majority, their money has little value. [...] Further, the real distribution differences as between the social groups are made in direct and natural forms. [...] Distribution in other words relates to social group directly through state allocation or through direct contact.[56]

Mohun's revision

Starting out from the idea that 'the classical Trotskyist position is somewhat incomplete'[57] – and consistent with the newer concept of a 'transitional society' used by Mandel and others – the British economist Simon Mohun (b. 1949) proposed an interpretation of the Soviet Union based on an analogy about the transition from feudalism to capitalism. Such an interpretation was, Mohun admitted, doomed to be inadequate from the outset, but it could suggest a theoretical direction. Namely, just as the transition from feudalism to capitalism could be understood only *after* capitalism was consolidated, the transition from

---

[55] Ticktin 1979–80b, p. 132.
[56] Ticktin 1973, pp. 36–7.
[57] Mohun 1980, p. 282.

capitalism to communism could only be fathomed once communism had been established. Until such time, any analysis would necessarily be inadequate: 'For as long as the communist mode of production does not exist, it can only be described in terms of deductions based on the negation and transcendence of capitalist categories'.[58] This problem also occurred in discussions about the Soviet Union: 'The USSR may be a transitional formation, but there is only analysis of what it is transitional from.'[59]

With this limitation in mind, *heuristic parallels* could nevertheless be drawn.[60] The transition from feudalism to capitalism had, after all, taken place in two stages. Initially, there had been a *formal subsumption* of labour to capital, in which 'inherited methods of production' were used and 'there remained a substantive unity of the labourer with the means of production within the labour process itself'.[61] In a second phase, this unity was broken and a *real subsumption* of labour to capital occurred.[62] Real subsumption became possible when the lateral growth of formal subsumption had ended, because (i) the relevant geographical space (in this case, initially the nation-state) was exhausted, and (ii) so many workers had been absorbed into the production process that further accumulation could not be realised by increasing the workforce or intensifying labour.

Analogously, Mohun delineated two stages in the transition from capitalism to communism. As the first stage, the nationalisation of the means of production occurred:

---

[58] Mohun 1980, p. 240.

[59] Mohun 1980.

[60] Mohun 1980, p. 242, characterises these parallels as 'suggestive rather than isomorphic, involving certain *forms* of contradictions in order to arrive at an understanding of their *content* in what is an entirely novel historical transition'.

[61] Mohun 1980, p. 240.

[62] Compare Marx: in the first instance, 'capital subsumes the labour process as it finds it, that is to say, it takes over an *existing labour process*, developed by different and more archaic modes of production [i.e., formal subsumption]. [...] If changes occur in these traditional established *labour processes* after their takeover by capital, these are nothing but the gradual consequences of that subsumption. The work may become more intensive, its duration may be extended, it may become more continuous or orderly under the eye of the interested capitalist, but in themselves these changes do not affect the charachter of the actual labour process, the actual mode of working.' (Marx 1976, p. 1021.) Real subsumption implies the establishment of specifically capitalist labour processes, and simultaneously, 'the corresponding *relations of production*. Between the various agents of production and above all between the capitalist and the wage-labourer' (Marx 1976, p. 1024).

There is a unity created within the labour process between the collective worker and the nationalised means of production; but this unity constitutes only a *formal* subsumption of the means of production to labour, since the means of production exist only as they have been developed under capitalist relations, and capitalist technology has a built-in authoritarian character – its principles of design being based on the priority of the subsumption of labour to capital.[63]

A second, still hypothetical step, was the *real subsumption* of the means of production to labour, i.e. their *socialisation*. To take this second step, 'the continual extension of the revolution' was required, both geographically ('so as ultimately to incorporate the world economy within the nexus of socialized relations and realise for the first time the benefits of an integrated and cooperative world economy', and democratically ('via the continual extension of democratic, proletarian control over social processes').[64]

Mohun's central thesis was that the Soviet Union had remained 'stuck' in the first phase of the transition. Already three years after the revolution of 1917, the Bolsheviks had lost their support among the majority of the population, due to the experience of civil war and 'war communism'. If free elections had been held at that time, they would have ended in a defeat of Lenin and his supporters. That was the main reason why the Communists restricted political freedom more and more. The Communist Party then substituted for the working class, with corruption and degeneration as its result. A bureaucracy developed which owed its power to the defeat of the German Revolution on the one side, and the Bolshevik victory in the Civil War on the other. This double political isolation became 'a necessary condition for the survival, and even extension, of bureaucratic privilege'.[65] Thus, an ideology of 'socialism in one country' followed logically from the total situation, and the new society remained locked in the *formal* subsumption of the means of production, with the associated 'continued reproduction of the separation of the working class from the product it creates'.[66]

---

[63] Mohun 1980, p. 241.
[64] Ibid.
[65] Mohun 1980, p. 268.
[66] Mohun 1980, p. 273.

As the Soviet economy subsequently developed further, the limits of this formal subsumption became increasingly visible, because the number of centrally planned products grew explosively (eight times between 1952 to 1968) – with the result that planning became more and more complex. The blocked transition to real subsumption thus led to growing inefficiency. The USSR lacked an intrinsic dynamic: 'The bureaucracy plays no objectively necessary role in the production process, and its control over the surplus product therefore depends on the maintenance of political control.'[67] The workers were – even though they sold their labour for money – *not* wage-workers in a capitalist sense:

> Rather, since there are no market processes to generate incentives to productivity or threats to employment, there is a significant degree to which the worker is tied to the means of production within the industrial labour process (even more obviously true in agriculture) whereby partial control over the individual labour process is devolved to the individual worker. This partial control, in conditions of alienation and atomization, is expressed in poor quality and a large degree of inefficiency. This concrete reality reflects both the formal subsumption of the means of production to labour and the alienated form of this subsumption via its mediation by bureaucratic control.[68]

With this analysis, Mohun created a bridge between the theory of the degenerated workers' state and Ticktin's theory (see Section 6.iv). At the same time, his approach implied a criticism of Mandel, who had not given the formal (and bureaucratically mediated) subsumption of the means of production a central place in his analysis, but, instead, emphasised a contradiction between (non-capitalistic) planning and (capitalistic) market forces.

> But if the plan is associated with non-capitalist production relations, and the market with bourgeois distribution relations [...], it is still unclear why this is essentially and centrally contradictory unless the distribution relations are allowed some bourgeois effects on production relations. Since the market phenomena of capitalism are ruled out (crises of overproduction of capital and of commodities), then the only effect is via the avariciousness

---

[67] Mohun 1980, pp. 283–4.
[68] Mohun 1980, p. 282.

of those who make the plan. In other words, the psychological desire for consumption privileges defines the bureaucracy at the heart of the plan-market contradiction. [...If] it is the plan-market contradiction which yields a bureaucracy, then that bureaucracy can only be defined in terms of its psychological motives. If on the other hand it is argued that it is the existence of the bureaucracy which yields the plan-market contradiction, then it is clearly not the plan-market contradiction which defines the transition but the contradictions surrounding the origins and continuation of bureaucratic rule.[69]

6.iii. Theories of bureaucratic collectivism

Stojanović

After the demise of Djilas, a second theoretician of the new class society emerged in Yugoslavia during the second half of the 1960s: Svetozar Stojanović (b. 1931), a philosopher who became internationally known as one of the moving spirits behind the critical journal *Praxis*.[70] After writing some initial articles about the topic,[71] Stojanović published his book *Between Ideals and Reality*[72] in 1969, which was, to a large extent, devoted to ethical questions of socialism, but also contains several chapters about East-European society. Contrary to those who, like Kuroń and Modzelewski, believed that the establishment of bureaucratic rule was inevitable, Stojanović insisted on the existence of historical possibilities for choice. In his view, there was no 'iron law' such that revolutions inevitably degenerated. The establishment of a new ruling class could be prevented by the stubborn struggle of consistently revolutionary forces.[73] Thus, in principle, 'Two possibilities are being laid bare as a consequence of the crisis of capitalism: statism and socialism.'[74]

---

[69] Mohun 1980, pp. 285–6.
[70] About Stojanović, see the 'Translators Introduction' in Stojanović 1973. About the Praxis group, see Marković 1975; Marković and Cohen 1975.
[71] See for example Stojanović 1967; the response by Pečulić 1967; and the reply in Stojanović 1968.
[72] Stojanović 1973, first published in Belgrade in 1969.
[73] Stojanović 1973, pp. 40–1.
[74] Stojanović 1973, p. 39.

In the case of statism – a category which Stojanović applied to the Soviet Union, but not to Yugoslavia – the state apparatus is the collective owner of the means of production which exploits the workers (in contrast to Djilas, Stojanović does not delineate differentiations within the bureaucracy). This could hardly be considered an original thesis anymore, but the novelty of Stojanović's theory inhered in a number of considerations which he presented with regard to the 'statist class'.

In the first place, Stojanović pointed out that the 'statist class' deviated in an essential respect from traditional ruling classes, because its economic power grew out of political power, while the reverse applied to the bourgeoisie. This observation took Djilas's conclusion that the new ruling 'class' historically originated as a *political* class one step further.

Secondly, Stojanović tried – much more clearly than previous supporters of the theory of 'bureaucratic collectivism' – to justify the application of the concept of 'class' to the political élite. The term 'ruling caste', which Trotsky had used occasionally, seemed incorrect to Stojanović because a 'caste' is an exclusive social group reproducing itself on the basis of inherited characteristics – and that did not apply to the Soviet bureaucracy. Likewise, he deemed the term 'social stratum' inappropriate, because it signified an ideological mystification. The only term suitable to describe the relations realistically was the concept of a *class*, because that concept was based on a categorical symmetry, defined as follows: 'statist class – working class'.[75] Stojanović's assumption, it seems, was that an oppressed class could be oppressed only by a ruling *class*. Consistent with this assumption, he was even prepared to define a group as a class which, by his own testimony, was determined politically, and not economically.

Critical Rizzi supporters: Carlo and Melotti

After the rediscovery of Bruno Rizzi[76] and the publication of the critiques by Djilas and Kuroń/Modzelewski, the odds were that at least those parts of Rizzi's *The Bureaucratisation of the World* analysing the Soviet Union would also be republished. This did indeed happen in 1967, when a new Italian

---

[75] Stojanović 1973, p. 49.
[76] See Chapter 5, note 20.

edition appeared.[77] Approximately from that time, the Italians Antonio Carlo (b. 1941) and Umberto Melotti (b. 1940) developed theories which, in essential respects, were consistent with Rizzi's train of thought.

In contrast to Rizzi, the sociologist Carlo rejected the idea that the bureaucracy constituted an homogenous and monolithic bloc. Nor did he perceive a universal historical tendency in bureaucratic collectivism. In his 1971 treatise *The Socio-Economic Nature of the USSR*, Carlo concurred with Kuroń and Modzelewski's view, although he did not indicate this very clearly. Just like the latter two, Carlo perceived a connection between the industrialisation process outside the capitalist world market and the emergence of a 'ruling class'. The central thesis was that a bureaucratic-collectivist society could only arise in countries where the productive forces were only at a rather low level. Admittedly, the system could also be imposed on more highly developed countries (such as the GDR and Czechoslovakia, after World War II), but, within a short time, this would necessarily lead to serious crises. The reason was that bureaucratic planning was effectively possible only in an underdeveloped country. As soon as the productive forces developed more, and reached a level comparable to contemporary developed capitalism, then bureaucratic planning became unmanageable. Carlo claimed this had been proved clearly in the Soviet Union. Thus, while, in the initial phase of bureaucratic planning (the first Five Year Plan), the number of factors to be taken into account was still relatively small, already during the second Five Year Plan the planners ran into difficulty, because the productive forces raised by the first plan had caused an enormous expansion of data and conditions to be reckoned with:

> The economic structure of a poor, predominantly agricultural country can certainly not be compared to that of an advanced industrial country. Even if the range of products is kept quite narrow, the simple growth of production poses a series of problems relating to adjustment, merging and increasing the complexity of the preceding choices, in the sectors of transport, maintenance, storage and distribution.[78]

---

[77] Rizzi 1967. At the beginning of the 1960s, Rizzi had again made himself heard in a few publications. See among others Rizzi 1962.

[78] Carlo 1971. This version was not accessible to me, and I therefore cite from the reprint with the same title published in 1975, p. 85; English translation, p. 55.

204 • Chapter Six

As soon as other planning goals were realised, the total structure of the economy acquired a more complex character.

> It becomes clear that planners have an enormous job calculating and forecasting the direction of the economy. Even with the aid of electronic computers, their problems could not be overcome given the present rate at which the productive forces are developing.[79]

Carlo's point was that social complexity and bureaucratic planning calculations were incompatible. Even if one supposed that the USSR was assisted by millions of highly developed computers – which was far from being the case – so that one would be able to plan every operation by each individual worker, then the implementation of such an extremely detailed plan would still be practically impossible:

> To the extent that such a mechanism becomes immensely complex, it would have to work as a mathematical model so large and complex that it cannot be questioned and readjusted every day. Such a system would imply a bureaucratic apparatus of immense dimensions and strength in order to follow every act of every worker, in turn implying an increase in the non-productive costs and therefore waste. Thus, the main dysfunction that computers were supposed to eliminate, re-emerges once more.[80]

At some point, the plan would thus inevitably become a brake on the development of the productive forces. As soon as the system arrived at this point, then in theory only two possibilities remained: either a return to market-oriented production – which would solve the calculation problems 'automatically' – or else a 'real' socialist economic planning.

Thus, the crisis of bureaucratic planning was the most important expression of the contradiction between the productive forces and the relations of production in bureaucratic collectivism. Other expressions were the disproportionalities between department I (capital-goods sector) and department II (consumer-goods sector) previously identified by Kuroń and Modzelewski, and the low labour productivity and poor product quality, resulting from the fact that workers in the Soviet system had no direct interest in the production of high-quality goods:

---

[79] Carlo 1975, p. 85; English translation, p. 56.
[80] Carlo 1975, p. 86; English translation, p. 56.

The Soviet workers, feeling that the factory does not belong to them, that the aims of the plan are not theirs, adopt a totally indifferent attitude. [...] This workers' rejection combines with managerial decisions. Thus, overly heavy tractors can be produced because the plan established the objective in terms of weight, managers can profit if the stipulated goal is surpassed, and the proletariat sees no good reason to produce high quality products to enlarge the bureaucracy's fortunes. [...] They know that, given the need for labor power, they cannot be dismissed when there is no reserve army to replace them. Denied power, freedom and an acceptable standard of living, they react with the lowest possible rhythm and quality of work.[81]

In the same way as Stojanović, among others, had argued, Carlo believed that underdeveloped countries which sought to industrialise outside of capitalist relations had an historic choice of two possibilities: socialism or bureaucratic collectivism. In particular, developments in the People's Republic of China had, in his view, made it clear that bureaucratic collectivism was not the only way out for non-industrialised countries.

For the emergence of a bureaucratic-collectivist structure, the primary condition was that the bureaucratic apparatus could attain independence vis-à-vis all social classes. In the Soviet Union, it had been shown just how this happened. After the socialist revolution of 1917 became bogged down (civil war etc.), the national bourgeoisie had insufficient power to restore its rule, on the one hand, while, on the other hand, the exploited classes were not yet strong enough to give substance to a socialist perspective (Carlo, incidentally, also believed such a process of bureaucratic autonomisation had occurred in Egypt).[82]

There was, in Carlo's opinion, little chance that bureaucratic collectivism would establish itself in many countries. In the first place, imperialism was less and less inclined to let matters get that far, and, secondly, revolutionary movements in the Third World were becoming increasingly powerful and conscious, so that countervailing forces existed 'from below'. What Carlo therefore really claimed here – although he did not say so explicitly – was that bureaucratic collectivism only had its chance in phases of a low level of class struggle nationally and internationally (the similarity with Trotsky's

---

[81] Carlo 1975, p. 95; English translation, p. 63.
[82] Carlo 1975, pp. 107–9; English translation, pp. 71–2.

judgement about the historically brief duration of the phenomenon of socialist transition is, in this respect, quite remarkable).

The political scientist Umberto Melotti endorsed Carlo's analysis of bureaucratic collectivism, but differed in his assessment of the conditions from which it originated. Melotti criticised Carlo by arguing that any distinction between underdeveloped and developed countries, or rich and poor countries, was completely 'un-Marxist' unless one referred to the dominant *mode of production* – something which Carlo did not do. As an alternative hypothesis, Melotti proposed that: 'In fact, as history shows, bureaucratic collectivism takes root, not in underdeveloped countries *per se*, [...] but in countries already based on the Asiatic mode of production.'[83]

This did not mean that 'Asiatic' countries could only develop in the direction of bureaucratic collectivism. The case of India showed that a transition to an (underdeveloped) capitalism was possible:

> Further refining our argument, we could assert that bureaucratic collectivism is the typical form of development of countries based on the Asiatic or semi-Asiatic [!] mode of production that have not been subjected to the capitalist mode of production as a prolonged and penetrating external influence.[84]

Carlo rejected this criticism, and insisted that Russia in 1917 had been capitalist, and that the *mir* had not survived the nineteenth century – whereas Asiatic relations in China had been only a remnant around 1925–7, the country being already included in imperialist competition at that time.[85]

Fantham/Machover

In the 1970s, Big Flame was founded in Liverpool and later also in other British cities. This was a small political group inspired by Italian organisations such as *Lotta Continua* which inclined towards spontaneism.[86] Big Flame energetically opposed Trotskyism[87] and began at the end of the 1970s to develop its own analysis of the Soviet Union.

---

[83] Melotti 1971, pp. 146–7; English translation, p. 149.
[84] Melotti 1971, p. 147; English translation, p. 150.
[85] Carlo 1972, pp. 85–6.
[86] For background information, see: Howell 1981.
[87] See, in particular, Thompson and Lewis 1977.

The most important contribution to the debate was the pamphlet *The Century of the Unexpected* by the mathematician Moshé Machover (b. 1936), a well-known left-socialist author, and his collaborator John Fantham.[88] In this text, the authors expressed ideas which showed an affinity with the work of Carlo and Melotti. They started their analysis with the observation that the bureaucratic régime – which they called 'state collectivism' – had not spread all across the world, but had remained limited to a particular part of the world:

> While country after country in the *underdeveloped* part of the world came under state collectivism, the developed capitalist world has remained virtually immune to it. [...] Historical evidence suggests that Stalin's Russia did in fact represent a new form of society, but one which spread only in the underdeveloped part of the world.[89]

From this observation, they reached the conclusion that state collectivism appeared in regions where the possibility of 'normal' capitalist development was excluded, while the socialist world revolution (which could resolve the problems of these countries via planning and international co-operation) was not on the agenda. State collectivism was a mode of production which ran parallel to capitalism, and had as its task the development of the productive forces in those countries where capitalism was no longer able to do so.[90]

Just like Kuroń and Modzelewski, Fantham and Machover viewed the accumulation of means of production in the form of use-values as the 'motor' of state collectivism. However, they went one step further than the Polish authors, because they also tried to explain why a direct connection existed between prioritising the development of department I (capital-goods sector) and the self-interest of the bureaucracy. According to Fantham and Machover, there were three reasons why the bureaucracy considered the production

---

[88] Fantham and Machover 1979.

[89] Fantham and Machover 1979, p. 3. This passage could have been written by Antonio Carlo, but the authors seem to be unaware of this. They do, however, explicitly criticise Melotti. The theoretical similarity with the Italian was, according to Fantham and Machover, 'purely formal', since they did not assume 'pre-existence of an Asiatic mode of production.' (Fantham and Machover 1979, p. 6.) This explains why, contrary to Melotti, they treated countries like Angola and Mozambique as state-collectivist, but not Iran and Egypt.

[90] Fantham and Machover 1979, p. 11.

of means of production essential. First, industrialisation as such justified the system, as well as the leading role of the bureaucracy in it. Second, by attempting to reproduce its own power, the bureaucracy made use of its central instrument of power, namely that part of the social product which ended up in the accumulation fund. The greater the accumulation fund, the more powerful and successful the bureaucracy was. Third, the pressure exerted by capitalist encirclement necessitated the forced expansion of the military part of the state apparatus, and thus also the expansion of industrial 'hardware'.[91] And, just like Carlo, Fantham and Machover identify limits of bureaucratic 'planning' with its inability to steer a complex industrial society.[92]

The argument which Fantham and Machover offered to justify their use of the concept of 'class' in referring to the bureaucracy is interesting. Next to the categorical symmetry which we already encountered in Stojanović's theory, they mentioned the fact that the élite was socially stable and reproduced itself. In addition, they believed that one should interpret the concept of 'class' in a broad sense:

> Class is not a suprahistorical category. It is not just that each mode of production has its own classes specific to it. Also the very concept of what it is to be a class at all differs between modes of production. In other words not only classes themselves but the very category of class are different modes of production. Thus while the bureaucracy may not be a class in the sense in which this term is used for capitalism, it can still be a class in the sense appropriate to state collectivism.[93]

---

[91] Fantham and Machover 1979, p. 16. As regards the third argument (capitalist pressure), Fantham and Machover themselves referred to an affinity with Cliff: 'Indeed the observation is a very rational and useful insight. However we feel it is blown out of all perspective when it forms one of the bases for the state capitalism thesis.'

[92] Fantham and Machover 1979, p. 15.

[93] Fantham and Machover 1979, p. 18. Upon the publication of Fantham and Machover's opus, a debate broke out within Big Flame, in which positions were taken which varied from support (Bill Campbell), partial agreement (state collectivism could also emerge in developed countries – Paul Thompson) to rejection from an apologetic perspective (Gavin MacLean). See Big Flame 1980.

Sweezy

As noted earlier, the prominent American Marxist Paul Marlor Sweezy (1910–2004)[94] had developed a sympathy for the Chinese critique of the Soviet Union in the 1960s. But, contrary to the likes of Bettelheim, Sweezy continued to maintain certain reservations.[95] When the Chinese party leadership declared in 1963 that Yugoslavia had replaced socialism with capitalism through a peaceful counter-revolution,[96] Sweezy dissented (Yugoslavia was, in his eyes, still socialist), but he did endorse the interpretation that in principle 'a revision [of socialism to capitalism] can take place without violent counterrevolution or foreign invasion'.[97] In the wake of the invasion of Czechoslovakia in 1968, Sweezy tried to prove that both Tito's Yugoslavia and Dubček's Czechoslovakia, as well as the Soviet Union and its allies were gradually reverting back to capitalism – be it at different tempos.[98]

In 1970, Sweezy wrote that the germs of counterrevolution had been sown in the beginning of the 1920s, when the working class had, to a large extent, disintegrated through civil war and foreign invasions. The Bolshevik Party had, at that time, lost its organic class basis, and thus had to battle on in a substitutionist way:

> The Party established a dictatorship which accomplished epic feats of industrialization and preparation for the inevitable onslaught of the imperialist powers, but the price was the proliferation of political and economic bureaucracies which repressed rather than represented the new Soviet working class; and gradually entrenched themselves in power as a new ruling class.[99]

---

[94] The economist Sweezy – a student of Schumpeter – had after an initial 'all Harvard career: undergraduate, graduate student, and instructor in the economics department' developed towards the left during World War II and subsequently withdrew from the academic world; in 1947, he co-founded the independent Marxist journal *Monthly Review*. Until the 1960s, Sweezy was politically sympathetic to Soviet Communism. See Jacoby 1987, pp. 177–8; Foster 2004; Howard and King 2004.
[95] See also Section 6.i.
[96] Anon. 1963.
[97] Sweezy and Huberman 1964, p. 588.
[98] Sweezy 1968.
[99] Sweezy 1970, p. 19.

About the precise nature of this new ruling class, Sweezy remained silent; he made it clear however in several contributions to the discussion that he saw nothing in theories of 'state capitalism'.[100] In 1976, he wrote:

> I thought I was quite careful to make clear that I couldn't accept Bettelheim's easy identification of the USSR as 'capitalist', preferring in the present state of our knowledge to leave open the question of the precise nature of the exploitative class society which has developed in the USSR.[101]

This agnostic theory about classes – limited to a reference about 'a ruling class [...] of a new type'[102] – later made way for a somewhat more elaborate conception. According to Sweezy's later interpretation, the Soviet Union was a society without economic laws of motion of the kind that characterised capitalism:

> it follows that the ruling class lacks a structural framework within which to carry out its self-imposed responsibility to manage the total social capital. It must generate its own goals since it cannot simply internalize and be guided by those of an underlying autonomously functioning economy.[103]

The only motive that drove the bureaucracy was the conservation and strengthening of its privileged class position. In order to do so, it had to do two things: (i) to maintain the capital-labour relation, i.e. the relation of exploitation, which meant repression as well as attempts to improve the standard of living gradually; (ii) resist the permanent threat posed by capitalist encirclement, which led to forced accumulation, opportunist diplomacy (the Hitler-Stalin pact, for example) etc. Both imperatives were mutually contradictory because high rates of accumulation, which were necessary for 'peaceful coexistence', undermined the policies necessary to maintain the capital-labour relation. At the same time, however, it became clear that the Soviet society lacked an internal drive towards expansionism that was so typical of capitalism.[104]

---

[100] The lengthy debate with Bettelheim became famous and parts of it were reprinted in Sweezy and Bettelheim 1971.
[101] Sweezy 1976b, p. 16.
[102] Sweezy 1978.
[103] Sweezy 1985a, p. 108.
[104] Sweezy 1985a, pp. 109–11.

6.iv. Theories of the new mode of production without a (consolidated) ruling class

As the shortcomings of the three traditional approaches (state capitalism, degenerated workers' state, bureaucratic collectivism) became clearer, an increasing need was felt among critical Marxists for a new vision. The attempts of the past were almost forgotten; the searchers were thus, in a sense, theoretically empty-handed. Since the validity of the unilinear schema was meanwhile being questioned everywhere,[105] many felt free to speculate about the existence of 'byways' in history, and unforeseen social formations. In addition, some could, at least tendentially, free themselves from a narrow interpretation of historical materialism, according to which the dynamics of the historical process would be 'in the last instance' determined by the development of the productive forces.

Pioneers: Arthur, Naville, Altvater/Neusüss

The first Western-Marxist attempts to develop a new approach, around 1970, were still somewhat uncertain and relatively vague. Early initiatives for a new conceptualisation were due to the young British philosopher Chris Arthur, the retired French sociologist Pierre Naville, and the West-German economists Elmar Altvater and Christel Neusüss.

Arthur (b. 1940) stayed, comparatively speaking, closest to the Trotskyist interpretation. He voiced his opinion that, in a nationalised economy, the strict separation between political and economic spheres was no longer possible, and that the bureaucratic élite, for that reason, not only possessed *political* power (as Trotsky claimed) but also *economic* power. The bureaucracy organised both production and distribution, and did so as an independent power which served only itself. Whether the bureaucracy then could plausibly considered as a class, was a question difficult to answer for Arthur, because he did not know 'how a class is defined'.[106] Therefore he preferred not to pronounce on the issue, and, instead, sought to provide a description of the social-historical position of the bureaucracy:

---

[105] As shown *inter alia* by the Communist debates about the succession of modes of production in the British magazine *Marxism Today* (from 1961) and in the French journal *La Pensée* (from 1964).

[106] Arthur 1972, p. 185. This article by Arthur was a revised version of Biro 1969.

The bureaucracy (particularly once in power in society) is a social layer developed on the basis of functional differentiation in the workers' organisations and post-revolutionary institutions; a layer that soon develops interests of its own, becoming a conservative force strangling further revolutionary development. However, precisely because of its origin in the process of proletarian revolution itself, the distinction between the proletariat and the bureaucracy is more ill-defined and variable than the sharp distinction between capitalist property owners and the proletariat. This means that the 'space' between capitalism and pure socialism can be filled by an almost infinite variety of transitional forms, in the assessment of which more than one dimension must be taken into consideration: inequalities in income, distribution of power, even ideological criteria that may help to determine the direction of change, etc.[107]

From this characterisation, it is already evident that Arthur considered Soviet society as post-capitalist, and therefore as being closer to socialism than to capitalism.[108]

Pierre Naville (1904–93)[109] took a significantly less positive view of Soviet society. In his book *Le Salaire socialiste*, which, at some points, recalls the views of Laurat, he made it clear that, in his opinion, it was not a post-capitalist society, but a capitalist formation in the form of state socialism. In fact, the essence of the matter was that the working class exploited *itself*:

In fact, state socialism is a sort of grouping of co-operatives functioning according to a series of laws inherited from capitalism, and co-ordinated centrally by the brutal hand of a bureaucracy. The workers there are in a sense 'their own capitalists', exploiting 'their own labour'. They will thus reproduce the type of inequalities characteristic of relations dominated by the law of value, although it is no longer private owners which assure this reproduction.[110]

---

[107] Arthur 1972, p. 190.

[108] This explains why, completely in the Trotskyist tradition, he sees the USSR as 'still worth defending' despite shortcomings (Arthur 1972, p. 190).

[109] The sociologist Naville belonged in the 1920s to the prominent French theoreticians of surrealism. He was a Communist from 1925 to 1928, then a Trotskyist until 1939. He was a co-founder of the Fourth International in 1938 and of the Parti Socialiste Unifié in 1960. See the autobiographical fragments in Naville 1987 and overviews of Naville's thought in Düll 1975, pp. 235–52, and Eliard 1996.

[110] Naville 1970, p. 152.

This is what Naville called 'mutual exploitation', in which the workers sold their labour-power to their own class. Given the 'commercial function of the capacity to work'[111] the system stayed capitalist, although there was no longer any capitalist class. With this thesis, Naville situated himself 'halfway between the Trotskyist theory and the theory of state capitalism'.[112]

Impressed by the events in Czechoslovakia in 1968, Elmar Altvater (b. 1938) and Christel Neusüss (1937–87) in the following year published an analysis in *Neue Kritik*, the theoretical organ of the socialist student movement. This analysis aimed 'to comprehend the contradictions in socialist societies, which were acutely focused by the military intervention'.[113] Given the context in which they made their contribution, they used in particular data concerning Czechoslovakian society to substantiate their argument. The intended scope of the essay was however broader: Czechoslovakia was, so the authors contended, 'exemplary' for the whole Eastern Bloc.

Altvater and Neusüss interpreted the countries of the Eastern Bloc as 'transitional societies', in which the bureaucracy was socially completely autonomised, and not accountable to any class. The bureaucracy was therefore able to direct the economic process itself, in accordance with its own whims. At the same time, this dominant élite had not been able to acquire the social legitimacy which 'ordinary ruling classes' had. This made their position in power uncertain; the bureaucracy felt permanently compelled to justify its existence and the extension of its power by the forced development of the productive forces:

> Bureaucracies in socialism [are] more than in capitalism forced to prove their socially relevant efficiency: their performance reports refer to high economic growth rates, rapid industrialisation, educational opportunities for all strata of the population, successes in the scientific-technological area etc. The equation of economic efficiency with the construction of socialism, i.e. the integration of revolutionary goals for which the masses had overthrown capitalism, in bureaucratically abbreviated efficiency calculations represents the attempt of the bureaucracy to evade the dangers issuing from its revolutionary origins.[114]

---

[111] Naville 1970, p. 180.
[112] That, at least, was the characterisation of Ernest Mandel, in Mandel 1970b, p. 21.
[113] Altvater and Neusüss 1969, p. 19.
[114] Altvater and Neusüss 1969, p. 22.

Economic efficiency meant higher economic growth rates. High economic growth rates could, in the longer term, be realised only by the development of the economic sector which produces means of production:

> The economic growth rate is dependent on the capital productivity of the invested funds, and/or the rate of return on investments. The former is the higher, the smaller the rate of return; but the rate of return and/or the capital coefficient (the only expression for the rate of return in the absence of a temporal dimension) is dependent on the structure of all productive funds of a national economy. From this it can be inferred that the productivity of individual projects cannot be calculated without referring back to complementary projects. When complementarity of the production structure does not already exist on the basis of a high degree of industrialisation, then the complementarity complex must first be created. This however requires development of the industries creating means of production.[115]

In this way, the priority attached to the expansion of heavy industry followed logically from the social position of the ruling bureaucracy.

To the degree that industrialisation advanced, however, the bureaucracy itself increasingly constituted a brake on further economic growth. In the transitional societies, there were two specific factors which, above all others, had a negative effect in this context. On the one hand, the growth of the productive forces in a system of central planning meant that, in the longer term, bureaucratically-commanded planning goals became less realistic. Central planning without democracy of the producers (workers' self-management) implied the establishment of gross target figures which restricted the autonomy of enterprises as much as possible. The expansion and increasingly more complex nature of the economic structure turned out to result in a growing discrepancy between the figures centrally fixed by the plan and the real world; economic resources were consequently increasingly misdirected, which retarded the growth process.[116] On the other hand, the waste of productive resources increased, and could be kept down to acceptable levels less and less. Attempts to curb waste by means of more and more quantitative indicators and details had an effect opposite to what

---

[115] Altvater and Neusüss 1969, pp. 28–9, note 17.
[116] Altvater and Neusüss 1969, p. 22.

was intended; the control function was just made more difficult, because the system became even more complex and unwieldy.[117]

Both tendencies created difficulties for the bureaucracy, because it could no longer adhere to its own immanent legitimation criterion, namely high efficiency. If this situation became visibly contradictory, then the bureaucracy would try to reform itself. This was, Altvater and Neusüss argued, the real background of the structural adjustments implemented in the course of the 1960s in many East-European countries. These reforms were, however, doomed to failure in the longer term, because bureaucratic rule persisted. If the bureaucracy tried to solve the economic problems by giving the masses more possibilities for participation in decision-making (a concession in the direction of a producers' democracy) then 'conflicts could emerge, of the kind which became a public issue in the USSR'.[118]

The debate in 'Links'

Arthur, Naville and Altvater/Neusüss had developed their ideas independently of each other, in Britain, France and West Germany respectively. This practice of working separately, each within their own national boundaries, lessened in subsequent years, but was not completely overcome. In the Federal Republic of Germany, the debate in the journal *Links* during the years 1973–7 played an essential role in stimulating Western thinking about the Soviet Union.

The discussion started with a series of articles by Johann Eggert, who wrote about a new type of society of which the laws of motion were still almost unknown. He proposed to call this form of society *'étatist'* and opined that its essential nature could no longer be understood with a traditional concept of property:

> If one takes ownership of the means of production as the decisive class criterion, then Soviet society today is a classless society, since private and/ or social ownership of *Kolkhoz* farmers does not serve capital accumulation and the whole population consists de facto of wage workers. If however one takes control as the core of the Marxist theory, then Soviet society is an antagonistic society shaped by contradictions of interests.

[117] Altvater and Neusüss 1969, p. 31.
[118] Altvater and Neusüss 1969, p. 51.

A fundamental contradiction existed, according to Eggert, between juridical ownership and the real interests of the leading élite. The contradiction between the majority of the population and the élite was, however, not a traditional contradiction between classes – since it was not based primarily on property relations – but another form of social antagonism. This explains why Eggert referred to the élite with concepts like 'quasi-class', 'class-section' and 'leading social group'. The power of this ruling 'quasi-class' was created by the division between intellectual and manual labour, which, until now, had been the cause of the bureaucratisation of all workers' organisations and workers' states.[119]

Eggert's contribution evoked many responses. It would be inappropriate to discuss them all here, because they were varying in quality and often did not advance the discussion. Thus, there were authors who entered into debate with Eggert from a clearly apologist perspective[120] and there were others who – although less clearly apologist – emphasised more strongly than Eggert the deforming influences of capitalism, and, on that basis, continued to refer to Soviet society as a 'transitional society'.[121]

An innovative contribution was made by Hansgeorg Conert (1933–2004), who discussed the contradictions within Soviet society more specifically. Starting out from the Marxist thesis that, within every mode of production, the productive forces at a certain point conflicted with the relations of production, Conert tried to clarify that the conditions for a change in production relations were quickly ripening in the USSR. Among the contradictions arising from the tension between productive forces and relations of production, he cited the inability to 'economise the expenditure on materialised and living labour individually and socially'. Additionally, he mentioned the difficulty arising from this to improve the use-value characteristics of industrial products, and the contradiction between increasing socialisation of the production process and the lack of socialisation of decision-making processes. The fundamental dysfunctionality of the modern Soviet Union was, according to Conert, expressed in particular in two aspects, namely inefficiency and undemocratic management structures (two aspects which were related to each other).[122]

---

[119] Eggert 1973.
[120] Haumann 1974; Meyer 1974.
[121] Schmiederer 1973 stated that 'capitalism has after-effects', while Altvater 1973 stated that it was 'fundamentally correct' to call the USSR a transitional society.
[122] Conert 1974.

About two and a half years later, the debate in *Links* had a sequel, prompted by the extradition of Wolf Biermann from the GDR. A very controversial contribution by Manfred Scharrer[123] unleashed fresh debates, in which some participants argued in a more nuanced way than in the first phase. Thus Schmiederer, who had, four years earlier, still considered capitalist influences to be very important for the analysis of actually existing socialism, now became significantly more critical:

> We continue to allow ourselves to be blocked by a tradition – of the Third International – which says that one should not forget the adverse circumstances of the Russian Revolution; that the capitalists take all of the blame; that it takes time to change a country and its people; that this society is building socialism.

Fully consistent with this view, Schmiederer also did not refer to a 'transitional society' anymore, but to an independent formation. In this new society, social cohesion (the synthesis) was not, as in capitalism, established via economic laws asserting themselves behind the backs of the producers, nor via direct socialist socialisation. 'The producers are the object of social processes. This also creates domination.'[124]

Like Schmiederer, Conert also tried to approach Soviet society as an independent formation. He pointed to the existence of unsolved methodological problems, arising from the fact that the categories used to study bourgeois societies were not adequate to analyse Soviet society. He therefore argued for investigating social reality empirically first, and for dispensing with labels that were attached too hastily.[125]

Two contributions again took up the theme of the division between intellectual and manual labour referred to by Eggert's opening essays. A group of authors raised the question of whether the rule of the bureaucracy ultimately had its roots in the continuation of Taylorist labour processes: 'We are not very surprised that among workers reduced to appendages of the

---

[123] Scharrer 1976, republished in *Links*, 84 (1977) by the editors to stimulate discussion even though parts were thought to be unfraternal because of unfair criticism of other socialists. Scharrer's central thesis was that most left-wing intellectuals are the victim of an *economistic* interpretation of Marx, leading to 'the logical fascination with the Plan', even though the plan subjugated the workers more brutally than the law of value does in capitalist society.
[124] Schmiederer 1977.
[125] Conert 1977.

machine and the leading and controlling hierarchies, a direct socialisation and/or the often cited "free association" could not emerge.'[126]

The political scientist Hans Kaiser (1935–79) and the historian Wolfgang Eichwede (b. 1942) expressly endorsed this thought. They pointed out that the Russian Bolshevik idea of revolution implied a close connection between a hierarchical organisational structure based on a given division of labour, on the one hand, and, on the other hand, the ideals of a socialist society. The power of the Leninist theory inhered precisely in this combination. After all, the vanguardist pretence of the party corresponded remarkably well with the hierarchical structure of the production process. This enabled the party to triumph everywhere over the workers' councils and the trade unions to triumph over the factory committees across the whole of society. The historical result was a bureaucratic élite with a dual character: a functioning leader of labour processes, and a relatively autonomous controller of the political sphere.[127]

Dutschke and his critics

Influenced by the reviving discussion about modes of production from the end of the 1950s onwards, some authors tried to improve their insight into Soviet society using analogies with older types of society. In particular, Wittfogel, who, as we saw earlier, made a connection with the Asiatic mode of production in his book *Oriental Despotism* (1957), was a source of inspiration.

For some time, the theory presented by the former student leader Rudi Dutschke (1940–79)[128] in his 1974 dissertation and subsequent articles was a topic of controversy.[129] Dutschke believed that the concept of the Asiatic mode of production was the best analytical tool to unlock the history of Russia and the Soviet Union. Concurring with Wittfogel – whom he praised in his writings[130] –

---

[126] SZ Tübingen 1977.

[127] Eichwede and Kaiser 1977.

[128] More biographical data in Chaussy 1983, Miermeister 1986 and Karl 2003.

[129] Dutschke 1974; Dutschke 1977; Berkhahn and Dutschke 1977–8; Dutschke 1975.

[130] Wittfogel 'belonged to the few Communists and Socialists, who elaborated the Asiatic conception of Marx and Engels in a limited way'. Dutschke 1974, p. 27, note 15.

Dutschke dated the beginning of the 'Asiatisation' of Russia back to the conquests of the Tatars in the thirteenth century. Since that time, he argued, the country – already strongly influenced in geography and agriculture by Asia – had distanced itself more and more from Europe. Pre-revolutionary Russia was characterised by Dutschke as a 'semi-Asiatic mode of production'[131] – a label not further specified – which, under different historical circumstances, could display both feudal and capitalist features, but which nevertheless did not change in essence. Dutschke acknowledged that, with this thesis, he had arrived at 'a certain conflict with Marx and Engels',[132] but he was sufficiently heterodox not to regard this as a problem.

Dutschke demarcated two developmental phases in the old Russia: a semi-Asiatic feudalisation begun under Peter the Great, and a semi-Asiatic state capitalism developing during the nineteenth century. The semi-Asiatic state capitalism necessarily had to stagnate, because its semi-Asiatic basis remained decisive, and the capitalistically modelled industry was, as it were, 'sprinkled' over the top.[133] Agriculture remained the economic base, while industry was a superstructure.[134] In these circumstances, the only realistic socialist perspective would have been to use peasant resistance to industrialisation under 'proletarian leadership' as a launching pad for an agrarian communism based on the *obshchina*.[135] Lenin and the Bolsheviks had, however, opted for another route: they took West-European civilisation as their exemplar, and promoted the industrialisation that had previously been 'sprinkled' full throttle. This choice was not an historical inevitability; the objectively given number of developmental possibilities had been small, but there never existed any *absolute* necessity to opt for the Bolshevik approach.[136] Admittedly, the New Economic Policy in the 1920s did mean an initial break with the old relations, but, around 1930, 'Asiatic despotism' re-established itself at a new and higher level.[137] With all the 'Asiatic tricks', the ruling class consolidated its position of power. The 'Asiatic imperialism' established in this way[138]

---

[131] Dutschke 1974, p. 55.
[132] Ibid.
[133] Dutschke 1974, p. 77.
[134] Dutschke 1974, p. 116.
[135] Dutschke 1974, pp. 122–4.
[136] Dutschke 1975, p. 269.
[137] Dutschke 1977.
[138] Berkhahn and Dutschke 1977–8, p. 82.

tended towards aggression, because it could partly transcend its internal weaknesses through expansion.[139]

Criticism

Dutschke's contributions attracted many responses. Criticism concentrated especially on five points. To begin with, it was noted that Dutschke did not define his concepts more closely, so that it remained unclear in particular what the term 'semi-Asiatic mode of production' really referred to. Not without justification, Wolf-Dietrich Schmidt wrote that Dutschke should be regarded 'more as the inventor than as the researcher and discoverer of new social formations'. Dutschke's reply, namely that he meant by semi-Asiatic 'the lowest form of the Asiatic mode of production', the fusion 'of the agricultural "infantile form" and Asiatic despotism' was, in this context, neither clarifying nor an adequate reply.[140]

Several authors noted that Dutschke had not really analysed Russia and the Soviet Union, but had restricted himself to the reception of certain writings by Marx and Engels about Russia. This invited the reproach that he had engaged in 'quotation mongering' and adopted an 'unhistorical' and 'dogmatic' method of working.[141]

It was furthermore noted that the construct of feudal and state capitalist forms of a semi-Asiatic mode of production (whatever that was understood to be) was extremely dubious. Valić pointed out that every capitalism in every formation was initially *ad hoc* and non-organic:

> Famine, immiseration etc. are nothing more than the accompanying phenomena of primitive accumulation, which occurred just as much in England, Belgium and Silesia as today in Brazil, Chile, and Indonesia. If Dutschke instead argues from the assumption that in Russia capitalism did not originate organically, he mystifies primitive accumulation. *Nowhere* did capitalism emerge 'organically'.[142]

---

[139] Dutschke 1977.
[140] Schmidt 1975, p. 992; Dutschke 1976, p. 97.
[141] Kössler 1979, pp. 116–17. Schmidt 1975 made the criticism that Dutschke had changed the 'historical-concrete formulation of the problem' into 'an orthodox one'.
[142] Valić 1975, p. 72.

That aside, the question remained to what extent a rapid growth of the productive forces was possible both before and after 1917 within an Asiatic mode of production which, after all, was characterised by stagnation.[143]

Finally, Breuer made the criticism that Dutschke's alternative for the Leninist-Stalinist development in the Soviet Union (the revival of the old peasant communities) was completely ahistorical and irrational. Breuer spoke of an unjustified romanticism which 'could only grasp the absolute historical power of subjectivity by constantly shutting out real history'.[144]

Zimin

Like Dutschke, the East-European dissident Alexandr Zimin also joined in the revived debate about modes of production. Zimin, an old-guard Bolshevik who, in the 1920s, had belonged to the United Opposition, and later spent many years in Stalin's concentration camps,[145] published a number of *samizdat*-style essays during the 1970s in which he tried to define the nature of the Soviet society.[146] In contrast to Dutschke, Zimin aimed to use the category of the Asiatic mode of production only as a heuristic instrument. Thus, Zimin did not seek to draw attention to 'Asiatic' elements in Soviet society – although he did not deny their existence – but, rather, to a parallel which, in his opinion, existed between the Asiatic mode of production and the East-European formation.

This parallel resulted from Zimin's own variant of a unilinear interpretation of history. He postulated that there was one 'main road' in human development, namely the classic sequence of slavery-feudalism-capitalism. This main road did have variations, deviations and exceptions, but existed as a whole dynamic. Its development was a fluid process, in which one stage always necessarily led to the next one. For that reason, Zimin adhered to what he calls 'a general theory of the three-stage character of the progress of class society'.[147] The Asiatic mode of production did not fit into this schema:

---

[143] Valić 1975, pp. 69–73.
[144] Breuer 1974, p. 591.
[145] Laetitia Cavaignais, 'Préface' in Zimine 1982, pp. 7–24.
[146] A number of these essays were published in French: Zimine 1982. The essay which is most important, in my opinion, was Zimin 1977. Further works included Zimin 1984.
[147] Zimin 1977, p. 117.

The stagnant character of the society of the Asiatic mode of production means that a society of that sort does not grow into anything, and leads nowhere. It possesses neither laws of development nor social forces that could take it out of the limits which fetter it, enabling it to advance to a higher stage of society.[148]

The stagnant character of the Asiatic mode of production was, according to Zimin, the result of a failed transition from primitive tribal communities to a slave society.

For Zimin, the existence of the Asiatic mode of production therefore clarified a number of issues:

i)   Under certain circumstances, a fundamental deviation could occur in some countries from unilinear development.

ii) As result of such a deviation, a specific mode of production could be formed, which did not correspond at all to any stage of the unilinear sequence and which also did not form a transitional phase between stages in the sequence. Nevertheless, such a deviating mode of production was capable of a durable and stable existence.

iii) Such a deviating mode of production lacked the internal power which enabled a development back to the main road of historical development.

iv) The deviating mode of production could for some time establish itself on a large area of the planet.

v)   The deviating mode of production emerged in historical circumstances where a transition occurred for the first time from a classless to a class society. There was, as it were, no experience yet with such a transition, and thus history could create 'a mongrel and freakish social formation' without internal dynamics.

These conclusions led Zimin to his main point, in which he situated the Soviet Union within the broad sweep of history:

Just as happened in the great change in man's history from pre-class to class society, so in the great change from class to classless society, in the countries in which the change began it was accomplished with a violation of the natural course of the maturation of a new socio-economic formation,

---

[148] Zimin 1977, p. 127.

prepared by the historical progress of mankind. This violation was expressed in a radical distortion of this formation and in the establishment, instead of it, of a social order which, though stable, led nowhere in its growth and development and was in this sense stagnant, a social order which thrust society into a blind alley and which had to be eliminated if the road was to be opened for the natural succession of socio-economic formations required by historical progress. And to the place which in the age of the first change was occupied by the Asiatic mode of production there corresponds, in the present age of history's second great change, the place occupied by the society of Stalin's 'complete socialism', which has spread over one-sixth of the globe and with variations of minor significance has been extended to several other countries.[149]

Zimin's vision is summarised in the schema below:

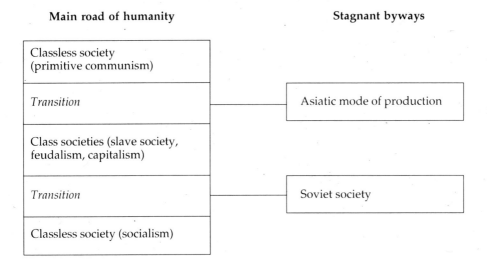

Soviet society was neither capitalist nor socialist, nor a transitional phase between them. It involved an historical impasse, a society 'in the doldrums' where economic growth was significantly lower than in contemporary capitalism or in 'the first phase of communism', and in which no essential internal development in any area (socio-psychological, intellectual, moral, etc.) occurred.

---

[149] Zimin 1977, pp. 130–1.

Zimin denied the existence of classes in the strict sense of the word within the Asiatic mode of production (he spoke of 'functional classes') because, so he argued, no clearly definable antagonism existed between exploiters and exploited. As regards the Soviet Union, Zimin referred to an élite which he described as 'a numerous class-like social stratum of state and quasi-state agents'.[150]

After pointing to parallels between the Asiatic mode of production and Soviet society, Zimin also drew attention to the different historical contexts in which both dead-end modes of production operated. Firstly, while the Asiatic mode of production originated in a milieu of numerous fragmented and mutually isolated village communities, Soviet society flourished in an epoch in which human society had become a global totality. Accordingly, the development of the Soviet mode of production was, from the beginning, strongly influenced by this environment.

Secondly, in consequence of global interdependence, developments in different parts of the world reinforced each other. Partly because of this, the intervals between social transformations became shorter:

> Nowadays it is impossible for a situation to occur as was natural in the age of transition from pre-class to class society, when one country could maintain inviolable for centuries and millennia the foundations of its social order, walled off from the changes going on in the rest of the world, even in neighbouring areas, and experiencing no influence from outside. Such self-isolation can now be kept up only for incomparably shorter periods of time.[151]

And, thirdly, while the Asiatic mode of production could be undermined only from the outside and not from the inside, Soviet society could definitely be influenced in a socialist direction from within, specifically by the revolutionary consciousness of the working class.[152]

Zimin thus perceived a rapidly growing significance of the subjective factor in the 1970s and 1980s. He did not believe in the historical inevitabilism of some other authors:

[150] Zimin 1977, p. 132.
[151] Zimin 1977, p. 139.
[152] Zimin 1977, p. 140.

The stable society, leading nowhere, and in that sense stagnant, of Stalin's 'complete socialism', which by its appearance and spread violated and distorted the sequence of socio-economic formations, though it proved to be possible, was not and is not historically *inevitable*, even in the area in which it arose.[153]

Zimin's theory however received hardly any comment in the Western-Marxist discussions.

Digression: Sohn-Rethel, Damus and the 'social synthesis'

In the newer debates about the Soviet Union, the concept of 'social synthesis' played a not inconsiderable role. This concept was developed by the German-British economist Alfred Sohn-Rethel (1899–1990). In his study *Intellectual and Manual Labour. A Critique of Epistemology* (first published in 1970, revised in 1972 and published in English in 1976) the concept is defined as follows:

> Every society made up of a plurality of individuals is a network coming into effect through their actions. How they act is of primary importance for the social network; what they think is of secondary importance. Their activities must interrelate in order to fit into a society, and must contain at least a minimum of uniformity if the society is to function as a whole. This coherence can be conscious or unconscious but exist it must – otherwise society would cease to be viable and the individuals would come to grief as a result of their multiple dependencies upon one another. Expressed in very general terms this is a precondition for the survival of every kind of society; it formulates what I term 'social synthesis'.[154]

Fundamentally, Sohn-Rethel distinguished between two types of social synthesis. On the one hand, *production societies*, which are at least potentially classless societies, formed a synthesis in the sphere of production, through labour processes; and, on the other hand, *appropriation societies*, which formed a synthesis through activities which by nature are different and temporally separated from labour processes. In such societies, non-working agents appropriated the products of labour. This could happen through one-sided

---

[153] Zimin 1977, p. 141.
[154] Sohn-Rethel 1972, pp. 19–20.

appropriation (robbery, theft, tributes, on a voluntary basis) or through bilateral appropriation (commodity exchange).[155] Sohn-Rethel devoted himself in particular to the study of this latter variant. Characteristic of the societies based on mutual appropriation, in his view, is the existence of money, as the embodiment of abstract exchange (i.e. exchange indifferent to what is exchanged) which constitutes the social synthesis.[156]

The West-German political scientist Renate Damus (b. 1940) used Sohn-Rethel's concept of social synthesis in several publications to analyse East-European social formations. Although she focused in particular on the GDR, she indicated regularly that her approach could also be applied to other East-European societies and the Soviet Union. Her point of departure was that these formations could not be considered as capitalist.[157] The social synthesis, after all, did not occur anymore through exchange. Two possibilities therefore remained: either the devolution of domination, and thus simultaneously real socialisation; or a new form of domination, characterised by direct oppression.

In the East-European formations, the latter option had been realised. It consisted of a central plan by which economic activity was initiated, dominated, prohibited and so forth, which, on the one hand, showed that no capitalist exchange-synthesis occurred, yet, on the other hand, did not prove that the rule of the working class really existed. The core problem was:

> whether despite the statification of the ownership of means of production, despite central planning or despite partial abolition of commodity production, new structures of domination have been formed, of a kind which means that government is executed only *for* the producers and not, in the framework of the given possibilities, *by* the producers [...].[158]

Direct rule could be exercised through personal dependence or through bourgeois 'forms of association'. In societies like the Soviet Union, the latter was the case:

---

[155] Sohn-Rethel 1972, pp. 123–4.

[156] Relevant in connection with his social theory is Sohn-Rethel 1971. A summary overview of Sohn-Rethel's ideas is provided by Kratz 1980. Of interest also are Dickler 1978 and Heinz and Hörisch 2006. An attempt to apply the theory of Sohn-Rethel in an apologetic way to 'actually existing socialism' is Brokmeier 1974.

[157] See the debate between Damus and the 'state capitalist' Buddeberg: Buddeberg 1976 and Damus 1976.

[158] Damus 1973, p. 29.

Direct rule, which does not resort to bourgeois forms of association can only be conceived in terms of personal interdependencies. Therefore bourgeois forms of association are in this case a necessary correlate of direct rule, since it projects the passive citizen who is oriented to his private sphere and equates living standards with private consumption.[159]

Damus thus distinguished, even if not explicitly, between four forms of social cohesion, which I summarise in the diagram below.[160]

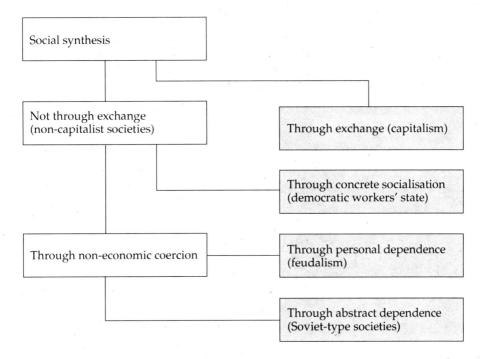

Just as in capitalism, the worker in Eastern Europe appears as *homo duplex*: she is, as Marx put it, both *bourgeois* and *citizen*. In the existing postcapitalist society, social synthesis through exchange had been abolished, but, in its place, socialisation has not emerged. Individuals were therefore objects for the

---

[159] Damus 1974b, p. 99.

[160] In a later publication, Damus defined the concepts of direct and concrete or immediate socialisation more explicitly: 'A direct socialisation would mean that it would be forced from individuals by other mechanisms than capitalism. Immediate [socialisation] would mean that it would be accomplished by the conscious actions and relations of members of society'. Damus 1978a, p. 132.

direct exercise of power. Not only did this lead to conflict, but technological progress was also obstructed, since the absence of democratic correctives has the consequence of swelling the bureaucratic apparati.[161] In fact, Damus thus characterised the East-European societies as *hybrid* formations, in which the planned economy, extra-economic compulsion and abstract relations of dependence formed a contradictory unity. The social synthesis was consciously achieved, but not democratically.[162]

Bahro and his critics

In the *magnum opus* of Rudolf Bahro (1935–97)[163] entitled *The Alternative in Eastern Europe* and first published in 1977, the influences of the downfall of the unilinear conception of history were noticeable. One of the most important features of the work of this East-German dissident was that he tried to link his analysis of 'actually existing socialism' to a more general vision of world-historical development. Bahro explicitly resisted any unilinear sequence, and claimed that in pre-colonial times, numerous regions outside Europe (like Mexico, Peru, Central America, India, China, Africa and the Middle East) featured remnants of the Asiatic mode of production.[164] Here again, the influence of Wittfogel was visible, although Bahro did not cite him in *The Alternative*.[165]

According to Bahro, world history could in broad outline be summarised by a *trilinear* schema in which, under the influence of diverse environmental circumstances, one primeval civilisation differentiated itself into three types of society. These three secondary formations (Asiatic mode of production,

---

[161] Damus 1974a, pp. 181, 190.

[162] Damus 1978b.

[163] Bahro, who initially seemed embarked on a career as functionary in the East German Socialist Unity Party (after his studies first as a 'party-agitator' in Oderbruch, then as editor of the university paper of Greifswald, then referent at the *Gewerkschaft Wissenschaft* and adjunct chief editor of the FDJ-journal *Forum*), worked since the invasion of Czechoslovakia in his leisure hours at his book about 'actually existing socialism'. In August 1977 he was arrested for 'espionage' and in the next year sentenced to eight years detention. After a campaign in the West during October 1979, he was freed, whereupon he moved to West Germany. Herzberg and Seifert 2002.

[164] Bahro 1977, pp. 72–3.

[165] 'In a discussion with Wittfogel and Dutschke in Dusseldorf in 1979, Bahro acknowledged the influence of Wittfogel which he had not publicly documented in his book'. Senghaas 1980b, p. 134.

slave society, feudalism) existed side by side, and all emerged directly from prehistoric society. Feudalism endogenously created the conditions for its supersession by capitalism. The Asiatic mode of production, by contrast, was stagnant, and found its symbol in the eternal turning wheel of Buddhist doctrine. After the core areas of slave society were absorbed by feudalism, and feudalism had developed into capitalism, two types of society confronted each other on a world scale: capitalism and the Asiatic mode of production. Confronted with capitalist imperialism, the 'Asiatic' countries had only two possibilities: either submit to underdevelopment and join the 'Third World', or take an alternative development route external to capitalism in order to industrialise in a non-capitalist way.[166]

This theory can be schematically represented as follows:

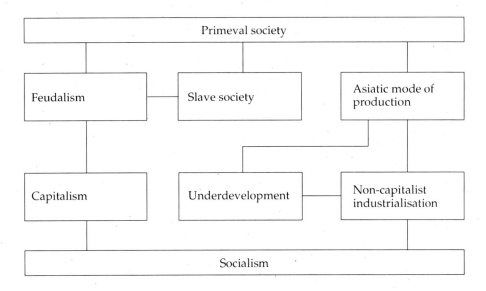

Bahro submitted the 'non-capitalist road' to closer investigation. His point of departure was that the abolition of private property, as happened in the Soviet Union, was evidently no panacea, since there existed several contradictions which were older and more persistent that capitalism. These contradictions were: the domination of men over women; the domination of the city over the countryside; and the domination of intellectual labour over manual labour:

---

[166] Bahro 1977, pp. 59–78.

These three phenomena, which Marxism has always conceived as economic relations, already provide the fundamental elements of the social *division of labour* and of the *state*, and moreover an entire epoch before private property in the means of production makes its historical appearance. And abolition of private property on the one hand, overcoming the division of labour and the state on the other, can now be separated by a whole epoch in time on the far side of capitalism.[167]

When a country abolished private property, the old contradictions again became dominant. In this case, then particularly 'the earlier element of the division of mental and manual labour emerges once again as autonomous factor of class formation, and does so as long as this division of labour is at all reproduced'.[168]

Using the example of the Soviet Union, Bahro tried to substantiate this interpretation. He demarcated three phases: pre-revolutionary Czarist Russia as a peripherally industrialised country; the time of the October Revolution and Stalinism, as a phase of industrialisation; and, finally, the post-Stalinist phase.

Bahro interpreted the pre-revolutionary relations of Czarist Russia mainly as agrarian despotism, i.e. agrarian relations with an Asiatic mode of production. Within that framework, he argued, feudal social relations also existed, which had by no means been cleared away after the emancipation of the peasantry in 1861, as well as capitalist relations, especially in the cities. Feudalism and capitalism, in Bahro's vision, were, just as with Dutschke, relatively marginal phenomena within a dominant Asiatic mode of production. So much is also implied by the fact that Bahro explicated the relationship between these three elements with a geological metaphor. At the beginning of the twentieth century, he wrote, three formations were sedimented one on top of the other in Russian society:

(a) At the bottom, the Asiatic formation: the Tsarist bureaucracy together with the orthodox state church and the peasantry. (b) On top of this, since the abolition of serfdom, an only half liquidated feudal formation, which had however never fully extricated itself from the earlier first formation:

---

[167] Bahro 1977, pp. 54–5; English edition, p. 47.
[168] Bahro 1977, p. 91; English edition, p. 77. That Bahro, in elaborating the theme, neglected the male-female contradiction is noted by Plogstedt 1979.

ex-landlords and ex-serfs in conflict over the land. (c) Finally, uppermost, and orientated in a few towns, the modern capitalist formation: industrial bourgeoisie and wage-labourers.[169]

The Bolshevik Revolution had eradicated the capitalists, as well as the half-bureaucratic, half-feudal big landowners. What remained was mainly the peasant base of Czarism. The October Revolution was therefore primarily not a socialist revolution, but

> above all the first *anti-imperialist revolution* in what was *still a predominantly pre-capitalist country*, even though it had begun a capitalist development of its own, with a socio-economic structure half-feudal, half-'Asiatic'.[170]

The function of the revolution, therefore, could not even in principle be the construction of socialism. Instead, its real function was the rapid industrialisation of Russia on a non-capitalist basis, which was, in fact, Asiatic. The statification of relations, the fusion of party and state, the Stalinist terror – all this and more only signified the reshaping of an agrarian despotism into an industrial despotism: the construction of an Asiatic mode of production on an industrial basis. The whole Stalinist development was therefore historically inevitable:

> The Bolshevik seizure of power in Russia could lead to no other social structure than that now existing, and the more one tries to think through the stations of Soviet history, [...] the harder it becomes to draw a limit short of even the most fearsome excesses, and to say that what falls on the other side was absolutely unavoidable.[171]

Bahro cited four factors which, he claimed, made the developments in the Soviet Union inevitable. Apart from (i) the (half-) Asiatic past of Russia[172] he identified: (ii) the external pressure put on the country by imperialist countries and their technological supremacy. This continual external threat explained to a large extent the Stalinist excesses, given the 'siege neurosis' it

[169] Bahro 1977, p. 104; English edition, p. 88.
[170] Bahro 1977, p. 58; English edition, p. 50.
[171] Bahro 1977, p. 106; English edition, p. 90.
[172] Bahro is rather imprecise in his characterisation of pre-revolutionary Russia; sometimes he refers to an 'Asiatic mode of production', at other times a 'semi-Asiatic' one.

created. (iii) The necessity for primitive accumulation, which obviously had to involve a lot of violence. (iv) The antagonistic character of the productive forces themselves. The machinery of the production processes could not possibly be socialist already, and so Taylorist techniques had to be reproduced from capitalism.

When the industrialisation process had, in its main respects, been completed (not only in the Soviet Union, but also in the East-European countries), a new contradiction between the productive forces and the relations of production became visible. At the latest since the 'Prague Spring', it had become visible to all how 'actually existing socialism' (Bahro's term for the East-European formation) stagnated:

> The monopoly of disposal over the apparatus of production, over the lion's share of the surplus product, over the proportions of the reproduction process, over distribution and consumption, has led to a bureaucratic mechanism with a tendency to kill off or privatize any subjective initiative. The obsolete political organization of the new society, which cuts deep into the economic process itself, blunts its social driving forces.[173]

Having sketched the outlines of the history of actually existing socialism in the Soviet Union, Bahro then tried to give a more detailed picture of this form of society, guided by his experiences in the GDR. He attached great importance to the 'social synthesis' as starting point for his analysis, and therefore distinguished within social labour between two kinds of activities: labour which has the social synthesis as such as objective ('general labour') and labour which does not have this synthesis as objective ('specific activities').[174]

This distinction could, Bahro argued, be applied to all societies which feature a division of labour in which one group dominates another. In fact, every process of class formation centred on this contradiction of general and specific labour. In very ancient class societies, intellectual labour as such was already socially leadership activity. But even in the ancient mode of production, a large part of the intellectual work was no longer performed by

---

[173] Bahro 1977, p. 12; English edition, p. 11.
[174] Bahro 1977, p. 174. Bahro's interest in the concept of social synthesis points to the influence of Damus. And, indeed, Bahro claims that Damus defended 'a theoretical conception close to my own' (ibid., p. 453). Inversely, Damus dedicated her book *Der reale Sozialismus* to Bahro, and commented in a foreword that 'Reading the book by Bahro for me confirmed fully the correctness and relevance of my analysis'.

the ruling élite, but by slaves. What the rulers reserved for themselves was the function of social synthesis. Gradually, the scope of intellectual labour in more complex societies had penetrated into all kinds of social sectors, such that, ultimately, the 'general labour' in actually existing socialism which accomplished the social synthesis only formed a fraction of all intellectual labour.

Within the total social labour of actually existing socialism, Bahro distinguished five different functional levels:

1. Simple and schematic compartmentalised and ancillary work.
2. Complex specialist empirical work.
3. Reproductive specialist work in science.
4. Creative specialist work in science.
5. Analysis and synthesis of the natural and social totality.[175]

These functional levels were the foundation of the social stratification of actually existing socialism. While, in capitalism and earlier class societies, property relations determined social stratification, in actually existing socialism – after the forms and limitations of capitalist private property had fallen away – social stratification resulted from the division of labour as such. Social stratification, therefore, arose from the structure of labour processes themselves, as well as from the structure of managerial labour in society, such as it was institutionalised within the state. It was not so much the differentiation of labour functions itself which caused the stratification, but the subordination of individuals to this stratification:

> The demarcation of the various spheres that is institutionalized and constantly reproduced by way of technical-economic and educational policy, the dominating tendency towards the confinement and restriction of individuals to particular levels of function, is what produces the pyramidic organization of the social collective worker in the process of production and management organized according to the division of labour.[176]

While, in this way, actually existing socialism was built up from different social strata, this stratification also contained an antagonism. Two contradictions

---

[175] Bahro 1977, p. 197; English edition, p. 194, table 1.
[176] Bahro 1977, pp. 192–5; English edition, p. 165.

divided society. Firstly, there was a contradiction between the top of the bureaucratic and economic apparatus, and those who are directly engaged in production, in which Bahro included the majority of the technical-economic and technical-scientific specialists. Secondly, there was the contradiction between production workers and the specialists:

> As a result of the fact that technique and technology, together with the requirements for economic handling of material, machinery and labour-time confront the workers in the capacity or function of state capital, the entire technical-economic staff, including the specialists and even the most minor managerial employees are viewed with mistrust and suspicion.[177]

Simplifying somewhat, one could say that, according to Bahro, a primary contradiction existed between the étatist élite and the workers in the production apparatus, but that, within this larger cluster of oppressed parts of the population, a sub-contradiction also existed between specialists (functional levels 2, 3, and 4) and ordinary workers (function level 1) – (see diagram).

Fundamental changes in the Eastern form of society could, Bahro argued, occur only from the middle group of specialists. Hidden behind this idea was the thought that the lowest strata of society in all historical situations were fundamentally restricted in their action radius, precisely because those strata by necessity could not or did not have a synthetic overview of society. 'The immediate needs of the subaltern strata and classes are always conservative, and never positively anticipate a new form of life.'[178]

The workers could, according to Bahro – at this point he turns into a Leninist – only achieve a trade-union consciousness[179] and their interest groups did not anticipate any new culture. That is why the working class cannot emancipate itself under its own steam: 'New perspectives only arise if, in a more general

[177] Bahro 1977, pp. 196–7.
[178] Bahro 1977, p. 174; English translation, p. 148.
[179] Bahro 1977, p. 229.

social crisis, a fraction of the upper strata or classes – or more effectively, a new "middle class" – organises the mass of the oppressed for a reformation or revolution.'[180]

Hence, not the workers, but the specialists formed the new subject of historical change. The specialist, and especially the engineer, was destined to take society's leadership into his hands in the next phase. Admittedly, the labour of the engineer was not yet 'synthetic' in nature,

> But his subjection to scientific-technical specialism has given him a capacity
> for abstraction which, even if originally applied to a non-human 'purely
> objective' and not socially conceived object of nature and technique,
> and for all its confinement by mechanism, positivism and scientism, can
> subsequently be deployed as a tool for subjective reflection, and thereby
> also for historical reflection.[181]

The people with the highest consciousness (mainly specialists) ought to be regrouped in a new party, the 'League of Communists' which would try 'to establish the predominance of an integral behavioural tendency in the perspectives of general emancipation, among all groups and strata of society.'[182] Workers might also be allowed to join this League, on the condition that they recognised that the restrictions on their self-actualisation were social in nature. As soon as they had gained such an insight, they behaved as intellectuals.[183] Once in power, the League of Communists had to 'take the sting' out of the class struggle, 'by the accelerated integration of the under-developed classes, and the productive employment of the non-parasitic elements from the privileged classes'.[184]

Through a grandiose reshaping of society 'from the top to the bottom', a situation could be achieved in which the whole population became capable of synthetic, general labour.[185]

Criticisms. The breadth of Bahro's vision as well as the fame which he acquired after his imprisonment by the authorities in the GDR ensured that

---

[180] Bahro 1977, p. 175; English translation, pp. 148–9.
[181] Bahro 1977, p. 206; English translation, p. 175.
[182] Bahro 1977, p. 430; English translation, p. 361.
[183] Bahro 1977, p. 433.
[184] Bahro 1977, p. 307; English translation, p. 260.
[185] Bahro 1977, p. 371.

his interpretations stimulated a wide-ranging discussion among Western Marxists. In a sense, the debate about the nature of East-European societies really became a public controversy (among the Left) only with Bahro's contribution. Even his strongest critics acknowledged that his book *The Alternative* was an important landmark, even just because of the political effect it had. Thus Hillel Ticktin, who, in other respects, had little sympathy for Bahro's substantive ideas, declared, for example, that 'It is possible that for a time the discussion on Eastern Europe will have to be divided between pre-Bahro and post-Bahro.'[186]

The literature published about Bahro since 1977 is so extensive that any short summary is difficult. Amidst the welter of responses and critiques, it does seem, however, as though the debate centred on a number of specific themes. Firstly, the method adopted by Bahro was a point of discussion. Jürgen Miermeister correctly observed that Bahro changed repeatedly his methodological levels, and apparently also conflated these levels, by transposing one to another without mediations. Initially, he set out from Russia, the Soviet Union and their semi-Asiatic base, the history of Czarist bureaucracy and its continuation under the Bolsheviks. Then he suddenly shifted to a discussion of contemporary social reality in the GDR, apparently assuming, in so doing, that the structural-analytical aspects deduced from Russian history could be identified directly in 'this half of a country'. After that, Bahro allegedly used conclusions he deduced from the contemporary GDR 'in poor generalisations' to extrapolate his general alternative for 'proto-socialist' society.[187] As a corollary, Bahro was also criticised on the ground that his super-historical analogy between the Asiatic mode of production and Soviet society had resulted from the fact that, having started out from a general-philosophical vision of human history, he drew direct political conclusions without the 'mediating link' of a specific historical analysis.[188]

The objection concerning empirical analysis as the 'missing link' was expressed more especially by those critics who missed more profound reflections on economics in Bahro's thought. Ticktin spoke in this regard of 'the Achilles heel of all left East European oppositionists with the exception

---

[186] Ticktin 1978–9, p. 133.
[187] Miermeister 1977.
[188] Anon. 1977.

of those who favour the market'.[189] Precisely because Bahro intended more
or less to repeat Marx's critique of capitalism in the case of actually existing
socialism,[190] it was striking that, in realising this intention, he did not venture
beyond a few scattered, though illuminating, descriptions.[191]

Secondly, the validity of Bahro's general interpretation about the course
of world history was doubted. Just as Kössler had reproached Dutschke for
his careless use of the concept of the Asiatic mode of production, Spohn
reproached Bahro for elevating the Asiatic mode of production to the status
of a universal force in the historical process, on the basis of rather facile
and inadequate reflections. Spohn also argued that Bahro's concept of non-
capitalist industrialisation, which implied that, while private property was
evaded, new industries nevertheless became articulated with the Asiatic mode
of production, should be treated with suspicion:

> The despotic state form of many underdeveloped countries can legitimately
> be explained from their historical backwardness in the context of a developed
> world market, i.e. it represents a specific combination of distinct capitalist
> relations and historically very diverse pre-capitalist formations. The category
> of the non-capitalist road to industrialisation is historically too unspecific,
> and moreover it assumes an independence from the capitalist mode of
> production and a nature which is principally different from it, which in
> reality cannot be found in history.[192]

A third point of criticism was that Bahro had characterised Stalinism as
inevitable. From orthodox-Trotskyist quarters, in particular, this view prompted
strong objections. Bahro's claim that the Stalinist dictatorship was already
present in germinal form in the October Revolution was contested by Mandel,
who argued that this theory was just as nonsensical as the idea 'that Hitler
and Auschwitz were inevitable since January 1919 or since the Wall Street

---

[189] Ticktin 1978–9, p. 133.
[190] Bahro 1977, p. 14; English edition, p. 12: 'Marx later gave his preliminary work
on *Capital* of 1859 the title *A Contribution to the Critique of Political Economy*. If I model
my own title on this great prototype, and call my text "Towards a critique of actually
existing socialism", I am well aware how far removed my critique of this actually
existing socialism still is from that degree of elaboration and coherence that Marx
achieved only some twenty years after his *Economic and Philosophical Manuscripts*'.
[191] Erbe 1978, p. 60.
[192] Spohn 1978, p. 13. See in this context also Givsan 1978.

crash in 1929 at the latest'.[193] Pierre Frank argued along similar lines.[194] Daniel Bensaïd took the argument further. If Bahro was right, he said, then one would have to conclude that 'October 1917 was not a proletarian revolution, but a new type of revolution (more bourgeois in the classical sense, and not yet proletarian), opening the road to a new period of transition.' In such an idea, he immediately detected the old legacy of 'bureaucratic collectivism' and 'state capitalism'.[195] The possibility that workers could be an important force in a revolution, but that the social-historical result of their efforts did not necessarily have to be a workers' state, was unacceptable for Bensaïd. By contrast, Helmut Fleischer, who originally was a member of the Trotskyist movement, expressly defended Bahro's vision. Both among the supporters and opponents of Bahro's historical inevitabilism, what remained undiscussed was the source of the toughness of objective relations in post-revolutionary Russia, and what efficacy 'the subjective factor' could have had under those conditions.[196]

Fourthly, a frequent criticism in socialist circles was that Bahro ignored the strategic relevance of the East-European working class, since the driving force of the cultural revolution he desired was the intelligentsia. A large number of authors agreed that there was no sense in devising a 'strategy from above' in this way. For this reason, some branded Bahro a 'technocrat' whose system – if realised – would lead to more alienation and depersonalisation:

> The executors of capitalist management, those who destroy our lives in every nook and cranny, are the very people whom Bahro wants to elevate as evolutionary elite to the leading role. These are the specialists of urban planning, who in the traffic, the pedestrian zones, and the shopping centres have sanitised our daily city life into machines out of the living flesh. It is the labour organisers of Bahro's ilk themselves, who now propose to eliminate also in the information factories the last remnants of employee qualification. Exactly when Bahro appeals to the qualifications of specialists, he appeals to the qualification of management.[197]

---

[193] Mandel 1977.
[194] Frank 1978.
[195] Bensaïd 1980, pp. 58–9.
[196] Fleischer 1978.
[197] Anon. 1980, p. 53.

Others denied the possibility of transcending an industrial, hierarchical society without the working class as the driving force, and therefore saw Bahro as a powerless oppositionist, unable to fathom the dynamic of the current period of history.[198] But however Bahro might be described – whether as 'technocrat' or as 'revolutionary' who sometimes reasoned like a 'reformist communist and tactician' (Mandel) – the great importance of the working class was emphasised by all.

Finally, there were reservations about Bahro's analysis of the GDR, and, more generally, objections to his analysis of the functioning of contemporary 'actually existing socialism'. Bögeholz criticised, in particular, Bahro's idea that a pyramid of job designations could be deduced from the structure of the productive forces (with general labour at the top), and that the highest job designations necessarily had to become more and more generalised. This idea implied, Bögeholz argued, that a group of people apparently existed in present-day 'actually existing socialism' who already steered society in a conscious way. Such an interpretation ran into several objections. On the one hand, the phenomenon of the 'naturalness' of social relations controlled by no one was thereby excluded, while, on the other hand, one would logically conclude from such reasoning that the 'malevolence' of the existing élite alone was the root of all injustices.[199]

Schmiederer

The West-German political scientist Ursula Schmiederer (1940–89) criticised the synthesis theory proposed by Damus on the ground that it was insufficiently Marxist, and because the research findings it yielded were, on balance, rather meagre.[200] For all that, Damus's approach did influence its critics. Although they posed the problem less abstractly and categorically than Damus did, the question of the synthesis – what ensured the social cohesion of actually existing socialism? – clearly reappeared in the work by Schmiederer et al.[201] The foundational assumption of Schmiederer et al. was orthodox-Marxist:

[198] Ticktin 1978–9, pp. 138–9.
[199] Bögeholz 1978. Bögeholz responded to Erbe 1978.
[200] Schmiederer 1980b, p. 408.
[201] The first relevant publication was Rotermundt et al. 1977, followed by Rotermundt et al. 1979 and Schmiederer 1980a.

the establishment of a socialist society is only possible within a socialised capitalist society, with generalised commodity production and a generalised contradiction between wage-labour and capital. Only under such conditions, a social transformation was conceivable that would result in a social structure dominated by the conscious will of the producers (socialism).

The pre-revolutionary social situation that existed in Russia (or China) was, however, not socialised capitalistically in this way. A society [*Gesellschaft*] therefore did not exist, 'in the sense of a cohesive totality encompassing all individuals both objectively and subjectively, in the sense of the Marxian concept of a social totality'.[202] Russia was much more a structurally deformed society, due to the pressure of the world market, which possessed considerable power internationally, a strong state and a relatively weak economy. On the one hand, industrialisation beginning at the end of the nineteenth century created a weak bourgeoisie with strong ties to the hypertrophied state, which did not possess the energy or willingness to implement the 'historic task' of the bourgeois class, i.e. the establishment of a developed capitalist society. On the other hand, the working class was unable, under the given circumstances, to establish socialism.[203]

The October Revolution, in this way, became a rather two-faced event, because, while the capital relationship was negated, a socialist socialisation was not yet possible either. In post-revolutionary society, an historical necessity therefore existed for a factor of social cohesion (a synthesising instance) which was neither capitalist nor socialist (based on self-management). This factor could not be economic (like the market in capitalism) but had to be political. The party itself then became this factor: 'Since a necessity for socialisation existed neither naturally nor consciously among the producers, the necessity emerged for the party to take upon itself, tacitly, the integration and leadership of society.'[204]

Production could in that way be socialised along a direct and authoritarian route, while, for the rest, private production (in family households) continued to exist. Labour in the Soviet Union therefore did not have the free character in the dual sense conferred by capitalism. On the one hand, there was no

---

[202] Rotermundt et al. 1977, p. 14.
[203] Rotermundt et al. 1977, pp. 16–19.
[204] Rotermundt et al. 1977, p. 22.

freedom of means of production, because there was no private control over the means of production (at the same time, however, there was also no collective appropriation of those means of production, so that an alienated relation existed between workers and means of production). On the other hand, the worker was no longer free from personal dependence, since everybody was directly and collectively dependent on the state.

Peculiarly, Schmiederer et al. in the end nevertheless arrived at the same characteristic of the Soviet élite mentioned by Bahro and Damus – namely, they referred to a 'ruling layer'. They too believed that this élite led social development in a conscious way, not guided by self-interest, 'but in the interest of a bumpy and ever precarious "road" to socialism'.[205] Ultimately, it was therefore the consciousness of the élite which determined in which direction society developed. Herein lies the explanation why Schmiederer et al. contrasted the Chinese élite with the Soviet one, and assumed the Chinese one did 'better' than the Russian one. Although the structural conditions of the Russian and the Chinese Revolutions were, so it was argued, comparable, and both countries had to contend with the domination of the capitalist world market and the underdeveloped nature of the 'social individual', one could learn from this how different interpretations of socialism could combine with different developmental perspectives.[206]

The contributions of Schmieder et al. did not receive noteworthy responses.

Ticktin and his critics

The studies by Damus, Bahro, Schmiederer et al. had all assumed that conscious regulation of the economic process occurred in the Soviet Union 'from above'. Or, as one author who supported them in this claim formulated it, 'the socialisation of the means of production is a first step towards the elimination of economically determined domination. [...] The act of socialisation initiates the transition from the bourgeois primacy of economics to the primacy of politics.'[207]

---

[205] Rotermundt et al. 1979, p. 43.
[206] Rotermundt et al. 1979, p. 29.
[207] Altvater 1981, p. 2.

The British Marxist Hillel Ticktin (b. 1937) took a completely different approach.[208] From 1973, he tried to analyse the Soviet economy without assuming *a priori* that any planning occurred at all. Starting out from the finding that contemporary Soviet society was characterised by a gigantic waste of manpower, means of production and products – a phenomenon to which he devoted the largest part of his début article[209] – he asked himself where this waste, which seemed unpreventable and thus deeply rooted, actually came from. As a Marxist, he rejected out of hand the idea of many East- and West-European experts that the phenomenon was the direct consequence of the lack of market-oriented forces. To the contrary, Ticktin perceived in the strengthening or re-introduction of market forces an anti-democratic tendency, which would worsen the position of the working class in 'actually existing socialism'.[210]

His explanation of inefficiency was, therefore, based on the exact opposite of the pro-market reasoning: it was precisely the existence of insufficient, *because undemocratic*, planning in the Soviet Union that led to waste, and really to the practical impossibility of all planning as such. As regards the Soviet Union, Ticktin spoke of an economy that was not planned, but 'administered', one in which the élite trailed behind developments, and had, at best, only a very tenuous grip over society's production. Soviet 'planning' was, in his view, 'really no more than a bargaining process at best, and a police process at worst'.[211]

The roots of the system were, according to Ticktin, to be found in the 1920s, when a contradiction visibly emerged between planning and the market, given the economic backwardness of the country and the national isolation of the 'socialist' experiment. As the tensions between planning and market tendencies increased, overcoming the contradiction became more urgent. Forced collectivisation and forced industrialisation were the solution. The bureaucracy then elevated itself as a kind of 'Bonapartist' power above the contradictions, and simultaneously enclosed them within itself:

---

[208] Ticktin, originating from South Africa, studied in Cape Town, Kiev and Moscow. From 1965 he taught at the Institute of Soviet Studies in Glasgow and from 1973 was chief editor of *Critique. Journal of Soviet Studies and Socialist Theory*. Letter by Ticktin to the author, 11 November 1982.
[209] Ticktin 1973.
[210] See especially the debate between Ticktin and the 'market-socialist' Wlodzimierz Brus in Ticktin and Brus 1981.
[211] Ticktin 1978a, p. 46.

It constituted itself as a new elite which held the means of administration in its own hands and effectively destroyed all opposition forces, either directly through physical liquidation or indirectly through a process of atomisation so thoroughly and so deep that it made the régime unique in its power over the population.[212]

The power which the new élite exercised over the economy was admittedly wasteful from the beginning, since all plans were based on incomplete information, and bottlenecks occurred at many levels upon implementation. Yet, despite this, the planned economy led initially to rapid growth:

> the sheer advantages of the organised form of production predominated over the colossal waste which occurred in the early period. Furthermore, the wasteful nature of this growth was masked by the continued high level of surplus pumped out of the working class.[213]

As the economy became more complex through industrialisation, the ability of the élite to retain oversight over the whole situation was reduced:

> The more intensive and the more complex is the economy the longer the chain of command, and the less intelligible is industry to the administrators, and so the greater the distortions and their proportionate importance.[214]

Since planning had to be based on the rule of the majority – the working class – Soviet 'planning' could only lead to a series of conflicts, with the consequence that the instructions of the central planners were only followed insofar as they cohered with the personal interests of individuals. Soviet society thus featured not one law of motion as in capitalism, but two: on the one side, the 'law of organisation' and, on the other side, the 'law of private benefit or interest'.[215]

Both the élite and the working class were atomised, fragmented into innumerable individuals. For its part, the *élite* was forced to fight a battle on two fronts. On the one hand, it had to fight as a social group in order to reproduce its privileged position, and, on the other hand, its members had to fight internally as individuals to maintain their personal position and secure

---

[212] Ticktin 1978b, p. 43.
[213] Ticktin 1978b, p. 47.
[214] Ticktin 1973, p. 34.
[215] Ticktin 1973, p. 36.

their promotion. The *working class* was likewise atomised, because it did not possess its own trade unions or any other autonomous political organisations. The working class could influence production exclusively in a negative way, either by producing too little, or by supplying products that had no use-value. Because everyone, including the élite and the working class, pursued their own self-interest first and foremost, any efficient policy was ruled out. In fact, the social surplus-product was not truly controlled by anyone. The workers had a negative influence, and the élite had a partly positive influence on the surplus-product. But no one really knew

> what the surplus is, where it is or how big it is, there is no way that the elite can give instructions capable of fulfillment. It is simply not possible to give all the instructions to the various persons, along the chain of subordination such as would be necessary to ensure compliance with the original intentions of the Ministries.[216]

As a result, the contradiction within the sphere of production was no longer formed primarily by the contradiction between (exchange-) value and use-value, but was contained in use-values themselves:

> The contradiction lies in use-value itself. The use-value produced is defective in no small measure, with the result that the surplus-product produced is itself of a particular kind. Part is so defective that it is in fact useless, another part is acceptable but the constant cause of additional cost whether because of breakdowns, absence of spare parts or whatever, while a third part may not in itself be defective but is operated in such a way that it is rapidly assimilated to the rest of the surplus-product.[217]

Precisely this deficient control over the surplus-product was the reason why Ticktin considered it did not make sense to call the élite a 'ruling class'. The conflict between private interests and organisation, decisive for the whole society, also expressed itself within the élite itself, and therefore made this social group highly unstable. More specifically, Ticktin described the élite as

> a social group which is involved in the exploitation of the direct producers and has partial control over the surplus-product extracted, but which can

---

[216] Ticktin 1978a, p. 50.
[217] Ticktin 1976, p. 32.

maintain its exploitation only in the form of direct political measures, involving the use of the state.[218]

As a whole, Soviet society was therefore an unstable and hybrid structure, a 'false start' on the road to socialism. It was a form of society

> which has no viability as a mode of production but performs specific tasks and had its own exploitative ruling group. The state-capitalists argue that these societies are capitalist, while the workers' statists argue that they are on the lowest and deformed rung of socialism. The bureaucratic-collectivists argue that it is a new mode of production in which the ruling group effectively owns the means of production. None of these views offer a theory of development of these societies. They amount to little more than simple statements of a political kind.[219]

The question of why the October Revolution ultimately became a 'false start', i.e. within which world-historical context the whole development took place, remained unanswered in Ticktin's writings.

Criticism of Ticktin's theory concentrated on two interconnected points. It was alleged by various authors that Ticktin exaggerated waste in the Soviet Union. If the situation was really so disastrous as Ticktin claimed, then – Mandel argued – it would become incomprehensible how the country had been able to transform itself from an underdeveloped country into a superpower within the space of one generation:

> It would be more correct to say that the 'central economic feature of the USSR' is growth plus waste, growth in spite of ('growing') waste, real growth beside growing waste. [...] It characterises the USSR as something quite different from a stagnant or regressive society which is basically wasteful and nothing else (e.g. the Roman empire in decadence).[220]

In addition, it was noted that two economic sectors could, in fact, be distinguished in the Soviet Union: a military-industrial sector which, compared to capitalism, did deliver 'high-quality' products and the civil

---

[218] Ticktin 1978a, p. 55.
[219] Ticktin 1978a, p. 61.
[220] Mandel 1974, p. 25.

sector, which was plagued by waste. In that sense, the Soviet economy was said to be both efficient and inefficient.[221]

That the Soviet Union featured both efficient and inefficient sectors, was, according to Klinger, itself one of the indications that the élite was definitely able to steer the social process. Thereby, social development became a consciously directed process, and one could no longer speak intelligibly about 'laws of motion' which take shape 'behind the backs of the producers'. The only dynamics the system had were the decisions and directives at the central level. If these were absent, the economy would grind to a halt. The main precondition for the functioning of the totality was the loyalty of the majority of the population. If that was present, the field of action of the élite remained limited only by 'the boundaries of its own power as centres of decision-making'.[222]

With the last-mentioned insight, the central theme of the newer controversies about the Soviet Union was touched upon: if the élite was not a class, and therefore not bound by the traditional laws of social formations based on class contradictions, did this mean that they autonomously and consciously steered the economic process – with the implication that abhorrent developments could be ascribed to 'wrong policy' or 'malevolence' – or was the élite bound by other 'laws' which were related to the fact that it constituted only the apex of a thoroughly bureaucratised society with its inherent tendencies?

The Hungarian 'New Left'

In the course of the 1960s, a circle of 'liberal-Marxist' philosophers and sociologists formed around György Lukács known as the 'Budapest School'. The most important representatives of this current (András Hegedüs, Agnes Heller, György Márkus and others) were, for quite some time, rather moderate in their critique of East-European socialism.[223] For a number of them, life was nevertheless made so difficult during the 1970s that, around 1977, they emigrated temporarily or permanently to the West.

---

[221] Klinger 1981, pp. xxiv–xxv. Klinger bases himself on Zaslavsky 1978.
[222] Klinger 1981, pp. xx–xxix.
[223] See for example Hegedüs 1976 and Hegedüs et al. 1976a. Background information in Lukács 1973; Rivière 1974; Szelényi 1977; Becker 1978; Arato 1987.

Meanwhile, however, a younger generation of dissident intellectuals made their appearance who either abandoned Marxism, or sought to be Marxist as well as oppositionist.

An important role in the last-mentioned network of intellectuals was played by the philosophers György Bence (b. 1941) and János Kis (b. 1943), who had both broken with the Budapest school, and argued for a strategy of 'radical reforms'.[224] Bence and Kis became known in the West as critics of the Soviet Union when they published an essay about the problematics in the journal *Les Temps Modernes*[225] under their collective pseudonym of 'Marc Rakovski'.[226] Shortly thereafter, they also published a more extensive critique of East-European society, under the title *Towards an East European Marxism*.[227] In the latter work, they defended the thesis that Soviet-type societies were neither socialist nor capitalist, nor a combination of both, but, instead, class societies *sui generis*. To understand these societies properly, they argued, a revision of the (unilinear) Marxist schema was unavoidable:

> [I]t is necessary to reconsider the whole traditional structure of historical materialism. [...] In spite of the key role which historicism played in Marx's thought, he was unable to avoid the implications of the unilinear evolutionism which dominated the social sciences of his period. [...] Within the traditional structure of historical materialism there is no place for a modern social system which has an evolutionary trajectory other than capitalism and which is not simply an earlier or later stage along the same route.[228]

---

[224] Bence and Kis 1980.

[225] Lomax 1982.

[226] Rakovski 1974. This article was part of a series of publications in Western journals. See for example the critique of André Gorz in Rakovski 1976 together with the reply by Gorz, 'Pour une critique des forces productives. Réponse à Marc Rakovski' in the same issue.

[227] Rakovski 1978.

[228] Rakovski 1978, p. 15. The attempts by Bence and Kis to analyse Soviet societies remained limited. Their contributions concentrated on theoretical-methodological questions; for the rest, they perceived in 'actually existing socialism' a class society without capital or labour, in which both antagonistic classes possessed a low level of class consciousness, and the rulers were not collective owners of the means of production.

Apparently, this longing for a 'non-Marxian' historical materialism around that time also affected other Hungarian intellectuals. Already in 1974, the economist Ivan Szelényi (b. 1938) and the novelist György Konrád (b. 1934) completed a manuscript in which they tried to develop a new analytical framework for Soviet-type societies. Repression prevented the publication of the work for quite some time; only in 1979 did it become accessible for a broader public as *The Intellectuals on the Road to Class Power*.[229]

Konrád and Szelényi compared three forms of society in their study: the Asiatic mode of production, capitalism and socialism (by which they meant Soviet-type societies). They did not, however, define these societies in Marxist terms, as modes of production, but, rather, with the aid of Karl Polanyi's models of economic integration and the Weberian concept of rationality.[230] As is known, Polanyi distinguished four kinds of economic systems: the system of household economy (autarchy), and the reciprocal (symmetric), redistributive (centralised) and exchange-based (market) systems.[231] Konrád and Szelényi adopted these distinctions, and then distinguished *within* the redistributive system between two variants: the *traditional* system, in which the distributing centre is legitimated by tradition, and the *modern* system, in which that centre is justified rationally.[232] The first redistributive system they equated with the Asiatic mode of production, the second with actually existing socialism.

We could schematically present the forms of society distinguished by Konrád and Szelényi as follows:

---

[229] In 1978, the Hungarian edition was published in Vienna with the title *Az értelmiség útja az osztályhatalomhoz*. I have used the English translation: Konrad and Szelényi 1979. In the foreword of this edition, Szelényi describes the experiences of the authors and their manuscript.

[230] Konrad and Szelényi 1979, p. 48.

[231] Polanyi 1957, Chapters 4 and 5.

[232] This distinction between traditional and rational legitimation obviously recalls Weber's distinction between traditional domination which is based on 'the sanctity of the order and the attendant powers of control as they have been handed down from the past, "have always existed"' and bureaucratic rule – 'the exercise of control on the basis of knowledge' (Weber 1972, pp. 129, 130; English translation, pp. 311, 313).

	Asiatic mode of production	Capitalism	Socialism
Economic model	Redistribution	Exchange	Redistribution
Legitimation	Traditional	Rational	Rational
Relationship between economic and political power	Fused	Separate	Fused

Actually existing socialism thus shared characteristics with both other systems, but was simultaneously – in the terminology of Bence and Kis – a society *sui generis*.[233] Within the system of rational redistribution, everything depended on knowledge. Whoever wanted to belong to the redistributing élite had to possess specialist capacities or, to put it differently, had to be an intellectual. Herein lay the reason why Soviet-type societies featured a dichotomous class structure:

> At one pole is an evolving class of intellectuals who occupy the position
> of redistributors, at the other a working class which produces the social
> surplus but has no right of disposition over it. [...] an ever larger fraction
> of the population must be assigned to the intermediate strata.[234]

Although structural social contradictions existed, the intelligentsia itself did not constitute a stable and matured ruling class. Konrád and Szelényi – who, incidentally, did not always use consistently the categories they themselves developed – distinguished between the 'ruling élite' whose members could take important decisions themselves, and a broader stratum of intellectuals. Under Stalin, all power was based on the first-mentioned group, but, subsequently, the élite also tried to co-opt large parts of the intelligentsia:

> In arrogating all power to itself, however, the ruling elite internalised the
> conflicts existing within the intellectual class; [...] if it wished to stabilise

---

[233] Konrád and Szelényi did note a certain historical continuity between traditional and modern redistribution. It seems they were influenced by Wittfogel's *Oriental Despotism*, because they claim that the Russian medieval rulers 'adapted [the Asiatic model of social organisation] to European conditions'. The semi-Asiatic system formed in this way adapted to the changing circumstances, and was finally encompassed by the modern redistribution. Konrad and Szelényi 1979, pp. 88–142.

[234] Konrad and Szelényi 1979, p. 145.

its power it must reach a compromise with the intellectual class, give up its power monopoly, and settle for a hegemony of power within a system of shared rule.[235]

In this sense, the intelligentsia was a ruling class *in statu nascendi*.[236]

The prominent members of the 'Budapest School' who had emigrated in the middle of the 1970s to the West, in due course formulated a critique of the Soviet Union and its allies which was more radical than they had made during their dissident period in Hungary. After initial attempts by Ferenc Féher,[237] Fehér, Heller and Márkus[238] in 1983 together published the study *Dictatorship over Needs*,[239] a substantive work in which – incorporating many previous attempts – a distinctive theory about 'actually existing socialism' was formulated. These authors not only paid attention to political and economic aspects, but also to law, ideology and philosophy. I will limit myself here to examining the two first-mentioned aspects.

Fehér et al. explicitly rejected theories of the degenerated workers' state, state capitalism and bureaucratic collectivism. Although they were of the opinion that the élite had consolidated itself as a separated, homogenous social group,[240] they also drew attention to essential differences between this group and a ruling class in the Marxian sense:

> The members of the apparatus are not constrained to act in a definite way by the position they occupy in the structure of social production; they have to follow consciously the rules and objectives pre-set by the apparatus – otherwise they would be sanctioned. [...] This type of social grouping (quite contrary to the case of class) is based on the primacy of a

[235] Konrad and Szelényi 1979, pp. 186–7.
[236] See also Szelényi 1978–9.
[237] Fehér 1978 and 1980.
[238] Agnes Heller (b. 1929), a philosopher and pupil of Lukács, was excommunicated from the party on the ground of 'mistaken and revisionist views'. Later however she was rehabilitated, and accepted at the Academy of Sciences. After her protest against the invasion of Czechoslovakia, she was again expelled. Because of the great political pressure exerted on her, she left Hungary in 1977 with her husband, the literature researcher Ferenc Fehér (b. 1933) who also was a pupil of Lukács. The philosopher György Márkus (b. 1934) who taught Bence and Kis had studied at the Lomonosov University in Moscow and was, like Heller, expelled in 1973 from the Hungarian Academy of Sciences. See Rivière 1974 and 'Bio-bibliographische Anmerkungen' in Hegedüs et al. 1976, pp. 183–7.
[239] Fehér, Heller and Márkus 1983.
[240] Fehér, Heller and Márkus 1983, pp. 112, 114.

definitely organised group ('corporation') over the individual and it is this which makes the central objective of class analysis – the question of how individuals in a similar objective position reach a common consciousness and organisation – objectless as far as the ruling stratum of these societies in concerned.[241]

Fehér et al. accordingly believed that, instead of the concept of *class*, the concept of *the apparatus* could perform a useful analytical function. The nationalised means of production were not the collective property of bureaucrats – as Rizzi and others had claimed – but of the bureaucratic apparatus as such. An analogy could, these Hungarian Marxists argued, be drawn with the church in feudal Europe, in which property was also corporate.[242]

Just like Ticktin and others, Fehér et al. accentuated the 'anarchic' character of the economies led by this apparatus. They pointed out that planning was far from effective, and, indeed, they went so far as to claim that the command economy embodied the 'exact opposite' of planned economy.[243] That the whole system was able to survive at all, was, in their view, attributable especially to the fact that, beside the official economy, a market economy still existed, which comprised (small) private enterprises as well as a relational economy which via contacts, friendships etc. informally 'regulated' the supply of desired goods (including means of production). As a result, a 'grey' secondary redistribution of incomes occurred and – to a lesser extent – of means of production.[244]

Facing the corporative ruling group, there was an unorganised and amorphous group of direct producers, which, in fact, could not be described as a 'class' anymore than the élite. The lower strata had admittedly shown that they could rise up in explosive revolts, but just as significant was that, after the repression of such revolts, the seemingly almost completely disintegrated ruling apparatus could restore its power again in short order.[245]

---

[241] Féher, Heller and Márkus 1983, pp. 116–17.
[242] Féher, Heller and Márkus 1983, pp. 68–9. The reference is therefore to an *Anstalt* (compulsory association) in the sense that Max Weber applies the term: 'a corporate group the established order of which has, within a given sphere of activity, been successfully imposed on every individual who conforms with certain specific criteria', Weber 1972, p. 28; English translation, p. 138.
[243] Féher, Heller and Márkus 1983, p. 78.
[244] Féher, Heller and Márkus 1983, pp. 99–103.
[245] Féher, Heller and Márkus 1983, p. 127.

All in all, three mutually related processes typified Soviet-type societies: the attempts of the apparatus to shape society after its 'own image' (étatist homogenisation), an antagonistic dichotomy between commanding and commanded labour, and multidimensional group interests, structured by the social division of labour.[246]

Campeanu

Writing under the pen-name of Felipe García Casals, an East-European dissident in 1980 published a number of extremely abstract 'Theses on the Syncretic Society', in which a theory was developed that appeared to refer to the debates current at that time about the 'articulation' of modes of production.[247] Subsequently, it turned out that the Romanian Pavel Campeanu (1920–2003) was hiding behind the pseudonym of García Casals.[248]

Just as Carlo and others had done, Campeanu took the phenomenon of underdevelopment as his starting point. He considered that, for countries underdeveloped by capitalism, there were, in principle, three 'choices': acquiescence, which meant the continuation of underdevelopment; resistance to imperialism by instating a new imperialism (e.g. Germany, Japan); or the Leninist revolution, which combined anti-imperialism and anticapitalism. This last-mentioned strategy was, as history taught, focused on its task:

---

[246] Féher, Heller and Márkus 1983, p. 130.

[247] García Casals 1980a. In an editorial notice accompanying this text it is noted: 'This paper was purportedly written under a pseudonym by a fairly prominent official in one of the East European countries. [...] We do not authenticate its East European origins; rather, we are publishing this piece solely because of its intrinsic interest for Western scholars.' The 'Theses' were republished in the same year with a new 'Introduction'. See García Casals 1980b.

[248] See Campeanu 1986, I, p. ix: 'A few years ago I sent some American academic colleagues a thesis I was working on. I hoped to obtain their critical comments. To my surprise, they arranged, in my absence, to have it published [...].' About Campeanu the book states among other things that: 'He joined the Communist Youth League in 1935 and the Romanian Communist Party in 1940. From 1941 until 1944 he was imprisoned for antifascist activity. Campeanu received a Ph.D. in sociology from the Stefan Gheorghiu Academy in 1960, and from that year until 1980 was head of the Opinion-Polling Department of Romanian television. [...] He is the author of numerous articles published in Romania and elsewhere, and of ten books. [...] He has served as a communications expert with UNESCO [...]. Campeanu was awarded the Prize of the Romanian Academy in 1964 and again in 1977.' (p. 187) See also the semi-autobiographical reflections in Campeanu 2003.

It has promoted the lasting elimination of external imperialist domination and of internal capitalist domination; it has promoted an accelerated industrialization; but it has not promoted the effective transition to a socialist organization of society.[249]

Campeanu's Leninist road was 'syncretic': elements from different types of societies were combined. The forced implantation of a revolutionary social structure in underdeveloped economic relations led to a 'disarticulation', a contradiction between society and economy. A third element was necessary which contained the effects of this contradiction: the (strong) state apparatus. Society as a whole therefore lacked an organic internal bond: 'Premature socialism represents a non-system whose goal is to become a system by harmonizing the economic organization with the social one (and not the other way round).'[250] This then was the reason why little insight was gained by using traditional Marxist concepts. In particular, it was doubtful whether the concept of 'modes of production' under those circumstances could be meaningfully applied.

Campeanu elaborated his thesis by indicating which elements were combined in 'premature socialism'. As socialist elements he itemised, among others, the absence of a ruling class; the considerable facilities for education, housing, social security and recreation; the great vertical mobility, etc. As capitalist elements, he included the compulsion to sell labour-power; the wage form; the market distribution of consumer goods; the absence of influence of wage-workers on decision-making etc. As precapitalist (feudal) elements, he listed, among others, the absence of effective workers' organisations; the low level of labour productivity in comparison to the technological possibilities; and the importance of personal dependencies. A confluence of all these factors into one process occurred:

[T]he various modes of production [...] are articulated in one single economic process. The syncretism of the economy does not consist, therefore, in the plurality of the modes of production, but rather in the heterogeneity of the single functioning mode of production.[251]

---

[249] García Casals 1980a, p. 234.
[250] García Casals 1980a, p. 235.
[251] García Casals 1980a, p. 237.

6.v. Summary

The period after 1968 witnessed the broadest, most varied, and intense debate about the nature of the Soviet Union since the October Revolution of 1917. Although theoretical development of the older currents around Gluckstein (Cliff) and Trotsky-Mandel stagnated, at the same time numerous new hypotheses were proposed. Maoist-inspired authors like Holmberg, Nicolaus, Bettelheim and Chavance defended a new version of the state-capitalist interpretation, which differed from older variants especially in two respects: (i) the transition to capitalism was no longer dated at 1917 or around 1929, but *circa* 1956; (ii) Soviet capitalism was no longer defined as one big capital, but as a conglomerate of many small capitals protected by the state.

Several new versions of 'bureaucratic collectivism' were also formulated. More strongly than Rizzi, Burnham, Shachtman et al., they emphasised the unique character of the alleged new ruling class. It was claimed to have, for example, not an economic but a political foundation (Stojanović), it was claimed that it was not a class in the sense in which capitalism structured classes (Fantham and Machover), or it was claimed that it did not possess an endogenous dynamic (Sweezy).

The most striking feature of this period, however, was the strong revival of interpretations which depicted the Soviet Union as a society *sui generis*, where a consolidated ruling class was said to be absent altogether. The current of 'classless' interpretations, which contained many variations, advanced a number of viewpoints which, in part, could be included in the new generation of 'bureaucratic-collectivist' theories. Thus many authors drew a connection between the underdevelopment of Czarist Russia (specified by some as the existence of a (half-) Asiatic mode of production) and the rise of the 'new system', which, for that reason, could be considered as a kind of non-capitalist development dictatorship (Carlo, Melotti, Dutschke, Bahro, Schmiederer et al., Campeanu).

Secondly, many authors emphasised the contradiction between intellectual and manual labour, or an aspect of it, as the essential cause of social contradictions (Eggert, S.Z. Tübingen, Eichwede and Kaiser, Damus, Bahro, Konrád and Szelényi).

Thirdly, attention was focused on structural imbalances in the Soviet economy: it was claimed that there was a growing contradiction between productive forces and production relations, increasing inefficiency or waste

(Carlo, Altvater and Neusüss, Conert, Ticktin, Féher et al.). Some authors even went so far as to characterise the Soviet Union as an historical impasse (Zimin, Ticktin).

A fundamental difference of opinion however existed about the question of whether the political élite consciously directed the social process (Damus, Bahro, Schmiederer et al.), or whether it was seriously restricted in its leadership capacity by structural causes (Ticktin, Fehér et al.).

Chapter Seven

The Collapse and Its Aftermath:
From 1985 to the Present

The appointment in March 1985 of Mikhail S. Gorbachev as General Secretary of the CPSU heralded the demise of the Soviet Union. Very soon after accepting his post, Gorbachev went public with hitherto unprecedented official criticisms of the social, economic and political structures of the USSR. During the plenary session of the Central Committee of the CPSU in June 1987, he presented his 'basic theses' and called for *perestroika* [restructuring] of the economy. The attempts at 'modernisation' that followed – such as the Law on State Enterprises (1987), the Joint Venture Law (1987) and the Law on Cooperatives (1988) – were nevertheless accompanied by an accelerating economic decline: output levels fell, while prices rose. At the same time, the new politics of *glasnost* [openness] – which, for a while, gave Gorbachev a positive image in the West – facilitated the expression of social, ethnic and nationalist protest.

The failed conservative coup d'état in August 1991 dealt a death-blow to Gorbachev's intended reform project. In the weeks after the coup, more and more Soviet republics declared their independence; in November 1991, Boris Yeltsin decreed the dissolution of the CPSU in the Russian Republic; and, in December, the Soviet Union was formally dissolved altogether in favour of a Commonwealth of Independent States (initially involving the Russian, Ukranian and Belorussian republics). The 'free fall' in the direction of an unregulated market capitalism continued in subsequent years. The economic crisis and a 'dirty war' in Chechnya sometimes caused resistance and revolts, but more often led to demoralisation among the population. In 2000, President Yeltsin was succeeded by his protégé Vladimir Putin, whose policy has focused on restoring a 'strong state' which can keep economic forces in the country under control, promoting a work ethic, taking tough action against separatists, and projecting a new military grandeur.

7.i. Theories of (state) capitalism

The current around Cliff and its critics

The downfall of the Soviet Union necessitated an important but seldomly explicitly recognised theoretical about-turn for Tony Cliff and his supporters. After all, they had originally assumed that state capitalism represented a *higher* stage of development than Western capitalism. Thus Cliff had, in 1948, referred to the USSR as 'the extreme theoretical limit which capitalism can reach' and as 'a transition stage to socialism, this side of the socialist revolution'.[1] In the 1940s, this interpretation had some plausibility, because the Soviet economy seemed more dynamic than that of the West. But, when it became clear in subsequent decades that the Soviet economy had run into a structural impasse, Cliff and his supporters de-emphasised this aspect of their theory, without, however, offering any explicit defence of the revision.[2] Initially, they could hardly conceive of a *collapse* of state capitalism and the regression to a 'lower' stage of private capitalism which that would imply. As late as 1987, Mike Haynes criticised anyone who believed that the crisis of Soviet society was terminal, and that it was rooted in the unique characteristics of the USSR. Haynes argued specifically that:

[1] Cliff 1948a, p. 62; reprint 2003, p. 58.
[2] See also *Aufheben* 1997, p. 34.

i)   The Soviet economy has historically shown itself to be a dynamic economy.

ii) The dynamic of this economy arises from its competitive interaction with the West.

iii) This dynamic is internalised in the Soviet Union and reproduced in its wider relations.

iv) [The] Soviet economy has shown sufficient drive to not only prevent the gap with the advanced West widening but to narrow it both absolutely and relatively.[3]

Haynes did not deny that the Soviet economy was experiencing difficulties, but he emphasised that 'crisis is a *relative* concept'[4] and that 'economic difficulties and constraints affect all of the world's major economies'.[5] The 'existing rigid and ossified structures' had certainly slowed down the accumulation process in the Soviet Union, and – together with a number of 'drag factors' – caused a 'falling rate of profit',[6] but the consequences of that development should not be exaggerated. Precisely because the Soviet economy, despite its specific characteristics, was capitalist like so many other economies, 'we can consider a whole series of stopping points before we arrive at free market capitalism'.

But, around 1990, it became more and more apparent that the Soviet economy was no longer capable of withstanding competition from the West. In the summer of 1990, Chris Harman accordingly argued that rapid industrialisation under Stalinist rule was able to take place from the 1930s until the 1960s because external trade links during those years had been reduced to a minimum; this policy had subsequently reached a limit, because of the growing internationalisation of the world economy. In the long run, the USSR had not been able to avoid the impact of a new international division of labour. The consequence was a 'normal' accumulation crisis, which forced the bureaucracy 'to try to change its ways'.[7]

---

[3] Haynes 1987, p. 13.
[4] Haynes 1987, p. 14.
[5] Haynes 1987, p. 15.
[6] Haynes 1987, p. 27. Haynes named four 'drag factors': (1) the maturation of the economy; (2) its low level of development; (3) the arms burden; and (4) the relative isolation of the economy.
[7] Harman 1990b, p. 154.

This interpretation continued to be the dominant one. Thus, Mike Haynes and Pete Glatter explained in 1998, through the 1970s and 1980s it had become increasingly clearer that 'from a global point of view, Russia had the wrong type of industry in the wrong place; plants were too large, turning out too diversified a range of products with equipment that was less efficient than that elsewhere in the world economy'.[8] Radical interventions in the system had become unavoidable, even although these had seriously divided the ruling class.[9] The provisional result was 'paralysing confusion evident everywhere', a hybrid combination of markets, state capital and mafia practices, with substantially the same people in power who had also ruled in the Soviet Union.

Criticisms. Much of the criticism of the position of Cliff and his supporters related to methodological issues, and amounted, in essence, to the idea that they could define the USSR as 'state-capitalist' only by reasoning with dubious analogies of the following sort:

i.   in capitalism of type X, Y occurred;
ii. Y occurred in the Soviet Union;
iii. therefore, the Soviet Union is capitalist.

Frank Füredi gave several examples which he regarded as representative of this schematic style of argumentation, including Cliff's 'discovery' that there were cases within capitalism where use-values had become the aim of capitalist production (namely, war economies). 'Since use-values are also the aim of Soviet production it followed, once again, that both systems were the same.'[10] Füredi considered this analogy not just logically flawed, but also empirically false; even in capitalist war-economies, the production of use-values was never a goal in itself:

> The production of use-values remained very much subject to the law of value. As the British ruling class knows only too well, it didn't get its guns

---

[8] Haynes and Glatter 1998, p. 49.
[9] Haynes and Glatter 1998, p. 49. Cliff 1991 had earlier pointed out, that introducing 'a real market economy' in the USSR would have meant 'a massive amount of unemployment', and that this problem had split the ruling class 'in all sorts of ways which are always shifting'.
[10] Richards 1987, p. 101.

for free. The discipline of the law of value imposed itself most painfully through the loss of important foreign assets, which Britain had to sell off to meet debts run up with the USA.[11]

Mandel commented that theories of capitalism like those by Cliff failed to explain why no crisis of overproduction had occurred in the Soviet Union since the late 1920s.[12] Of course, the former USSR had been experiencing 'a specific systemic crisis', but this crisis was very different in nature: 'you cannot explain empty shops to be just a variant of (over) full shops, underproduction of use values as a variant of overproduction of commodities'.[13]

Daum and his critics

In 1990, the mathematician Walter Daum presented a new theory of capitalism developed in previous years by the small New York-based League for the Revolutionary Party.[14] Partly inspired by James/Dunayevskaya and Kuroń/Modzelewski,[15] Daum proposed in his book *The Life and Death of Stalinism* both a new periodisation of the transition to capitalism, and a new definition of capitalism itself. Until the middle of the 1930s, he argued, developments had occurred as Trotsky had analysed them, but, in subsequent years – 1936 being the turning point – a counterrevolution had occurred, culminating in a restoration of capitalism. This change was the result of two developments: *internally*, the first Five Year Plan had led to chaos: 'Disproportions were rampant: factories lacked materials and workers; inflation skyrocketed through 1933, and in that year there was a precipitous and unplanned decline in investments.'[16]

And, *externally*, the defeat of the German workers' movement and the international advance of fascism had dealt a heavy blow. In response to this double crisis, the Stalinist bureaucracy made a new turn. Foreign policy from now on became definitely counterrevolutionary, as shown by the deliberate

---

[11] Richards 1987, p. 102.
[12] Mandel 1992, p. 141.
[13] Mandel 1992, pp. 141–2.
[14] The League for the Revolutionary Party was founded in 1976 after a conflict in the Revolutionary Socialist League, which, in turn, had emerged from a split in 1973 from the International Socialists in the United States. See Landy 1997.
[15] Daum 1990, p. 22.
[16] Daum 1990, p. 165.

undermining of the resistance against the Francoists in Spain and the promotion of 'popular-front' policies elsewhere. From 1934–5, 'the USSR has always played a conservative role on the world stage, safeguarding its own interests both in collaboration and in conflict with Western imperialism'.[17] On the domestic front, a drastic turn to the right occurred: Russian nationalism was promoted while minority nations were oppressed, and the Great Purges were instrumental in establishing tight political control over the party, the army and industrial bureaucracies. Competition between workers was encouraged (Stakhanovism), piece wages became increasingly common and labour laws became increasingly strict.

Formally speaking, the Soviet economy was also centralised further in these years via a planning system which, in practice, meant 'administration by fiat'.[18] But this planning, in reality, strongly promoted the decentralisation of the economy – a fact 'overlooked by Marxists of every stripe'.[19] Crucial had been the introduction in 1936 of economic accountability for enterprises, through which Soviet firms became legally independent.

Managers, whose economic stake was in their own firms' success, not in that of society, became agents of the economic laws of capital. They sought to discipline their workers and to accumulate, centralise and modernise capital – not according to the needs of the nation and certainly not according to the needs and rights of the workers – but in order to maximise the value and surplus-value at their disposal. The central bureaucracy, representing the interests of the rulers as a whole, had to balance its demands against the specific interests of its local agents.[20]

Daum called the system emerging in this way a 'pseudo-socialist capitalism' or 'statified capitalism'.[21] This capitalism did not compete on the world market with Western capitalism, as Cliff argued, but, to the contrary, strove for autarchy, 'capitalism in one country'. In contrast to Mandel, Cliff and others, Daum did not believe that competition was an essential aspect of capitalism. He defined the essential driving force of capitalism as 'the drive to accumulate, the struggle between capital and labor, at bottom the exploitation

---

[17] Daum 1990, p. 171.
[18] Daum 1990, p. 176.
[19] Daum 1990, p. 177.
[20] Daum 1990, p. 180.
[21] Daum 1990, p. 197.

of proletarians through the wage system'.[22] As soon as 'the surplus labor is extracted through wage labor' in an economy, then capitalism existed.[23] Competition, however, was only a 'surface manifestation' of this drive to accumulate surplus labour.[24]

The striving for autarchic accumulation was 'a natural choice for nationalist rulers in formerly colonized or economically backward countries since it helps them keep surplus value at home; it perpetuates the nation where traditional capitalism can no longer do'.[25] The system's primary social aim of production was *'to preserve and maximize the value of the national capital as a whole* – that is, the state-owned capital within the national boundaries'.[26]

This primary goal operated 'in conjunction – and often at variance – with the narrower goals of local and sectoral bureaucrats: maximizing the value of the firm or sector they are responsible for'.[27] So there was competition after all, but only *within* the domestic economy (cf. Bettelheim). The expressions of this system were 'pseudo-planning' (i.e. bureaucratic management from the top), priority of production over consumption, and a declining rate of accumulation since the 1930s – except for the postwar recovery years – which resulted from the tendency of the rate of profit to decline.

Criticisms. Supporters of the theory of the degenerated workers' state criticised both Daum's periodisation and his characterisation of Soviet capitalism. As regards the first point, if indeed a structural change had occurred in the USSR during in the years 1936–9, how then was it possible that the state structure and even the dictator had remained the same beforehand and afterwards? 'In going over the work methods, the exploitation, the labour code, the purges and the terror', Al Richardson wrote, Daum 'is unable to surmount the problem that the state that implemented them was the same state before and after, which had developed by uninterrupted stages from 1917 onwards.'[28]

---

[22] Daum 1990, p. 50.
[23] Daum 1990, p. 27. '[The] wage-labor relation is the foundation of the bourgeois state.'
[24] Daum 1990, p. 51.
[25] Daum 1990, p. 197.
[26] Daum 1990, pp. 196–7.
[27] Daum 1990, p. 197.
[28] Richardson 1991, p. 36.

Peter Main and Clair Heath criticised in particular Daum's interpretation of capitalism. They reproached him not only for adopting a 'normative' approach – in which an 'ideal type' of capitalism was constructed and the elements of this ideal type were compared with the Soviet Union – but also argued that Daum's ideal type of capitalism itself was untenable. After all, wage-labour occurred not only under capitalism, but also in the post-capitalist transitional society, although its content changed. In a transitional economy, 'wages remain the *form* in which surplus labour is extracted', but 'the wage form no longer expresses the relations of exploitation between capitalist and worker'.[29] Implicitly, Daum seemed to recognise this, because wage-labour was also important in the 1917–36 period, yet Daum did *not* define this earliest period as capitalist.[30]

Main and Heath also made short shrift of the idea that there was capitalist competition in the Soviet Union between enterprises and sectors: 'If there were real competition there would be losers, firms which were inefficient would go out of business and the capital they represented would be destroyed. But this is exactly what did not happen in the Soviet Union.'[31]

Joseph Green, a Marxist-Leninist supporter of a state-capitalism theory, reproached Daum for being inconsistent. After all, Daum claimed that the supposed 'decentralisation' from the 1930s onwards had been of great importance, but he called the same process 'a secondary, surface phenomenon when it was called "competition"'. 'What he offers the reader with one hand (recognition of competitive phenomena in the Soviet economy), he takes back with the other (denigration of the theoretical importance of competition).'[32]

---

[29] Main and Heath 1994, p. 146. The authors base themselves here on Marx's 1875 *Critique of the Gotha Programme*, in the first section of which Marx wrote that 'What we are dealing with here is a communist society, not as it has *developed* on its own foundations, but, on the contrary, just as it *emerges* from capitalist society, which is thus in every respect, economically, morally and intellectually, still stamped with the birth-marks of the old society from whose womb it emerges. Accordingly, the individual producer receives back from society – after the deductions have been made – exactly what he gives to it. [...] Here, obviously, the same principle prevails as that which regulates the exchange of commodities, as far as this is the exchange of equal values. Content and form are changed, because under the altered circumstances no one can give anything except his labour, and because, on the other hand, nothing can pass to the ownership of individuals except individual means of consumption.' Marx 1989, pp. 85–6.

[30] Main and Heath 1994, p. 153.

[31] Main and Heath 1994, p. 157.

[32] Green 1998, p. 34.

Sapir

In the 1980s and early 1990s, the French ex-Maoist economist Jacques Sapir (b. 1947) published a number of books and articles about the class character of the Soviet Union, in which he explored the idea mooted by the Polish economist Oskar Lange that the Soviet Union was a *'sui generis war economy'*:[33]

> I think that, essentially, it can be described as a *sui generis* war economy. Such methods of war economy are not peculiar to socialism because they are also used in capitalist countries in war time. They were developed in the First and Second World Wars. In capitalist countries similar methods were used during the war. [...] It shows clearly that such methods of centralised planning and management are not peculiar to socialism, that they are rather techniques of a war economy. The difficulty starts when these methods of war economy are identified with the essence of socialism and are considered essential to socialism.[34]

Inspired by Bettelheim, Chavance and the so-called regulation school,[35] Sapir interpreted the USSR as a capitalist society that continually existed in an exceptional situation. In *L'Économie mobilisée* (1990), his most important book on the subject, he denied strongly that the Soviet economy was 'one big enterprise'; instead, he regarded it much more as a permanent war economy, in which the state directed industry and agriculture through guaranteeing demand for output. This 'mobilised economy' had emerged already *before* the October Revolution, in 1915–16, and had, despite several political overturns and changes in form, persisted until the end of the 1980s.[36]

> In using the term mobilised economy, one refers in fact to commodity-producing economies, that is to say, where producers and consumers are

---

[33] Lange wrote literally that 'the first period of planning and management in a socialist economy, at least according to our present experience, has always been characterised by administrative management and administrative allocation of resources on the basis of priorities centrally established. Economic incentives are in this period replaced by moral and political appeals to the workers, by appeals to their patriotism and socialist consciousness. This is, so to speak, a highly politicised economy, both as regards the means of planning and management and the incentives it utilises.' Lange 1970, pp. 101–2.

[34] Sapir 1997, pp. 102–3.

[35] For a brief overview of the regulation school, see Boyer 2004.

[36] Sapir 1997, p. 32.

separated, but *non-commercially*, in which the validation of production does not take place through the sale (or lack of sale) of the goods concerned.[37]

Because the state guaranteed the purchase of outputs for a fixed price, the system acquired a different dynamic from ordinary capitalism. Individual enterprises strove for profit-maximisation by maximising their output volumes. They did not compete with each other in sales, but with regard to *input costs*, because they aimed to acquire as many employees and means of production as possible for the lowest possible price. The profit of enterprises no longer functioned as an objective instrument of control, so that other means were necessary to monitor enterprises.[38]

Within this system, 'normal' investment cycles[39] emerged, but, in the long run, a general crisis of the mobilised economy as such was also a possibility. This was evident in three ways:

By the rhythm of growth, which should be superior to that of its potential adversaries to assure a catch-up, overcoming backwardness at a human level (to the order of one or two generations or more); by the technological level of production, which should assure the rulers that they would not be excluded from any options; finally, by the degree of internal social conflicts.[40]

In the Soviet Union, the general crisis of the 1980s led to *perestroika* and *glasnost* as well as to a 'demobilisation' of the economy, i.e. the 're-introduction of commercial practices and functioning'.[41]

Chattopadyay and his critic

The publication of Charles Bettelheim's magnum opus *Class Struggles in the USSR* stimulated the Indian-Canadian economist Paresh Chattopadhyay[42] to new reflections about the Soviet Union over a number of years, which in 1994 were made available in his book *The Marxian Concept of Capital and*

---

[37] Sapir 1997, pp. 38–9.
[38] Sapir 1997, pp. 45–7, 59–89.
[39] Sapir 1997, pp. 120–4; also Sapir 1989.
[40] Sapir 1990, p. 129; see also Sapir 1980.
[41] Sapir 1990, p. 142.
[42] Year of birth not available (communication by Paresh Chattopadhyay, 10 June 2005).

the Soviet Experience. Originally, in the early 1980s, Chattopadhyay had still defined the October Revolution as a proletarian revolution, 'immediately aimed more against the bourgeois state power than against the bourgeois mode of production'.[43] At that time, he argued that a proletarian revolution would, in the first instance, always lead to a dictatorship of the proletariat combining capitalist and socialist elements:

> The dictatorship of the proletariat is not, as such, a complete negation of capital (as a relation); it is rather the conscious preparation for this negation. Capital (along with commodity production) continues to exist over a period for the fundamental reason that the immediate producers cannot collectively dominate overnight the objective conditions of production and it is precisely the task of the proletarian dictatorship to ensure this domination through uninterrupted class struggles during the whole transition period.[44]

Only when the social relations were changed in such a way that the working class came to dominate the objective conditions of production, socialism could, as the first phase of communism, begin. That, however, failed to happen, because, around 1930, capital had been able to consolidate its power. In later years, Chattopdahyay revised this argument implicitly and began to deny the proletarian content of the October Revolution, because 'first, the seizure of power was not a self-emancipating act of the laboring masses (themselves) [...], and secondly – as a natural consequence – the regime issued in October was not the proletariat organised as the ruling class, the very first step in a socialist revolution'.[45] In this second, revised interpretation, as expounded in his book, the October Revolution was in fact a *bourgeois* revolution which introduced *capitalist* production relations in a pre-capitalist environment. Stalin's 'revolution from above' represented no more than a change in social form:

> What basically happened was that wage labor was generalised extremely rapidly and on a vast scale, combined with constraints and special operational forms of the economy not inconsistent with a capitalist 'war

---

[43] Chattopadhyay 1981 (II), p. 1104.
[44] Chattopadhyay 1981 (I), p. 1066; (III), p. 1157.
[45] Chattopadhyay 1994, p. 154. See also the substantiation of this thesis in Chattopadhyay 2004, pp. 117–23.

economy in peacetime,' particularly given the 'catching up with and surpassing' exigency of capital accumulation in a situation of economic-technological backwardness.[46]

In contrast to Cliff and his supporters, Chattopadhyay thought that the Soviet Union could be studied 'as a basically closed economy', although he did not deny the significance of international economic relations.[47] In order to prove that the Soviet Union as isolated unit of analysis was nevertheless capitalist, Chattopadhyay had to show not just that the workers were 'free' wage-workers in Marx's sense – which he did by pointing to the separation of 'free' workers from their means of production[48] –, but he also had to make plausible the idea that competition between capitals occurred *within* the USSR, even though the Soviet Union was one big conglomerate. He accomplished this by appealing to Marx's distinction between 'total social capital' and 'many capitals'. In *Capital*, Volume II, Marx had written that 'each individual capital forms only a fraction of the total social capital, a fraction that has acquired independence and been endowed with individual life, so to speak, just as each individual capitalist is no more than an element of the capitalist class'.[49] Chattopadhyay deduced from this idea that 'each capital is *not* independent in an *absolute* sense'.[50] In the Soviet Union, the social total capital was centralised in the state, while the individual enterprises formed individual capitals. Total social capital was the '*essential* reality', while singular capitals were the '*phenomenal* reality'.[51]

Competition of capitals existed, according to Chattopadhyay,

> whenever the process of total social production is split among *reciprocally autonomous* units of production each of which, based on the double freedom of the producers, exchanges with other units the products of labor in (money) commodity form, whatever be the specific juridical *form* of property in the means of production or the specific *form* of exchange of commodities (including labor power as a commodity).[52]

---

[46] Chattopadhyay 1994, p. 158.
[47] Chattopadhyay 1994, p. xiii; 2004, pp. 112–13.
[48] Chattopadhyay 1994, pp. 13, 50.
[49] Marx 1978, p. 427.
[50] Chattopadhyay 1987, p. 7; Chattopadhyay 1994, pp. 20, 42–4.
[51] Chattopadhyay 1994, p. 12; Chattopadhyay 1992, pp. 77, 114.
[52] Chattopadhyay 1994, p. 54.

The competition between separate capitals was proved by 'the exchange of the means of production, taking the commodity form, between Soviet enterprises based on wage labor'.[53]

The accumulation process which emerged through this competition was based on extensive growth. Because of 'the shortage of cadres and skilled workers, availability of labor force with a low level of education, and largely underutilised natural wealth of the country', extensive growth was the obvious choice in the first instance by mobilising unused energy and raw materials.[54] In this accumulation process, the growth of the means of production had the absolute priority over producing consumer goods. But this type of growth obviously encountered 'an insurmountable resource barrier', as had become apparent during the Seventh Plan, 1961–5.[55] The step to intensive accumulation could however not be made: 'Soviet capitalism continued to function as a mobilization economy and was unable to demobilize itself with corresponding changes in economic organization following the requirements of enlarged reproduction in the new situation.' In this way, an *absolute overaccumulation crisis* emerged, culminating in a terminal crisis of the system.[56] The collapse only meant a change in form of capitalism, as indicated also by 'workers' massive *indifference* to the changes, initiated – as usual – from "above"'.[57]

Criticism. When Chattopadhyay proposed some of his ideas in the 1980s, the Belgian Marxist Guy Desolre attacked him on several fronts. Not only did Desolre advance empirical arguments against the claims that generalised commodity production and competition between enterprises existed in the USSR, but he also attacked Chattopadhyay's 'translation' of Marx's concept of 'social total capital' to Soviet society. Desolre argued that this was just playing with words, rather than a serious interpretation of Marx:

> Marx referred to *total social capital* and to *social capital* (the capital of directly associated individuals) in two totally different ways. It is therefore useless

---

[53] Chattopadhyay 1994, p. 50.
[54] Chattopadhyay 1994, p. 86.
[55] Chattopadhyay 1994, p. 88.
[56] Chattopadhyay 1994, p. 40. Chattopadhyay follows Marx (1981, p. 260) who stated that the 'absolute overproduction of capital' occurs when the fall of the rate of profit would be accompanied by 'an absolute decline in the mass of profit [...], so that the mass of surplus-value, too, could not be increased'.
[57] Chattopadhyay 1994, p. 159.

if one tries to make him say that the two could be conflated in one capital only, of which the members of the bureaucracy would somehow be the collective shareholders.[58]

Fernandez

Neil Fernandez (b. 1964) was active in various British anti-Bolshevik communist projects since the 1980s, such as the journal *A Communist Effort* (1984–5) and the London-based 'Red Menace' collective (1989–90).[59] In his book *Capitalism and Class Struggle in the USSR* (1997), Fernandez tried to develop an autonomist analysis.[60] Elaborating on earlier publications,[61] Fernandez sought to show that what he considered the three defining characteristics of capitalism (namely commodities, wage-labour and production for profit) had all existed in the Soviet Union.

In order to prove that the Soviet economy was based on the production, distribution and consumption of commodities, Fernandez examined each of these aspects of the economy. The sphere of consumption posed few problems, because 'the basic relationship was one of purchase and sale'.[62] Proof was more difficult with regard to the distribution of producer and consumer goods; these, after all, occurred through barter and competition between enterprises and, as far as the wholesaling of consumer goods were concerned, fairs. Fernandez, however, defines these as relations of exchange, and therefore as renewed commodification.[63] The argumentation became more complex with regard to the sphere of production. Fernandez concluded that the workers were exploited, while managers competed with each other and with the members of the central bureaucratic élite for supplies and personnel, using a 'characteristic mix of manoeuvring, negotiation, bargaining, and bureaucratic diktat'.[64]

> Certainly, this competition did not operate in a market form; nor could bureaucrats pass on their portions of control to those whom they individually

---

[58] Desolre 1983, p. 229.
[59] Personal communication by Fernandez to the author, June 2005.
[60] The book was 'a contribution to the same area of critique' as the works of Michael Lebowitz (1992) and, especially, Felton Shortall (1994). Ibid.
[61] See especially Fernandez 1989.
[62] Fernandez 1997, p. 117.
[63] Fernandez 1997, pp. 118–22.
[64] Fernandez 1997, p. 126.

chose as their successors. Instead, control was passed on through a mixture of bureaucratic appointment and unofficial *blat* distribution, including via the inheritance of privilege and the 'education' system.[65]

Despite these observations, Fernandez nevertheless identified capitalist relations in this sphere as well:

> [Since] there was privative appropriation, and there was also competition among bureaucrats (post-holders) each of whom possessed a portion of control over the means of production (and hence over the extraction of the surplus product), then it is clear that this competition was itself neither more nor less than the *system wherein portions of such privatively-appropriated control were exchanged*. And anything exchanged (and mediated through labour) is by definition a commodity.[66]

Labour-power was a commodity in the USSR, because 'the wage-packet given to the worker in return for her labour-power was real rather than nominal'.[67] And, finally, the Soviet Union featured also a constant striving to accumulate a surplus applied for expanded production.

After he believed to have proved in this way that the USSR was not just based on generalised exchange, but also featured a generalised drive for accumulation, Fernandez concludes 'It follows that it was capitalism.'[68] But not a state capitalism (a category which Fernandez regards as having no valid application), because 'privative appropriation always held full sway in the USSR'[69] – and not a Western capitalism either, where 'considerations of currency-dominated accumulation' were supreme.[70] Rather, it was a kind of bureaucratic capitalism:

> wherein portions of control over labour-power, labour, the product, and the productive forces in general – portions taking the form of permission, clout and *blat* – were negotiated, exchanged, and crucially, invested in production with the aim of accumulation.[71]

---

[65] Fernandez 1997, p. 127. *Blat* is the use of personal contacts, influence or bribery to acquire goods and services.
[66] Ibid.
[67] Fernandez 1997, p. 129.
[68] Fernandez 1997, p. 132.
[69] Fernandez 1997, p. 140.
[70] Fernandez 1997, p. 137.
[71] Fernandez 1997, pp. 136–7.

In this system, money had taken the form of 'bureaucratic forms of permission, and, more generally, *blat*'.[72]

Aufheben

The autonomist group *Aufheben* originating from Brighton, England developed a theory of capitalism in the late 1990s which tried to integrate insights from Ticktin's analysis. They argued Ticktin had, in the last instance, wrongly characterised the USSR – on the one hand, because he saw the essence of capitalism in terms of the operation of the law of value, and, on the other hand, because he did not see through the reified nature of the categories of political economy[73] – but, nevertheless, Ticktin had 'given the most plausible explanation and description of the decline and fall of the USSR'.[74] Ticktin's writings clarified that any understanding of the USSR had to 'explain the systematic waste and inefficiencies that it produced. If the USSR was in any way capitalist it must have been a deformed capitalism'.[75]

The group rejected 'the vulgar interpretation of orthodox Marxism which simply sees capitalism as a profit driven system based on private property and the "anarchy of the market"'.[76] Not the law of value formed the essence of capitalism, but 'the self-expansion of alienated labour: the creative and productive power of human activity that becomes an alien force that subsumes human will and needs to its own autonomous expansion'.[77] The fact that Soviet workers were separated both from means of production and means of subsistence made the USSR a capitalist society, even although virtually no private ownwership of means of production existed. But this conclusion was only the beginning. Because, if the Soviet Union was capitalist, why did it feature so many chararacteristics which *prima facie* were not capitalist? If no commodity production occurred, how then could there be value and surplus-value?[78]

---

[72] Fernandez 1997, p. 142.
[73] *Aufheben* 1998, pp. 40–1.
[74] *Aufheben* 2000, p. 32.
[75] *Aufheben* 1998, p. 38.
[76] *Aufheben* 2000, p. 30.
[77] Ibid.
[78] Ibid.

To solve this problem, *Aufheben* developed an idiosyncratic theory which combined ideas taken from Ticktin and Bordiga. The group proposed 'to follow Ticktin and consider the USSR as a transitional social formation, but, following insights of Bordiga and the Italian Left, we do not propose to grasp the USSR as having been in transition from capitalism, but as a social formation in transition *to* capitalism'.[79] After the proletarian revolution of 1917 had led to nothing and a new state bureaucracy had seized power, *national capitalist development* was on the agenda. Because of the underdeveloped nature of the Russian economy, this required first of all the growth of the stock of productive capital. Because, until that time, merchant capital and money-capital had restricted industrial development, the new élite was forced to restrict the free operation of markets. In this way, a 'productivist' variant of an early capitalist society emerged. The associated suppression of money capital meant that money was reduced to 'a mere fleeting means of circulation'.[80] The value of capital could not be expressed in money, but only in use-values.

In this underdeveloped capitalism, the producer goods and consumer goods being created did have the commodity form, and only a limited type of commodity circulation occurred, but in a way different from developed capitalism: 'the values of the commodities produced by each capital were not validated or realised through the act of their transformation into money but were *pre-validated* by their recognition as values by the state'.[81] Thus money was functional especially for productive capital, and was not a generalised independent expression of value. This had two consequences. Firstly, the buying power of money remained limited:

> While everyone needed money, it was insufficient to meet all needs. As a consequence, non-monetary social relations had to be preserved. Influence and favours with those in authority, client relations, etc. – that is the system known as 'blat' – became salient features of the Soviet bureaucracy as means of gaining access to privileged goods or as a means of getting things done.[82]

---

[79] *Aufheben* 2000, pp. 33, 46.
[80] *Aufheben* 2000, p. 44.
[81] *Aufheben* 2000, p. 43.
[82] *Aufheben* 2000, p. 44.

Secondly, the restricted function of money meant that wages hardly functioned as material incentives, because why should one work harder, if one could buy nothing with the additional earnings? Because the forced accumulation process additionally led to shortages of labour, the managers had neither a 'carrot' nor a 'stick' to control the workers.

> Confronted by the imperative to appropriate surplus-value in the form of increased production imposed through the central plan on the one hand, and the power of the workers over the labour-process on the other hand, the management of the state enterprises resolved the dilemma by sacrificing quality for quantity. This was possible because the technical and social needs embodied in the use-values of the commodities they produced were not derived from those who were to use these commodities, but were prescribed independently by the central plan.[83]

The result was an endemic production of defective use-values. And, to the extent that defective use-values from one branch of production were utilised in other branches, 'the chronic production of useless products' increased.[84]

As a whole, the Soviet Union was a kind of deformed capitalism, in which capital predominantly accumulated in the form of use-values, while these use-values themselves were, to an important extent, defective.

> Hence, whereas in a fully developed capitalism the class conflicts at the point of production are resolved through the waste of recurrent acute economic crises which restore the industrial reserve army and the power of capital over labour, in the USSR these conflicts were resolved through the chronic and systematic waste of defective production.[85]

Sandemose

The Norwegian philosopher Jørgen Sandemose (b. 1945), who incorporated the insights of among others Tony Cliff, Rita di Leo and Hillel Ticktin in his writings, worked on his own theory of state capitalism from the 1970s onwards.[86] This theory was first systematically presented in his book *State*,

---

[83] *Aufheben* 2000, p. 45.
[84] *Aufheben* 2000, p. 46.
[85] Ibid.
[86] See in particular Sandemose 1976.

Religion, Economy (2002), which demonstrated an ambitious general analysis of diverse 'capitalist forms'. Sandemose endorsed Cliff's thesis that the Soviet Union constituted 'one big capital'. But he did not share Cliff's idea that this capital, considered in isolation, was 'one big factory'. To the contrary, he argued that the *real subsumption* of labour under capital had never succeeded in the USSR; there was only a *formal subsumption*.[87] Soviet capital showed the same characteristics as the manufactories described by Marx, in which 'the organisation of the social labour process is [...] a combination of specialised workers'.[88] In both cases, 'the workers had a very great autonomy, and capital is constantly compelled to wrestle with the subordination of the workers.'[89]

Because most means of production within the Soviet Union were not tradeable commodities, unlike consumer goods, Sandemose treats the total surplus-value as being equal to the state income from the turnover tax on means of consumption.[90] Next, he attempts to render plausible – using economic reproduction schemes – that the manufacturing character of Soviet capital only permitted 'absolute surplus-value', and thus reached an inevitable limit, while any transition to real subsumption appeared impossible, both because productive investments would reduce the size of the working class and cause a falling rate of profit, and because the inherent position of power of the working class prevented such a development. It seemed that the growth of the arms industry as a 'non-reproductive' sector could provide a way out for some time, but this ultimately also failed to prevent the terminal crisis of the system.[91]

Resnick/Wolff and their critics

In 2002, the US economists Stephen Resnick (b. 1938) and Richard Wolff (b. 1942) – associated with the postmodernist-Marxist journal *Rethinking Marxism* – presented a 'capitalist' characterisation of the Soviet Union in their book *Class Theory and History*.[92] They based themselves on a unique

---

[87] Sandemose 2002, p. 203. See also Mohun's theory, discussed in 6.ii.
[88] Marx 1976, p. 508; Sandemose 2002, pp. 223–4.
[89] Sandemose 2002, pp. 490, 202–3.
[90] Sandemose 2002, pp. 209–10.
[91] Sandemose 2002, pp. 450–65.
[92] See also their preparatory studies: Resnick and Wolff 1993, 1994a, 1994b, 1994c, 1994d.

class theory, according to which society must be viewed as a totality of overdetermined processes, i.e. a complex whole in which every process 'is determined by each and every other process constituting that society'.[93] There existed innumerable 'entry points' to explore this totality, and no one entry point can be conceived as 'the essential cause or determinant of any other process(es) in the society'.[94] Marxian social theory's entry point was class, defined here as the economic process of 'producing and appropriating surplus labor'.[95]

In Resnick and Wolff's theory, two kinds of class processes exist: fundamental and subsumed. The fundamental class process concerns the production of the surplus-product by one class for the other. Subsumed class processes encompass the distribution of this surplus-product between other classes. In a capitalist society, productive workers and industrial capitalists are personifications of the fundamental class process, while landlords, unproductive workers or supervisory managers are personifications of subsumed class processes.[96]

Thus, by highlighting the social organisation of surplus, Resnick & Wolff claimed that the Soviet Union was state-capitalist, where state capitalism is defined as the co-existence and interaction of two processes, namely capitalist production, appropriation and distribution of the surplus on the one side, and, on the other side, 'processes that place state officials (rather than private individuals) in the class position of appropriators and distributors of the surplus'.[97]

On the assumption that there was no socialism or communism in the Soviet Union, but, instead, an exploitative class structure, Resnick & Wolff provided two arguments for the existence of capitalist production, appropriation and distribution. In the first place, they claimed that there exist only three 'basically different kinds of exploitative class structures' (slave, feudal and capitalist), and that two of them – slavery and feudalism – certainly did not dominate in the USSR, leaving capitalism as the only other possibility.[98] Moreover, the

---

[93] Resnick and Wolff 1987, p. 2.
[94] Resnick and Wolff 1987, p. 26.
[95] Resnick and Wolff 1987, p. 20.
[96] Resnick and Wolff 1987, pp. 109–63; see also Resnick and Wolff 2002, pp. 51–81.
[97] Resnick and Wolff 2002, p. 85.
[98] Resnick and Wolff 2002, pp. 88–90.

Soviet workers were faced with a kind of structural coercion very similar to capitalist relations: 'workers "freedoms" from individual property in means of production or means of survival other than employment in state-owned enterprises under exploitative conditions led them to "choose" to sell their own labor power.'[99]

On the basis of these considerations, Resnick & Wolff elaborately reconstructed the historic rise and downfall of the Soviet Union. State capitalism, in their view, began already with the revolution of 1917, which was not a revolution but a reform, a transition from one form of capitalism to another.[100] Just like Bettelheim, whose work inspired these authors,[101] they explained this development *subjectively*, by referring to the consciousness of the leadership:

> Unable to conceptualize, let alone disseminate, the class (qua surplus labor) issue, Soviet political, economic, and cultural leaders were unable to take advantage of the truly revolutionary change they had actually created in their own society. On the class issue, they were as theoretically underdeveloped as the supposedly backward farmers they sought to manage.[102]

The new state capitalism interacted with 'continuing and pervasive private ancient, feudal, capitalist, and through the 1930s even communist class structures at different social sites.'[103] 'Under war communism and the NEP, the new state and the Communist Party succeeded in developing that state capitalism: more industrial output, workers and capacity.'[104] This development did not however occur without contradictions: 'When war communism's contradictions overwhelmed its benefits in accumulating capital for state capitalist industry and for the USSR's survival, NEP arrived. When the NEP's contradictions overwhelmed its benefits for the same goals, the collectivization of agriculture arrived'[105] – a process in which, though briefly, 'communist class structures' became visible.[106]

---

[99] Resnick and Wolff 2002, p. 90.
[100] Resnick and Wolff 2002, pp. 151–2.
[101] Resnick and Wolff 2002, p. xiv, note 6.
[102] Resnick and Wolff 2002, p. 247.
[103] Resnick and Wolff 2002, p. 164.
[104] Resnick and Wolff 2002, p. 229.
[105] Resnick and Wolff 2002, p. 230.
[106] Resnick and Wolff 2002, pp. 245–7.

The new accumulation structure experienced more and more difficulties in the course of the following decades. Job security stood in the way of the automation of production processes (replacement of workers by machines) and the continuous growth of the number of unproductive workers (clerks, managers, etc.) meant a growing imposition on the surplus-product. 'The Soviet state could neither appropriate enough surplus in state capitalist enterprises nor siphon enough surplus away from other class structures nor find other revenues sufficient to secure its own survival even to the end of the 1980s.'[107] The restoration of the private capitalism, which had been abolished in 1917, was the result.

The rise and downfall of Soviet state capitalism ultimately expressed a broader trend in the twentieth century:

> The century's first half displays tendencies of transition from private to state capitalisms. The second half moves in the reverse direction. The specific problems of the private capitalisms inherited from the nineteenth century included their growing difficulties in appropriating enough surplus to secure their non-class conditions of existence. These problems eventuated in crises that were resolved by solutions that ranged from state-regulated to state-managed to state-owned-and-operated capitalisms. The rightist versions in Nazi-Germany, fascist Italy, and Imperial Japan focused on military aggression. On the left, the post-1917 USSR was the longest sustained and most globally influential of these statist solutions. In the reverse movements provoked by the 1970s crises of state-regulated, state-managed and state-run capitalisms, the solutions entailed returns to various form of more private capitalism. The post-Soviet return to private capitalism has been the starkest example.[108]

Criticisms. Simon Clarke considered the study by Resnick/Wolff methodologically weak, among other things because they devoted no attention to the forces of production, and because

---

[107] Resnick and Wolff 2002, p. 310.
[108] Ibid.

Marx's analysis did not centre on *who* appropriated the surplus, but on the prior question of the *social form* of the production and appropriation of a surplus, which cannot be separated from the question of the social basis of the power to appropriate a surplus. A surplus cannot be conceptualised independently of the social form of its production and appropriation, so it is impossible to identify *whom* it is who appropriates the surplus without an analysis of the social form of its production, which Resnick and Wolff do not provide.[109]

Clarke strongly denied that capitalism was the dominant social form of production in the USSR, except possibly in the period of the New Economic Policy in the 1920s. He offered a series of empirical arguments:

Goods and services were not produced as values, so production was not and could not be subordinated to the production and appropriation of surplus value. Enterprises and organisations were required to deliver particular goods and services at particular times to other enterprises and organisations. They were required to provide means of collective consumption and wages to their workers according to centrally determined norms. Prices were attached to goods and services, so that enterprises and organisations could nominally make profits and losses, but these were accounting prices that reflected the physical allocations in the central plan, and monetary balances were purely accounting balances. Money played a significant role only in the payment of wages and in workers' spending, with wages, prices and taxes again adjusted to secure a material balance. Labour was not freely mobile, and wages and the intensity of labour varied considerably between branches of production, while there was no competition between enterprises and organisations and so no tendency to the reduction of labour-time to that socially necessary. The necessary labour-time was determined by centrally defined technical norms, according to the particular equipment installed, to accomodate the very uneven development of the forces of production.[110]

---

[109] Clarke 2004, p. 357.
[110] Clarke 2004, p. 359.

Henry Reichman considered the subjective explanation of the 'failure' of the October Revolution in terms of the inadequate political consciousness of the leadership 'of limited utility at best and certainly non-Marxist (or non-materialist)'.[111] Moreover

> if the success of communism is dependent on its leaders' command of the kind of theoretical sophistication evidenced by Resnick and Wolff, then communism will only succeed under a system even more elitist than Lenin's: Those who 'understand theory' would be like Plato's philosopher-kings.[112]

7.ii. The theory of the degenerated workers' state

Already in 1933, Trotsky had warned that the 'further unhindered development of bureaucratism' in the Soviet Union 'must lead inevitably to the cessation of economic and cultural growth, to a terrible social crisis and to the downward plunge of the entire society'.[113] This prediction seemed to be fully confirmed by the events of 1989–91. But, nevertheless, the theoreticians of the 'degenerated workers' state' found themselves in a difficult predicament with the collapse of the Soviet Union. When, in the 1940s and 1950s, Stalinism had proved more persistent than Trotsky had expected, they had attributed a longer lease of life to the Soviet Union than the 'orthodox' standpoint permitted. To justify this revision, two kinds of arguments could in principle be made: either that contingent historical developments had somehow delayed the collapse, or else that the Soviet Union was structurally more robust than Trotsky had believed. Impressed by the victories of the Soviet armies in World War II and the apparent rapid growth of the Soviet economy afterwards, the second type of argument prevailed for a long time. Typical were the views of Ernest Mandel, who claimed for many years that the Soviet Union would, due to collectively owned means of production, central planning and the state monopoly of foreign trade, be able to develop to ever-higher economic levels. But, even though he continued to maintain for a long time that, on the whole, the

---

[111] Reichman 2004.
[112] Ibid.
[113] Trotsky 1933a, p. 8; English edition, p. 115.

planned Soviet economy was *superior* to capitalist economy,[114] he became much more aware, partly under the influence of Ticktin's writings, of 'monstrous waste and imbalances'.[115] In 1987, he accordingly characterised Soviet society as 'a product of the combination of dynamism and immobility':

> The movement results from the economic and social growth, which is impressive over the long term even if this is slowing down year by year. This growth has profoundly changed the country from what it was in 1940, 1950 or even 1960. The immobility results from the bureaucratic stranglehold on the state and society as a whole. This is an obstacle to future growth. [...] This is the contradiction which is today dominant in the Soviet Union.[116]

Mandel upheld this historical assessment until his death.[117] To explain *perestroika*, he referred to the inability of the Soviet bureaucracy to shift from extensive to intensive growth, with the consequence that 'the Soviet economy missed the boat of the third technological revolution'. The result was Gorbachev's closer collaboration with capitalism.[118]

From the middle of the 1980s, Mandel began to see the downfall of the Soviet economy also in a broader, historically comparative perspective. In particular, he signalled a parallel with the Asiatic mode of production (in classical China, etc.):

---

[114] Mandel 1979a, p. 135. This is a constant theme in Mandel's writings. More than twenty years earlier he has stated: 'The Soviet Union maintains a more or less even rhythm of economic growth, plan after plan, decade after decade, without the progress of the past weighing on the possibilities of the future [...]. All the laws of development of the capitalist economy [...] which provoke a slowdown in the speed of economic growth [...] are eliminated.' Germain 1956, p. 17.

[115] Mandel 1978c, pp. 147–8.

[116] Mandel 1987, p. 8.

[117] Mandel 1992, p. 144. Bureaucratic management 'robs the entire economy of any form of economic rationality' (Mandel 1991a, p. 35).

[118] Mandel 1992, p. 145. In the late 1980s, some erstwhile Mandel supporters, analogously to Isaac Deutscher in the 1950s, began to believe that a part of the Soviet élite led by Gorbachev would enable a transition to socialist democracy without a central role being played by the working class. Thus Tariq Ali stated (Ali 1988, p. xiii): 'Gorbachev represents a progressive, reformist current within the Soviet elite, whose programme, if successful, would represent an enormous gain for socialists and democrats on a world scale. [...] In order to preserve the Soviet Union, Gorbachev needs to complete the political revolution [...] but one based on an abolition of the whole nomenklatura system of privileges on which the power of the Soviet bureaucracy rests.'

In the initial phases of each dynasty, the objective function of the bureaucracy
was to protect the state and the peasantry from the encroachment of the
landed nobility (gentry) in order to permit expanded reproduction (irrigation
works, socialization of the surplus product, guarantee of adequate labour
productivity in the villages, etc.). [...] In this way the bureaucrat remains
dependent on the arbitrariness of the state, never secure in his position. [...]

Therefore, in the second half of each dynastic cycle, an integration of the
landed nobility (gentry) and the bureaucracy often took place. Bureaucrats
became private property owners, first of money and treasure, and then of
the land. [...] To the extent that the state bureaucrats merge with the landed
nobility, the centralization of the social surplus product is undermined;
the state power is weakened; the pressure on the peasantry increased. The
income of the peasantry is reduced; the productivity of agricultural labour
falls; flight from the land, peasant revolts, banditism, uprisings become
common. In the end, the dynasty falls.[119]

In the Soviet Union, something similar happened, according to Mandel. Initially,
in the period 1929–50, there was an 'absolute scarcity of consumption goods'.
But, when this had been overcome, a growing fraction of the bureaucracy
began to push for 'decentralized control over the means of production and
the surplus product'.[120] Central planning was thereby undermined, and 'the
tendency toward the restoration of capitalism' grew.

In summary, the Soviet Union and similar societies are experiencing the
beginning of a transformation of portions of the bureaucracy into a 'ruling
class' – not a 'new bureaucratic ruling class' but the old well-known class
of capitalist and private owners of the means of production.'[121]

Such a restoration could, however, occur only *after* an historic social and
economic defeat of the working class, but, he argued, 'This defeat has not
yet taken place.'[122]

Peter Main and Claire Heath chose a different angle from Mandel, by
adducing contingent historical developments to explain why Trotsky's
prediction seemed to have been realised only after half a century's delay.

[119] Mandel 1985, p. 240.
[120] Mandel 1985, p. 241.
[121] Ibid.
[122] Mandel 1985, p. 242.

Main & Heath pointed out that, after finishing *The Revolution Betrayed* in 1936, Trotsky never wrote any detailed, systematic analyses of the Soviet Union again. But precisely in the last four years of his life, i.e. in the period 1937–40, 'a system of control of the economy' had been established 'which enabled Stalinism to survive longer than Trotsky had predicted'.[123] This system, as described by Mark Harrison,[124]

> was based around the creation of a network of Gosplan plenipotentiaries who were empowered to take whatever action they thought necessary to complete projects that had been prioritised by the political leadership. This same system was instrumental in allowing the maintenance of war production after the invasion of 1941 and for the astonishing creation of new war industries in Siberia prior to the counter-attack of 1943. Thereafter, in the reconstruction phase, the regime was able to utilise the lessons (as well as the actual blueprints, very often) of the First and Second Plans to rebuild the most important infrastructural and industrial projects with much lower 'overhead costs' than in the thirties. In other words, Trotsky's assumption that the economic dislocation caused by bureaucratic planning would eventually reach a pitch where economic collapse would cause the downfall of the regime, was offset by developments of which he appears to have known nothing.[125]

Chattopadhyay identified an important anomaly for the theory of the degenerated workers' state. If the Soviet economy had really been *superior* to capitalism, how was it possible that a restoration of capitalism could have occurred 'without any massive resistance of the producers'?[126]

7.iii. Theories of bureaucratic collectivism

The theoreticians of the new class society also began to relativise the power and efficiency of the bureaucracy. While, previously, Rizzi, Burnham and others had characterised the Soviet Union as a well-oiled, smoothly functioning social system, capable of competing with capitalism in every respect, more emphasis was now put on internal contradictions.

---

[123] Main and Heath 1994, p. 159.
[124] Harrison 1985.
[125] Main and Heath 1994, p. 159.
[126] Chattopadhyay 1994, p. 159.

Loone

In 1990, the Estonian philosopher Eero Loone (b. 1935) argued that the Soviet Union was 'some kind of pre-capitalist socio-economic formation'.[127] The weak dynamic of the productive forces – through which the USSR imported more innovations than it exported – and the virulence of ethnic conflicts suggested as much. Moreover, numerous precapitalist aspects could be found in the Soviet Union, such as slavery in the Gulag, corvée labour at the *kolkhoz* farms, and the feudal renting out of means of production.[128] Quite possibly, elements of the Asiatic mode of production had also been present. The owners of the means of production were not individuals, but collectives, namely the hierarchies around the Politburo, the Party and the Government. Loone did not state unambiguously how, in his view, Soviet society should be characterised, but it was in any case clear to him that 'an advance towards capitalism would be a good thing in the Soviet Union'.[129]

Brenner and his critic

In some writings published in 1989–91, the US historian Robert Brenner (b. 1943), who had previously become famous for his path-breaking contributions to the debate about the European transition from feudalism to capitalism,[130] also portrayed the Soviet Union as a form of society which showed a resemblance with precapitalist societies. The Soviet Union, in his view, was more like 'an old regime society – based on a mix of coercion and corruption – than it resembles advanced capitalism'.[131] Politically, he thus aligned himself with theoreticians of bureaucratic collectivism such as Joseph Carter, who had also characterised the USSR as reactionary.

The logic of the system, according to Brenner, was to be found in the non-capitalist way in which the surplus-product was extracted from the direct producers. The bureaucratic ruling class strove to maximise the total social surplus, because 'the greater the social surplus available to it, the more easily it can achieve any particular aim(s) it might have'.[132] In order to realise this

---

[127] Loone 1990, p. 789. See also Loone 1992, pp. 215–31.
[128] Loone 1990, pp. 782–3.
[129] Loone 1990, p. 791.
[130] Aston and Philpin (eds.) 1985.
[131] Brenner 1991a, p. 29.
[132] Brenner 1991a, p. 27.

maximal output, the bureaucracy was compelled to utilise the labour-power of every worker: 'There is no interest in a surplus army of unemployed if you own the means of production and you are trying to maximize output.'[133] The consequence was a certain attachment of the workers to the means of production (as, for example, Mohun has postulated):

> While workers have little control over their means of production and subsistence, they also have had secure employment. The bureaucracy cannot, as a rule, find it in its own interest to lay people off or fire them. The bureaucracy cannot therefore successfully use the workers' dependence upon unemployment, as can capital, to render them *economically dependent* upon the bureaucracy.
>
> On the contrary, the bureaucracy must seek strictly to control labor mobility so that workers do not capitalize on the bureaucracy's insatiable demand to have their wages bid up by competing firms. Because workers are thus essentially *merged* with their means of production and subsistence, the bureaucracy finds it difficult to subject them to managerial control. Instead, the bureaucracy must squeeze out its surplus by forcing it from the workers, ultimately through its total control of the armed forces and the police.

Because there was no real labour market, labour-power was no commodity either.

This 'quasi-feudal society' owed its dynamic to an important extent to its capitalist surroundings, which forced the rulers to re-invest the surplus and accumulate. At the same time, this accumulation process was structurally handicapped, on the one hand because the productive units and their managers were not stimulated to innovate and produce in response to demand; and, on the other side, because the workers had no say over the surplus, yet also could not be fired from their jobs. For some time, substantial growth could be realised by driving people from the countryside into urban factories, but, at a certain point, this possibility was exhausted. Afterwards, the régime depended on technological innovation at enterprise level for further growth, but, because the possibilities for implementing such innovation in the system were very limited, the process occurred 'at best very haltingly'.[134]

---

[133] Brenner 1989, p. 28.
[134] Brenner 1991a, p. 29.

Given that, at the same time, military and political competition with capitalism continued and because this competition ultimately depended on economic productivity, reforms were inevitable, initially in the form of attempts 'to get the advantages of a market society within that set of non-capitalist property relations'.[135] When that proved unsuccessful, the alternative became capitalism or democratic socialism.

Criticism. Alex Callinicos advanced four arguments in reply to Brenner.[136] Firstly, he claimed that Brenner's explanation of stagnation in the Soviet Union remained too general; what exactly had caused the rise and decline of the assumed bureaucratic mode of production to occur in such an extraordinarily short time (only seventy years)? Secondly, Brenner had underestimated the lack of freedom of the Soviet workers, because labour turnover had also been great in the heyday of the Stalinist era, and, in the period following the Second World War, a genuine labour market had existed, which allocated workers between sectors, regions and enterprises. Thirdly, Brenner had underestimated the efficiency of Stalinism; for a long time, the growth rate in the USSR was high, and the fact that the production of consumer goods trailed behind was due above all to prioritising the arms industry. Finally, Brenner allegedly operated with an 'abstract and normative theory of capitalism',[137] meaning he failed to recognise that within capitalism 'state direction of the economy for the purposes of military competition' could occur.[138]

Finger

An analysis similar to Brenner's was developed after the collapse of the Soviet Union by Barry Finger, a member of the editorial board of the magazine *New Politics* (founded by the ex-Shachtman supporter Julius Jacobson).[139] Finger set out from the idea that 'bureaucratic command economies are necessarily a one-way system, which, by choking off all feedback from below, precludes

---

[135] Brenner 1989, pp. 28–9.
[136] Callinicos 1995, pp. 136–8.
[137] Callinicos 1995, p. 139.
[138] Callinicos 1995, p. 137.
[139] See the contributions in memory of Julius Jacobson (1922–2003) in *New Politics*, New Series, 9–3 (Summer 2003).

a continuous correction process'.[140] This structural defect inevitably caused system-specific obstacles:

> Consequently, disproportionalities cannot be detected until large, multiple bottlenecks dam up the system. But the rate at which the economy can grow is critically dependent, in the final analysis, upon the mass of surplus-labor which can effectively be reapplied. Without an operative feedback mechanism, bureaucratic planning lacks the sensitivity to anticipate and locate potential disruptions.[141]

Seen this way, the continuing priority given to the development of heavy industry became explicable:

> Offsetting this requires an enormous reserve of spare parts, inventories, intermediate goods and semi-finished products, in short, a colossal tie-up of necessary labor in social overhead before an hour of surplus-labor can actually be expended. This is reflected in the hypertrophic growth of the producer goods sector.[142]

The implication was that economic growth undermined itself. The larger the economy became, the more 'points of potential disruption' emerged, with the effect 'that every actual percentage increase in productivity that does occur results in a smaller increment in final output than would be the case under capitalism'.[143] Taking into account the fact that a large part of output was 'sub-standard, even unusable', it became clear that bureaucratic collectivism also contained a tendency towards crisis. This crisis could be postponed for some time by the intensification of labour and by increasing the number of hours worked per year, but these forms of extensive expansion had their limits:

> Output growth, unlike under capitalism, is essentially separated and indeed critically independent of improvements in labor productivity. The *extraction of surplus-labor is primarily an extensive process which is, in effect, exhausted when the absolute limits to the growth of the collective working day are reached.*[144]

---

[140] Finger 1995, p. 173.
[141] Finger 1995, p. 174.
[142] Ibid.
[143] Ibid.
[144] Finger 1995, p. 176.

The point at which these limits were reached depended, among other things, on the natural growth rate of the population, the input of the rural population, and the possibility to draw workforces and material inputs from other countries via 'imperialism'. In the USSR, the end was in sight in the 1980s. Especially the intermediate strata (including the factory and enterprise managers) revolted, because they lacked political power and received instructions which could not be put into practice. The more the central ministries disintegrated, the greater the power of the managers became. But they failed to accomplish any smooth transition to capitalism, given the lack of a viable monetary system and effectively functioning markets:

> Without massive economic intervention on the part of the West, the new
> men of power may find themselves unable to walk on capitalist legs, without
> heavy reliance on bureaucratic crutches.[145]

7.iv. Theories of a new mode of production without a (consolidated) ruling class

Füredi

In his 1986 book *The Soviet Union Demystified*, the English sociologist Frank Füredi (b. 1947), at that time a leader of the Revolutionary Communist Party,[146] presented an analysis of the Soviet Union which was, to a large extent, inspired by the work of Hillel Ticktin. But, while Ticktin's work remained fragmentary, Füredi offered an ambitious synthesis which tried to integrate Ticktin's empirical observations (about waste, class, and so forth).[147]

---

[145] Finger 1995, p. 178.

[146] The Revolutionary Communist Party (RCP) was formed in 1981 out of the Revolutionary Communist Tendency (RCT), which in 1976 split from the Revolutionary Communist Group (RCG). The RCG was founded in 1974 after the expulsion of a group called the 'Revolutionary Opposition' from the International Socialists (now called the Socialist Workers' Party). See Freeman 1986, pp. 52–3. In the course of the 1990s, the RCP distanced itself from an explicitly Marxist stance and the organisation formally dissolved in 1997–8.

[147] The *Aufheben* group reproached Ticktin because he failed to provide a 'systematic political economy of the USSR', but they argued this was 'no accident' (*Aufheben* 1998, p. 32). Füredi's book could be seen as a rebuttal of this critique.

After October 1917, the postrevolutionary government had faced the question of how the economy could be regulated, a question which became even more acute because of a ruinous civil war and the defeat of revolution in Europe. In 1921, the answer had been sought in more market economy, but the New Economic Policy quickly became a threat for the new régime. For the sake of its own survival, the Stalinist bureaucracy was, from 1929, forced to reduce the influence of the law of value. By abolishing markets, the governing élite acquired a degree of control over society's resources. But this control was very limited because of poor information flows and insufficient expertise.

> Soviet industrialisation was achieved, not through effective economic management, but by sweeping aside all the social and political obstacles that stood in its way. [...] In terms of rational planning, the industrialisation drive lacked conscious direction and appeared more like a form of planned anarchy.[148]

The growth of the productive forces thus occurred 'despite planning targets rather than because of them'.[149]

The crucial point here was that abolishing regulation of production by the law of value did not automatically provide mastery over society's resources. And that was precisely the problem with which the Soviet bureaucracy constantly wrestled:

> In the absence of economic regulation, the Soviet social formation has no inherent tendency to socialise labour or to establish a national division of labour. While the exchange of commodities provides capitalism with a mechanism for extending the social division of labour, the Soviet Union has no such mechanism at its disposal. [...]
>
> The attempt to give coherence to the economy through a plan and the use of success indicators establishes only a technical unity among producers. Different producers depend on each other for particular products, giving the Soviet division of labour a semblance of coherence. But a technical relationship is not a substitute for a social division of labour. It does not solve the problem of the efficient utilisation of social labour, nor does it

---

[148] Füredi 1986, p. 98.
[149] Füredi 1986, p. 99.

necessarily lead to harmony or co-operation. This is why, ever since the thirties, there has been a tendency towards the breakdown of the technical division of labour in the Soviet Union.[150]

Because both a market and a real plan were lacking, the distribution of labour-time occurred in large part spontaneously, which meant that 'successful state policy is the exception, not the rule'.[151]

The individual enterprises could only survive if they succeeded in weakening the forces of spontaneity. For that reason, they aimed to achieve maximal self-sufficiency: 'the goal of any enterprise manager is to reduce his reliance on the overall division of labour to a minimum, to gain the best chance of reaching centrally-imposed performance targets'.[152] Hence local managers made informal agreements with other enterprises about the supply of raw materials and labour. Barter, theft and black marketeering were the logical consequences:

> The ultimate welfare of the enterprise depends on the resources and inputs it can obtain, rather than on its achievement of output targets. Hence production units tend to try to meet targets with the minimum of effort. The whole organisation of the enterprise is shaped by this conservative approach. This explains why economic experiments which rely on enterprise initiative do not work.[153]

The forces of spontaneity also led to hoarding resources, to waste of raw materials, and to products of inferior quality: 'The aim of the individual enterprise is to meet formal targets – it has no responsibility for selling its products.'[154]

That innovation took place despite managerial conservatism was, therefore, mainly the result of pressure from the centre. The central bureaucracy could influence developments by its control over material resources, by the import of new technologies from the capitalist West, by the introduction of certain material incentives, and by threats of violent coercion. But the possibility of directing economic development in this way tendentially declined, as was evident from decreasing economic growth since the end of the 1950s.

---

[150] Füredi 1986, p. 102.
[151] Füredi 1986, p. 115.
[152] Füredi 1986, p. 124.
[153] Füredi 1986, p. 117.
[154] Füredi 1986, p. 127.

As industry becomes more complex, increases in investment have less and less effect in sustaining growth. More investment can no longer substitute for the absence of an internal dynamic of development. Not only is Soviet investment becoming more inefficient, but the high cost of production threatens to limit the availability of investment resources. The Soviet bureaucracy cannot indefinitely rely on mobilising new resources to invest in industry. Unless industry itself generates more resources for investment, the tendency towards crisis will be exacerbated.[155]

Repeated attempts of the central bureaucracy to turn the tide with reforms and disciplinary measures failed.

Within this logic of the system, the bureaucratic élite should be viewed as a 'political order', a social group whose power had a *directly political* character, and which could not become a class because the Soviet social formation itself blocked this development. The workers, by contrast, did form a real class, but this class differed from the working classes in capitalism, because labour-power was not sold in labour markets, and because the relationship between wages and living standards deviated from that under capitalism.[156] Füredi proposed to call the Russian working class a 'proletariat': 'In common with the proletariat in other societies, Soviet workers own nothing but their capacity to work. In contrast to capitalist society however, the capacity to work in the Soviet Union does not assume a commodity form.'[157]

Stalinism represented a kind of development dictatorship, and could therefore nestle most easily in less-developed countries. 'Stalinism seemed most appropriate when capitalism was most backward', and 'the more economically advanced a country was, the less applicable the Stalinist model proved to be'. For example, 'whereas the Soviet system could achieve some success in China, in Czechoslovakia, a country that was fairly highly industrialised before the Stalinist takeover, the new system produced economic regression'.[158]

In 1989, Füredi reached the conclusion that the bureaucracy faced a fatal dilemma: 'Unless fundamental change takes place, the Soviet system faces economic breakdown', but 'if it introduces wider market relations it risks

---

155 Füredi 1986, p. 121.
156 Füredi 1986, p. 179.
157 Füredi 1986, pp. 179–80.
158 Richards 1989, p. 102.

disintegration.'[159] Whatever the outcome might be, it was not predictable, according to Füredi:

> The intrinsic volatility of the Soviet system means that the bureaucracy itself is scarcely in control of its own destiny. It is, however, difficult to avoid the conclusion that if present trends continue, the result will be either the restoration of capitalism, or the strengthening of forces committed to the capitalist option. Underlying trends are rarely transformed directly into reality, but they do indicate the general direction of events.[160]

Ticktin and his critics

In a 1987 article, Ticktin argued, in line with his previous publications, that the USSR had no real social classes in the Marxian sense. The workers in his view did not sell their labour-power, but only alienated it:

> In the first place, the worker effectively receives his means of subsistence simply on the basis of being registered as employed and everyone has to be employed on pain of exile, imprisonment or worse. His education, health, housing, utilities, public transport are either free or cost very little, while his food and consumer goods are effectively obtained through a form of rationing either directly or indirectly through queuing. Wages only nominally vary according to skill level. Thus workers receive not rewards so much as a subsistence level irrespective of their performance or even the nature of their work. In the second place, the worker retains control over his labour process so that he does not actually sell control over his labour power.
>
> The result, to sum up, is that the worker has to work by instruction of the state. He does not have a choice to sell his labour power or not. He can move his point of employment within strictly defined limits, but the movement has less to do with competitive sale of labour power than discontent with the job itself. There is no unemployment so that there is no real competition among workers for jobs.[161]

---

[159] Richards 1989, p. 106.
[160] Ibid.
[161] Ticktin 1987, p. 17.

Because every worker 'works at his own individual rate', 'there can be no abstract labour'.[162] And, if abstract labour was absent, atomised 'direct dependence' took its place.[163] As soon as 'the social nature of production forces its way through society the power of the workers will be unmediated', and the power of the élite would be broken.[164] In other words:

> the day that the workers can establish themselves as a class movement, on that day the society will have been overthrown. No further battles will be necessary, since the conditions for such a movement, the decline of the secret police, and the atomisation of society are the only instruments that exist for the maintenance of exploitation as it stands.[165]

Again and again, Ticktin stressed his own position that the USSR was in a permanent crisis but that only the workers could overthrow the system. In *Origins of the Crisis in the USSR*, completed in 1991 and published in 1992 he summarised his interpretation, stating

> but this does not imply that the USSR will break down tomorrow. On the contrary, the USSR has its own form of limited stability as well as its own form of decay. The USSR is a regime that cannot permit opposition to exist, and hence its decline can only take the form of disintegration of the system. The pulling apart of the poles of the system, so that the social groups, factions, and economic categories each stand in opposing and non-cooperating forms, is the form of disintegration. In the end, the disintegration must reach a point where the workers will constitute their own collectivity and so become a class and make their own bid for power.[166]

Fully consistent with this view, Ticktin did not regard the collapse of the USSR as a transition to capitalism, because that required the consent of the workers, and they would give it only if they were offered a genuine prospect of a higher standard of living. The East-German workers perceived this as a real possibility, 'simply by crossing to West Germany', but the Soviet workers

---

[162] Ticktin 1987, p. 18.
[163] Ticktin 1987, p. 19.
[164] Ibid.
[165] Ibid.
[166] Ticktin 1992a, p. 14. 'The whole dynamic of the system is toward its own demise and overthrow by the workers.' Ticktin 1992a, p. 87.

lacked any such prospect.[167] The real introduction of capitalist relations would have two important implications. Firstly, large-scale unemployment would need to be introduced, given that Soviet workers were used to full employment and control over the work process. Workers would obviously strongly resist such a policy. And, secondly, competitive market relations would have to be established, which, under the given circumstances seemed impossible:

> Even if a capital market is assumed, the so-called natural monopolies would continue. The utilities, transport, housing, health, and education would either be in a monopoly sector or in the state sector. Manufacturing could not be made competitive either, except on an international scale. The automobile, aircraft, shipbuilding, computer, electronics, and extractive industries are all examples of industries where cartels exist in the West, or else there are very few firms in any one country. The point, again, is that the USSR needs genuine free competition to establish quality control, control over prices, and control over the direct producers. But a monopoly or a cartel will simply keep the system going as it now stands. The USSR needs not just competition but a raging competition to reestablish capitalism with all its controls over the worker. [...] The market on this showing cannot be introduced except by returning to the nineteenth century. In other words, it cannot be done.[168]

In an article written in 2000, Ticktin acknowledged that the disintegration of the Soviet Union had generated 'a weak potential bourgeoisie',[169] but, at the same time, he continued to maintain his position that no real transition to capitalism had occurred:

> Since prices mean little when barter is used and workers are not paid, while workers cannot sell their labour power when they are seldom paid and continue to work much as they did under the old system, the basis of the word capitalism rests on the existence of capitalists and the abolition of the old system of centralised planning. As the latter is a negative condition, we are left only with the existence of owners of privatised enterprises and

[167] Ticktin 1992a, p. 172.
[168] Ticktin 1992a, pp. 174–5. See also Ticktin 1993, pp. 123–30.
[169] Ticktin 2000, p. 28.

finance capital. In reality both privatised enterprises and finance capital are closely enmeshed with the state and bureaucracy.

One can only call the former USSR countries capitalist if the categories of money, prices, capital, wages, wage-labour are looked at in a purely formal and superficial manner. It is absolutely clear that all categories exist only in a partial and highly conflicted and contradictory form.[170]

The collapse of the USSR thus led only to a further disintegration and hybridisation of society – 'a prelude either to further disintegration or to another revolution'.[171]

Criticism. Ticktin was criticised on several fronts by supporters of the theory of state capitalism. The Cliff supporter John Molyneux alleged that Ticktin had broken with Marxism. If it was true, as Ticktin asserted, 'that the whole idea of social classes is not applicable to the USSR [...] then what he is saying is that Marxism is not applicable to the USSR'.[172] And if there were no classes in the USSR there could be no class conflict either. So how could Ticktin then explain the existence of an enormous repressive apparatus?

The only answer he can give in terms of his analysis is that the Soviet state is a product of conflict between various social groups (elite, intelligentsia, workers, etc.), but if this explanation is valid for the Soviet state it opens the door to non-class theories of other states. In other words we are once again moving away from Marxism.[173]

---

[170] Ticktin 2000, p. 40. Ticktin's supporter Donald Filtzer had predicted in 1991: 'Any marketisation of the Soviet economy will have to take place on the basis of the existing structures, where large, monopolistic enterprises with a long history of distorting planning criteria to improve their financial position will simply carry this behaviour over into the new economic system. Given the size of production units and the persistence of dire shortages, there will be nothing to prevent this. In this situation, the law of value – the spontaneous regulator of the capitalist economy – would be seriously distorted and eroded. There would be no "pure market" and no "pure capitalism" of independent, competitive producers allocating resources according to market demand. Rather, the tendencies towards corruption and managerial and ministerial appropriation of newly privatised enterprises are likely to continue.' (Filtzer 1991, p. 1002)

[171] Ticktin 2000, p. 41. Ticktin placed the failed transition in the broader context of a global transitional epoch, characterised by 'the decline of the old forms, being replaced by forms neither capitalist nor socialist.' (Ticktin 1987, p. 23) See also Ticktin 1992a, pp. 182–7.

[172] Molyneux 1987, p. 131.

[173] Molyneux 1987, p. 132.

In addition, Ticktin's analysis was not free from ambiguity; he did not clearly explain what he meant by 'exploitation in the USSR' and he said nothing about the character of other 'Communist' countries which structurally resembled the Soviet Union, from Eastern Europe to Kampuchea; nor did his analysis offer 'criteria for deciding whether the USSR is historically progressive or reactionary in relation to Western capitalism'.[174] And, finally, Ticktin paved the way for a new ideology of 'socialism in one country', because if the Soviet Union had its own developmental laws, independently from world capitalism, every reason existed to believe that in different circumstances other countries could also develop according to a 'socialist law of motion', external to capitalism.

Less critical than Molyneux was the *Aufheben* group, which, as we saw, sympathised with Ticktin's views, but also accused him of breaking with Marx's critique of political economy at one point. Ticktin had claimed that the Soviet workers did not sell their labour-power, because they maintained substantial control over the use of their labour.[175] But, according to Marx, there was a difference between the sale of labour-power (the capacity to work) and the actual use of that labour-power (the consumption of labour-capacity) that followed it. Therefore,

> The fact that the workers in the USSR were able to assert considerable control over the labour process does not necessarily mean that they did not sell their labour-power. It need only mean that, given the state guarantee of full employment, the workers enjoyed an exceptionally favourable position with regard to management and were able to resist the full subsumption of labour-power to the commodity form within the labour process.[176]

Cox

The political scientist Michael Cox (b. 1945), who was already from 1974 involved with Ticktin's journal *Critique*, raised a subject which usually played almost no role in the Western-Marxist theories about the nature of the Soviet Union, namely foreign policy. Starting out from the idea that Soviet society

---

[174] Ibid.
[175] *Aufheben* 1998, p. 36.
[176] *Aufheben* 1998, p. 40; see also *Aufheben* 2000, p. 45.

was structurally unstable, Cox argued that the foreign policy of the Soviet élite should not be seen as 'anti-capitalist' or 'imperialist', but, rather, as a result of a fundamental vulnerability:

> As long as it continues with its flawed economic system which has not caught up with and cannot overtake the West, the Soviet elite will always have to take what amounts to extraordinary external (as well as internal) measures to remain in being. It is not just the bureaucracy which is insecure, but the whole system. This has produced an ambivalent relation with world capitalism. On the one hand, Soviet weakness has forced it to seek accommodation with the West. This is the real meaning of peaceful co-existence. On the other hand, the same weakness has pushed it into opposition with the world capitalist system in order to reduce the attraction and the pressure which the latter can exert against the Soviet social order.[177]

Only against this background could the apparently inconsistent politics of the USSR be understood. This politics involved mostly 'forward defence'. Support given to Communist parties in other countries should be seen as a means to exert pressure against the Western bourgeoisies; the East European *cordon sanitaire* was intended to weaken Western pressure on the USSR; and support given to anti-imperialist movements was intended to yield allies in the fight against the West. In all cases, the primary aim however was not the destruction, but the weakening of global capitalism.[178]

Arthur

The philosopher Chris Arthur, who had in the 1960s been among the first to argue that the Soviet Union was a new form of society without a consolidated ruling class, presented an analysis in 2000 which extended this original analysis, incorporating the arguments of Ticktin and Füredi.[179] Setting out from the difference and the dialectical connection of formal and material determination, Arthur argued that, in the USSR, 'capital's metabolism was disrupted without an alternative being established'.[180] A consolidated

---

[177] Cox 1987, p. 158.
[178] Ibid.
[179] Arthur 2000.
[180] Arthur 2000, p. 121.

capitalism is an organic system, because the form of capital ('self-valorising value') forms a perfect complement for the content (a factory system with its specific division of labour and hierarchy of control as a means to appropriate surplus-labour). In the Soviet Union, the capitalist form was abolished, but the content had remained:

> As far as *social form* is concerned capitalism was destroyed in the USSR. It is not meaningful to speak of the system as having had value, surplus value, or capital accumulation [...]. There was the price form, and the wage form, but this in no way represented some appearance-form of value, since these forms were rather fixed within a totally administered system. [...]
>
> What remained, however, was the *materialisation of capital*, namely the factory system. [...] The entire human/material configuration of capital's technique was replicated. But without the objective economic regulator of value measures. [...] The great difference with capitalism is that the lack of an objective value regulator leaves the mechanism without a spring, i.e. there is no drive for capital accumulation.[181]

One result, according to Arthur, was that (as Brenner had postulated earlier) a kind of feudalisation of labour relations had occurred: 'Strictly speaking there was no separation of workers from the conditions of production – the Soviet manager was stuck with the workers just as the feudal estate carried its complement of serfs.'[182] The system thus embodied the *negation* of capital, but not the *supersession* of capital. There existed no organic cohesion of society, and therefore also no mode of production.

Behrens

Fritz Behrens (1909–80) was one of the most well-known economists of the German Democratic Republic.[183] As director of the central statistics bureau of the GDR in the mid-1950s, he gained insight into the inefficiency of a command economy already at an early stage. In 1956 he criticised 'actually existing socialism' with this background, but he later partly recanted under pressure of the party. In private, however, he kept working at dissident manuscripts

---

[181] Arthur 2000, pp. 98–9.
[182] Arthur 2000, p. 115.
[183] Steiner 1990, 1992.

which, because of political repression, were shifted between many different
hiding places. Only some time after Behrens's death were a few of his texts
published (in the early 1990s).[184]

Influenced in his studies by Trotskyism, council communism and Wittfogel,
Behrens adopted the classical-Marxist view that capitalism entered its phase
of decline with the outbreak of World War I. The old competitive form of
capitalism had disintegrated in the first decades of the twentieth century, and,
out of the subsequent crisis of bourgeois society as a whole, two new forms of
society had emerged: monopoly capitalism in the West, and state monopolism
in the East: 'The centralisation of capital and thereby the decision-making
power over production is *capitalist* in the hands of national or super-national
monopolies, and socialist in the hands of states controlled by a party and state
bureaucracy; monopolism and state monopolism'.[185] Both variants showed
the same hierarchical-élitist structure.[186]

Soviet society had its roots in the semi-Asiatic relations of prerevolutionary
Russia, but at the same time showed modern characteristics: 'While the Asiatic
mode of production [...] was a transitional society – between prehistoric
society and class societies – from which a capitalist but also a socialist society
could emerge, the mode of production of actually existing socialism is *not* a
transitional society anymore, but [...] an independent social formation.'[187]

State monopolism was not an alternative for capitalism, nor (as Bahro
claimed) a preparation for socialism, but a 'mutation for the worse' because
this new mode of production excluded the possibility of democratisation, and
reduced people to the status of infants without a voice of their own.[188]

Behrens seems to have doubted whether the ruling élite should be defined
as a class. At one point, he calls the élite '*not yet* a class in the old sense',[189] but,
in another context, he mentions two 'basic classes' – the ruling bureaucracy
and the dominated producers – and describes them as follows:

> The ruling *bureaucracy* has a *hierarchical-élitist* structure with many divisions
> and is stratified from top to bottom with numerous privileges, which are

---

[184] Behrens 1990, 1992.
[185] Behrens 1992, p. 62.
[186] Behrens 1992, p. 36.
[187] Behrens 1990–I, p. 89.
[188] Behrens 1992, pp. 96, 245; Behrens 1990–I, p. 89.
[189] Behrens 1992, p. 85.

not just purely material in nature. The chief privilege is the monopoly over information, which is created and maintained by the education and training system based on appointments and selection. Here, more than anywhere, the rule 'knowledge is power' applies. [...]. The bureaucracy has no control, if there is no self-control for the purpose of preventing tendencies of resistance within the ruling power pyramid. It is in all cases and spheres not elected but appointed. The bureaucracy is unproductive and lives from the exploitation of the producers but its structure differs in essential respects from the hierarchical-élitist structure of a ruling class.

The class of producers is described by Behrens as the industrial collective worker. The surplus-product created by this collective worker has the appearance of surplus-value which, through sale of labour-power, is transferred to the bureaucracy – with the difference that the 'silent compulsion of economic relations' typical for capitalism is replaced by 'the vocal compulsion of political power'.[190]

The ruling class or 'strategic élite'[191] had revolutionary roots, but its radical goals had, in the course of time, degenerated into apologism: Leninism became a legitimating ideology.[192] This about-turn had both objective and subjective causes:

> *Objectively*, because the Russian Revolution in 1917 remained isolated precisely in a country which was economically and culturally backward; *subjectively*, precisely because the Leninist organisational principle emerged in the context of a failed bourgeois-democratic revolution within Tsarist Russia, and not in industrially developed Western Europe, which was ripe for a socialist revolution.[193]

The formation of the 'socialist' bureaucracy's power had fatal consequences. Even the achievements of bourgeois democracy were abolished, while militarism and nationalism spread like cancers through society, as shown by

---

[190] Behrens 1990–II, p. 41. A page later, Behrens again doubts his concept of class: 'We leave aside the question of whether the bureaucracy in a state-established actually existing socialism is or is not yet a class in the true sense of the word. In any case it is a [...] stratum, which had all the power and privileges which a ruling class has, including that of incompetence' (Behrens 1990–II, p. 42).

[191] Behrens 1992, p. 35.

[192] Behrens 1992, p. 239.

[193] Behrens 1992, p. 78.

the 'grotesque display of medals, which the bureaucrats and militarists in actually existing "socialism" mutually award themselves'.[194] At the same time, the élite – although not always consistently – gave support to revolutionary liberation movements.[195]

This whole development was not historically inevitable. At the end of World War I, a real possibility existed to establish socialism, but, due to historical contingencies, a different development took place. Undesirable side-effects from the point of view of the revolutionary subject became the main effect, i.e. the ultimate result.[196] The future was also uncertain. Behrens saw two possibilities: either a transition to capitalism would occur, making the bureaucracy a definite ruling class, or a self-managing society based on council democracy would come into being.[197]

Campeanu

Campeanu elaborated his earlier, concisely formulated, theory in three books, which examined successively the origin, development and downfall of Soviet-type societies.[198] In these publications, the concept of syncretism occupied a central place, which was now described in the following way:

> A state of stabilized disarticulation between the forces of production and the class structure in a particular society. What is specific is not disarticulation, which can also occur in other societies, but its stabilization, a quality belonging exclusively to societies born of anticipatory revolutions. This disarticulation, or break in correspondence, occurs at the deepest and most basic level of a society, but in its manifest form appears as a dysfunctionality in the presumptive mediators of the two terms of the correspondence, i.e., relations of ownership and relations of production.[199]

Stalinist syncretism, according to Campeanu, was the product of two successive and contrary 'desynchronizations'. Firstly, there was the desynchronisation of backwardness, or the attempt to carry through a revolution in the

---

[194] Behrens 1992, p. 84.
[195] Behrens 1992, p. 85.
[196] Behrens 1992, pp. 62–3, 199, 228.
[197] Behrens 1992, pp. 85, 96, 149.
[198] Campeanu 1986, 1988, 1990.
[199] Campeanu 1988, p. 9.

imperialist era which was simultaneously anti-feudal, anti-bourgeois and anti-imperialist.[200] Subsequently, the anticipatory desynchronisation, namely the Leninist strategy, 'centered on the possibility of replacing anti-industrial capitalism with pre-industrial socialism'.[201] The combination and stabilisation of both processes led under Stalinism to a system based on extra-economic constraint, in which the economy was subordinated to non-economic power, and the relations of production were reshaped into relations of submission.[202]

The crisis of the system was nothing more than a new phase of desynchronisation: 'anticipation ultimately grinds to a halt in stagnation'.[203] Gradually, a number of 'specific changes, failures, and unresolved crises' had accumulated,[204] which forced the system to revise its regulatory mechanisms. This gave rise to new desynchronisations, because 'old structures are being demolished at a more rapid pace than alternative structures are being built'.[205]

7.v. Summary

In the 1980s and 1990s, the three 'classical' Western-Marxist theories of the Soviet Union (degenerated workers' state, bureaucratic collectivism and state capitalism) appeared to have lost ground. These approaches had all emerged in the 1930s and 1940s, when the internal contradictions of Soviet society were less visible to Western observers than in later years. These theories had tended, like their non-Marxist counterparts of the same vintage, to picture the USSR as a *relatively stable* social system. The extremely rapid collapse of the Soviet Union prompted explicit or unacknowledged theoretical revisions.

Parallel to the relative stagnation of the approaches of Mandel, Shachtman, Cliff and others, new interpretations emerged. On the one hand, the interpretation of the *Critique* current (Ticktin et al.) gained more influence, and, on the other side, a renewed growth occurred of theories of Soviet capitalism

---

[200] This is a theme in Campeanu 1986.
[201] Campeanu 1988, p. 7.
[202] Campeanu 1988, p. 124.
[203] Campeanu 1990, p. 11.
[204] Campeanu 1990, p. 129.
[205] Campeanu 1990, p. 134.

which, more or less in the tradition of Bordiga and Bettelheim, often claimed that there had never been any *state* capitalism the Soviet Union, but, instead, a special variant of *competitive* capitalism.

Increasingly dominant in all currents of thought became the idea that the Soviet Union had embodied a model of economic growth which, although it had initially been successful using extensive methods of industrialisation and extra-economic coercion, could not maintain its economic and military position in the competition with 'globalising' world capitalism, because of growing inefficiencies and the absence of a transition to intensive growth.

Chapter Eight

In Lieu of a Conclusion

> Any statement can be held true come what
> may, if we make drastic enough adjustments
> elsewhere in the system.
>
> W.V. Quine

A broad spectrum of Marxist theories and fragments of theories was examined in previous chapters. Numerous attempts were made to understand the nature of Soviet society, some with solid empirical foundations, but most lacking them; some very consistent and carefully thought-out, others illogical and superficial. What they all had in common was not so much their scientific content, which varied strongly among the different contributions, but their common striving to analyse a phenomenon crucial for Marxists in a critical way, using categories borrowed from or – rightly or wrongly – ascribed to Marx. In what follows, I will try first of all to identify the main issues and themes in the historical survey I have presented. Afterwards, I will discuss in greater detail certain meta-theoretical aspects of the overall course of theoretical development in Western-Marxist thought about the Soviet Union.

To obtain an (admittedly schematic) impression of the scope of the Western-Marxist debate about the Soviet Union over the years, I have presented the number of original publications for each period in the table below:[1]

---

[1] This table is compiled on the basis of the bibliography. For each entry, the earliest

Period	Number of publications	Percentage of the total	Publications per year per period
1917–28	28	3.6	2.33
1929–40	53	6.8	4.42
1941–56	130	16.6	8.13
1957–68	63	8.0	5.25
1969–85	402	51.3	23.65
1986–2004	107	13.7	5.63
Total	783	100.0	8.90

This table does not tell us a great deal. With some qualifications, one could infer that the scope of debate from 1917 gradually increased, declined somewhat in the 1957–68 period, grew explosively after 1968 and declined significantly again since the 1980s.

A closer examination of frequencies suggests that, within the distinguished periods, there were peaks. Significant years appear to be 1938 (the debate over Trotsky's *The Revolution Betrayed*), 1941 (the Shachtman-Burnham-Trotsky debate), 1947–8 (the debate around the European editions of Burnham's *Managerial Revolution*), 1951–3 (the Yugoslav controversy), 1958 (the debate over Djilas's *The New Class*), 1974–80 (when many writings on the topic were constantly being published), and 1990 (the collapse).

The growth in scope of the debate in the period 1917–56 is, at first sight, paradoxical. After all, precisely in this period, the community which concerned itself with these questions grew smaller. After parts of the communist and social-democratic movements had initially participated in the discussion, in the end only 'various smaller groups of the Western Left'[2] were still concerned with the Soviet Union in a critical-Marxist manner. At the same time, however, we have to conclude that *within* this dwindling circle the debates became more intense.

In the period 1956–68, the most important theories had crystallised, and the political situation in the West did not promote further innovative developments. After May '68 in Paris and the Prague Spring, however, a turning-point point was reached: a rather broad Marxist Left emerged, only

---

year of publication was used. Articles published in series and books comprising several volumes were included as single items.

[2] Fehér, Heller & Márkus 1983, p. 8.

parts of which directly continued the tradition of older currents. As the radicalisation in the 1980s ebbed away, interest in the debate about the Soviet Union also declined.

We can also view matters from a somewhat different angle. In my introduction, I mentioned three clusters of factors which influenced the theorising about the Soviet Union: the perception of the West, the perception of the Soviet Union and the interpretation of the Marxist analysis of society. Tentatively, I also indicated that each of these three influences went through several phases. Both Western capitalism and the Soviet Union were, for some time, experienced as unstable, then as stable and dynamic, and then again as increasingly unstable – until the breakdown of the USSR. The interpretation of the Marxist social analysis developed from a restricted schematism, via a rigid unilinearism to an ever-broadening multi-linearism.

If we combine these three influences schematically, then we obtain approximately the result shown in the table below:

Period	Perception of Western capitalism	Perception of the Soviet Union	Interpretation of Marxist social analysis
1917		Unstable	Open to a limited extent
	Unstable (decline)		
1929			
1952		Stable/ dynamic	Closed
1956	Stable/ dynamic		
1968		Stability declining	
1985	Stability declining		Increasingly open
		Crisis and collapse	
1991	The only vital system		

It does not seem unreasonable to assume that critical theorising was promoted by (i) openness within Marxist circles and (ii) instability of the reference societies (Western capitalism and the Soviet Union). While the second factor tends to discount the new events that keep occurring, which were – precisely because of that instability – not predictable, the first factor makes it possible to identify a multiplicity of competing hypotheses to explain these developments.

Viewed in this way, the preconditions for critical theorising about the Soviet Union were most favourable in the periods 1917–29 and 1968–85, and least favourable in the intervening years. If, in addition, we take into account that the Soviet Union in the period 1917–29 had not yet assumed its qualitatively new, Stalinist structure, then it is not surprising that, precisely after 1968, the discussion about 'actually existing socialism' became most intensive.

Theoretical development from 1917–2005 appears to fall in four clearly different phases:

i)   The period 1917–29, in which classical unilinearism dominated, and postrevolutionary societies were only analysed in terms of a transition to socialism which was either successful, or historically impossible, or doomed to failure.

ii) The period 1929–68, in which – in the wake of the Stalinist transformation – it was generally recognised that a new type of society had emerged in the Soviet Union. Three main variants were offered in these years: (i) the theory of state capitalism and (ii) the theory of the degenerated workers' state, both of which still adhered rather closely to the unilinear schema, as well as (iii) the theory of bureaucratic collectivism, according to which the bureaucracy operated as a new ruling class. That aside, cautious attempts at a fourth approach ('theories without label') emerged in the beginning of the 1940s (Pedrosa, Hilferding) and especially in West Germany in the early 1950s, but these remained relatively isolated, and were forgotten again.

iii) The period 1968–85, during which the debate strongly revived, the fourth approach gained much more prominence, and the three old approaches tended to stagnate.

iv) The period after 1985, in which the intensity of the debate was reduced and especially the number of new theories of (state) capitalism proliferated.

A posteriori, the first phase (1917–29) appears as no more than a transitional period of orientation, because the terms for all the later debates were fixed in the 1930s, at which time people like Weil, Trotsky, Worrall and others formulated the main perspectives which negatively or positively dominated the discussion.

Some critics of the Soviet Union discussed in this book

	Capitalism	Bureaucratic collectivism	Degenerated workers' state	Other
1917–28	Gorter Pannekoek Rühle Korsch			Kautsky Luxemburg
1929–41	Miasnikov Adler Wagner Worrall Pollock	Laurat Weil Rizzi Burnham Shachtman Pedrosa	Trotsky	Hilferding
1941–56	Grandizo/Péret James/Dunayevskaya Castoriadis/Lefort Cliff Bordiga	Guttmann	Mandel	Sternberg Cycon Frölich Kofler
1956–68		Djilas Kuroń/ Modzelewski		Wittfogel Rosdolsky Boeuve Marcuse

1968–85	Mattick
	Holmberg
	Bettelheim
	Di Leo
		Stojanović
		Carlo
		Melotti
		Fantham/
		  Machover
		Sweezy
			Mohun	Dutschke
				Zimin
				Bahro
				Schmiederer
				Ticktin
				Konrád/
				  Szelényi
				Féher *et al.*
				Campeanu

1985–2005	Daum Sapir Chattopadhyay Fernandez *Aufheben* Resnick/Wolff Sandemose	Brenner Finger	Main/Heath	Füredi Cox Behrens

After the – quite possibly confusing – multitude of theories described in previous chapters without an overall theoretical evaluation, it now seems appropriate to confront the various approaches with their own pretensions. I hope to show that all 'classical' variants conflict in essential respects with Marx's own theory, and, in addition, occasionally run counter to the facts or violate logical principles.

To begin with, let us examine the theories of (state) capitalism, of which a large number of protagonists have been reviewed. If we disregard for a moment the fact that these theoreticians identified different dates for the establishment of a capitalist formation in the Soviet Union,[3] then what is most striking in the first instance is how much they *differed* in their interpretations about the real essence of (state-) capitalism. Schematically, we could distinguish between four different perspectives:

i) Most theorists emphasised that capitalism is predicated on the existence of a working class which does not rule society. For some, that characteristic was really already sufficient in itself to define a society as capitalist (James, Mattick, Di Leo), but some others added other criteria. Thus, Worrall mentioned as a second condition the production of surplus-value, and Holmberg the fact that means of production were applied for the purpose of exploiting the wage-workers.

ii) Bordiga, Bettelheim, Chattopadhyay et al. emphasised the separation between individual enterprises, who attempt to realise 'profit' and exchange goods among themselves via 'market contracts'. Bordiga considered this a sufficient condition to speak of capitalism; Bettelheim added the separation between wage-labour and capital.

iii) Grandizo spoke of capitalism when wages were minimised, and surplus-value was used for investment and unproductive consumption.

iv) Finally, Cliff saw the essence of capitalist society in the competition between capitals motivated by profit maximisation.

Grandizo's description is undoubtedly farthest removed from Marx's. After all, talk of surplus-value already implies the existence of capitalism, and thus

---

[3] As dates are mentioned: *1929* (Cliff, James et al.), *1936* (Daum), and *1956* (the early Bettelheim et al.). The theoreticians who used the term capitalism instead of state capitalism (Rühle, Gorter, Pannekoek, the later Bettelheim, Chattopadhyay, Resnick/Wolff) tended towards treating *1917* as starting point.

a *petitio principii* is involved. Definitions based on wage-labour then make an orthodox impression; Marx himself had written in *Capital* that

> The capitalist epoch is therefore characterised by the fact that labour-power, in the eyes of the worker himself, takes on the form of a commodity which is his property; his labour consequently takes on the form of wage-labour.[4]

If, however, one reduces Marx's conception to such a passage, he is done an injustice. Capitalism for him was, after all, a complex and dynamic system, in which wage-labour was only one important aspect. Thus, Marx also mentioned 'commodity production and commodity circulation' as 'general prerequisites of the capitalist mode of production'.[5] Essential, in his opinion, was especially the *generalisation* of commodity production (labour-power and labour products) by capitals, in a market ruled by competition.

According to Marx, competition therefore constituted another *essential* characteristic of capitalism. Thus he referred in *Capital* to 'the basic law of competition, which political economy has so far failed to grasp, the law that governs the general rate of profit and the so-called prices of production determined by it'[6] and, in the *Grundrisse*, he wrote:

> Free competition is the real development of capital. By its means, what corresponds to the nature of capital is posited as external necessity for the individual capital; what corresponds to the concept of capital, is posited as the external necessity for the mode of production founded on capital. The reciprocal compulsion which the capitals within it exert on each other, on labour etc. (the competition among workers is only another form of the competition among capitals) is the *free*, at the same time the *real* development of wealth as capital.[7]

So capitalism, in Marx's view, constituted a unity of several 'moments', of which wage-labour was only one. If this fact is accepted, then the mentioned authors fail to prove the existence of business competition in the Soviet Union in the Marxian sense, i.e. arising in some or other way out of the immanent logic of the system, and thereby fail to prove the existence of a Soviet

---

[4] Marx 1976, p. 274.
[5] Marx 1976, p. 473.
[6] Marx 1981, pp. 127–8.
[7] Marx 1973, pp. 650–1.

state capitalism. If some supporters of the 'state-capitalist' interpretation, by contrast, treat wage-labour either as the most important, or as the only condition for the definition of capitalism, this is possibly due their limited knowledge of Marx's political-economic writings. Wage-labour is, after all, discussed in the *first* volume of *Capital*, while competition is dealt with more extensively only in the *third* volume.

A second problem is raised by the question of whether, within the assumed Soviet state capitalism, a ruling class existed. Some authors did not express a definite view in this regard, and denied only the existence of private capitalists, but a remarkable number of authors explicitly denied that Russian capitalism was ruled by a *bourgeoisie*. Thus, according to Wagner, Pollock and Bordiga, such as class is completely absent, Worrall claims that the bureaucracy exercises the function of a bourgeoisie which is lacking, and Grandizo and Péret refer to an 'immature' bourgeoisie. All of this again runs counter to Marxian orthodoxy. In his *Grundrisse*, Marx stated among other things that

> The production of capital and wage labourers is thus a chief product of capital's valorization process. [...] It is posited in the concept of capital, that the objective conditions of labour – and these are its own product – take on a *personality* towards it, or, what is the same, that they are posited as the property of a personality alien to the worker. The concept of capital contains the capitalist.[8]

Marx thus clearly assumed that a capitalist class is a *conditio sine qua non* for capitalism.

In fact, only two representatives of the state-capitalism theory took an approach compatible with an orthodox definition of capitalism: Cliff and Bettelheim. Both assumed the existence of a bourgeoisie in the Soviet Union, and both believed that competition existed. Bettelheim believed this competition existed in the domestic economy, while Cliff believed he could identify it at the international level.

Cliff's approach forces him to reduce competition essentially to the arms race: a competition over military capacity. That, however, is still in conflict

---

[8] Marx 1973, p. 512. See also the *Theories of Surplus Value*: 'The *capitalist*, as capitalist, is simply the personification of capital, that creation of labour endowed with its own will and personality which stands in opposition to labour. [...] if one eliminates the capitalists, the means of production cease to be *capital*.' Marx 1972, p. 296.

with orthodoxy. The arms race, after all, did not involve mainly commodities produced for an open market, and therefore cannot be considered as trade based on capitalist competition. In the Marxian view, each capital seeks to realise the value of the commodities produced by selling them through commercial trade, and that is not possible by just displaying them (or destroying them).[9] Bettelheim's approach, by contrast, based its orthodoxy on the denial of reality. His thesis, as Sweezy rightly observed, is contrary to the facts, because Soviet enterprises were unable to determine prices, wages, suppliers and recipients by themselves.[10]

Ultimately, we are forced to the conclusion that not a single theory of state capitalism succeeded in being both orthodox-Marxist as well as consistent with the facts.

The second main theoretical variant was the theory of the *degenerated workers' state*. We saw previously how Trotsky characterised the Soviet bureaucracy as a parasitic social stratum, which, from the sphere of distribution, had *temporarily* seized political power within the workers' state. From an orthodox-Marxist perspective, there are again several essential problems involved here.

Firstly, there is the question of the *temporary nature* of the bureaucratic phenomenon. Trotsky's thought, in this respect, showed a clear logic: the Russian working class, with the victory of 1917 still fresh in its memory, would sweep aside the élitist outgrowth which tried to rob the fruits of its revolutionary efforts. If, by any chance, that did not happen then, after some time, the old revolutionary self-confidence would ebb away, and the élite would acquire the possibility of transforming itself into a new ruling class. One can obviously question whether, within the Soviet working class

---

[9] 'Even though the excess value of the commodity over its cost-price arises in the immediate process of production, it is only in the circulation process that it is realized'; 'Whatever the surplus-value capital has pumped out in the immediate production process and expressed in commodities, the value and surplus-value contained in these commodities must first be realized in the circulation process' (Marx 1981, pp. 134 and 966).

The argument adduced here notably by Callinicos (1995, p. 137) that 'state direction of the economy was a pervasive feature of Western capitalism in the first half of the twentieth century' is not convincing; the point is that, in the West (including the extreme case of Nazi Germany), competition between capitals continued *within* the domestic economy.

[10] See Section 6.i.

of the 1930s, the 'lessons of the revolutionary struggles and the conclusions of Bolshevik strategy' were still very much alive, as Trotsky claimed.[11] But, if that had been the case, then one could have regarded Trotsky's thesis as consistent with Marxist orthodoxy. After all, in Marx himself we encounter similar ideas.[12] Problems, however, arise when Trotsky's intellectual heirs write, even in recent times, that: 'In the scales of history, the question remains as Trotsky posed it in 1939. But the "time frame" was erroneous.'[13] The force of Trotsky's argument is thereby undone, because the specific (and Marxian) considerations which originally brought the author of *The Revolution Betrayed* to his thesis are now tacitly eliminated, and replaced by an abstract generality ('the scales of history').

A second difficulty inheres in the distinction which the theory of the degenerated workers' state makes between the sphere of production and the sphere of distribution. This distinction conflicts with Marx, who always emphasised that *both* should be considered as part of a cohesive totality:

> In the shallowest conception, distribution appears as the distribution of products, and hence as further removed from and quasi-independent of production. But before distribution can be the distribution of products, it is: (1) the distribution of the instruments of production, and (2), which is a further specification of the same relation, the distribution of the members of the society among the different kinds of production.
>
> [...] To examine production while disregarding this internal distribution within it is obviously an empty abstraction; while conversely, the distribution of products follows by itself from this distribution which forms an original moment of production.[14]

A third problem is posed by the fact that Trotsky only ascribed a distributive and parasitic function to the bureaucracy, and thereby denied that it could have roots in the productive sphere. From an orthodox standpoint, this idea

---

[11] Trotsky 1931, p. 11; English translation, p. 224.

[12] Rubel 1960.

[13] Mandel 1980, p. 62.

[14] Marx 1973, p. 96. Actually, this deviation from Marxian orthodoxy was not exclusive to Trotsky. It has been noted by other authors that the autonomisation of the sphere of distribution was present among many theoreticians educated in the Second International. See for example the critical analysis of Hilferding's *Das Finanzkapital* (1910) in Stephan 1974.

is impossible to sustain. The Soviet bureaucracy, after all, led the enterprises, and hence also the production processes. In *Capital*, Marx wrote about such coordinating work:

> The work of supervision and management necessarily arises everywhere when the direct production process takes the form of a socially combined process, and does not appear simply as the isolated labour of separate producers. It has, however, a dual nature.
>
> On the one hand, in all labour where many individuals cooperate, the interconnection and unity of the process is necessarily represented in a governing will, and in functions that concern not the detailed work but rather the workplace and its activity as a whole, as with the conductor of an orchestra. *This is productive labour that has to be performed in any combined mode of production.*
>
> On the other hand [...] this work of supervision necessarily arises in all modes of production that are based on opposition between the worker as direct producer and the proprietor of the means of production. The greater this opposition, the greater the role that this work of supervision plays.[15]

This dual character of the leadership function obviously also applied to Soviet enterprise management, which, on the one side, tried to organise production, and, on the other side, simultaneously embodied the oppression of the workers. Clearly, the corollary must be that at least an important part of the Soviet bureaucracy was not exclusively parasitic, but also performed *productive* labour in the Marxian sense.

A final problem concerns not so much a matter of orthodoxy, but of logic. It inheres in the separation between the political and economic spheres. This separation was logical and theoretically consistent, since the working class was viewed as being economically the ruling class, but politically powerless. Be that as it may, the peculiar thing is that, precisely in a planned economy, political and economic power *cannot* be so separated. Whoever formulated and supervised the implementation of the plan, and thus possessed political power, obviously also ruled the economy.

If we combine these objections, it appears that the theory of the degenerated workers' state is in part unorthodox, and in part illogical.

---

[15] Marx 1981, p. 507 (translation corrected and emphasis added – MvdL).

The third variant is the collection of theories of *bureaucratic collectivism* (a new type of society with a ruling class). Seen from the perspective of Marxian orthodoxy, this current is also confronted with three essential objections.

The first and most important difficulty is obviously that the theory *as a whole* does not fit in a Marxian framework. It probably does not need to be argued again that Marx conceived of only one possible type of postcapitalist society: a communist or socialist one. The idea that, after capitalism, there could be another additional and complete historical stage (Weil, Rizzi, and Burnham) was completely alien to him. Likewise, the thesis that underdeveloped ('semi-feudal' or 'semi-Asiatic') countries could experience a pattern of development different from a capitalist one, does not fit his approach: 'The country that is more developed industrially only shows, to the less developed, the image of its own future.'[16]

Secondly, the protagonists of this current – leaving aside the various different dates given for the beginning of the new society[17] – offered mutually contradictory interpretations of the foundation of the rule of the bureaucratic class. Some, like Weil and Burnham, considered that bureaucratic power was *economically* based. Others, like Djilas and Stojanović, thought that the basis of power should be sought in the *political* sphere. The first-mentioned interpretation is contrary to the facts: the élite came to power by a political route. Its power grew out of its domination of the state apparatus (which, in its turn, ruled the enterprises) and not from the direct rule of the enterprises themselves. This was true both in a collective and in an individual sense. The last-mentioned interpretation breaks with Marx – and its defenders are usually also aware of this. After all, Marx deduced political power from economic power:

> The specific economic form, in which unpaid surplus-labour is pumped
> out of direct producers, determines the relationship of rulers and ruled, as
> it grows directly out of production itself and, in turn, reacts upon it as a

---

[16] Marx, 'Preface to the First Edition', in Marx 1976, p. 91. Marx mentioned an important exception to this thesis: the *obshchina*, which, under particular conditions, might enable Russia to skip over the intermediate capitalist stage. But also in this case, Marx obviously did not envisage a transition to a new type of class society in the sense of Carlo, Melotti, or Fantham/Machover, but a direct transition to socialism.

[17] Two interpretations were advanced: *1917–21* (Burnham, Sweezy and others) and *1929* (Shachtman and others).

determining element. Upon this, however, is founded the entire formation of the economic community which grows up out of the production relations themselves, thereby simultaneously its specific political form. It is always the direct relationship of the owners of the conditions of production to the direct producers – a relation always naturally corresponding to a definite stage in the development of the methods of labour and thereby its social productivity – which reveals the innermost secret, the hidden basis of the entire social structure and with it the political form of the relation of sovereignty and dependence, in short, the corresponding specific form of the state.[18]

A third problem is that, if the theoreticians of bureaucratic collectivism are correct, a ruling class emerged which did not exist as a class before it came to power. In all relevant writings by Marx, it was assumed that *first* antagonistic classes emerge from the relations of production, that these classes *then* acquire political consciousness and carry on a struggle with each other on a broad scale, and that, finally, after a fundamental social transformation, a previous subaltern class is established as the new ruling class. Prior to coming to power, the bureaucratic 'class' however comprised at most parts of the intelligentsia and the 'labour aristocracy', and could hardly be said to form a class fighting against the Soviet working class.

The theory of the 'new ruling class' therefore cannot pretend consistency with Marxian orthodoxy anymore than both of the other main variants.

In this light, it becomes perfectly clear that Soviet society can hardly be explained in orthodox-Marxian terms at all. If it is accepted that the USSR was not communist in a Marxian sense, the analysis becomes almost impossible: which categories should one use to analyse a society in which oppression and exploitation exist, but in which no ruling class in the strict sense (whether the working class, bourgeoisie or collective bureaucracy) can be identified? In which, as a consequence, no logical social and economic dynamic can be recognised?

The emergence of a 'fourth current' which denied that the Soviet Union had a distinct mode of production is, against this background, quite

---

[18] Marx 1981, p. 927.

understandable – even although the rapid spread and elaboration of theories 'without label' after 1968 was probably not the result of a systematic analysis of the strengths and weaknesses of the old theories.

This conclusion does not imply that the old theories are of no use whatever in further theoretical developments. Nor do I wish to argue that they lack any practical political utility as a meaningful orienting device. In the theories discussed, sub-theoretical themes or *topoi* recur, not limited to one perspective. I can identify eleven of these:

i)   The Bolshevik and later the Stalinist régime constituted a *modernisation dictatorship*: given the underdevelopment of the socio-economic relations in 1917, it was inevitable that in the first instance forced industrialisation and accumulation occurred. It required social compulsion, and led to a dictatorial régime. We encounter this *topos* among others in the writings of Adler, Kofler, Rosdolsky, Kuroń and Modzelewski, Marcuse, Mattick, Carlo, Melotti, Fantham and Machover, Schmiederer and Campeanu.

ii)   The Soviet Union manifested *analogies with the Asiatic mode of production*: Stalinism was not a variant of 'Eastern despotism', but did resemble it strongly in some respects. Analysis of classical Chinese society, for example, has heuristic value in studying Soviet society. This *topos* is found among others in the writings of Sternberg, Frölich, Zimin, Konrád/ Szelényi and Mandel. Closely related to this theme is the idea of Gorter, Pannekoek, Wagner, Wittfogel and others, that Russia and the Soviet Union traditionally belonged to a completely *different* economic, political and cultural sphere from 'the West'.

iii) Soviet society was a *'bastard' formation*, an 'illegitimate' phenomenon, a cul-de-sac along the high road of human history. Representatives of this *topos* are Kautsky, Zimin, Ticktin and Füredi, and one could quite possibly also include Laurat and Shachtman.

iv)   Bolshevism and/or Stalinism were historically limited, *temporary phenomena*: within a matter of years, it had to make way for another, more durable formation. This *topos* – close to the one just mentioned, but not identical to it – is found in the writings of Kautsky, Trotsky, and Pedrosa.[19]

---

[19] The opposite – Stalinism as a long-lasting phenomenon – was really only defended in the 1950s by the theoretically-less-interesting Trotskyist Michel Raptis (Pablo).

v) Soviet society embodied a transitional stage between class society and a classless society, and therefore showed *parallels with the transitional stage from a classless society*. This *topos* was articulated by Rizzi, Zimin and Bahro.

vi) Stalinism and fascism or national socialism were two variants of the same form of society. This *topos* – which is obviously also known in theories of totalitarianism – is found among defenders of the theory of state capitalism (Rühle, Pollock) and among defenders of the theory of a new mode of production (Laurat, Weil, Rizzi, Burnham).[20]

vii) In the Soviet Union, there was *a subordination of the economy to politics*, or, put differently, *a completely autonomised state*. Representatives of this *topos* are Hilferding and Pedrosa, Damus and Schmiederer et al.

viii) The power of the ruling élite was based on the *separation of intellectual and manual labour* (knowledge as the basis of domination). We encounter this *topos* in theories of the managerial class (Weil, Burnham) but also in the writings of Cycon, Eggert, the S.Z. Tübingen, Eichwede and Kaiser, as well as Konrád and Szelényi. A somewhat deviant variant (the élite as a sector of the leading workers) is defended by Bahro.

ix) Workers in the Soviet Union were not 'free wage-workers' in the Marxian sense: because they could ultimately only supply their labour-power to one employer and additionally had the obligation to work, an important element of Marxian 'freedom' disappeared, namely the freedom of choice 'between different exploiters'. This *topos* is found in the writings of Rizzi, Burnham, Guttman, Mohun and Brenner.

x) The longer the Soviet Union existed, the stronger was the growth of inefficiency, or, as some authors put it, a contradiction developed between productive forces and relations of production. This *topos* emerged in the 1970s (Carlo, Ticktin, Conert, Fehér et al.).[21]

xi) The dynamic of the Soviet Union was shaped by its competition with the West; even in peacetime, Soviet society could be characterised as a *war economy* (Cliff, Sapir).

---

[20] Trotsky referred to many 'superstructural' similarities between fascism and Stalinism, but emphasised, at the same time, the difference in the economic base of both régimes (capitalist versus workers' state). See, for example, Trotsky 1940a.

[21] The theme of inefficiency as such was naturally raised already much earlier by, among others, Trotsky, Guttmann and Mandel.

Some of these themes could perhaps be building blocks for a 'post-Marxian' analysis. But, even if that is not the case, we can use the collapse of the Soviet Union to test the various theories formulated before that collapse. The historian E.P. Thompson already noted in the late 1970s that the different hypotheses about the dynamics and class character of the Soviet Union could only be definitively proved or falsified through 'the *praxis* of eventuation'. However, he warned:

> The result, when brought within the scrutiny of future historians, may appear to confirm one hypothesis, or may propose a new hypothesis altogether. Any such 'confirmation', if it should arise, can never be more than approximate: history is not rule-governed, and it knows no sufficient causes: and if future historians suppose otherwise they would be falling into the error of *post hoc ergo propter hoc*.[22]

---

[22] Thompson 1978, p. 49.

Chapter Nine
Meta-theoretical Note

I will now try to analyse the theoretical developments I described meta-theoretically; I will, in other words, try to formulate a theory about these theoretical formations. In so doing, I am inspired, among other things, by the newer diachronic interpretation of science.[1] My aim here is to make a modest contribution to the establishment of a model for the development of political discourses in the history of the labour movement.

My point of departure is that political theories of the kind discussed in this study are *relatively autonomous* with respect to their social bearers. They are *autonomous* in the sense that, once formulated, they are bound by a certain internal logic. They are also *relatively* autonomous given that they also fulfill social functions (they can for example contribute to the social cohesion of a political group) and are thereby restricted in their 'freedom of movement'. What does the internal structure of the mentioned political discourses look like, in that case?

---

[1] While the older theory of science was mainly preoccupied with statically interpreted problems (the relationship between theory and experience, formal models of scientific explanations etc.) the new theory of science, the beginning of which coincided approximately with the first edition of Thomas Kuhn's *The Structure of Scientific Revolutions* (1962), is clearly aware of the dynamic character of scientific development. The description of this new approach as 'diachronic' is based on Diederich 1974.

Just as with every other construct of the intellect, it is also true of political discourses that they are founded on more or less explicitly defined concepts. These concepts (such as 'capitalism', 'working class') can be, for the most part, rather vague. By this I mean that the user of a given concept both recognises objects which definitely can or cannot be encompassed by the concept, as well as objects of which it is not obvious whether they can be subsumed under the concept. Many of the concepts used in Western Marxism were directly taken from Marx's work, although the content which the user imputed to it did not necessarily match the meaning Marx gave to it exactly.

Concepts can be equivalents, or have a different degree of generality. I call two concepts 'equivalent' if the referents (i.e. the objects indicated by them) of one concept are equal to the referents of another concept. If all the referents of concept A are also the referents of concept B, but not vice versa, then I call B more general than A.[2]

In the development of a political theory, concepts are constantly being replaced by other concepts. This can occur in three ways: either through the substitution of an equivalent concept, or through the substitution of a less general concept (specification), or through substitution of a more general concept (generalisation). Each of these changes already implies political-theoretical choices. Think, for example, of the substitution of 'the revolutionary subject in capitalism' by the equivalent 'the working class', or the substitution of 'workers' states' by the more concrete 'the Soviet Union'.

The concepts form the building blocks out of which more or less complex discourses are constructed. They are combined in statements which are related to the object of the discourse: Soviet society. Incidentally, not all the statements belonging to the discourse refer in an immediate sense to the object; there are also more general statements, which nevertheless are indispensable for the discourse.

I would suggest that every political theory consists of three subsets of statements, such that these three subsets are necessary and sufficient to distinguish that theory from all other theories. These three subsets are the following:

---

[2] I owe this terminology to Nowak 1977, p. 101.

(a) *The set of principles*. To this set belong statements with a high degree of generality, which are considered applicable to more objects than are dealt with by the theory. An example of a principle is Marx's thesis 'that the emancipation of the working classes must be conquered by the working classes themselves'.[3] This statement obviously can be applied not only to the Soviet Union in the twentieth century, but also to all other situations in which a working class has existed, exists, or will exist. Statements of principle characterise a specific situation, or indicate how a specific situation can be reached or eliminated. The Marx quote suggests for example – assuming two related concepts (working class and emancipation) – under which conditions an initial situation (an unemancipated working class) can be transformed into a second (the working class is emancipated). Principles are also political and not 'value-free' in nature. Their implications are both descriptive and prescriptive,[4] they describe analytically and politically (morally) judge a situation. Just like the concepts from which they are constructed, principles can, of course, also be formulated with greater or lesser generality, and, in that sense, be replaced by equivalents, or statements which are more general or more concrete.

(b) *The set of observations*, or – what amounts to the same in this context – of the facts. To this set belong statements considered to describe a particular aspect of the social object of the theory. Obviously bare empiria are not involved here, but politically pre-fabricated constructions. 'A fact by itself', Znaniecki wrote with justification, 'is already an abstraction; we isolate a certain limited aspect of the concrete process of becoming, rejecting, at least provisionally, all its indefinite complexity.'[5] Hence it is quite possible that different political discourses do not assume the same observations or facts. While one theory will, for example, claim that 'means of production in the Soviet Union are commodities', another theory will consider that this statement is in conflict with reality.

---

[3] Marx 1992, p. 82.

[4] This is not exceptional, given that even in the 'apolitical' purely scientific theories such admixtures can occur. To mention just one example: the philosopher Paul Feyerabend criticised the mentioned work by Kuhn because of its 'ambiguity of presentation': 'are we here presented with *methodological prescriptions* which tell the scientist how to proceed; or are we given a *description*, void of any evaluative element, of those activities which are generally called "scientific"? Kuhn's writings, it seems to me, do not lead to a straightforward answer.' Feyerabend 1970, p. 198.

[5] Znaniecki 1919, p. 83.

(c) *The political core*. This set consists of the conclusions drawn from observations and principles. Together, they constitute statements about the social object which are the essence of the theory. Within the political core, more-or-less explicitly prescriptive statements can be distinguished. Thus, for example, the political core of the Maoist theory (as elaborated by Bettelheim) could be summarised in three conclusions:

i) the Soviet Union was, from the 1950s onwards, subject to capitalist relations, in which enterprises were separated from each other, and workers were separated from means of production;

ii) the Soviet state had, from the end of the 1950s, become a state-capitalist institution;

iii) in the Soviet Union a social revolution became necessary.

In the 'ideal' case, the construction of a certain political discourse is completely consistent; the concepts are continually used in the same way, and the reasoning is watertight. Obviously, this is not always the case, not here any more than in other kinds of argumentation:

> Logical compatibility, partial or total, may exist and yet also go unnoticed or not be responded to for a variety of reasons, as is also the case with the so-called inconsistencies within an individual's mind. The individual can live quite well with a number of inconsistencies, simply by shifting them around in different contexts, by forming ad-hoc or sometimes more general rules of exception, inclusion and exclusion, by developing an astonishing resourceful casuistry of definitions of a situation in ways that avoid cognitive hardships. It is only under special circumstances [...] that the usual escape hatches of time and circumstances have been closed and the individual is forced to cope with his inconsistencies. The same holds for scientific theories; we have learned to live with their inconsistencies which are partially explained away or may go unnoticed or not cared for most of the time. It is only under exceptional circumstances that they become relevant and that the difference matters [...].[6]

Assume, however, that the argumentation of a certain discourse is completely consistent. Then the critic will be able to attack the political core exclusively

---

[6] Nowotny 1975, pp. 39–40.

in an indirect way. Through the concepts, the principles and observations thus form a protective belt around the political core, as symbolised in the following schema:

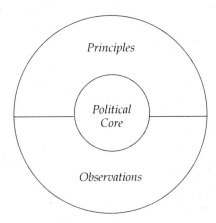

Critics who want to eliminate the political core of a theory can adopt one or more of the following offensive strategies:

i)   contest the adequacy of certain concepts used in the discourse;
ii) make visible inconsistencies in the argumentation of the discourse;
iii) contest the validity of certain observations, which are important for the discourse;
iv) introduce new or alternative observations, which cannot be integrated in the discourse in a consistent way;
v)   contest the applicability of certain principles, which are important for the discourse;
vi) introduce new or alternative principles, which cannot be integrated in the discourse in a consistent way.

Very probably, the supporters of the discourse under threat will continually be able to resist these attacks, if they are prepared to replace or abandon parts of the argumentation at the foundations of the political core. (That the credibility of the discourse can thereby be put in question is another matter, which I will discuss later.) Two kinds of defensive strategies are open to the supporters of a discourse: (i) direct immunisation, whereby the whole old discourse is maintained through stating that the attackers just use different concepts, and/or declaring that the new principles and/or observations are irrelevant or not valid; (ii) indirect immunisation, whereby statements in the protective belt are eliminated or replaced. Both strategies could, obviously, be combined. Direct immunisation is only possible if the attackers do not contest the consistency of the discourse. If they do so (effectively), then indirect immunisation is inevitable, which also happens if the attackers, in the eyes of defenders, justifiably contest certain principles and/or observations and/or supplement them with new principles and/or observations.

An illustration may well clarify this abstract interpretation. As example, I will reconstruct the debate between Cliff and the Fourth International discussed in Chapter 4. During the debate, two principles were put in question:

Principle 1: A violent proletarian revolution is a necessary condition for the establishment of a workers' state.

Principle 2: A violent anti-proletarian revolution is a necessary condition for the dissolution of a workers' state.

These two principles were, originally, considered as implying each other, and together formed part of Trotskyist orthodoxy. In their debate about these principles, the opponents based themselves on the same observations:

Observation 1: The East-European people's democracies were not the outgrowth of violent proletarian revolutions.

Observation 2: The East-European people's democracies had become, to a large extent, identical to the Soviet Union *qua* social structure during the period 1947–50.

Observation 3: The Soviet Union was a workers' state during the first years after 1917.

Observation 4: In the Soviet Union, no violent anti-proletarian revolution occurred between 1917 and 1950.

Now, the argument offered by Cliff was as follows:

i)   Principle 1 is correct.
ii) From Principle 1 and Observation 1, it follows that the East-European people's democracies cannot be workers' states (Conclusion 1).
iii) From Conclusion 1 and Observation 2, it follows that the Soviet Union was not a workers' state *anno* 1950 (Conclusion 2).
iv) From Conclusion 2 and Observation 3, it follows that the dissolution of the workers' state had occurred between 1917 and 1950 (Conclusion 3).

v) From Conclusion 3 and Observation 4, it follows that Principle 2 is *incorrect* (Conclusion 4).

The argumentation of the Fourth International was put together in a different way:

i) Principle 2 is *correct*.
ii) From Principle 2 and Observations 3 and 4, it follows that the Soviet Union *anno* 1950 had to be a workers' state (Conclusion 1).
iii) From Conclusion 1 and Observation 2, it follows that the East-European people's democracies were workers' states (Conclusion 2).
iv) From Conclusion 2 and Observation 1, it follows that Principle 1 is *incorrect* (Conclusion 3).

The Fourth International therefore succeeded in protecting the political core of its theory (the Soviet Union remained a workers' state) by sacrificing Principle 1.[7] For Cliff, however, Principle 1 was more important than the political core of the old Trotskyist discourse. His preservation of Principle 1, however, led to sacrificing Principle 2, and the formulation of a new political core ('the Soviet Union *anno* 1950 is state-capitalist' – a political core which does not, of course, necessarily follow from the rejection of the old political core).

Obviously, Cliff could also have followed another argumentation strategy, by putting into question one or more observations. In that case, one could have maintained both principles. Indeed, in a later stage, other figures than Cliff followed this alternative strategy.[8] This strategy involves abandoning Observation 4; it is claimed that, around 1930, a violent anti-proletarian revolution did take place, in the form of forced collectivisation and forced introduction of five-year plans. This new observation I call Observation 4*. The reasoning then takes the following form:

---

[7] Principle 1 was not explicitly rejected by the Fourth International. Rather, Principle 1 was revised in the sense that workers' states could also be established through interventions 'from above', provided this intervention was carried out by a workers' state. The absence of proletarian revolution in the 'structurally assimilated' countries was therefore indirectly compensated. Cf. the 'definitive' official standpoint of the Fourth International as formulated by the Third World Congress in 1951 (Fourth International 1951, and Frank 1951).

[8] This was communicated to me personally by Cliff's collaborator Duncan Hallas during a conversation in London, July 1979.

i)   Principle 1 is *correct.*

ii) From Principle 1 and Observation 1, it follows that the East-European people's democracies were not workers' states (Conclusion 1).

iii) From Conclusion 1 and Observation 2, it follows that the Soviet Union anno 1950 was not a workers' state (Conclusion 2).

iv) From Conclusion 2 and Observation 3, it follows that the dissolution of the workers' state has occurred between 1917 and 1950 (Conclusion 3).

v)   From Conclusion 3 and Observation 4* it follows that Principle 2 is *correct.*

These examples raise the question of why some (groups of) people apparently endlessly adhere to a political core, and are prepared to replace or eliminate observations and principles again and again, while other (groups of) people at a given moment think that these sacrifices in the protective belt go too far, and thus are prepared to eliminate the political core itself. It is clear that the course of development of political discourses is, on the one side, not purely accidental – in particular, given the argumentative determinants – but that, on the other side, there exists no immanent necessity either. In each case, a generally accepted 'truth criterion' which could force a decision between the correctness or incorrectness of a discourse is lacking.

This conclusion leads inevitably to the inference that the course of theoretical development must also be seen as the result of external determinants. External influences can cause a political core, however immunised, to appear no longer plausible, and lose all support, or, alternatively, cause a new core to become rapidly popular in relatively broad circles.

In this perspective, a straight-line evolution does not occur, but, rather, a complex selection process; the discourses develop through a chain of branches, in which alternative possibilities for progress are visible, or where forgotten approaches ('dead branches') can be re-introduced, or where parallel lines hitherto separated from each other can be combined.[9]

In order to analyse the operation of external influences more closely, it seems useful to introduce the sociological concept of *regulative ideas*. By this are meant the more-or-less explicitly stated normative requirements, which the

---

[9] For a closely related vision on the development of pure science, see Böhme, van den Daele and Krohn 1972, pp. 302–16.

users of political discourses impose on these discourses. The most important regulative ideas, in my view, include the following:

a) The discourse must cohere with (or, in a weaker sense, not clearly conflict with) the observations of the users.
b) The discourse must cohere with (or, in a weaker sense, not clearly conflict with) the principles of the users.
c) The discourse must, in the eyes of users, not be manifestly inconsistent.
d) The discourse must cohere with (or, in a weaker sense, not clearly conflict with) political traditions highly valued by the users (e.g. 'Marxism').
e) The discourse must be politically useful, i.e. enable an orientation in the everyday political realities.

This summary does not pretend to be complete. Nor do I want to argue by it that all users of a political discourse attach the same weight to each of these regulative ideas.

Along two routes, regulative ideas can cause users of a discourse to abandon the political core of that discourse:

a) Accepted regulative ideas can be affected by the immunisation of the discourse. The reasons why continuing immunisation seems necessary could be theoretical attacks, or new experiences (which make it necessary to incorporate new observations and/or principles in the discourse).
b) New regulative ideas by the users of the discourse seem to be in conflict with that discourse (although that discourse did cohere with regulative ideas accepted already earlier).

References

This bibliography lists two categories of publications. Those marked * are the primary literature of this study; they refer to Marxist theories of the class nature of the Soviet Union elaborated since 1917, in English, German, French, Italian, Spanish, Swedish, Norwegian, Danish and Dutch. Included are the original editions of books and articles and, if known, English translations of texts originally published in other languages. Translations and reprints (including anthologies) as well as publications which only refer to the topic in passing, have not been included. I have aimed for completeness, knowing, however, that it is unlikely to be realised. Texts not marked * contain information important for the understanding of the primary literature.

*Abendroth, Wolfgang 1978, 'Weder Strategie noch – insgesamt – richtige Analyse, aber eine wichtige Quelle zum Problem des gegenwartigen Entwicklungsstadiums des realen Sozialismus', *Das Argument*, 107: 60–6.
*Abosch, Heinz 1970, 'Leo Trotzki und der Sowjetstaat', *Neue Rundschau*, DXXXI, 3: 564–78.
*Abosch, Heinz 1975, *Trotzki und der Bolschewismus*, Basel: Ed. Etcetera.
*Abramowitsch, R. 1930, 'Revolution und Konterrevolution in Russland', *Die Gesellschaft*, II: 532–41.
*Abramowitsch, R. 1932, 'Stalinismus oder Sozialdemokratie', *Die Gesellschaft*, I: 133–47.
*Abramovitch, Raphael R. 1947, 'From Socialist Utopia to Totalitarian Empire', *Modern Review*, I: 249–65; also in *Left*, 130 (August): 176–82.
Accornero, Aris et al., 1985, *Simone Weil e la condizione operaia*, Rome: Ed. Riuniti.
*Adler, Alexandre et al., 1978, *L'URSS et nous*, Paris: Editions Sociales.
Adler, Frank 1985–6, 'Rizzi's Honor', *Telos*, 66 (Winter): 105–9.
*Adler, Friedrich 1932, 'Das Stalinsche Experiment und der Sozialismus', *Der Kampf*, 25: 4–16.
*Adler, Friedrich 1933, 'Zur Diskussion über Sowjetrussland. Ein Briefwechsel mit Karl Kautsky', *Der Kampf*, 26: 58–69.
Adler, Les K. and Thomas G. Paterson, 1970, 'Red Fascism: The Merger of Nazi Germany and Soviet Russia in the American Image of Totalitarianism, 1930's–1950's', *American Historical Review*, 75, 4 (April): 1046–64.
Ahlberg, René 1976, *Die sozialistische Bürokratie*, Stuttgart: Kohlhammer.
*Ahlberg, René 1979, *Sozialismus zwischen Ideologie und Wirklichkeit. Die marxistische Systemkritik seit Leo Trotzki*, Stuttgart: Kohlhammer.
*Alfa [Amadeo Bordiga] 1946, 'La Russia Sovietica dalla rivoluzione ad oggi', *Prometeo*, 1 (July): 24–38.
Ali, Tariq 1988, *Revolution from Above. Where is the Soviet Union Going?*, London: Hutchinson.
*Altvater, Elmar 1973, 'Der sozialistische Nationalstaat. Etatistische Gesellschaft oder Übergangserscheinung', *Links*, 50 (December): 15–18.
*Altvater, Elmar 1981, 'The Primacy of Politics in Post-Revolutionary Societies', *Review of Radical Political Economics*, XIII, 1 (Spring): 1–10.
*Altvater, Elmar and Christel Neusüss 1969, 'Bürokratische Herrschaft und gesell-schaftliche Emanzipation. Zur Dialektik soziökonomischer Reformen in der Übergangsgesellschaft', *Neue Kritik*, 51–52: 19–51.

*Alvin, Milton 1941a, 'Russia – A Workers' State', *New International*, VII: 27–30.
*Alvin, Milton 1941b, 'For the Defence of the S.U.', *New International*, VII: 184–7.
Ambrosius, Gerold 1981, *Zur Geschichte des Begriffs und der Theorie des Staatskapitalismus und des staatsmonopolistischen Kapitalismus*, Tübingen: J.C.B. Mohr (Paul Siebeck).
*Amin, Samir 1984, 'Expansion or Crisis of Capitalism? (Are the U.S.S.R. and China Capitalist?)', *Contemporary Marxism*, 9: 3–17.
*Amodio, Luciano 1973, 'La rivoluzione bolscevica nell'interpretazione di Rosa Luxemburg', *Annali Istituto Giangiacomo Feltrinelli*: 289–325.
Anderson, Kevin 1988, 'Raya Dunayevskaya, 1910 to 1987, Marxist Economist and Philosopher', *Review of Radical Political Economics*, 20, 1: 62–74.
Anderson, Perry 1976, *Considerations on Western Marxism*, London: New Left Books.
*Anderson, Perry 1983, 'Trotsky's Interpretation of Stalinism', *New Left Review*, I, 139 (May-June): 49–58.
*Andreff, W. 1978, 'Capitalisme d'Etat ou monopolisme d'Etat en URSS? Propos d'étape', in *Economie politique de la planification en système socialiste*, edited by M. Lavigne, Paris: Economica.
*Andreff, W. 1980, 'L'URSS et eux', *Critique socialiste*, 40: 53–67.
*Andreff, W. 1983–4, 'Marxisme en crise cherche sociétés socialistes: à propos des thèses de P.M. Sweezy et de B. Chavance', *Babylone*, 2–3: 100–24.
*Anon. 1947, 'The Russian Question Today', *Fourth International*, VIII, 9 (November-December): 259–73.
*Anon. 1951, 'Answer of SWP to Natalia Trotsky's Letter', *The Militant*, 4 June.
Anon. 1954, 'Cronaca della riunione', *Il Programma Communista*, III–21 (11–25 November).
Anon. 1955a, 'La riunione interfederale di lavoro a Napoli il 24–25 aprile', *Il Programma Comunista*, IV–9 (7–21 May 1955).
Anon. 1955b, 'La grandi questioni storiche della rivoluzione in Russia. La riunione interfederale di Genova del 6 e 7 agosto 1955', *Il Programma Comunista*, IV–15 (26 August–8 September 1955).
*Anon. 1958, *Milovan Djilas en de nieuwe klasse*, Amsterdam: Spartacusbond.
Anon. 1963, 'Is Yugoslavia a Socialist Country?', *Peking Review*, 27 September.
*Anon. 1968, *How The Soviet Revisionists Carry Out All-Round Restoration of Capitalism in the USSR*, Beijing: Foreign Languages Press.
*Anon. 1977, 'Bahros "Alternative". Analyse und Kritik', *Spartacus*, 38: 20–2.
Anon. 1980, 'Ein Technokrat im Gewand des Propheten: Bhagwan Bahro', *Autonomie*, New Series, 4–5.
*Anon. 1981a, *Sozialistische Revolution in einem unterentwickelten Land. Texte der Menschewiki zur russischen Revolution und zum Sowjetstaat aus den Jahren 1903 bis 1937*, Hamburg: Junius.
Anon. 1981b, 'Nils Holmberg – ett liv för socialismen', *Marxistisk Forum*, 3: 19–25.
Anon. 1987, 'Rae Spiegel (Raya Dunayevskaya) (1910–1987)', *Cahiers Léon Trotsky*, 31: 125-6.
*Arato, Andrew 1978, 'Understanding Bureaucratic Centralism', *Telos*, 35 (Spring): 73–87.
*Arato, Andrew 1985, 'Between Reductionism and Relativism: Soviet Society as a World System', *Telos*, 63 (Spring): 178–87.
Andrew Arato 1987, 'The Budapest School and Actually Existing Socialism', *Theory and Society*, 16: 593–619.
*Arato, Andrew and Mihaly Vajda 1980, 'The Limits of the Leninist Opposition. Reply to David Bathrick', *New German Critique*, 19 (Winter): 167–75.
Ardelt, Rudolf G. 1984, *Friedrich Adler: Probleme einer Persönlichkeitsentwicklung um die Jahrhundertwende*, Vienna: Österreichischer Bundesverlag.
*Ariat, André 1946, 'Le régime soviétique est-il socialiste?', *Masses – Socialisme et Liberté*, 2 (15 March): 22–4 and 3 (June): 20–2.
Aron, Raymond 1953, 'La Russie après Staline', *Preuves*, 32 (October): 5–13.
*Arthur, Chris J. 1972, 'The Coming Soviet Revolution', in N. Krasso (ed.), *Trotsky – The Great Debate Renewed*, St Louis: New Critics Press.

Arthur, Chris J. 1984, 'What Is Stalinism?', *International*, 9, 1 (January–April): 11–14.
*Arthur, Christopher J. 2000, 'Epitaph for the USSR: A Clock Without a Spring', *Critique*, 32–33: 91–122. [Slightly shortened version in Arthur, *The New Dialectic and Marx's 'Capital'*, Leiden: Brill, 2002.]
Aston, T.H. and C.H.E. Philpin (eds.) 1985, *The Brenner Debate. Agrarian Class Structure and Economic Development in Pre-Industrial Europe*, Cambridge: Cambridge University Press.
Aufheben 1997, 'What Was the USSR? Towards a Theory of the Deformation of Value under State Capitalism (I)', *Aufheben*, 6 (Autumn): 4–39.
Aufheben 1998, 'What Was the USSR? Towards a Theory of the Deformation of Value under State Capitalism (II): Russia as a Non-Mode of Production', *Aufheben*, 7 (Autumn): 26–41.
Aufheben 1999, 'What Was the USSR? Towards a Theory of the Deformation of Value under State Capitalism (III): Left Communism and the Russian Revolution', *Aufheben*, 8 (Autumn): 24–44.
Aufheben 2000, 'What Was the USSR? Towards a Theory of the Deformation of Value under State Capitalism (IV)', *Aufheben*, 9 (Autumn): 29–46.
Avrich, Paul 1984, 'Bolshevik Opposition to Lenin: G.T. Miasnikov and the Workers' Group', *The Russian Review*, 43: 1–29.
Badia, Gilbert 1974, 'Rosa Luxemburg und Lenin', in *Rosa Luxemburg oder Die Bestimmung des Sozialismus*, edited by Claudio Pozzoli, Frankfurt am Main: Suhrkamp.
*Bahne, Siegfried 1962, 'Trotsky on Stalin's Russia', *Survey*, 41 (April): 27–42.
*Bahro, Rudolf 1977, *Die Alternative. Zur Kritik des real existierenden Sozialismus*, Frankfurt am Main: EVA. [*The Alternative in Eastern Europe*, trans. David Fernbach, London: New Left Books, 1978.]
Baran, Paul and Paul Sweezy 1966, *Monopoly Capitalism*, New York: Monthly Review Press.
*Barrot, Jean [Gilles Dauvé] 1972, *Le mouvement communiste (Essai de définition)*, Paris: Champ Libre.
*Barrot, Jean [Gilles Dauvé] and François Martin 1974, *Eclipse and Re-Emergence of the Communist Movement*, Detroit: Black & Red.
*Bartsch, Günter 1962, 'Von Trotzki zu Djilas', *Die Neue Gesellschaft*, IX, 3: 216–20.
Bass, Robert and Marbury, Elizabeth (eds.) 1959, *The Soviet-Yugoslav Controversy, 1948–58: A Documentary Record*, New York: Prospect Books.
Bathrick, David 1978, 'The Politics of Culture: Rudolf Bahro and Opposition in the GDR', *New German Critique*, 15 (Autumn): 3–24.
*Bauer, Otto 1919, 'Karl Kautsky und der Bolschewismus', *Der Kampf*, 12: 661–7.
Bauer, Otto 1936, *Zwischen zwei Weltkriegen? Die Krise der Weltwirtschaft, der Demokratie und des Sozialismus*, Bratislava: Eugen Prager.
*Bayar, Ali 1992, 'La théorie de Marx et le mode de production partitique', *Revue d'études comparatives est-ouest*, 2–3 (June–September): 211–27.
Becker, Gabriel 1978, 'The Left in Hungary', *Critique*, 9 (Spring-Summer): 135–42.
*Becker-Panitz, Helmut et al. 1977, '"Realer Sozialismus" und realer Sozialismus. Bedingungen und Chancen einer sozialistischen Entwicklung in Gesellschaften sowjetischen Typs', *Jahrbuch Arbeiterbewegung*, 5: 9–37.
*Becker-Panitz, Helmut et al. 1979, *Die Sowjetunion und Europa. Gesellschaftsform und Aussenpolitik der UdSSR*, Frankfurt am Main: Campus.
*Behrens, Fritz 1990, 'Der real existierende Sozialismus', *Utopie kreativ*, 2 (October): 85–9 and 3 (November): 39–44.
*Behrens, Fritz 1992, *Abschied von der sozialen Utopie*, edited by Hannamaria Loschinski, Berlin: Akademie-Verlag.
*Bell, Daniel 1958, 'Ten Theories in Search of Reality: The Prediction of Soviet Behavior', *World Politics*, X, 3 (April): 327–65.
Bell, Daniel 1959, 'The Strange Tale of Bruno R.', *The New Leader*, 28 September: 19–20.
Bell, Daniel 1971, 'The Post-Industrial Society: The Evolution of an Idea', *Survey*, XVII, 2: 102–68.

Bell, Daniel 1988, 'The End of Ideology Revisited (Part I)', *Government and Opposition*, 23, 2, Spring: 131–50.

*Bellis, Paul 1979, *Marxism and the U.S.S.R. The Theory of Proletarian Dictatorship and the Marxist Analysis of Soviet Society*, Basingstoke: Macmillan.

Bence, György and Janos Kis 1980, 'On Being a Marxist: A Hungarian View', *The Socialist Register*, 1980: 263–97.

*Bensaïd, Daniel 1972, 'Révolution socialiste et contre-révolution bureaucratique', *Critiques de l'économie politique*, 7–8: 116–49.

*Bensaïd, Daniel 1980, 'Lecture de Rudolf Bahro – Trois incohérences théoriques et leurs conséquences politiques', *Critique communiste*, 30: 53–65.

Beradt, Charlotte 1969, *Paul Levi. Ein demokratischer Sozialist in der Weimarer Republik*, Frankfurt am Main: EVA.

Bergman, Jay 1987, 'The Perils of Historical Analogy: Leon Trotsky on the French Revolution', *Journal of the History of Ideas*, 48: 73–98.

*Berkhahn, Günter and Rudi Dutschke 1977–8, 'Über die allgemeine reale Staatssklaverei. Die Sowjetunion in der russischen Geschichte', *L'76*, 6: 135–62 and 9: 64–90.

Berle, Adolf and Gardiner Means 1932, *The Modern Corporation and Private Property*, New York: Macmillan.

Bernstein, Howard R. 1981, 'Marxist Historiography and the Methodology of Research Programs', *Studies in Marxist Historical Theory* [= *History and Theory, Beiheft 20*]: 424–49.

*Bessaignet, Pierre 1947, 'Réponse à une théorie de la bureaucratie nouvelle', *La Revue Internationale*, 18 (October): 103–11.

*Bettelheim, Charles 1947, 'Une mystification: la "révolution directorale"', *La Revue Internationale*, 16 (June): 387–97.

*Bettelheim, Charles 1968, *La Transition vers l'économie socialiste*, Paris: Maspero.

*Bettelheim, Charles 1969, 'On the Transition between Capitalism and Socialism', *Monthly Review*, 20, 10 (March): 1–10.

*Bettelheim, Charles 1970a, *Calcul économique et formes de propriété*, 2 vols., Paris: Maspero. [*Economic Calculation and Forms of Property. An Essay on the Transition Between Capitalism and Socialism*, New York: Monthly Review Press, 1975.]

*Bettelheim, Charles 1970b, 'More on the Society of Transition', *Monthly Review*, 22, 7 (December): 1–14.

*Bettelheim, Charles 1971, 'Dictatorship of the Proletariat, Social Classes, and Proletarian Ideology', *Monthly Review*, 23, 6 (November): 55–76.

*Bettelheim, Charles 1974, *Les luttes de classes en URSS (1917–1923)*, Paris: Maspero/Seuil. [*Class Struggles in the USSR: First Period, 1917–1923*, New York: Monthly Review Press, 1976.]

*Bettelheim, Charles 1977, *Les luttes de classes en URSS (1923–1930)*, Paris: Maspero/Seuil. [*Class Struggles in the USSR: Second Period, 1923–1930*, New York: Monthly Review Press, 1978.]

Bettelheim, Charles 1978, *Questions sur la Chine après la mort de Mao Tse-toung*, Paris: Maspero.

[Bettelheim,Charles 1979], 'Interview mit Charles Bettelheim', in Kommunistischer Bund, *Texte zur Stalinfrage*, Hamburg: Jürgen Reents Verlag.

*Bettelheim, Charles 1982, *Les luttes de classes en URSS (1930–1941): Tome premier: Les dominés*, Paris: Maspero/Seuil.

*Bettelheim, Charles 1983, *Les luttes de classes en URSS (1930–1941): Tome deuxième: Les dominants*, Paris: Maspero/Seuil.

*Bettelheim, Charles 1985, 'The Specificity of Soviet Capitalism', *Monthly Review*, 37, 4 (September): 43–56.

*Bettelheim, Charles and Gilles Martinet 1948, 'Marxisme et démocratie', *La Revue Internationale*, 20 (January–February): 33–43.

*Beyerstedt, Horst-Dieter 1987, *Marxistische Kritik an der Sowjetunion in der Stalinära (1924–1953)*, Frankfurt am Main: Peter Lang.

*Big Flame 1980, *The Nature of So-Called Socialist Societies,* London: Big Flame International Committee.

*Binns, Peter 1975, 'The Theory of State Capitalism', *International Socialism,* I, 74 (January): 20–5. [Revised reprint in Peter Binns, Tony Cliff and Chris Harman, *Russia: From Workers' State to State Capitalism,* London: Bookmarks, 1987.]

*Binns, Peter and Duncan Hallas 1976, 'The Soviet Union. State Capitalist or Socialist?', *International Socialism,* I, 91 (September): 16–27.

*Binns, Peter and Haynes, Mike 1980, 'New Theories of Eastern European Class Societies', *International Socialism,* II, 7 (Winter): 18–50.

Birchall, Ian 2003, 'Michael Kidron (1930–2003)', *International Socialism,* II, 99 (Summer): 103–13.

*Biro, B. [Chris J. Arthur] 1969, 'Workers' States – Problems of Transition', *Marxist Studies,* I, 4: 6–20 and 5: 5–17. [Abridged version: C.J. Arthur, 'The Revolution Betrayed', *Radical Philosophy,* 3 (Winter 1972): 2–9.]

*Bleibtreu-Favre, Marcel 1951, 'Where Is Pablo Going?', in *Trotskyism versus Revisionism: A Documentary History,* I, edited by Cliff Slaughter, London: New Park Publications, 1974.

Blick, Karen 1995, 'Adam Westoby', *Revolutionary History,* 5, 4 (Spring): 194–5.

*Blum, Léon 1947a, 'Révolution socialiste ou révolution directorale', *La Revue Socialiste,* New Series, 7 (January): 1–10. ['Socialist or Managerial Revolution?', *Modern Review,* I (1947): 118–29.]

Bock, Hans Manfred 1969a, *Syndikalismus und Linkskommunismus van 1918–1923. Zur Geschichte und Soziologie der FAUD (S), der AAUD und der KAPD,* Meisenheim am Glan: Anton Hain.

Bock, Hans Manfred 1969b, 'Zur Geschichte und Theorie der Holländischen Marxistischen Schule', in Anton Pannekoek and Herman Gorter, *Organisation und Taktik der proletarischen Revolution,* edited by Hans Manfred Bock, Frankfurt am Main: Neue Kritik.

*Bögeholz, Hartwig 1978, 'Bahros Klassentheorie', *Prokla,* 33: 147–59.

Böhme, Gernot, Wolfgang van den Daele, and Wolfgang Krohn 1972, 'Alternativen in der Wissenschaft', *Zeitschrift für Soziologie,* 1, 4: 302–16.

*Boella, Laura 1979, 'Eastern European Societies', *Telos,* 41 (Autumn): 59–75.

Boggs, Grace Lee 1993, 'Thinking and Acting Dialectically: C.L.R. James, the American Years', *Monthly Review,* 45, 5 (October): 38–50.

Boggs, Grace Lee 1998, *Living for Change: An Autobiography,* Minneapolis: University of Minnesota Press.

*Bongiovanni, Bruno 1979, 'Il destino della burocrazie e la dissoluzione del trotskismo', *AnArchos,* 3 (Autumn): 221–39.

*Bongiovanni, Bruno 1982, 'La natura sociale dell'URSS e l'impervia terza via', *Belfagor,* 37, 2 (March): 223–32.

*Bongiovanni, Bruno (ed.) 1975, *L'antistalinismo di sinistra e la natura sociale dell' URSS,* Milan: Feltrinelli.

*[Bordiga , Amadeo] 1951, 'La controrivoluzione maestra', *Battaglia Comunista,* XII, 18, 29 August–12 September.

*[Bordiga, Amadeo] 1952a, 'Dialogato con Stalin', *Il Programma Comunista,* I, 1, 10–24 October – I, 4, 20 November–4 December.

*[Bordiga, Amadeo] 1952b, 'Il Marxismo dei cacagli', *Battaglia Comunista,* XIII–8 (7–30 April).

*[Bordiga, Amadeo] 1952c, 'Le gambe ai cani', *Battaglia Comunista,* XIII–II (20 May–9 June).

[Bordiga, Amadeo] 1953, *Dialogato con Stalin,* Milan: Edizioni Prometeo.

[Bordiga, Amadeo] 1954–5, 'Russia e rivoluzione nella teoria marxista. Rapporto alla riunione interfederale di Bologna', *Il Programma Comunista,* III, 21: 11–25 November 1954–IV: 22 April–6 May 1955.

*[Bordiga, Amadeo] 1955a, 'Struttura economica e sociale della Russia d'oggi. Rapporto alla riunione di Napoli', *Il Programma Comunista,* IV, 10: 25 May–4 June–IV, 14: 28 July–25 August.

*[Bordiga, Amadeo] 1955b, 'La Russia nella storia mondiale, nella Grande Rivoluzione e nella società contemporanea. Sintesi della relazioni di Bologna, Napoli e Genova', *Il Programma Comunista*, IV, 15: 26 August–8 September and IV, 16: 9–23 September.

*[Bordiga, Amadeo] 1955–57, 'Struttura economica e sociale della Russia d'oggi. Rapporto alla riunioni di Napoli e Genova', *Il Programma Comunista*, IV, 17: 23 September–7 October 1955–V, 4: 18 February–2 March 1956 and V, 11: 18 May–1 June 1956–VI, 12: 6 June–21 June 1957.

*[Bordiga, Amadeo] 1956a, 'Dialogato coi morti: il XX Congresso del Partito Comunista Russo', *Il Programma Comunista*, V, 5: 3–17 March–V, 10: 6–18 May.

*[Bordiga, Amadeo] 1956b, *Dialogato coi morti*, Milan: Edizioni di 'Il Programma Comunista'.

*[Bordiga, Amadeo] 1976, *Struttura economica e sociale della Russia d'oggi*, Milan: Edizioni Il Programma Comunista.

Borgognone, Giovanni 2000, *James Burnham: totalitarismo, managerialismo e teoria delle élites*, Prefazione Bruno Bongiovanni, Aosto: Stylos.

*Borillin, B. 1929, 'Lenin über die "Ökonomik der Transformation"', *Unter dem Banner des Marxismus*, III: 834–68.

Bornstein, Sam and Al Richardson 1986, *The War and the International. A History of the Trotskyist Movement in Britain 1937–1949*, London: Socialist Platform.

*Boston Study Group 1981, 'More on *The Myth of Capitalism Reborn*', *Monthly Review*, 32, 10 (March): 60–2.

*Bostulo, Pablo 1981, 'Materialismo histórico y "socialismo real": Una crítica de Bahro', *Argumentos*, 41: 55–7.

*Bourdet, Yvon 1969, 'Otto Bauer et la Russie soviétique. Quatre lettres inédites d'Otto Bauer à Karl Kautsky', *International Review of Social History*, XIV: 468–78.

[Bourrinet, Philippe] 1981, *La gauche communiste d'Italie*, Brussels: Courant Communiste International.

Boyer, Robert 2004, *Théorie de la régulation. 1. Les fondamentaux*, Paris: La Découverte.

Braunthal, Julius 1965, *Victor und Friedrich Adler. Zwei Generationen Arbeiterbewegung*, Vienna: Verlag der Wiener Volksbuchhandlung.

*Braverman, Harry 1954, 'Russia and Socialism', *The American Socialist*, I, 9 (September): 6–8.

Braverman, Harry 1967, 'The Successes, the Failures, and the Prospects', *Monthly Review*, 19, 6 (November): 22–8. [Also in Leo Huberman et al., *Fifty Years of Soviet Power*, New York: Monthly Review Press, 1967.]

Bresciani, Dario 2001, 'Bordiga ou de l'attentisme?', *Cahiers Léon Trotsky*, 75 (October): 23–5.

*Brendel, Cajo 1990, 'Wat voor samenleving schiep de Russische Oktoberrevolutie?', *Daad en Gedachte*, 26, 3 (April): 3–8 and 26, 4 (May): 4–8.

*Brenner, Robert 1989, [no title], *Workers' Liberty*, 12–13 (August): 28–9.

*Brenner, Robert 1991a, 'The Soviet Union and Eastern Europe (I) The Roots of the Crisis', *Against the Current*, 30 (January–February): 27–31.

Brenner, Robert 1991b, 'The Soviet Union and Eastern Europe (II): Nature of the Transition', *Against the Current*, 31 (March–April): 40–5.

*Breuer, Stefan 1974, 'Utopie als Affirmation. Bemerkungen zu Rudi Dutschkes "Versuch, Lenin auf die Füsse zu stellen"', *Leviathan*, 2: 572–96.

*Brokmeier, Peter 1974, 'Über die Bedeutung Sohn-Rethels für eine materialistische Theorie der Übergangsgesellschaften in Osteuropa', in *Übergangsgesellschaft: Herrschaftsform und Praxis am Beispiel der Sowjetunion*, edited by Peter W. Schulze, Frankfurt am Main: Fischer Taschenbuch Verlag.

*Brossat, Alain 1980, 'La révolution culturelle chez Rudolf Bahro', *Critique Communiste*, 30: 39–51.

Broué, Pierre 1982a, 'Le Mouvement trotskyste en Amérique Latine jusqu'en 1940', *Cahiers Léon Trotsky*, 11 (September): 13–30.

Broué, Pierre 1982b, 'Sur l'histoire du Parti Communiste Tchécoslovaque', *Revue Française de Science Politique*, 32: 270–4.

Brzezinski, Zbigniew K. 1961, *The Soviet Bloc. Unity and Conflict*, New York: Praeger.

*Bubis, Mordecai Donald 1988, 'Débat sur la question russe en 1937', *Cahiers Léon Trotsky*, 35 (September): 39–55.

*Bucharin, Nikolai 1925, *Karl Kautsky und Sowjetrussland*, Vienna: Verlag für Literatur und Politik.

*Buci-Glucksmann, Christine 1982, 'L'Austro-marxisme face à l'expérience soviétique. Aux origines d'une "troisième voie"?', in *L'URSS vue de gauche*, edited by Lilly Marcou, Paris: Presses Universitaires de France.

Buckmiller, Michael 1973a, 'Marxismus als Realität. Zur Rekonstruktion der theoretischen und politischen Entwicklung Karl Korschs', *Jahrbuch Arbeiterbewegung*, 1: 15–85.

Buckmiller, Michael 1973b, 'Zeittafel zu Karl Korsch – Leben und Werk', *Jahrbuch Arbeiterbewegung*, 1: 103–6.

Buckmiller, Michael 1976, *Karl Korsch und das Problem der materialistischen Dialektik. Historische und theoretische Voraussetzungen seiner ersten Marx-Rezeption (1909–1923)*, Hannover: SOAK.

Buckmiller, Michael 1981, 'Bibliographie der Schriften von Paul Mattick 1924–1981', *Internationale wissenschaftliche Korrespondenz zur Geschichte der deutschen Arbeiterbewegung*, 17: 197–224.

Buckmiller, Michael and Götz Langkau (eds.) 1974, 'Karl Korsch: Briefe an Paul Partos, Paul Mattick und Bert Brecht, 1934–1939', *Jahrbuch Arbeiterbewegung*, 2: 117–249.

*Buddeberg, Manfred Paul 1976, 'Wer herrscht in den "nachkapitalistischen" Gesellschafen und warum? Eine Kritik an Renate Damus', *Prokla*, 22: 125–48.

Buhle, Paul (ed.) 1986, *C.L.R. James: His Life and Work*, London: Allison & Busby.

Buhle, Paul 1988, *C.L.R. James. The Artist as Revolutionary*, London: Verso.

*Buick, Adam 1975, 'The Myth of the Transitional Society', *Critique*, 5: 59–70.

*Buick, Adam 1997–8, 'Why the Russian Revolution Wasn't a Proletarian Revolution', *New Interventions*, 8, 2 (Winter): 7–10.

Buick, Adam 2004, 'Introduction', in Rudolf Sprenger, *Bolshevism. Its Roots, Role, Class View and Methods*, Translated from the German by Integer, Sawbridgeworth: Redline.

*Buick, Adam and John Crump 1986, *State Capitalism: The Wages System under New Management*, London: Macmillan.

[Burnham, James and Joseph Carter] 1937, *Socialist Workers Party Bulletin*, 2.

Burnham, James 1938a, 'From Formula to Reality', *Socialist Workers Party Bulletin*, 5: 11–25.

Burnham, James 1938b, 'Roosevelt Faces the Future', *New International*, 4 (February): 43–5.

Burnham, James 1939, 'The Future of Roosevelt', *New International*, 5 (September): 26–3.

*Burnham, James 1941, *The Managerial Revolution. What Is Happening in the World*, New York: John Day Company.

Busino, Giovanni et al. 1989, *Autonomie et autotransformation de la société: la philosophie militante de Cornelius Castoriadis*, Geneva: Droz.

*Bust-Bartels, Axel and Georg Stamatis 1975, *Zur Produktionsweise und Theorie der Übergangsgesellschaften*, Giessen/Lollar: Achenbach.

Cabaud, Jacques 1960, *L'Expérience vécue de Simone Weil*, Paris: Plon.

*Caillosse, Jacques 1989, 'La question du Thermidor soviétique dans la pensée politique de Léon Trotsky', *Cahiers Léon Trotsky*, 37 (March): 5–85.

*Callinicos, Alex 1979, 'Maoism, Stalinism and the Soviet Union', *International Socialism*, II, 5 (Summer): 80–8.

*Callinicos, Alex 1981, 'Wage Labour and State Capitalism: A Reply to Peter Binns and Mike Haynes', *International Socialism*, II, 12 (Spring): 97–117.

*Callinicos, Alex 1992, 'Rhetoric Which Cannot Conceal a Bankrupt Theory: A Reply to Ernest Mandel', *International Socialism*, II, 57 (Winter): 147–60.

Callinicos, Alex 1995, *Theories and Narratives. Reflections on the Philosophy of History*, Cambridge: Polity Press.

*Callinicos, Alex 1996, 'State in Debate', *International Socialism*, II, 73 (Winter): 117–26.

*Calvin [ps.] 1975, 'Theories of State Capitalism', *Revolutionary Perspectives*, 1: 6–16, [Revised version in *Revolutionary Perspectives*, 19 (1982): 8–31.]

*Camatte, Jacques 1974, 'Bordiga et la révolution russe: Russie et necessité du communisme', *Invariance*, VII, Second Series, 4.

Camatte, Jacques 1975, 'Introduction', in Amadeo Bordiga, *Structure économique et sociale de la Russie d'aujourd'hui: II, Développement des rapports de production après la Révolution bolchevique*, Paris : Ed. de l'Oubli.

*Camatte, Jacques 1978a, *Capital et Gemeinwesen. Le 6e chapitre inédit et l'oeuvre économique de Marx*, Paris: Spartacus.

*Camatte, Jacques 1978b, *Community and Communism in Russia*, London: David Brown.

*Campeanu, Pavel 1986, *The Origins of Stalinism. From Leninist Revolution to Stalinist Society*, trans. Michael Vale, Armonk: M.E. Sharpe.

*Campeanu, Pavel 1988, *The Genesis of the Stalinist Social Order*, trans. Michael Vale, Armonk: M.E. Sharpe.

*Campeanu, Pavel 1990, *Exit. Toward Post-Stalinism*, trans. Michael Vale, Armonk: M.E. Sharpe.

Campeanu, Pavel 2003, *Ceausescu. From the End to the Beginning*, New York: Columbia University Press.

*Campbell, Bill 1980, 'The Class Nature of the Soviet Union and its Implications for Marxist Theory', in Big Flame 1980.

*Cannon, James P. 1954, 'Trotsky or Deutscher?', *Fourth International*, XV, 1 (Winter): 9–16.

Cannadine, David 1984, 'The Present and the Past in the English Industrial Revolution 1880–1980', *Past and Present*, 103 (May): 131–72.

*Cardorff, Peter [Peter Kulemann] 1976, 'Hegemonialbürokratismus gegen National-bürokratismus. Über einige Aspekte des "Internationalismus" der bürokratisierten Übergangsgesellschaften', *Die Internationale*, 9: 101–46.

*Carillo, Santiago 1977, *Eurocomunismo y estado*, Barcelona: Editorial Critica. [*Eurocommunism and the State*, London: Lawrence & Wishart, 1977.]

*Carlo, Antonio 1971, 'La natura socio-economica dell'URSS', *Giovane Critica*, 26 (Spring 1971): 2–75; reprint in Antonio Carlo, *La natura socio-economica dell'URSS*, Milan: Centro Studi Terzo Mondo, 1975. ['The Socio-Economic Nature of the USSR', *Telos*, 21 (Fall 1974): 2–86.]

*Carlo, Antonio 1972, 'Sulla natura sociale dell'URSS. Riposta a Rizzi e a Melotti', *Terzo Mondo*, 15: 74–86.

*Carlo, Antonio 1980, 'The Crisis of Bureaucratic Collectivism', *Telos*, 43 (Spring): 3–31.

Carlo, Antonio 1989, 'Contradictions of Perestroika', *Telos*, 79 (Spring): 29–46.

Carlo, Antonio and Umberto Melotti 1977, 'In Memory of Bruno Rizzi', *Telos*, 33 (Fall): 142–3.

*Carter, Joseph [Joseph Friedman] 1938, 'The Class Nature of the Stalinist State', *Socialist Workers Party Bulletin*, 5.

*Carter, Joseph [Joseph Friedman] 1941, 'Bureaucratic Collectivism', *New International*, 7: 216–21.

*Cartwright, Perry 1980, 'Managerial Society – The Next Stage of Human History', *Monthly Review*, 31, 11 (April): 58–60.

Castilho, José and Marques Neto 1996, *Mario Pedrosa e o Brasil*, São Paulo: Fundação Perseu Abramo.

[Castoriadis, Cornelius] 1949, 'Socialisme ou Barbarie', *Socialisme ou Barbarie*, 1 (March): 7–46. ['Socialism or Barbarism', in Castoriadis 1988.]

Castoriadis, Cornelius 1973, 'Introduction', in Castoriadis, *La Société Bureaucratique*, I: *Les rapports de production en Russie*, Paris: UGE: 11–61. ['General Introduction', in Castoriadis 1988.]

Castoriadis, Cornelius 1975, 'An Interview with Cornelius Castoriadis', *Telos*, 23 (Spring): 131–55.

*Castoriadis, Cornelius 1978–79, 'The Social Regime in Russia', *Telos*, 38 (Winter): 32–47.

Castoriadis, Cornelius 1988, *Political and Social Writings*, I: *From the Critique of Bureaucracy to the Positive Content of Socialism*, trans. David Ames Curtis, Minneapolis: University of Minnesota Press.

*Challinor, Raymond 1948, '"State Capitalism" – A New Order', *Left*, 140 (June): 137–41.

Challinor, Ray[mond] 1995, 'The Perspective of the Long Haul', *Workers' Liberty*, 21 (May): 27–8.

Chattopadhyay, Paresh 1972, 'On the Political Economy of the Transition Period', *Monthly Review*, 24, 4 (September): 12–29.

*Chattopadhyay, Paresh 1981, 'Rise of Social Capitalism in the USSR', *Economic and Political Weekly*, 24: 1063–8, 25–26: 1103–20 and 27: 1157–61.

*Chattopadhyay, Paresh 1983, 'Post-Revolutionary Society: Socialism, Bureaucracy or Social Capitalism?', *Revue des Pays de l'Est*, 1–2: 199–224.

*Chattopadhyay, Paresh 1987, 'On the Marxian Category of "Competition of Capitals" and its Relevance for the "Postrevolutionary" Economy', *Research in Political Economy*, 10: 3–25.

*Chattopadhyay, Paresh 1990, 'La dynamique de l'économie soviétique à la lumière de l'analyse marxienne de l'accumulation du capital', *Economie appliquée*, 2: 5–32.

*Chattopadhyay, Paresh 1992, 'Economics of Shortage or Specificity of Capital Accumulation? The Soviet Case – A Marxian Perspective', *Research in Political Economy*, 13: 75–121.

*Chattopadhyay, Paresh 1994, *The Marxian Concept of Capital and the Soviet Experience*, Westport: Praeger.

*Chattopadhyay, Paresh 2004, 'The Soviet Question and Marx Revisited: A Reply to Mike Haynes', *Historical Materialism*, 12, 2: 111–28.

*Chaulieu, Pierre [Cornelius Castoriadis] 1949, 'Les rapports de production en Russie', *Socialisme au Barbarie*, 2 (May–June): 1–66. ['The Relations of Production in Russia', in Castoriadis 1988.]

*Chaulieu, Pierre [Cornelius Castoriadis] and Claude Montal [Claude Lefort] 1946, 'Sur le régime et contre la défense de l'URSS', *Bulletin Interieur*: PCI, 31 (August). ['On the Regime and Against the Defense of the USSR', in Castoriadis 1988.]

*Chaulieu, Pierre [Cornelius Castoriadis] and Claude Montal [Claude Lefort] 1947, 'Le problème de l'URSS et la possibilité d'une troisième solution historique', *L'URSS au lendemain de la guerre. Matériel de discussion préparatoire au IIe congrès de la IVe Internationale*, III (February). ['The Problem of the USSR and the Possibility of a Third Historical Solution', in Castoriadis 1988.]

Chaussy, Ulrich 1983, *Die drei Leben des Rudi Dutschke. Eine Biographie*, Darmstadt: Luchterhand.

*Chavance, Bernard 1977a, 'On The Relations of Production in the USSR', *Monthly Review*, 29, 1 (May): 1–13.

*Chavance, Bernard 1977b, 'Remarques sur la réponse de Paul Sweezy', *Les Temps Modernes*, 375 (October): 34–9.

*Chavance, Bernard 1980a, *Le Capital socialiste*, Paris: Le Sycomore.

*Chavance, Bernard 1980b, 'Une alternative existant réellement? Notes sur le livre de Rudolf Bahro', *Les Temps Modernes*, 412 (November): 794–808.

*Chavance, Bernard 1981, 'La nature du système soviétique. Questions et enjeux', *Les Temps Modernes*, 419 (June): 2198–213.

*Chavance, Bernard 1983, *Le système économique soviétique*, Paris: Le Sycomore.

*Chavance, Bernard 1983–4, 'Pourquoi le capitalisme étatique? Réponse à "Marxisme en crise cherche sociétés socialistes"', *Babylone*, 2–3 (Winter): 126–42.

*Chavance, Bernard 1985, 'Economie et politique dans *La Dictature sur les besoins*', *Les Temps Modernes*, 468–469 (July–August 1985): 103–33.

*Ciaramelli, Fabio 1987, '"Socialisme ou Barbarie" e la questione sovietica', *MondOperaio*, 40,1: 100–6.

*Ciliga, Ante 1938, *Au Pays du Grand Mensonge. Problèmes et documents*, Paris: Gallimard. [Anton Ciliga, *The Russia Enigma*, Westport: Hyperion, 1973.]

*Clarke, George [Bert Cochran] 1953, 'Stalin's Role – Stalin's Future', *Fourth International*, XIV, 1 (January–February): 5–13.

*Clarke, Simon 1990, 'Crisis of Socialism or Crisis of the State?', *Capital & Class*, 42 (Winter), 19–29.

*Clarke, Simon 1992, 'Privatization and the Development of Capitalism in Russia', *New Left Review*, I, 196 (November–December): 3–41.

*Clarke, Simon 1993, 'The Crisis of the Soviet System', in Clarke et al., *What About the Workers? Workers and the Transition to Capitalism in Russia*, London: Verso.

*Clarke, Simon 2004, 'Resnick and Wolff's *Class Theory and History*', *Research in the History of Economic Thought and Methodology. A Research Annual*, 22–A: 355–63.

*Claudin, Fernando 1978, 'Die Debatte um die Natur des "realen Sozialismus" und ihre politischen Konsequenzen', *Kritik*, 16: 123–7.

*Clawson, Pat and James Keenan 1979, 'Economism Exposed – Bettelheim on the Bolshevik Revolution', *The Insurgent Sociologist*, IX, 1: 80–8.

Clecak, Peter 1973, *Radical Paradoxes. Dilemmas of the American Left 1945–1970*, New York: Harper & Row.

Clementi, Andreina de 1971, *Amadeo Bordiga*, Turin: Einaudi.

Cless, Olaf 1978, '"Bürokratie" – Anmerkungen zu einem Schlagwort', in *Beiträge zur Sozialismusanalyse*, Volume I, edited by Peter Brokmeier and Rainer Rilling, Cologne: Pahl-Rugenstein.

Cliff, Tony [Ygael Gluckstein] 1947, 'All That Glitters Is Not Gold. A Reply to Germain's "From the ABC to Current Reading: Boom, Revival or Crisis?"', Revolutionary Communist Party, British Section of the Fourth International, *Internal Bulletin*, (September). [Reprint in Cliff, 2003.]

*Cliff, Tony [Ygael Gluckstein] 1948a, 'The Nature of Stalinist Russia', trans. C. Dallas, Revolutionary Communist Party, British Section of the Fourth International, *Internal Bulletin* (June). (Duplicated text, available at the International Institute of Social History, Amsterdam.) [Reprint in Cliff 2003.]

*Cliff, Tony [Ygael Gluckstein] 1948b, 'The Theory of Bureaucratic Collectivism: A Critique', Duplicated document, [Reprint in Cliff 2003.]

Cliff, Tony [Ygael Gluckstein] 1950, 'On the Class Nature of the "People's Democracies"', in *The Origins of the International Socialists*, edited by Richard Kuper, London: Pluto Press, 1971.

Cliff, Tony [Ygael Gluckstein] 1957, 'Perspectives of the Permanent War Economy', *Socialist Review*, 6, 8 (May): 5–6.

Cliff, Tony [Ygael Gluckstein] 1960, 'The Revolutionary Party and the Class, or Trotsky on Substitutionism', *International Socialism*, I, 2 (Autumn): 14–26.

*Cliff, Tony [Ygael Gluckstein] 1964–65, 'The End of the Road. Deutscher's Capitulation to Stalinism', *International Socialism*, I, 15 (Winter): 10–20.

Cliff, Tony [Ygael Gluckstein] 1979, 'Tony Cliff Interview', *The Leveller*, September.

Cliff, Tony [Ygael Gluckstein] 1991, 'Balance of Powerlessness', *Socialist Review*, September: 10–1.

Cliff, Tony [Ygael Gluckstein] 2000, *A World to Win. Life of a Revolutionary*, London: Bookmarks.

Cliff, Tony [Ygael Gluckstein] 2003, *Marxist Theory after Trotsky*, Selected Writings, Volume 3, London: Bookmarks.

Cohen, Stephen F. 1975, *Bukharin and the Bolshevik Revolution. A Political Biography 1888–1938*, New York: Random House.

Collins, Henry 1961, 'The Case for Left Reformism', *International Socialism*, I, 6 (Autumn): 15–19.

*Colyer, Tom 1947, 'Cork on Russia', *Left*, 133 (November): 247–50.

*Colyer, Tom 1948a, 'What Remains of the Russian Revolution?', *Left*, 136 (February): 32–6.

*Colyer, Tom 1948b, 'Our Attitude to Russia', *Left*, 138 (April): 73–80.

*Conert, Hansgeorg 1974, 'Zur Diskussion über die Sowjetgesellschaft', *Links*, 52 (February): 10–3 and 54 (April): 7–10.

*Conert, Hansgeorg 1977, 'Zur Kritik der Sowjetgesellschaft', *Links*, 87 (April): 15–18.

*Conert, Hansgeorg 1979, 'Über Konstitutionsmerkmale nachkapitalistischer Gesellschaften', *Das Argument*, 117: 716–29.

*Conert, Hansgeorg and Wolfgang Eichwede 1976, *Produktionsverhältnisse und Arbeiterklasse in der UdSSR*, Hannover: Landeszentrale für politische Bildung.

'Conférence de fondation de la IVe Internationale. Procès-verbaux de la conférence etablis selon les notes prises par un délégué américaine et un délégué francais' 1979, *Cahiers Léon Trotsky*, 1: 17–57.

Conner, Cliff 1973, 'From World War II to the Cold War', in *Towards a History of the Fourth International*, Part I, New York: Socialist Workers Party.

*Coolidge, David 1941, 'What is a Workers' State?', *New International*, VII: 116–9.

Corey, Lewis [Louis Fraina] 1934, *The Decline of American Capitalism*, New York: Covici, Friede.

*Cork, Jim 1947a, 'The Russian Question', *Left*, 128 (June): 134–9.

*Cork, Jim 1947b, 'Ridley on Russia', *Left*, 133 (November): 243–6.

*Cork, Jim 1948, 'What Remains of the Russian Revolution?', *Left*, 137 (March): 49–54.

Coser, Lewis 1954, 'But on other terms...', *Dissent*, 1, 3 (Summer): 234–41.

*Cox, Michael 1987, 'Perry Anderson and Leon Trotsky on *The Revolution Betrayed*', *Critique*, 20–1: 151–63.

Cox, Michael 1994, 'Trotsky – His Enemies and Friends and the Soviet Crisis', *Critique*, 26: 149–63.

*Cox, Michael (ed.) 1998, *Rethinking the Soviet Collapse. Sovietology, the Death of Communism and the New Russia*, London: Pinter.

*Craipeau, Yvan 1938, 'La Quatrième Internationale et la Contre-Révolution Russe', *Quatrième Internationale* (June), special issue: 81–5.

*Craipeau, Yvan 1976, 'U.S.S.R.: Comment amorcer le dégel', *Critique socialiste*, 24: 85–90.

*Craipeau, Yvan 1980, 'Trockij e la natura sociale dell'URSS', *Il Ponte*, 36: 11–12: 1440–61.

*Croan, Melvin 1962, 'Prospects for the Soviet Dictatorship: Otto Bauer', in *Revisionism. Essays on the History of Marxist Ideas*, edited by Leopold Labedz, London: George Allen and Unwin.

*C[ycon], D[ieter] 1952a, 'Die innerpolitischen Tendenzen in Sowjetrussland: Der Sieg der "Neuen Intelligenz"', *Funken*, III, 6 (November): 1–4.

*C[ycon], D[ieter] 1952b, 'Klassenstaat oder "Übergang zum Kommunismus"', *Funken*, III, 7 (December): 1–6.

*C[ycon], D[ieter] 1953a, 'Wirtschaftliche Perspektiven der Sowjetunion', *Funken*, III, 9 (February): 7–10.

*C[ycon], D[ieter] 1953b, 'Russische Probleme', *Funken*, III, 10 (March): 9–10.

D'Agostino, Anthony 1979, 'Ambiguities of Trotsky's Leninism', *Survey*, 24, 1 (Winter): 178–203.

*Dallemagne, Jean-Luc 1972, 'Charles Bettelheim ou l'identification des contraires', *Critiques de l'économie politique*, 7–8: 17–46.

*Dallemagne, Jean-Luc 1974, 'La dégénérescence de l'Etat ouvrier', in L.D. Trockij, *La nature de l'URSS*, Paris: La Brèche.

*Damen, Onorato 1977, *Bordiga: validità e limiti d'una esperienza nella sinistra italiana*, Milan: EPI.

*Damkjær, Søren 1979a, 'Bettelheim og teorien om overgangssamfundet', *Historievidenskab*, 17: 43–64.

*Damkjær, Søren 1979b, 'Den tyske skoles socialismeanalyse', *Historievidenskab*, 17: 161–9.

Damus, Renate 1973, *Entscheidungsstrukturen und Funktionsprobleme in der DDR-Wirtschaft*, Frankfurt am Main: Suhrkamp.

*Damus, Renate 1974a, 'Vergesellschaftung oder Bürokratisierung durch Planung in nachkapitalistischen Gesellschaften', *Leviathan*, 2: 179–98.

*Damus, Renate 1974b, 'Ist die Arbeit im Sozialismus Lohnarbeit? Zum Charakter der Arbeit in den nachkapitalistischen Gesellschaften Osteuropas', *Kursbuch*, 38: 92–102.

*Damus, Renate 1976, 'Zur Reproduktion von Herrschaft in nachkapitalistischen Gesellschaften', *Prokla*, 22: 149–59.

*Damus, Renate 1978a, *Der reale Sozialismus als Herrschaftssystem am Beispiel der DDR*, Giessen: Focus.

*Damus, Renate 1978b, 'Die Intelligenz als Potential des gesellschaftlichen Umwälzungsprozesses im "realen Sozialismus": nach Rudolf Bahro', *Prokla*, 31: 67–73.

Daniels, Robert V. 1960, *The Conscience of the Revolution. Communist Opposition in Soviet Russia*, Cambridge, MA.: Harvard University Press.

Datta, Satyabratta 1981, 'Sovjetrysslands historiska förutsättningar. En diskussion av Rudi Dutschkes Rysslandanalys och Leninkritik', *Häften för kritiska studier*, XIV, 3: 46–80.

*Daum, Walter 1990, *The Life and Death of Stalinism. A Resurrection of Marxist Theory*, New York: Socialist Voice.

David, Gérard 2000, *Cornelius Castoriadis: le projet d'autonomie*, Paris: Michalon.

Davy, Marie-Magdaleine 1956, *Simone Weil*, Paris: Ed. Universitaires.

Day, Richard 1973, *Leon Trotsky and the Politics of Economic Isolation*, Cambridge: Cambridge University Press.

*Day, Richard 1975, 'Preobrazhensky and the Theory of the Transition Period', *Soviet Studies*, 27, 2 (April): 196–219.

De Liagre Böhl, Herman 1973, *Herman Gorter. Zijn politieke aktiviteiten van 1909 tot 1920 in de opkomende arbeidersbeweging in Nederland*, Nijmegen: SUN.

De Liagre Böhl, Herman 1996, *Met al mijn bloed heb ik voor U geleefd. Herman Gorter 1864–1927*, Amsterdam: Balans.

*Denitch, Bogdan 1979, 'Eurocommunism and "The Russian Question"', *Telos*, 39 (Spring): 180–91. [Shortened version in *Dissent*, XXVI (Summer 1979): 326–30.]

*Desolre, Guy 1983, 'Commentaire de l'article de P. Chattopadhyay', *Revue des Pays de l'Est*, 1–2: 227–31.

Deutscher, Isaac 1949, *Stalin A Political Biography*, London: Oxford University Press.

*Deutscher, Isaac 1953, *Russia after Stalin*, London: Hamish Hamilton.

*Deutscher, Isaac 1954a, 'Réponse aux critiques', *Esprit*, 212 (March): 350–67.

*Deutscher, Isaac 1954b, 'The Future of Russian Society', *Dissent*, I, 3 (Summer): 221–34.

*Deutscher, Isaac 1954c, 'Russia: After Lenin and After Stalin', *The American Socialist*, I, 11 (November): 25–7.

Deutscher, Isaac 1954d, *The Prophet Armed. Trotsky: 1879–1921*, Oxford: Oxford University Press.

*Deutscher, Isaac 1955a, 'Russia in Transition', *Dissent*, II, 1 (Winter): 23–39.

Deutscher, Isaac 1955b, *Heretics and Renegades and Other Essays*, London: Hamish Hamilton.

Deutscher, Isaac 1959, *The Prophet Unarmed. Trotsky: 1921–1929*, Oxford: Oxford University Press.

Deutscher, Isaac 1963, *The Prophet Outcast. Trotsky: 1929–1940*, Oxford: Oxford University Press.

*Deutscher, Isaac 1967, *The Unfinished Revolution. Russia 1917–1967*, Oxford: Oxford University Press.

*Deutscher, Isaac 1969, 'The Roots of Bureaucracy [Ed. by Tamara Deutscher]', *Canadian Slavonic Studies*, III, 3: 453–72.

*Devaux, Jean 1972, 'Lénine et Trotsky et la transition au socialisme', *Critiques de l'économie politique*, 6: 26–46.

*Dévérité, Jules [Leo Kofler] 1951, *Marxistischer oder stalinistischer Marxismus?*, Cologne: Verlag für politische Publizistik.

Dhongy, Farrukh 2001, *C.L.R. James: A Life*, New York: Pantheon Books.

Dhoquois, Guy 1972, 'Per una critica dell'esotismo: a proposito di socialismo e di capitalismo di Stato', *Terzo Mondo*, 17: 72–8.

*Dickhut, Willi 1974, *Die Restauration des Kapitalismus in der Sowjetunion*, Stuttgart: Neuer Weg.

Dickler, Robert A. 1978, 'Die Gesellschaftstheorie Alfred Sohn-Rethels in historischer Perspektive', in *Symposium Warenform-Denkform. Zur Erkenntnistheorie Sohn-Rethels*, edited by Heinz D. Dombrowski, Ulrich Krause and Paul Roos, Frankfurt am Main: Campus Verlag.

Diederich, Werner (ed.) 1974, *Beiträge zur diachronischen Wissenschaftstheorie*, Frankfurt am Main: Suhrkamp.

*Diner, Dany 1977, 'Geschichtsbewusstsein und Sowjetkritik', *Links*, 91 (September): 16–17.

Dingel, Frank 1981, 'Paul Mattick (1904–1981)', *Internationale wissenschaftliche Korrespondenz zur Geschichte der deutschen Arbeiterbewegung*, 17: 190–7.

*Dittrich, Z.R. 1966, 'Wittfogel and Russia. On the Origins of Russian Autocracy', *Acta Historiae Neerlandica*, I: 53–66.

*Djilas, Milovan 1950, *On New Roads to Socialism. Address Delivered at the Pre-Election Rally of Belgrade Students, March 18, 1950*, Belgrade: Jugoslavenska knjiga.

*Djilas, Milovan 1951, 'Thèmes contemporaines: I, Apparences et essence de l'Union Soviétique', *Questions actuelles du socialisme*, 1–2 (March–April): 3–78. [Originally: *Savremene teme*, Belgrado: Borba, 1950.]

*Djilas, Milovan 1952, 'Class or Caste?', in Djilas, *Parts of a Lifetime*, New York: Harcourt Brace, 1975.

Djilas, Milovan 1956, 'The Storm in Eastern Europe', *The New Leader*, 19 November.

*Djilas, Milovan 1957, *The New Class. An Analysis of the Communist System*, New York: Praeger.

*Domanewskaja, Olga 1934–5, 'Der soziale Gehalt des Sowjetstaates', *Rote Revue*, 14: 267–7.

Draper, Hal 1959, 'Bruno R.', *New Leader*, 12 October: 29.

Draper, Hal 1962, 'Marx and the Dictatorship of the Proletariat', *Etudes de Marxologie*, 6: 5–73.

Draper, Hal 1999, 'Anatomy of the Rizzi Myth', *Workers' Liberty*, 57 (September): 29–31.

Drucker, Peter 1994, *Max Shachtman and His Left. A Socialist's Odyssey through the 'American Century'*, Atlantic Highlands: Humanities Press.

Dubiel, Helmut 1975, 'Kritische Theorie und politische Ökonomie', in Friedrich Pollock, *Stadien des Kapitalismus*, edited and introduced by Helmut Dubiel, Munich: C.H. Beck.

Ducombs, M. 1972, 'Le sens de réformes dans les économies de transition', *Critiques de l'économie politique*, 7–8: 150–61.

Düll, Klaus 1975, *Industriesoziologie in Frankreich. Eine historische Analyse zu den Themen Technik, Industriearbeit, Arbeiterklasse*, Frankfurt: EVA.

Dulles, John W.F. 1973, *Anarchists and Communists in Brazil 1900–1935*, Austin: Texas University Press.

Dulles, John W.F. 1983, *Brazilian Communism 1935–1945. Repression during World Upheaval*, Austin: Texas University Press.

Dunayevskaya, Raya [Rae Spiegel] 1944, 'A New Revision of Marxian Economics', *American Economic Review*, 34, 3 (September): 531–7.

Dunayevskaya, Raya [Rae Spiegel] 1945, 'Revision or Reaffirmation of Marxism? A Rejoinder', *American Economic Review*, 35, 3 (September): 660–4.

*Dunayevskaya, Raya [Rae Spiegel] 1958, *Marxism and Freedom. From 1776 until Today*, New York: Bookman.

*Dunayevskaya, Raya [Rae Spiegel] 1960, 'Bureaucratie et capitalisme d'Etat', *Arguments*, 17: 45–7.

*Dunayevskaya, Raya [Rae Spiegel] 1973, *Russia as State Capitalism*, Detroit: News & Letters.

*Dunayevskaya, Raya [Rae Spiegel] 1992, *The Marxist-Humanist Theory of State-Capitalism: Selected Writings*, Chicago: News & Letters.

*Dutschke, Rudi 1974, *Versuch, Lenin auf die Füsse zu stellen. Über den halbasiatischen und den westeuropäischen Weg zum Sozialismus. Lenin, Lukács und die Dritte Internationale*, West Berlin: Wagenbach.

*Dutschke, Rudi 1975, 'Der Kommunismus, die despotische Verfremdung desselben in der UdSSR und der Weg der DDR zum Arbeiteraufstand vom 17. Juni 1953', in Dutschke and Wilke (eds.) 1975.

*Dutschke, Rudi 1976, 'Antwort auf Schmidt und andere', *Das Argument*, 95: 92–106.

*Dutschke, Rudi 1977, 'Zur Sowjetgesellschaft. Das politisch ungeklärte Problem der Metamorphosen der asiatischen Produktionsweise', *Links*, 89 (June): 15–16.

*Dutschke, Rudi 1978, 'Wider die Päpste. Die Schwierigkeiten, das Buch von Rudolf Bahro zu diskutieren', in Ulf Wolter (ed.), *Antworten auf Bahros Herausforderung des realen Sozialismus'*, West Berlin Olle & Wolter. ['Against the Popes: How Hard It Is to Discuss Bahro's Book', in *Rudolf Bahro: Critical Responses*, edited by Ulf Wolter, White Plains: Sharpe, 1980.]

Dutschke, Rudi and Manfred Wilke (eds.) 1975, *Die Sowjetunion, Solschenizyn und die westliche Linke*, Reinbek: Rowohlt.

*Ebbing, Hans 1975a, 'Plan, pris og "profit" i Sovjetunionen', *Häften för kritiska studier*, VIII, 4: 29–44.

*Ebbing, Hans 1975b, 'Ridderne av den røde fane', *Kontrast*, 53: 9–27.

*Ebbing, Hans 1976, 'Til spørsmålet om arbeidskraftens varekarakter', *Vardøger*, 8: 152–66.

*Eggert, Johann 1973, 'Die Sowjetgesellschaft: eine sozialistische Gesellschaft?', *Links*, 45 (June): 8–10; 46 (July–August): 22–3 and 47 (September): 14–9.

*Eggert, Johann 1974, 'Über den sozialen Antagonismus in der Sowjetgesellschaft', *Links*, 57 (July–August): 16–19.

Entschiedene Linke 1926, 'Resolution zur Politik und Taktik der KPD und Komintern', *Kommunistische Politik*, 2 (April): 2–4.

*Eichwede, Wolfgang 1977, 'Fragen die jeden bewegen…und auf die es keine eindeutigen Antworten gibt', in Wolfgang Eichwede, Peter Knirsch and Boris Meissner, *60 Jahre Sowjet-Russland*, Hannover: Niedersächsische Landeszentrale fur Politische Bildung.

*Eichwede, Wolfgang and Hans Kaiser 1977, 'Sowjetgesellschaft. Zur bisherigen Diskussion in *Links'*, *Links*, 93 (November): 22–4.

*Elfferding, Wieland 1979, 'Gibt es in den sozialistischen Landern Herrschaftsverhältnisse?', *Das Argument*, 117: 730–4.

Eliard, Michel (ed.) 1996, *Naville: la passion de la connaissance*, Toulouse: Presses Universitaires du Mirail-Toulouse.

*Elleinstein, Jean 1975, *Histoire du phénomène stalinien*, Paris: Bernard Grasset.

Ellenstein, Jean 1979, *Staline, Trotsky, le pouvoir et la révolution*, Paris: Julliard.

Engels, Friedrich 1875, 'Letter to August Bebel' dated 18–28 March 1875, in Marx and Engels, *Collected Works*, Volume 45, Moscow: Progress, 1991.

Engels, Friedrich 1878, *Anti-Dühring. Herr Eugen Dühring's Revolution in Science*, in Marx and Engels, *Collected Works*, Volume 25, Moscow: Progress, 1987.

*Erbe, Günther 1978, 'Klassenantagonismus oder Schichtendifferenzierung. Bemerkungen zu Bahros Analyse der Sozialstruktur des realen Sozialismus', *Prokla*, 31: 57–65.

*Fabrègues, Bernard 1976–7, 'Eléments sur les formes spécifiques du capitalisme en URSS', *Communisme*, 25–6 (November–February): 4–25.

*Fagerlid, Olav 1974, 'Noen bemerkninger til Sæmund Fiskvik', *Vardøger*, 6: 152–8.

*Fantham, John and Moshe Machover 1979, *The Century of the Unexpected. A New Analysis of Soviet-Type Societies*, London: Big Flame.

*Farl, Erich 1973, 'The Genealogy of State Capitalism', *International*, 2, 1 (Spring): 18-23.
*Farl, Erich 1974, 'Is the U.S.S.R an Imperialist Country?', *International*, II, 3 (Summer): 23–6.
*Fehér, Ferenc 1978, 'The Dictatorship over Needs', *Telos*, 35 (Spring): 31–42.
*Fehér, Ferenc 1980, 'Paternalismo e dispotismo in URSS', *MondOperaio*, XXXIII, 4: 107–14.
*Fehér, Ferenc, Agnes Heller and György Márkus 1983, *Dictatorship over Needs. An Analysis of Soviet Societies*, Oxford: Basil Blackwell.
Fejtö, Férenc n.d. [1952], *Histoire des démocraties populaires*, I, Paris: Maspero.
Felix, Vs. 1951, 'Soziale Gegensätze in der UdSSR', *Funken*, I, 11 (April): 7–9.
Fenwick, J. [Hal Draper] 1948, 'The Mysterious Bruno R.', *New International*, XIV–XV (September): 215–18.
*[Fernandez, Neil] 1989, *Capitalism and Class Struggle in the USSR* [Subversion Discussion Paper 1], [Manchester]: no publisher.
*Fernandez, Neil 1997, *Capitalism and Class Struggle in the USSR. A Marxist Theory*, Aldershot: Ashgate.
Feyerabend, Paul 1970, 'Consolations for the Specialist', in *Criticism and the Growth of Knowle©e*, edited by Imre Lakatos and Alan Musgrave, Cambridge: Cambridge University Press.
*Filtzer, Donald 1978, 'Preobrazhensky and the Problem of the Soviet Transition', *Critique*, 9 (Spring-Summer): 63–84.
Filtzer, Donald A. 1991, 'The Contradictions of the Marketless Market: Self-Financing in the Soviet Industrial Enterprise, 1986–90', *Soviet Studies*, 43: 989–1009.
*Finger, Barry 1995, 'Russia Before the Deluge: Workers' State or Bureaucratic Collectivism?', *New Politics*, New Series, 5–2 (Winter), 168–79.
*Finger, Barry 1997, 'On Bureaucratic Collectivism', *New Politics*, New Series, 6–3 (Summer), 142–50.
*Fisch, William L. 1973, 'On the Political Economy of the Transition Period', *Monthly Review*, 24, 9 (February): 48.
*Fiskvik, Sæmund 1974, 'Til debatten om utviklinga i Sovjet', *Vardøger*, 6: 137–51.
*Flaherty, Patrick 1990, 'The State and the Dominant Class in the Soviet Perestroika', *Research in Political Economy*, 12: 253–94.
*Fleischer, Helmut 1978, 'Rudolf Bahros Beitrag zur Philosophie des Sozialismus', in *Antworten auf Bahros Herausforderung des 'realen Sozialismus'*, edited by Ulf Wolter, West Berlin: Olle & Wolter: 57–82. ['Bahro's Contribution to the Philosophy of Socialism', in *Rudolf Bahro. Critical Responses*, edited by Ulf Wolter, White Plains: M.E. Sharpe, 1980.]
*Fontaine, J.M. 1980, 'Gouverner par la terreur: Staline et les "transitions autoritaires"', *Critique socialiste*, 40: 75–85.
*Forest, F. [Rae Spiegel] 1942–3, 'An Analysis of Russian Economy', *New International*, VIII (December 1942): 327–32; IX (January 1943): 17–22 and IX (February 1943): 52–7.
Foster, John Bellamy 2004, 'The Commitment of an Intellectual. Paul M. Sweezy (1910–2004)', *Monthly Review*, 56, 5 (October): 5–39.
*Fournier, Laurent 1973, 'Capitalisme en Union Soviétique', *Communisme*, 2 (January–February): 50–70.
Fourth International 1946, 'The New Imperialist Peace and the Building of the Parties of the Fourth International', *Fourth International*, 9, 6 (June): 169–83.
*Fourth International 1947, 'The Russian Question Today', *Fourth International*, 10, 9 (November-December): 259–73.
Fourth International 1949, 'The Evolution of the Buffer Countries', *International Information Bulletin*, June.
Fourth International 1951, 'Class Nature of Eastern Europe' [Resolution of the Third World Congress, introduced by Pierre Frank], *Fourth International*, 12, 6 (November–December): 198–200.

Fourth International 1958, 'The Decline and Fall of Stalinism. Resolution adopted by the Fifth World Congress', *Fourth International*, 1 (Winter): 56–75.

*Fox, Michael 1991, 'Ante Ciliga, Trotskii, and State Capitalism: Theory and Tactics, and Re-Evaluation During the Purge Era, 1935–1939', *Slavic Review*, 50, 1: 127–43.

*Foxcroft, Helen Charlotte 1938, 'The Revolution Betrayed', *The Quarterly Review*, 535: 1–14.

*Franck, Sebastian [Henry Jacoby] 1953a, 'Russische Probleme', *Funken*, III, 9 (February): 1–4.

*Franck, Sebastian [Henry Jacoby] 1953b, 'Probleme einer marxistischen Analyse der russischen Gesellschaft', *Funken*, IV, 4 (September): 57–61.

*Franck, Sebastian [Henry Jacoby] 1958, 'Alte und neue Klassen', *Funken*, IX, 6 (June): 86–90.

Frank, Pierre 1951, 'Evolution of Eastern Europe' [Report to the 3rd World Congress], *Fourth International*, 12, 6 (November–December): 176, 213–18.

*Frank, Pierre 1975, 'Problèmes d'Union soviétique vus d'Union soviétique', *Quatrième Internationale*, New Series, 20–21 (Spring): 37–44.

*Frank, Pierre 1977a, '"Novateurs" et "conservateurs" dans la question de l'URSS', in Pierre Frank, *Le stalinisme*, Paris: Maspero. [Originally published in a supplement of the *Bulletin Intérieur* [International Secretariat of the Fourth International], July 1947.]

*Frank, Pierre 1977b, 'Die Klassennatur der Sowjetunion im Lichte ihrer Krisen', in *Entstalinisierung. Der XX. Parteitag der KPdSU und seine Folgen*, edited by Manfred Crusius and Manfred Wilke, Frankfurt am Main: Suhrkamp.

Frank, Pierre 1977c, *Le stalinisme*, Paris: Maspero.

Frank, Pierre 1978, 'War der "real existierende Sozialismus" historisch notwendig?', in *Antworten auf Bahros Herausforderung des 'realen Sozialismus'*, edited by Ulf Wolter, West Berlin: Olle & Wolter. ['Was "Actually Existing Socialism" Historically Necessary?', in *Rudolf Bahro. Critical Responses*, edited by Ulf Wolter, White Plains: M.E. Sharpe, 1980.]

Freeman, Mike 1986, 'The Road to Power', *Confrontation*, 1 (Summer): 32–89.

*Frölich, Paul 1952, 'Vom Wege zum Sozialismus', *Funken*, II, 11 (April): 9–14.

Frölich Paul 1967, *Rosa Luxemburg: Gedanke und Tat*, Frankfurt am Main: EVA.

*Frölich, Paul 1976, 'Beiträge zur Analyse des Stalinismus. Zwei unveröffentlichte Beiträge aus dem Nachlass', *Jahrbuch Arbeiterbewegung*, 4: 141–58.

*Frühling, Pierre 1974a, 'Reflexioner kring analysen av övergångssamhällena', *Zenit*, 37: 47–61.

*Frühling, Pierre 1974b, 'Synpunkter på M–L–forbundens "Sovjetanalys"', *Häften för kritiska studier*, VII, 7–8: 62–76.

*Frühling, Pierre 1976, 'Nils Holmberg och sovjetanalysen', *Häften för kritiska studier*, IX, 4: 50–60.

*Füredi, Frank 1986, *The Soviet Union Demystified. A Materialist Analysis*, London: Junius.

*Gandy, Ross 1976, 'More on the Nature of Soviet Society', *Monthly Review*, 27, 10 (March): 11–14.

*Gandy, Ross 1977, 'The East European Social Formation', *Monthly Review*, 29, 3 (July–August): 82–8.

*García Casals, Felipe [Pavel Campeanu] 1980a, 'Theses on the Syncretic Society', *Theory and Society*, IX, 2 (March): 233–60.

García Casals, Felipe [Pavel Campeanu] 1980b, 'Introduction', in García Casals, *The Syncretic Society*, translated from the French by Guy Daniels, White Plains: M.E. Sharpe.

*Gardoncini, Giovanni Battista 1978, 'Il sistema sovietica nel dibattito degli austro-marxisti', *MondOperaio*, XXXI, 10: 77–82.

Garstka, Dietrich and Werner Seppmann 1980, 'Aus der Lebensgeschichte Leo Koflers', in *Marxismus und Anthropologie. Festschrift für Leo Kofler*, edited by Ernst Bloch et al., Bochum: Germinal.

*Gates, Albert 1941, 'Burnham and his Managers', *New International*, VII: 144–8, 175–9.
*Gates, Albert 1958, 'Djilas' Indictment of Stalinism', *New International*, XXIV, 1 (Winter): 30–5.
Gaudillière, Jean-Paul et al. 2005, 'De l'autogestion ouvrière au mythe de Solidarnosc. Entretien avec Karol Modzelewski', *Mouvements*, 37 (January–February): 109–18.
*Geisslinger, Hans 1979, 'Die asiatische Produktionsweise – Fata Morgana oder historische Realität? Eine Antwort auf Florian Gellerts Essay "Rudolf Bahro und die asiatische Produktionsweise"', *Theorie und Praxis des Marxismus-Leninismus*, 1: 13–27.
*Gellert, Florian 1978, 'Rudolf Bahro und die Asiatische Produktionsweise', *Theorie und Praxis des Marxismus-Leninismus*, 3: 26–39.
Gerber, John 1989, *Anton Pannekoek and the Socialism of Workers' Self-Emancipation 1873–1960*, Dordrecht: Kluwer.
Germain, E. [Ernest Mandel] 1947a, 'De l'A.B.C. à la lecture courante: boom, reprise ou crise?', *Bulletin Intérieur du Secrétariat International*, II, 16 (July): 34–7.
Germain, E. [Ernest Mandel] 1947b, 'Projet de thèses de la 4e Internationale et le Stalinisme', *Bulletin Interieur du Secrétariat International*, November.
*Germain, E. [Ernest Mandel] 1951a, 'La théorie du "capitalisme d'Etat"', *Quatrième Internationale*, IX, 5–7 (May–July): 21–33.
Germain, E. [Ernest Mandel] 1951b, 'Zur Theorie des "Staatskapitalismus" in Sowjetrussland', *pro und contra*, 2, 7–8 (July–August) [German version of Germain 1951a.]
Germain, E. [Ernest Mandel] 1951c, 'The Theory of "State Capitalism"', *Fourth International*, XII, 5 (September–October): 145–56 [English version of Germain 1951a.]
*Germain, E. [Ernest Mandel] 1951d, 'Nochmals zur Theorie des "russischen" Staatskapitalismus', *pro und contra*, II, 11–12 (November–December): 172–6.
*Germain, E. [Ernest Mandel] 1952, 'Diskussion in der Sackgasse', *pro und contra*, III, 3–4 (March–April): 48.
Germain, E. [Ernest Mandel] 1956, 'Le 6e plan quinquennal', *Quatrième Internationale*, 14, 1–3 (March): 17–21.
*Germain, Ernest [Ernest Mandel] 1958, 'Prospects and Dynamics of the Political Revolution against the Bureaucracy', *Fourth International*, 1 (Winter): 75–81.
Gilcher-Holtey, Ingrid 1986, *Das Mandat des Intellektuellen. Karl Kautsky und die Sozialdemokratie*, West Berlin: Siedler.
Gillman, Joseph M. 1957, *The Falling Rate of Profit. Marx's Law and its Significance to Twentieth Century Capitalism*, London: Dennis Dobson.
*Givsan, Hassan 1978, 'Eine Kritik an Bahros alternativer Geschichsschreibung', in *Antworten auf Bahros Herausforderung des 'realen Sozialismus'*, edited by Ulf Wolter, West Berlin: Olle & Wolter. ['A Critique of Bahro's Alternative Writing of History', in *Rudolf Bahro. Critical Responses*, edited by Ulf Wolter, White Plains: M.E. Sharpe, 1980.]
*Goldman, Albert 1940, *Why We Defend the Soviet Union*, New York: Pioneer Publishers.
Goldner, Loren 1991, 'Amadeo Bordiga, The Agrarian Question and the International Revolutionary Movement', *Critique*, 23: 73–100.
*Golubović, Zagorka 1984, 'Why "Dictatorship Over Needs" is Not Socialism', *Praxis International*, 4: 322–34.
*Golubović, Zagorka 1985, 'Logical Fallacies or Ideological Justifications: Schaff's Arguments on the Socialist Character of "Really Existing Socialism"', *Praxis International*, 5: 86–93.
*Gomáriz, Enrique 1977, 'La discusión acerca de la URSS', *Zona Abierta*, 9–10: 151–71.
Goode, Patrick 1979, *Karl Korsch. A Study in Western Marxism*, London: Macmillan.
Gorman, Robert A. (ed.) 1986, *Biographical Dictionary of Marxism*, Westport: Greenwood Press.

*Gorter, Herman 1920a, *Offener Brief an den Genossen Lenin*, Berlin KAPD. [*Open Letter to Comrade Lenin*, London: Wildcat, 1989.]
*Gorter, Herman 1920b, *De wereldrevolutie*, Amsterdam, J.J. Bos. [*The World Revolution*, trans. H. Mcmillan, Glasgow: Socialist Information and Research Bureau, 1920.]
Gottraux, Philippe 1997, *'Socialisme ou Barbarie': un engagement politique et intellectuel dans la France d'après-guerre*, Lausanne: Payot-Lausanne.
Gottschalch, Wilfried 1962, *Strukturveränderungen der Gesellschaft und politisches Handeln in der Lehre von Rudolf Hilferding*, West Berlin: Duncker & Humblot.
*Gouldner, Alvin W. 1977–8, 'Stalinism: A Study of Internal Colonialism', *Telos*, 34 (Winter): 5–48.
Goutier, Jean-Michel et al. 1982, *Benjamin Péret*, Paris: Ed. Henri Veyrier.
*Graham, V. 1980, 'Some Notes on Big Flame's Contribution to the Discussion of Soviet Type Societies', in *The Nature of So-Called Socialist Societies*, London: Big Flame International Committee.
*Gransow, Volker 1978, 'Jenseits des Stalinismus?', *Das Argument*, 110: 535–45.
Gramonte, Concha 1977, 'Esbozo biografico revolucionario de G. Munis', Appendix II in G. Munis, *Jalones de derrota, promesa de victoria. Critica y teoria de la Revolución Española*, Bilbao and Madrid: Edita Zero.
Gras, Christian 1971, *Alfred Rosmer et le mouvement révolutionnaire international*, Paris: Maspero.
Grebing, Helga (ed.) 1981, *Fritz Sternberg (1895–1963). Für die Zukunft des Sozialismus*, Frankfurt am Main: Otto Brenner Stiftung.
*Green, Joseph 1998, 'On Walter Daum's "The Life and Death of Stalinism". Competition Among Soviet Enterprises and Ministries, and the Collapse of the Soviet Union', *Communist Voice*, 4, 4 (8 December): 31–44.
Greffrath, Mathias 1979, 'Die hydraulische Gesellschaft und das Gespenst der asiatischen Restauration. Gespräch mit Karl August Wittfogel', in Mathias Greffrath, *Die Zerstörung einer Zukunft. Gespräche mit emigrierten Sozialwissenschaftlern*, Reinbek: Rowohlt.
*Grilli, Liliana 1982, *Amadeo Bordiga, capitalismo sovietico e comunismo*, Milan: La Pietra.
Grimshaw, Anna 1989, 'C.L.R. James (1901–1989)', *Revolutionary History*, 2–3 (Autumn): 40–2.
*Grogan, Brian 1971, 'Further Developments (?) in State Capitalism', *International*, I, 6 (September–October): 29–40.
Grossmann, Henryk 1929, *Das Akkumulations- und Zusammenbruchsgesetz des kapitalistischen Systems (Zugleich eine Krisentheorie)*, Leipzig: Verlag von C.L. Hirschfeld.
*Guibeneuf, R. 1948, 'Remarques sur la méthode de J. Burnham', *La Revue Internationale*, 20 (January–February): 49–50.
Guillamón Iborra, Agustin 1993, 'Munis, vie et oeuvre d'un révolutionnaire méconnu', *Cahiers Léon Trotsky*, 50 (May): 85–98.
Gumnior, Helmut and Rudolf Ringguth 1983, *Max Horkheimer*, Reinbek: Rowohlt.
*Haberkern, Ernest E. and Arthur Lipow (eds.) 1996, *Neither Capitalism nor Socialism. Theories of Bureaucratic Collectivism*, Atlantic Highlands: Humanities Press.
Haferkorn, Katja and Peter Schmalfuss 1988, 'Für die Bolschewiki. Eine bisher unbekannte Arbeit Clara Zetkins vom Jahre 1918', *Beiträge zur Geschichte der Arbeiterbewegung*, 30: 620–31.
Hallas, Duncan 1980, 'Eastern European Class Societies', *International Socialism*, II, 9 (Summer): 128–30.
Hallas, Duncan, Raymond Challinor, and Ted Crawford 2000, 'Tony Cliff: Three Appraisals', *Revolutionary History*, 7, 4: 183–94.
*Hamon, Léo 1982, 'Rosa Luxemburg et la révolution russe', in *L'URSS vue de gauche*, edited by Lilly Marcou, Paris: Presses Universitaires de France.
Hampton, Paul 1999, 'Trotskyism after Trotsky? C'est moi!', *Workers' Liberty*, 55 (April): 37–9.
*Hannak, Jacques 1947, 'Die Revolution der Manager', *Die Zukunft*, I: 360–4.
Hansen, F.R. 1985, *The Breakdown of Capitalism. A History of the Idea in Western Marxism*, London: Routledge & Kegan Paul.

*Harman, Chris 1969–70, 'The Inconsistencies of Ernest Mandel', *International Socialism*, I, 41: 36–41.

*Harman, Chris 1977, 'Better a Valid Insight than a Wrong Theory', *International Socialism*, I, 100 (July): 9–13.

*Harman, Chris 1990a, 'The Storm Breaks', *International Socialism*, II, 46 (Spring): 3–93.

*Harman, Chris 1990b, 'From Trotsky to State Capitalism', *International Socialism*, II, 47 (Summer): 137–56.

*Harman, Chris 1990c, 'Criticism which Does not Withstand the Test of Logic''', *International Socialism*, II, 49 (Winter): 65–88. [Also published as 'L'URSS: un capitalisme d'Etat', *Quatrième Internationale*, 37–38 (August-September 1990): 55–73.]

Harmel, Claude 1973, 'Le marxisme de Lucien Laurat', *Est & Ouest*, New Series, XXV, 515 (16–30 September): 15–29.

*Harrer, Jürgen 1978, 'Anmerkungen zu Rudolf Bahro: "Die Alternative"', in *Beiträge zur Sozialismusanalyse*, vol. I, edited by Peter Brokmeier and Rainer Rilling, Cologne: Pahl-Rugenstein.

Harrison, Mark 1985, *Soviet Planning in War and Peace, 1938–45*, Cambridge: Cambridge University Press.

*Haug, Wolfgang Fritz 1979, 'Eurozentrismus bei Bahro und Dutschke', *Das Argument*, 116: 534–42.

*Haumann, Heiko 1974, '5 Thesen zu Johann Eggerts Artikelserie über die Sowjetgesellschaft', *Links*, 53 (March): 17–18.

Haupt, Georges et al. (eds.) 1986, *Karl Kautsky und die Sozialdemokratie Südosteuropas. Korrespondenz 1883–1938*, Frankfurt am Main: Campus.

Hautmann, Hans 1971, *Die verlorene Räterepublik. Am Beispiel der Kommunistischen Partei Deutsch-Österreichs*, Vienna: Europa Verlag.

*Haynes, Michael 1985, *Nikolai Bukharin and the Transition from Capitalism to Socialism*, London: Croom Helm.

*Haynes, Mike 1987, 'Understanding the Soviet Crisis', *International Socialism*, II, 34 (Winter): 3–41.

*Haynes, Mike 1994, 'The Wrong Road on Russia', *International Socialism*, II, 64 (Autumn): 105–13.

*Haynes, Mike 2002, *Russia 1917–2000: Class and Power*, London: Bookmarks.

*Haynes, Mike 2002, 'Marxism and the Russian Question in the Wake of the Soviet Collapse', *Historical Materialism*, 10, 4: 317–62.

*Haynes, Mike 2004, 'Rejoinder to Chattopadyay', *Historical Materialism*, 12, 2: 129–48.

Haynes, Mike and Pete Glatter 1998, 'The Russian Catastrophe', *International Socialism*, II, 81 (Winter): 45–88.

Haynes, Mike and Rumy Husan 2002, 'Whether by Visible or Invisible Hand: The Intractable Problem of Russian and East European Catch-Up', *Competition and Change*, 6, 3 (September): 629–87.

Hearse, Phil 1983, 'Perry Anderson on Stalinism', *International*, 8, 5 (November-December): 31–4.

Hegedüs, Andras 1976, *Socialism and Bureaucracy*, London: Allison & Busby.

Hegedüs, Andras et al. 1976a, *The Humanisation of Socialism. Writings of the Budapest School*, London: Allison & Busby.

Hegedüs, Andras et al. 1976b, *Die Neue Linke in Ungarn*, Vol. 2, Berlin: Merve.

*Heidt, Ulrich 1979, *Arbeit und Herrschaft im 'realen Sozialismus'*, Frankfurt am Main: Campus.

*Heidt, Ulrich and Elisabeth Mangeng 1974, 'Parteivergesellschaftung. Über den Zusammenhang von Transformationsprozess und nachrevolutionären Gesellschaftsstrukturen in den nachkapitalistischen Ländern sowjetischen Typs', in *Übergangsgesellschaft: Herrschaftsform und Praxis am Beispiel der Sowjetunion*, edited by Peter W. Schulze, Frankfurt am Main: Fischer Taschenbuch Verlag.

Heinz, Rudolf and Jochen Hörisch 2006, *Geld und Geltung. Zu Alfred Sohn-Rethels soziologischer Erkenntnistheorie*, Würzburg: Königshausen und Neumann.

Heiter, Heinrich 1986, 'Die Veränderung des Konzepts der Volksdemokratie infolge der Bipolarisierung Europas', in *Der Marshall-Plan und die europäische Linke*, edited by Othmar Nikola Haberl and Lutz Niethammer, Frankfurt am Main: EVA.

*Hellmann, Henry 1953, 'Der russische Popanz', *Funken*, III, 11 (April): 5–8.

*Henein, Georges 1958, 'Bruno R. et la "nouvelle classe"', *Le Contrat Social*, II, 6: 365–8.

*Hennicke, Peter (ed.) 1973, *Probleme des Sozialismus und der Übergangsgesellschaften*, Frankfurt am Main: Suhrkamp.

*Herer, S. 1978, 'L'URSS, Trotsky, le mode de production bureaucratique', *Dialectiques*, 24–25 (Autumn): 58–69.

Herrman, Friedrich Georg 1972–3, 'Otto Rühle als politischer Theoretiker', *Internationale wissenschaftliche Korrespondenz zur Geschichte der deutschen Arbeiterbewegung*, December 1972: 16–60 and April 1973: 23–50.

Herzberg, Guntolf and Kurt Seifert 2002, *Rudolf Bahro: Glaube an das Veränderbare. Eine Biographie*, Berlin: Links.

*Heuler, Werner 1977, 'Über Rudolf Bahros Buch "Die Alternative – Zur Kritik des real existierenden Sozialismus"', *Theorie und Praxis des Marxismus-Leninismus*, 1–2: 117–40.

*Heuler, Werner 1978, 'Für eine marxistische Kritik der politischen Ökonomie des "real existierenden Sozialismus" – ein Diskussionsbeitrag', *Theorie und Praxis des Marxismus-Leninismus*, 3: 4–25.

*Heuler, Werner 1979, 'Zur Diskussion über den Charakter der osteuropäischen Klassengesellschaften', *Theorie und Praxis des Marxismus-Leninismus*: 120–43.

Hilferding, Rudolf 1937, 'Letter to Karl Kautsky', 5 November 1937, Kautsky archive, International Institute of Social History, Amsterdam.

*Hilferding, Rudolf 1940, 'Gosudarstvennyj kapitalizm ili totalitarnoe gosudarstvennoe khoziaistvo?', *Sotsialisticheskii Vestnik*, 459: 92–3. ['State Capitalism or Totalitarian State Economy', *Modern Review*, 1 (1947): 66–71.]

*Hirszowicz, Maria 1976, 'Is there a Ruling Class in the USSR – A Comment', *Soviet Studies*, XXVII, 2 (April): 62–73.

*Hobson, Christopher Z. and Ronald D. Tabor 1988, *Trotskyism and the Dilemma of Socialism*, New York: Greenwood Press.

*Holmberg, Nils 1974a, *Fredlig kontrarevolution*, Uddevalla: Oktoberförlaget.

Holmberg, Nils 1974b, *Friedliche Konterrevolution*, I, West Berlin: Oberbaum Verlag. [German translation of Holmberg 1974a.]

*Horkheimer, Max 1942, 'Autoritärer Staat', in *Gesellschaft im Übergang. Aufsätze, Reden und Vorträge 1942–1970*, edited by Werner Brede, Frankfurt am Main: Athenäum Fischer Taschenbuch, 1972. ['The Authoritarian State', in *The Essential Frankfurt School Reader*, edited by Andrew Arato and Eike Gebhart, New York: Urizen Books, 1978.]

*Horner, K. [Anton Pannekoek] 1919, 'De groei van het kommunisme', *De Nieuwe Tijd*, XIV: 489–502.

*Hosfeld, Rolf et al. 1978, 'Bahros Kommunismus – eine Alternative?', *Das Argument*, 108: 241–50.

Howard, M.C. and J.E. King 2004, 'The Economic Contributions of Paul Sweezy', *Review of Political Economy*, 16, 4 (October): 411–56.

Howell, John 1981, 'Big Flame: Resituating Socialist Strategy and Organisation', *The Socialist Register 1981*: 207–20.

*Howl, Derek 1990, 'The Law of Value and the USSR', *International Socialism*, II, 49 (Winter): 89–113.

[Huberman, Leo and Paul Sweezy] 1961, 'The Sino-Soviet Dispute', *Monthly Review*, 13, 8 (December): 337–46.

[Huberman, Leo and Paul Sweezy] 1963, 'The Split in the Socialist World', *Monthly Review*, 15, 1 (May): 1–20.

*Huhn, Willy 1950a, 'Manager – keine soziale Revolution. Die Managergesellschaft bei Marx und Burnham', *pro und contra*, 3 (January): 15–22.

*Huhn, Willy 1950b, 'Karl Marx gegen den Stalinismus. Was Marx und Engels unter "Kommunismus" verstanden', *pro und contra*, 4 (February): 5–11.

*Huhn, Willy 1951, 'Lenins Staatskapitalismus 1917 bis 1922', *Funken*, II, 7 (December): 3–9.

*Huhn, Willy 1952, 'Trotzkis Bonapartismus', *Aufklärung*, II, 2: 89–104.

Huhn, Willy 1952–3, 'Etatismus, '"Kriegssozialismus", Nationalsozialismus in der Literatur der deutschen Sozialdemokratie', *Aufklärung*, II, 3: 162–80 and II, 4–6: 264–88.

*Hunter, Bill 1949, 'Is Russia Moving to Communism?', *Workers International News*, VIII, 1 (January–February): 8–23.

*Hussein, Mahmoud 1975, 'Sur *Les luttes de classes en URSS*', *Les Temps Modernes*, 346 (May): 1608–25.

Ihlau, Olaf 1969, *Die roten Kämpfer. Ein Beitrag zur Geschichte der Arbeiterbewegung in der Weimarer Republik und im Dritten Reich*, Meisenheim am Glan: Anton Hain.

Jacobson, Julius 1964–6, 'Isaac Deutscher: The Anatomy of an Apologist', *New Politics*, III, 4 (1964): 95–121 and V, 2 (1966): 47–85.

*Jacoby, Henry 1969, *Die Bürokratisierung der Welt. Ein Beitrag zur Problemgeschichte*, Neuwied: Luchterhand. Revised edition, Frankfurt am Main: Campus 1984. [*The Bureaucratization of the World*, trans. Eveline L. Kanes, Berkeley: University of California Press, 1973.]

Jacoby, Henry [1983], *Davongekommen. 10 Jahre Exil 1936–1946*. Frankfurt am Main: Sendler.

Jacoby, Henry and Ingrid Herbst 1985, *Otto Rühle zur Einführung*, Hamburg: Junius.

Jacoby, Russell 1981, *Dialectic of Defeat*, Cambridge: Cambridge University Press.

Jacoby, Russell 1987, *The Last Intellectuals. American Culture in the Age of Academe*, New York: Basic Books.

Jahn, Egbert 1974, *Kommunismus – und was dann? Zur Bürokratisierung und Militarisierung der Nationalstaaten*, Reinbek: Rowohlt.

*Jahn, Egbert (ed.) 1975, *Sozioökonomische Bedingungen der sowjetischen Aussenpolitik*, Frankfurt am Main: Campus. [*Soviet Foreign Policy: Its Social and Economic Conditions*. London: Allison & Busby, 1978.]

*James, C.L.R. 1964, 'Trotsky's "Revolution Betrayed"', *International Socialism*, I, 6 (Autumn): 25–9.

*James, C.L.R. 1969, *State Capitalism and World Revolution*, Detroit: Facing Reality.

James, C.L.R et al. 1972, *The Invading Socialist Society*, Detroit: Bewick.

James, C.L.R. 1980, *Spheres of Existence. Selected Writings*, London: Allison & Busby.

James, C.L.R. 1980, *Notes on Dialectics*, London: Allison & Busby.

*James, C.L.R. 1981, 'The Characteristics of Capitalism', *Monthly Review*, 33, 1 (May): 54–5.

James, Harold 1981, 'Rudolf Hilferding and the Application of the Political Economy of the Second International', *Historical Journal*, 24, 4: 847–70.

Jay, Martin 1973, *The Dialectical Imagination. A History of the Frankfurt School and the Institute of Social Research 1923–1950*, London: Heinemann.

Jedlicki, W. 1990, 'Ludwick Hass', *Revolutionary History*, 3–1 (Summer): 11–13.

*Jenssen, L.A. [Ludwig Jacobsen] 1951, *Um den Weg zum Sozialismus. II. Teil: Der Kampf um die Weltherrschaft und die Welteinheit*, Ulm/Donau: AJ. Schotola.

*Jenssen, L.A. [Ludwig Jacobsen] 1958, 'Djilas und die "Neue Klasse"', *Funken*, IX, 2 (February): 17–22.

*Jerome, W. and A. Buick 1967, 'Soviet State Capitalism? The History of an Idea', *Survey*, 62: 58–71.

*Jobic, Bernard 1972, 'La révolution culturelle et la critique de l'économisme', *Critiques de l'économie politique*, 7–8: 57–87.

*Johnson, Alan 1999, 'The Third Camp as History and a Living Legacy', *New Politics*, New Series, 7–3 (Summer), 135–65.

*Johnson, J.R. [C.L.R. James] 1941a, 'Russia – A Fascist State', *New International*, VII: 54–8.

*Johnson, J.R. [C.L.R. James] 1941b, 'Russia and Marxism', *New International*, VII: 213–16.

Johnstone, Monty 1968, 'Trotsky and the Debate on Socialism in One Country', *New Left Review*, I, 50 (July–August): 113–23.

*Joko [Joseph Kohn] 1929, 'Die russische Frage. Einige Grundfragen des Leninbundes', *Fahne des Kommunismus*, 3, 34 (13 September).

*Joravsky, David 1980, 'Commentary on Casals: Toward a Marxist Argument over Stalinism', *Theory and Society*, 9: 261–7.

Jost, Annette 1977, 'Rosa Luxemburgs Lenin-Kritik', *Jahrbuch Arbeiterbewegung*, 5: 77–103.

Jünke, Christoph 2006, *Leo Kofler: Leben und Werk (1907-1995)*, Hamburg: VSA.

*Kaiser, Hans 1980, 'Noch einmal: Zur Kritik der Sowjetgesellschaft', *Politikon*, 64 (March): 28-31.

*Kallscheuer, Otto 1976, 'Theoretische Aspekte der "Innenkritik" der sowjetischen Gesellschaften. Anmerkungen zur Analyse von Rakovski', *Politikon*, 50 (February): 10–19.

Karl, Michaela 2003, *Rudi Dutschke: Revolutionär ohne Revolution*, Frankfurt am Main: Verlag Neue Kritik.

*Katz, David H. 1977, 'Trotsky's *The Revolution Betrayed*. A Reappraisal', *Midwest Quaterly*, 18: 287–97.

*Kaufman, Adam 1954, 'Who Are the Rulers in Russia?', *Dissent*, I, 2 (Spring): 144–56.

Kautsky, Karl 1904–5, 'Die Bauern und die Revolution in Russland', *Neue Zeit*, 23–I: 670–7.

Kautsky, Karl 1917a, 'Die Aussichten der russischen Revolution', *Die Neue Zeit*, 35–II (6 April): 9–20.

Kautsky, Karl 1917b, 'Stockholm', *Die Neue Zeit*, 35–II (31 August): 505–12.

*Kautsky, Karl 1918, *Die Diktatur des Proletariats*, Vienna: Verlag der Wiener Volksbuchhandlung Ignaz Brand & Co.

*Kautsky, Karl 1919, *Terrorismus und Kommunismus. Ein Beitrag zur Naturgeschichte der Revolution*, Berlin: Neues Vaterland.

*Kautsky, Karl 1921, *Von der Demokratie zur Staats-Sklaverei. Eine Auseinandersetzung mit Trotzki*, Berlin: 'Freiheit'.

*Kautsky, Karl 1922, 'Rosa Luxemburg und der Bolschewismus', *Der Kampf*, 15: 33–44.

*Kautsky, Karl 1925a, 'Die Lehren des Oktoberexperiments', *Die Gesellschaft*, I: 374–80.

*Kautsky, Karl 1925b, *Die Internationale und Sowjetrussland*, Berlin: J.H.W. Dietz Nachf.

*Kautsky, Karl 1930, 'Georgien und seine Denker', *Die Gesellschaft*, I: 241–58.

*Kautsky, Karl 1931, 'Das bolschewistische Kamel', *Die Gesellschaft*, II: 342–56.

Kelly, Daniel 2002, *James Burnham and the Struggle for the World. A Life*, Wilmington: ISI Books.

*Kelly, Kevin D. 1985, 'Capitalism, Socialism, Barbarism: Marxist Conceptions of the Soviet Union', *Review of Radical Political Economics*, 17, 4 (Winter), 51–71.

Kellner, Douglas 1975–6, 'Korsch's Revolutionary Historicism', *Telos*, 26 (Winter): 70–93.

Kellner, Douglas 1984, *Herbert Marcuse and the Crisis of Marxism*, Basingstoke: Macmillan.

*Kendall, Walter 1962, 'Bruno Rizzi: Socialism and the Bureaucratic Society', *The Socialist Leader*, 3 November.

*Kent, W. 1941a, 'The Russian State', *New International*, VII: 148–51, 179–84.

*Kent, W. 1941b, 'What Is Capitalism?', *New International*, VII: 245–7.

Kern, Richard [Rudolf Hilferding] 1936a, 'Die Kehrseite der Rüstungskonjunktur', *Neuer Vorwärts*, 136 (19 January).

Kern, Richard [Rudolf Hilferding] 1936b, 'Grundlagen der auswärtigen Politik', *Neuer Vorwärts*, 179 (15 November), Supplement.

*Kidron, Michael 1961, 'Reform and Revolution. Rejoinder to Left Reformism', *International Socialism*, I, 7 (Winter): 15–21.

*Kidron, Michael 1969, 'Maginot Marxism – Mandel's Economics', *International Socialism*, 36 (April–May): 33–5.
Kidron, Michael 1968, *Western Capitalism since the War*, London: Weidenfeld and Nicholson.
Kidron, Michael 1977, 'Two Insights Don't Make a Theory', *International Socialism*, I, 100 (July): 4–9.
*Kief, Fritz 1953, 'Und wo bleibt der Mensch?', *Funken*, III, 9 (February): 4–6.
*King, Francis 2003, 'Class Theory and History', *Communist History Network Newsletter On-Line*, 14 (Spring), available at: <http://les1.man.ac.uk/chnn/chnn14fra.html>.
*King, P.C. 1948, 'What Remains of the Russian Revolution?', *Left*, 136 (February): 36–8.
Klemm, Bernd 1983, 'Paul Frölich (1884–1953). Politische Orientierung und theoretische Reflexionen von Linkssozialisten nach dem Zweiten Weltkrieg', *Internationale wissenschaftliche Korrespondenz zur Geschichte der deutschen Arbeiterbewegung*, 19: 186–229.
*Klinger, Fred 1981, 'Einleitung', in Hillel Ticktin et al., *Planlose Wirtschaft. Zum Charakter der sowjetischen Gesellschaft*, Hamburg: Junius.
*Klinger, Fred and Boris Reinstein 1977, 'Bahro – am Rande des revolutionären Marxismus?', *Was Tun*, 22 December: 13–18.
*Kofler, Leo 1952a, *Der Fall Lukács. Georg Lukács und der Stalinismus*, Cologne: Verlag für politische Publizistik.
*Kofler, Leo 1952b, *Das Wesen und die Rolle der stalinistischen Bürokratie*, Cologne: Verlag für politische Publizistik.
*Kofler, Leo 1958, 'Bemerkungen über den Stalinismus', *Funken*, II, 2: 26–9.
*Konrád, György and Ivan Szelényi 1979, *The Intellectuals on the Road to Class Power*, New York: Harcourt Brace Jovanovich.
Kornder, Hans-Jürgen, *Konterrevolution und Faschismus. Zur Analyse van Nationalsozialismus, Faschismus und Totalitarismus im Werk van Karl Korsch*, Frankfurt am Main: Peter Lang.
Korsch, Hedda 1972, 'Memories of Karl Korsch', *New Left Review*, I, 76 (November–December): 35–45.
*[Korsch, Karl] 1927a, 'Zehn Jahre Klassenkämpfe in Sowjetrussland', *Kommunistische Politik*, II, 17–18 (October).
*[Korsch, Karl] 1927b, 'Die Zweite Partei', *Kommunistische Politik*, II, 19–20 (December).
*Korsch, Karl 1932, '15 jaren Octoberrevolutie. Legenden en werkelijkheid van het socialisme in Sowjet-Rusland', *De Nieuwe Weg*, VII: 327–30.
*Kössler, Reinhart 1979, 'Zur Kritik des Mythos vom "asiatischen" Russland', *Prokla*, 35: 105–31.
*Kovar, A. 1972, 'La révolution prolétarienne et l'idéologisme – réponse au camerade B. Jobic', *Critiques de l'économie politique*, 7–8: 88–97.
*Krader, Lawrence 1978, 'Die asiatische Produktionsweise', in *Antworten auf Bahros Herausforderung des 'realen Sozialismus'*, edited by Ulf Wolter, West Berlin: Olle & Wolter. ['The Asiatic Mode of Production', in *Rudolf Bahro. Critical Responses*, edited by Ulf Wolter, White Plains: M.E. Sharpe, 1980.]
Kratz, Steffen 1980, *Sohn-Rethel zur Einführung*, Hannover: SOAK.
Kreter, Karljo 1986, *Sozialisten in der Adenauer-Zeit. Die Zeitschrift 'Funken'*, Hamburg: VSA.
*Krivine, Hubert 1992, 'Pays de l'Est: la nécessité d'un réexamen critique', *Critique communiste*, 113–114 (January): 31–4.
Krogmann, Angelica 1970, *Simone Weil*, Reinbek: Rowohlt.
*Krygier, Martin 1978, '"Bureaucracy" in Trotsky's Analysis of Stalinism', in *Socialism and the New Class: Towards the Analysis of Structural Inequality within Socialist Societies*, edited by Marian Sawer, Adelaide: Australian Political Studies Association Monograph, 19.
*Krygier, Martin 1979, 'The Revolution Betrayed? From Trotsky to the New Class', in *Bureaucracy – The Career of a Concept*, edited by Eugene Kamenka and Martin Krygier, London: Edward Arnold.

Kuhn, Thomas 1970, *The Structure of Scientific Revolutions*, Second Edition, Chicago: University of Chicago Press.

Kulemann, Peter 1978, *Die Linke in Westdeutschland nach 1945*, Hannover/Frankfurt am Main: SOAK/ISP.

*Kulkarni, Mangesh 1994, 'Theories of the Soviet System – A Retrospective Critique', *Economic and Political Weekly*, 29/31 (30 July): 2036–9.

*Kupferberg, Feiwel 1974a, 'Från Lenin till Brezjnev', *Zenit*, 36: 37–51.

*Kupferberg, Feiwel 1974b, 'Kommentar om övergångssamhället', *Zenit*, 37: 62–6.

*Kupferberg, Feiwel 1975, 'Klassförhållandena i Sovjetunionen. En kritik av trotskismen och stalinismen', *Marxistiska studietexter*, Volume 2, Stockholm: Förlaget Barrikaden.

*Kupferberg, Feiwel 1976, 'Om statssocialismen och vingklippta marknader', *Häften för kritiska studier*, IX, 4: 42–9.

*Kupferberg, Feiwel 1979, 'Bahros Alternativ', *Häften för kritiska studier*, XII, 6: 3–37.

Kurata, Minoru 1974, 'Rudolf Hilferding. Bibliographie seiner Schriften, Artikel und Briefe', *Internationale wissenschaftliche Korrespondenz zur Geschichte der deutschen Arbeiterbewegung*: 327–46.

*Kuroń, Jacek and Karol Modzelewski 1966, *List otwarty do partii*, Paris: Institut Littéraire SARL. [*Solidarność: The Missing Link? The Classic Open Letter to the Party by Jacek Kuroń and Karol Modzelewski*, edited by Colin Barker, London: Bookmarks, 1982.].

*Kusin, Vladimir V. 1976, 'Apropos Alec Nove's Search for a Class Label', *Soviet Studies*, 28: 274–5.

Lacapra, Dominick 1983, *Rethinking Intellectual History: Texts, Contexts, Language*, Ithaca: Cornell University Press.

*Lammers, Karl Christian 1979, 'Om overgangen til socialisme/kommunisme inden for den marxistiske tradition', *Historievidenskab*, 17: 13–41.

Landy, Sy 1997, 'Twenty Years of the LRP', *Proletarian Revolution*, 53 (Winter).

Lange, Oskar 1970, 'The Role of Planning in a Socialist Economy' (1958), in *Papers in Economics and Sociology*, translation edited by P.F. Knightsfield, Oxford [etc.]: Pergamon Press.

Langels, Otto 1984, *Die ultralinke Opposition der KPD in der Weimarer Republik*, Frankfurt am Main: Peter Lang.

Laschitza, Annelies 1996, *Im Lebensrausch, trotz alledem. Rosa Luxemburg: eine Biographie*, Berlin: Aufbau-Verlag.

*Laurat, Lucien [Otto Maschl] 1931, *L'économie soviétique. Sa dynamique. Son mécanisme*, Paris: Librairie Valois.

*Laurat, Lucien [Otto Maschl] 1939, *Le Marxisme en faillite? Du marxisme de Marx au marxisme d'aujourd'hui*, Paris: Ed. Pierre Tisne.

Laurat, Lucien [Otto Maschl] 1965, 'Le Parti Communiste Autrichien', in *Contributions à l'histoire du Comintern*, edited by Jacques Freymond, Geneva: Librairie Droz.

*Law, David 1976–7, [Review of Purdy 1976], *Critique*, 7 (Winter): 111–18.

*Law, David S. 1982, 'Trockij and Thermidor', in *Pensiero e azione politica di Lev Trockij*, edited by Francesca Gori, Florence: Leo S. Olschki, II.

*Lazitch, Branko 1957, 'Milovan Djilas et la "nouvelle classe"', *Le Contrat Social*, 1–5 (November): 310–14.

Lazitch, Branko and Milorad M. Drachkovitch 1973, *Biographical Dictionary of the Comintern*, Stanford: Hoover Institution Press.

Lebowitz, Michael A. 1992, *Beyond 'Capital': Marx's Political Economy of the Working Class*, London: Macmillan.

*Lebowitz, Michael A. 1986, 'Only Capitalist Laws of Motion?', *Monthly Review*, 38, 6 (November): 32–41.

*Lebrun, M. [Mário Pedrosa] 1940, 'Mass and Class in Soviet Society', *New International*, VI, 4: 87–91.

*Le Corre, Darius 1961, 'Pourquoi l'économie soviétique est un capitalisme d'Etat', *La Revue Socialiste*, New Series, 147 (November): 426–37.

*Le Corre, Darius 1965a, 'Oui, l'URSS est un capitalisme d'Etat', *La Revue Socialiste*, New Series, 181 (March): 293–308 and 183 (May): 466–82.

*Le Corre, Darius 1965b, 'Le profit en URSS: simple indice ou catégorie du capitalisme bureaucratique d'Etat?', *La Revue Socialiste*, New Series, 188 (December): 523–31.

*Le Corre, Darius 1966, 'Quelles sont les bases marxistes du capitalisme bureaucratique d'Etat de l'Union Soviétique?', *La Revue Socialiste*, New Series, 189–190 (January–February): 129–40; 191 (March): 256–72; 192 (April): 324–42; 193 (May): 474–87 and 194 (June): 79–98.

*Lee, Grace, Pierre Chaulieu [Cornelius Castoriadis] and J.R. Johnson [C.L.R. James] 1958, *Facing Reality*, Detroit: Correspondence.

*Lefort, Claude 1960, 'Qu'est-ce que la bureaucratie?', *Arguments*, 17: 64–81. ['What Is Bureaucracy?', in *The Political Forms of Modern Society. Bureaucracy, Democracy, Totalitarianism*, edited and introduced by John B. Thompson, Cambridge: Polity Press, 1986.]

Lefort, Claude 1976–7, 'An Interview with Claude Lefort', *Telos*, 30 (Winter): 173–92.

Lefranc, Georges 1966, 'Le courant planiste dans le mouvement ouvrier français de 1933 à 1936', *Le Mouvement Social*, 54: 69–90.

*Lenin, V.I. 1964 [1920], '"Left-Wing" Communism – An Infantile Disorder', trans. Julius Katzer, in *Collected Works*, Volume 31, Moscow: Progress.

*Lenin, V.I. 1974 [1918], 'The Proletarian Revolution and the Renegade Kautsky', trans. Jim Riordan, in *Collected Works*, Volume 28, Moscow: Progress.

*Lenz [Helmut Fleischer] 1950, 'Thesen zur russischen Frage. Die historische Einmaligkeit der russischen Entwicklung', *pro und contra*, 6 (June): 8–11.

*Leo, Rita di 1970, *Operai e sistema sovietico*, Bari: Laterza.

*Leo, Rita di 1977, *Il modello di Stalin*, Milan: Feltrinelli.

*Leonhard, Susanne 1953, 'Zur Russlandfrage', *Funken*, IV, 1 (June): 8–15.

*Leonhard, Wolfgang 1952, *Schein und Wirklichkeit in der UdSSR*, West Berlin: Freies Wort.

*Leser, Norbert 1985, 'Otto Bauers Haltung gegenüber dem Bolschewismus', in *Otto Bauer: Theorie und Politik*, edited by Detlev Albers, Horst Heimann and Richard Saage, West Berlin: Das Argument.

*Levi, Paul 1922, 'Einleitung', in Rosa Luxemburg, *Die russische Revolution. Eine kritische Würdigung*, Berlin: Gesellschaft und Erziehung.

*Lew, Roland 1983, 'La nature sociale des pays du "socialisme réel"', *Revue des Pays de l'Est*, 1–2: 233–48.

*Liebich, André 1977, 'Socialisme ou Barbarie. A Radical Critique of Bureaucracy', *Our Generation*, XII, 2 (Autumn): 55–62.

*Liebich, André 1981, 'I menscevichi di fronte alla costruzione dell' Urss', in *Storia del marxismo*, III–2, Turin: Einaudi.

*Liebich, André 1987, 'Marxism and Totalitarianism. Rudolf Hilferding and the Mensheviks', *Dissent*, 34 (Spring): 223–40.

*Liebman, Marcel 1965, 'Retour à Trotsky', *Les Temps Modernes*, 230 (July): 132–52.

*Linde, H. 1932, 'Die ideologische Vorbereitung der Intervention durch die II. Internationale', *Unter dem Banner des Marxismus*, VI: 19–41.

*Linden, Marcel van der 1979, 'Drie meningen', *Discorsi*, XII, 13 (2 May): 25–8.

*Linden, Marcel van der 1980, 'Siep Stuurman en het Oosteuropese raadsel', *De Internationale*, 26 (May): 28–33.

*Linden, Marcel van der 1981, 'Problemen bij de theorie van de gedegenereerde arbeidersstaat', *Toestanden*, 4 (December); 5–22.

*Linden, Marcel van der 1983, 'Het aktuele marxistische debat over de Sovjet-Unie', in Hans Kaiser et al., *Het Sovjetraadsel. Poging tot begrip van de Oosteuropese maatschappij*, Antwerp: Leon Lesoil – Toestanden.

*Linden, Marcel van der 1990, 'Wat voor samenleving werd voortgebracht door de Russische Oktoberrevolutie? Een andere visie', *Daad en Gedachte*, 26, 5 (June): 5–9.

Linden, Marcel van der 1998, 'Socialisme ou Barbarie: A French Revolutionary Group (1949–1965)', *Left History*, 5, 1: 7–37.

Livorsi, Franco 1976, *Amadeo Bordiga*, Rome: Editori Riuniti.

*Lobe, Henner 1978, 'Arbeitsteilung, Klassenherrschaft, Staat – Einige Thesen zur Bahro-Diskussion', *Theorie und Praxis des Marxismus-Leninismus*, 3: 40–9.

Lockwood, David 2000, *The Destruction of the Soviet Union. A Study in Globalization*, New York: St. Martin's Press.

*Lohmann, Karl-Ernst 1978, 'Gesellschaftliche Produktivkräfte und realer Sozialismus', *Das Argument*, 108: 230–40.

Lomax, Bill 1982, 'Hungary: The Rise of the Democratic Opposition', *Labour Focus on Eastern Europe*, V–3/4 (Summer): 2–7.

*Lombardo Radice, Lucio 1978, 'Staatssozialismus', in *Antworten auf Bahros Herausforderung des 'realen Sozialismus'*, edited by Ulf Wolter, West Berlin: Olle & Wolter. ['State Socialism', in *Rudolf Bahro. Critical Responses*, edited by Ulf Wolter, White Plains: M.E. Sharpe, 1980.]

*Loone, Eero 1990, 'Marxism and *Perestroika*', *Soviet Studies*, 42: 779–94.

Loone, Eero 1992, *Soviet Marxism and Analytical Philosophies of History*, London: Verso.

*Lovell, David W. 1985, *Trotsky's Analysis of Soviet Bureaucratization. A Critical Essay*, London: Croom Helm.

*Löw, Raimund 1980, *Otto Bauer und die russische Revolution*, Vienna: Europa Verlag.

*Löwy, Michael 1980, 'Sul concetto di "casta burocratica" in Trockij e Rakovskij', *Il Ponte*, XXXVI: 1462–70.

Lowy, A.G. 1969, *Die Weltgeschichte ist das Weltgericht. Bucharins Vision des Kommunismus*, Vienna: Europaverlag.

Lugowska, Urszula and August Grabski 2003, *Trockizm. Doktryna i ruch polityczny*, Warsaw: Widawnictwo 'Trio'.

*Lukács, Georg 1923, 'Kritische Bemerkungen über Rosa Luxemburgs "Kritik der russischen Revolution"', in Lukács, *Geschichte und Klassenbewusstsein. Studien aber marxistische Dialektik*, Berlin: Malik. ['Critical Observations on Rosa Luxemburg's "Critique of the Russian Revolution"', in Lukács, *History and Class Consciousness. Studies in Marxist Dialectics*, London: Merlin Press, 1971.].

*Lukács, György 1971, 'Critique de la bureaucratie socialiste', *L'Homme et la Société*, 20: 3–12.

Lukács, Georg 1973, 'Budapester Schule', *Praxis*, 2–3: 299–302.

*Luke, Tim 1985, 'On the Nature of Soviet Society', *Telos*, 63 (Spring): 187–95.

*Luke, Tim et al. 1984, 'Review Symposium on Soviet-Type Societies', *Telos*, 60 (Summer): 155–91.

*Lund, Ernest 1941, 'Basis for Defensism in Russia', *New International*, VII: 187–91.

*Lustig, Michael M. 1989, *Trotsky and Djilas: Critics of Communist Bureaucracy*, New York: Greenwood Press.

Luxemburg, Rosa 1916, 'Leitsätze über die Aufgaben der internationalen Sozial-demokratie' *Gesammelte Werke*, 4, Berlin [GDR]: Dietz Verlag, 1974: 43–7.

*[Luxemburg, Rosa] 1917a, 'Die Revolution in Russland', *Spartacus*, 4 (April): 3–4.

[Luxemburg, Rosa] 1917b, 'Der alte Maulwurf', *Spartacus*, 5 (May): 1–2.

Luxemburg, Rosa 1918–19, 'Rede für die Beteiligung der KPD an den Wahlen zur Nationalversammlung', *Gesammelte Werke*, 4, Berlin [GDR]: Dietz, 1974.

*Luxemburg, Rosa 1922, *Die russische Revolution. Eine kritische Würdigung*, Aus dem Nachlass herausgegeben und eingeleitet von P. Levi, Berlin: Gesellschaft und Erziehung. ['The Russian Revolution', trans. Bertram D. Wolfe, in *Rosa Luxemburg Speaks*, edited by Mary-Alice Waters, New York: Pathfinder Press, 1970.]

*Lynd, Staughton 1967, 'What Went Wrong?', *Monthly Review*, 19, 6 (November): 29–31.

McLellan, David 1983, 'Politics', in *Marx: The First Hundred Years*, edited by David McLellan, London: Francis Pinter.

*McNeal, Robert H. 1961, 'Trotsky's Interpretation of Stalin', *Canadian Slavonic Papers*, V: 87–97.

*McNeal, Robert H. 1977, 'Trotskyist Interpretations of Stalinism', in *Stalinism. Essays in Historical Interpretation*, edited by Robert C. Tucker, New York: W.W. Norton.

*McNeal, Robert H. 1982, 'Trockij and Stalinism', in *Pensiero e azione politica di Lev Trockij*, edited by Francesca Gori, [Milan]: Leo S. Olschki, II.

Macdonald, Dwight 1958, *Memoirs of a Revolutionist. Essays in Political Criticism*, New York: Meridian Books.

MacDonald, Dwight 1959, 'Bruno R.', *New Leader*, 16 November: 29–30.

MacIntyre, Alasdair 1961, 'Rejoinder to Left Reformism', *International Socialism*, I, 6 (Autumn): 20–3.

*Maclean, Gavin 1980, 'Sanctuary of the Disenchanted: Comments on "Century of the Unexpected"', in *The Nature of So-Called Socialist Societies*, London: Big Flame International Committee.

*Mänchen-Helfen, Otto 1932, *Russland und der Sozialismus. Von der Arbeitermacht zum Staatskapitalismus*, Berlin: J.H.W. Dietz Nachf.

*Maetzel, M. et al. 1979, 'Beiträge zur Diskussion über den Charakter des "real existierenden Sozialismus" und die Revisionismuskritik', *Theorie und Praxis des Marxismus-Leninismus*, 4: 38–119.

*Magdoff, Harry 1985, 'Are There Economic Laws of Socialism?', *Monthly Review*, 37, 3 (July–August): 112–27.

*Main, Peter and Heath, Clare 1994, 'Walter Daum – *The Life and Death of Stalinism*', *Permanent Revolution*, 10 (Spring-Summer): 140–63.

*Maitan, Livio 1992, 'Après la fin de l'URSS: quelle transition?', *Critique Communiste*, 116–117 (February–March), 5–12.

Malandrino, Corrado 1987, *Scienza e socialismo. Anton Pannekoek (1873–1960)*, Milan: Franco Angeli.

*Mallet, Serge 1974, *Bureaucracy and Technocracy in the Socialist Countries*, London: Spokesman.

*Malrieu, Jean 1947, 'La question de l'Etat', *La Revue Internationale*, 17 (Summer): 30–1.

Mandel, Ernest 1962, *Traité d'Economie Marxiste*, Paris: Julliard, 2 vols. [*Marxist Economic Theory*, trans. Brian Pearce, London: Merlin Press, 1968.]

*Mandel, Ernest 1965, 'La réforme de la planification soviétique et ses implications', *Les Temps Modernes*, 229 (June): 2161–86.

*Mandel, Ernest 1968a, 'Economics of the Transition Period', in *Fifty Years of World Revolution. An International Symposium*, edited by Ernest Mandel, New York: Merit Publishers.

[Mandel, Ernest] 1968b, 'Roman Rosdolsky (1898–1967)', *Quatrième Internationale*, 33 (April): 70–2.

*Mandel, Ernest 1969, *The Inconsistencies of State Capitalism*, London: International Marxist Group.

*Mandel, Ernest 1970a, *The Mystifications of State Capitalism*, London: International Marxist Group.

*Mandel, Ernest 1970b, 'Du "nouveau" sur la question de la nature de l'URSS', *Quatrième Internationale*, XXVIII, 25 (September): 12–24.

*Mandel, Ernest 1973a, 'Zehn Thesen zur sozialökonomischen Gesetzmässigkeit der Übergangsgesellschaft zwischen Kapitalismus und Sozialismus', in *Probleme des Sozialismus und der Übergangsgesellschaften*, edited by Peter Hennicke, Frankfurt am Main: Suhrkamp. ['Ten Theses on the Social and Economic Laws Governing the Society Transitional Between Capitalism and Socialism', *Critique*, 3 (Autumn 1974): 5–21.]

*Mandel, Ernest 1973b, 'Democrazia e socialismo nell'URSS in Trockij', *Annali Istituto Giangiacomo Feltrinelli*, XV: 843–64.

*Mandel, Ernest 1974, 'Some Comments on H. Ticktin's "Towards a Political Economy of the USSR"', *Critique*, 3: 23–6.

*Mandel, Ernest 1977, 'Bahros Bombe', *Was Tun*, 22 September: 10–12.

*Mandel, Ernest 1978a, 'Fatalismus als "Alternative"?', *Was Tun*, 2 March: 9–12.

*Mandel, Ernest 1978b, 'Sobre la naturaleza de la URSS [Interview]', *El Viejo Topo: Extra* 2: 30–6.

Mandel, Ernest 1978c, *The Second Slump. A Marxist Analysis of Recession in the Seventies*, trans. Jon Rothschild, London: New Left Books.

Mandel, Ernest 1979a, *Revolutionary Marxism Today*, London: New Left Books.

*Mandel, Ernest 1979b, 'Why the Soviet Bureaucracy is Not a New Ruling Class', *Monthly Review*, 31, 3 (July–August): 63–76. [A longer version is: 'Pourquoi la bureaucratie soviétique n'est pas une nouvelle classe dominante', *Quatrième Internationale*, XXXVIII, 1 (1980): 61–77.]

*Mandel, Ernest 1979–80, 'Once Again on the Trotskyist Definition of the Social Nature of the Soviet Union', *Critique*, 12: 117–26. [Almost identical is: 'The Laws of Motion of the Soviet Economy', *Review of Radical Political Economics*, XIII, 1 (Spring 1981): 35–9.]

*Mandel, Ernest 1985, 'Marx and Engels on Commodity Production and Bureaucracy. Theoretical Bases of the Marxist Understanding of the Soviet Union', in *Rethinking Marxism. Struggles in Marxist Theory. Essays for Harry Magdoff and Paul Sweezy*, edited by Stephen Resnick and Richard Wolff, Brooklyn: Autonomedia.

Mandel, Ernest 1987, 'The Significance of Gorbachev', *International Marxist Review*, 2, 4 (Winter): 7–39.

*Mandel, Ernest 1990, 'Une théorie qui ná pas résisté à l'épreuve des faits', *Quatrième Internationale*, 37–38: 75–96. ['A Theory Which has Not Withstood the Test of Facts', *International Socialism*, II, 49 (Winter 1990): 43–64.]

*Mandel, Ernest 1991a, *Beyond Perestroika. The Future of Gorbachev's USSR*, London: Verso.

*Mandel, 1991b, 'The Roots of the Present Crisis in the Soviet Economy', *Socialist Register 1991*: 194–210.

*Mandel, Ernest 1992, 'The Impasse of Schematic Dogmatism', *International Socialism*, II, 56 (Autumn): 135–72.

Mandelbaum, Kurt [Kurt Martin] 1974, *Sozialdemokratie und Leninismus. Zwei Aufsätze*, West Berlin: Rotbuch.

Manifesto 1946, 'Manifeste de la conférence d'Avril 1946 de la IVe Internationale aux travailleurs, aux exploités et aux peuples coloniaux du monde entier', *Quatrième Internationale*, April-May: 36–50.

*Marcoux, J. 1948, 'De Burnham à...Burnham', *La Revue Internationale*, 20 (January–February): 44–8.

*Marcuse, Herbert 1958, *Soviet Marxism. A Critical Analysis*, New York: Columbia University Press.

Marcuse, Herbert 1964, *One-Dimensional Man. Studies in the Ideology of Advanced Industrial Society*, Boston: Beacon Press.

*Marcuse, Herbert 1978, 'Protosozialismus und Spätkapitalismus – Versuch einer revolutionstheoretischen Synthese von Bahros Ansatz', *Kritik*, 19 (1978): 5–27. ['Protosocialism and Late Capitalism: Toward a Theoretical Synthesis Based on Bahro's Analysis', in *Rudolf Bahro. Critical Responses*, edited by Ulf Wolter, White Plains: M.E. Sharpe, 1980.]

Marković, Mihailo 1975a, 'La philosophie marxiste en Yougoslavie – le groupe Praxis', *L'Homme et la Société*, 35–36 (January–June): 5–28.

Marković, Mihailo 1988, 'Raya Dunayevskaya: Great Socialist Humanist Who Lived Her Philosophy All Her Life', *Praxis International*, 8, 3 (October): 372–4.

Marković, Mihailo and Robert S. Cohen 1975, *Yugoslavia: The Rise and Fall of Socialist Humanism. A History of the Praxis Group*, Nottingham: Spokesman.

*Markus, György 1981, 'Western Marxism and Eastern Societies', *Dialectical Anthropology*, 6: 291–318.

*Martin, Jean-Paul 1947, 'Quelques néo-staliniens de *La Revue Internationale*', *Quatrième Internationale* (September-October): 49–57.

Martin, Kurt [Kurt Mandelbaum] 1979, 'I Am Still the Same, but...', *Development and Change*, 10: 503–13.

*Martinet, Gilles 1947, 'Le socialisme et les sociétés de transition: de Trotsky à Burnham', *La Revue Internationale*, 17 (Summer): 12–30.

Marx, Karl 1972, *Theories of Surplus Value*, Part III, trans. Jack Cohen, London: Lawrence & Wishart.

Marx, Karl 1973, *Grundrisse. Foundations of the Critique of Political Economy (Rough Draft)*, trans. Martin Nicolaus, Harmondsworth: Penguin.

Marx, Karl 1976, *Capital. A Critique of Political Economy*, Volume 1, trans. Ben Fowkes, Harmondsworth: Penguin.

Marx, Karl 1978, *Capital. A Critique of Political Economy*, Volume 2, trans. David Fernbach, Harmondsworth: Penguin.

Marx, Karl 1981, *Capital. A Critique of Political Economy*, Volume 3, trans. David Fernbach, Harmondsworth: Penguin.

Marx, Karl 1989, 'Marginal Notes on the Programme of the German Workers' Party', in Karl Marx and Frederick Engels, *Collected Works*, Volume 24, Moscow: Progress.

Marx, Karl 1992, *The First International and After*, trans. David Fernbach, Harmondsworth: Penguin.

Masterman, Margaret 1977, 'The Nature of a Paradigm', in *Criticism and the Growth of Knowle©e*, edited by Imre Lakatos and Alan Musgrave, Cambridge: Cambridge University Press.

*Masuch, Michael 1977, 'Das Problem der Erklärung des "Stalinismus"', *Das Argument*, 106: 826–43.

*Masuch, Michael 1980, 'Hoe kon het in Marx' naam? De paradox van het stalinisme', *De Gids*, CXVIII, 2: 100–14.

*Matgamna, Sean 1998, 'Introduction: The Russian Revolution and Marxism', in *The Fate of the Russian Revolution. Lost Texts of Critical Marxism*, I, London: Phoenix Press.

*Matgamna, Sean 1999, 'Cliff's State Capitalism in Perspective', *Workers' Liberty*, 56 (June–July): 21–4, 37–54.

Mattick, Paul 1962, 'Marx and Keynes', *Etudes de Marxologie*, 5: 113–215.

*Mattick, Paul 1969, *Marx and Keynes. The Limits of the Mixed Economy*, Boston: Porter Sargent Publications.

Mautner, Wilhelm 1926, 'Zur Geschichte des Begriffes "Diktatur des Proletariats"', *Archiv für die Geschichte des Sozialismus und der Arbeiterbewegung (Grünberg-Archiv)*, 12: 280–3.

Meikle, Scott 1981, 'Has Marxism a Future?', *Critique*, 13: 103–21.

*Melotti, Umberto 1970–1, 'Marx e il Terzo Mondo', *Terzo Mondo*, 9 (1970): 11–28 and 11 (1971): 7–32.

*Melotti, Umberto 1971, 'Marx e il Terzo Mondo. Per uno schema multilineare della concezione marxiana dello sviluppo storico', *Terzo Mondo*, 13–14: 3–169. [*Marx and the Third World*, trans. Pat Ransford, Basingstoke: Macmillan, 1977.]

*Melotti, Umberto 1975, 'Modo di produzione asiatico e collettivismo burocratico. Una polemica sui paesi socialisti', *Critica Marxista*, XIII, 6: 169–72.

*Melotti, Umberto 1976, 'Il collettivismo burocratico', *Terzo Mondo*, 34: 108–12.

*Melotti, Umberto 1979, 'Socialismo e collettivismo burocratico nei paesi in via di sviluppo', *Terzo Mondo*, 37–38: 66–79.

Melville, Ralph 1992, 'Roman Rosdolsky (1898–1967) als Historiker Galiziens und der Habsburgermonarchie', in Roman Rosdolsky, *Untertan und Staat in Galizien. Die Reformen unter Maria Theriasia und Joseph II*, Mainz: Von Zabern.

*Men, L.L. 1986, 'The Capitalist Nature of the "Socialist" Countries: A Politico-Economic Analysis', in *Two Texts for Defining the Nature of the Communist Programme*, Hong Kong: International Correspondence.

Mergner, Gottfried 1973, *Arbeiterbewegung und Intelligenz*, Starnberg: Raith.

Merquior, J.G. 1986, *Western Marxism*, London: Paladin.

*Meyer, Ernst 1922, 'Rosa Luxemburgs Kritik der Bolschewiki', *Rote Fahne*, 15 January.

*Meyer, Gerd 1977, *Bürokratischer Sozialismus. Eine Analyse des sowjetischen Herrschafts-systems*, Stuttgart: Frommann-Holzboog.

*Meyer, Gerd 1979, *Sozialistische Systeme. Theorie- und Strukturanalyse*, Opladen: Leske + Budrich.

*Meyer, Gert 1974, 'Zum Problem der "etatistischen Bürokratie" in der UdSSR', *Links*, 53 (March): 18–20.

*Meyer, Gert 1977–8, 'Industrialisierung, Arbeiterklasse und Stalinherrschaft in der UdSSR', *Das Argument*, 106 (1977): 844–59; 107 (1978): 42–59 and 108 (1978): 202–21.

*Meyer, Gert 1978, 'Jean Ellensteins Darstellung des "Stalinschen Phänomens"', in *Beiträge zur Sozialismusanalyse*, I, edited by Peter Brokmeier and Rainer Rilling, Cologne: Pahl-Rugenstein.

*Meyer, Heinz 1953, 'Zum Sturze Berijas. Über das Verhältnis der einzelnen Machtgruppen im totalitären Staat', *Funken*, IV, 3 (August): 1–3.

*Meyer, Peter [Josef Guttmann] 1944, 'The Soviet Union: A New Class Society', *Politics*, March: 48–55 and April: 81–5.

*Meyer, Peter [Josef Guttmann] 1947, 'Reply to Leon Blum', *Modern Review*, I: 317–20.

*Miasnikoff, G. 1932, 'De klasse-grondslagen van den Russischen Sovjet-staat', *De Nieuwe Weg*, VII: 18–23, 38–45, 78–86, 107–15, 147–52, 181–86. [Originally: *Ocherednoi obman*. Paris (no publisher) 1931.]

Miasnikoff, G. 1939, 'Dictature et démocratie', *Cahiers d'Europe/Europäische Monatshefte*, 2 (February): 12–16.

*Miermeister, Jürgen 1977, 'Opposition(elle) in der DDR: Rudolf Bahro – nur zum Beispiel', *Zeitung für eine neue Linke*, II, 29: 18–20.

Miermeister, Jürgen (ed.) 1986, *Rudi Dutschke: mit Selbstzeugnissen und Bilddokumenten*, Reinbek bei Hamburg: Rowohlt.

*Migliardi, Giorgio 1985, 'I menscevichi e lo Stato Sovietico', in *L'Internazionale Operaio e Socialista tra le due guerre*, edited by Enzo Collotti, Milan: Feltrinelli.

*Miliband, Ralph 1975, 'Bettelheim and the Soviet Experience', *New Left Review*, I, 91 (May–June): 57–66.

*Miliband, Ralph 1979, 'A Commentary on Rudolf Bahro's *Alternative*', *The Socialist Register 1979*: 274–84.

*Möhner, F.K. 1979, 'Elemente für eine marxistische Phänomenologie der osteuropäischen Systeme – Thesen zum Buch "Die Intelligenz auf dem Weg zur Klassenmacht"', *Theorie und Praxis des Marxismus-Leninismus*, 3: 109–27.

*Mohun, Simon 1980, 'The Problem of the Soviet Union', *Research in Political Economy*, 3: 235–90.

*Molyneux, John 1987, 'The Ambiguities of Hillel Ticktin', *Critique*, 20–1: 131–4.

Montaldi, Danilo 1975, *Korsch e i comunisti Italiani. Contra un facile spirito di assimilazione*, Roma: Savelli.

*Morris, Jacob and Haskell Lewin 1976, 'More on the Nature of Soviet Society', *Monthly Review*, 27, 10 (March): 4–10.

*Morris, Paul 1991, 'The Crisis of Stalinism and the Theory of State Capitalism', *Permanent Revolution*, 9 (Summer-Autumn): 96–148.

*Mosley, Hugh 1978, 'The New Communist Opposition: Rudolf Bahro's Critique of the "Really Existing Socialism"', *New German Critique*, 15 (Autumn): 25–36.

Müller, Hans-Harald 1977, *Intellektueller Linksradikalismus in der Weimarer Republik*, Kronberg/Ts: Scriptor Verlag.

*Munis, G. [Manuel Fernandez Grandizo] 1946, *Los revolucionarios ante Rusia y el stalinismo mundial*, Mexico D.F.: Editorial 'Revolución'. [Simultaneously published as *Les révolutionnaires devant la Russie et le stalinisme mondial*, Mexico D.F.: Editorial 'Revolución', 1946.]

*Munis, G. [Manuel Fernandez Grandizo] 1948, *Jalones de derrota, promesa de victoria*, Mexico D.F.: Editorial 'Lucha Obrera'.

*Munis, G. [Manuel Fernandez Grandizo] 1975, *Parti-Etat, stalinisme, révolution*, Paris: Spartacus.

*Munis, Grandizo [Manuel Fernandez Grandizo] and Benjamin Péret 1967, *Pour un second manifeste communiste*, Paris: Losfeld.

Myers, Constance Ashton 1977, *The Prophet's Army. Trotskyists in America, 1928–1941*, Westport: Greenwood Press.

*Nair, K. 1972, 'Charles Bettelheim bouleverse la science', *Critiques de l'économie politique*, 7–8: 4–16.

A Natureza da USSR (Antologia) 1977, Porto: Afrontamento.

Nash, George H. 1976, *The Conservative Intellectual Movement in America since 1945*, New York: Basic Books.

Naville [Pierre] 1938, 'Extrait du rapport adopté par le 2e Congres du P.O.I. (Novembre 1937)', *Quatrième Internationale*, June: 78–81.

*[Naville, Pierre] 1947, 'L'Avenir est-il à la "classe directorale"?', *La Revue Internationale*, 16 (June): 385–7.

*Naville, Pierre 1958, 'Djilas et le "communisme national"', *Arguments*, 6: 13–16.

Naville, Pierre 1959, 'Un revenant: Bruno. R.', *Le Contrat Social*, III–1 (January): 60–1.

*Naville, Pierre 1960, 'La bureaucratie et la révolution', *Arguments*, 17: 47–64.

*Naville, Pierre 1962, 'Degenerazione burocratica e rivoluzione', *Tempi moderni dell'economia, della politica e della cultura*, 5: 121–34.

*Naville, Pierre 1970, *Le Nouveau Léviathan*, II: *Le Salaire socialiste*, Part I, Paris: Ed. Anthropos.

*Naville, Pierre 1972, 'La bureaucratie et les contradictions sociales en URSS', *Critique Socialiste*, 7: 54–63.

Naville, Pierre 1987, *Memoires imparfaites: le temps des guerres*, Paris: La Découverte.

*Naville, Pierre and Bruno Rizzi 1960, 'Une polémique sur la bureaucratie', *Arguments*, 20: 59–60.

Nettl, J.P. 1966, *Rosa Luxemburg*, Oxford: Oxford University Press.

*Neumann, Philipp 1971, 'Der "Sozialismus als eigenständige Gesellschaftsformation". Zur Kritik der politischen Ökonomie des Sozialismus und ihrer Anwendung in der DDR', *Kursbuch*, 23 (March): 96–142.

*Nicolaievski, Boris 1947, 'Nature de l'Etat soviétique. Capitalisme? Socialisme? Ou quoi?', *La Revue Socialiste*, New Series, 16 (December): 515–25.

*Nicolaievsky, Boris 1957, 'Zur Soziologie der Macht in der totalitären Diktatur', *Ostprobleme*, IX, 28: 974–86.

*Nicolaus, Martin 1975, *Restoration of Capitalism in the USSR*, Chicago: Liberator Press.

*Nitsche, Hellmuth 1984, *Antwort an Bahro und Genossen. Wesensmerkmale, Ergebnisse und Grenzen des realen Sozialismus*, Berne: Verlag SOI.

*Novack, George 1968, 'The Problem of Transitional Formations', *International Socialist Review*, 29, 6 (November–December): 17–34.

Novack, George 1973, 'Max Shachtman: A Political Portrait', *International Socialist Review*, 34, 2: 26–9, 44.

*Nove, Alec 1975, 'Is There a Ruling Class in the USSR?', *Soviet Studies*, 27, 4 (October): 615–38.

*Nove, Alec 1983, 'The Class Nature of the Soviet Union Revisited', *Soviet Studies*, 35, 3 (July): 298–312.

Nowak, Stefan 1977, *Methodology of Sociological Research. General Problems*, Dordrecht: Reidel.

Nowotny, Helga 1975, 'Controversies in Science: Remarks on the Different Modes of Production of Knowledge and Their Use', *Zeitschrift für Soziologie*, 4: 34–45.

Oakes, Walter J. [Ed Sard] 1944, 'Towards a Permanent Arms Economy?', *Politics*, February: 11–17.

*Occeña, Bruce and Irwin Silber 1980, 'Capitalism in the USSR? An Opportunist Theory in Disarray', *Line of March. A Marxist-Leninist Journal of Rectification*, I, 3 (October–November): 47–72.

*Öconomicus [Heinz Meyer] 1951, 'Zur Analyse der Ökonomie der UdSSR', *pro und contra*, II, 9 (September): 129–31.

*Öconomicus [Heinz Meyer] 1952, 'Zum Problem der russischen Bürokratie', *pro und contra*, III, 3–4 (March–April): 44–7.

*Olle, Werner 1974a, 'Zur Theorie des Staatskapitalismus. Probleme von Theorie und Geschichte in Theorien der Übergangsgesellschaft', *Prokla*, 11–12: 91–144.

*Olle, Werner 1974b, 'Zur Problematik der mao-strukturalistischen Theorie des Staatskapitalismus', in *Übergangsgesellschaft: Herrschaftsform und Praxis am Beispiel der Sowjetunion*, edited by Peter W. Schulze, Frankfurt am Main: Fischer Taschenbuch Verlag.

Orsini, Alessandro 2004, *L'Eretico della sinistra. Bruno Rizzi, elitista democratico*, Milan: Franco Angeli.

*Orso, A. [Amadeo Bordiga] 1948–52, 'Proprietà e Capitale', *Prometeo*, 10 (June–July 1948) – 14 (February 1950) and Series II, 1 (November 1950) and 4 (July–September 1952).

Orsoni, Claude 1981, 'Karl Korsch und die Russische Revolution', in *Zur Aktualität van Karl Korsch*, edited by Michael Buckmiller, Frankfurt am Main: EVA.

Orwell, George [Eric Blair] 1946, *James Burnham and the Managerial Revolution*, London: Socialist Book Centre.

*Pablo, Michel [Michel Raptis] 1951, 'Où allons-nous?', *Quatrième Internationale*, February-April: 40–50.

Pannekoek, Anton 1920, *Weltrevolution und kommunistische Taktik*, Vienna: Arbeiterbuchhandlung.

Pannekoek, Anton 1972, *Partij, raden, revolutie*, edited by Jaap Kloosterman, Amsterdam: Van Gennep.

Panaccione, Andrea 1987, *Kautsky e l'ideologia socialista*, Milan: Franco Angeli.

*Paramio, Ludolfo 1975, 'Sur la nature de l'Etat soviétique', *Les Temps Modernes*, 349–350 (August–September): 184–201.

*Paris, Rainer 1975, 'Class Structure and Legitimatory Public Sphere: A Hypothesis on the Continued Existence of Class Relationships and the Problem of Legitimation in Transitional Societies', *New German Critique*, 5 (Spring): 149–57.

*Park, Henry 1987, 'Secondary Literature on the Question of the Restoration of Capitalism in the Soviet Union', *Research in Political Economy*, 10: 27–58.

*Patri, Aimé 1947a, 'Une nouvelle classe dirigeante peut-elle exister?', *La Revue Internationale*, 18 (October): 96–102.

*Patri, Aimé 1947b, 'L'ère des "Organisateurs". Remarques à propos des conceptions de Burnham', *Masses – Socialisme et Liberté*, 11 (October-December): 23–5.

Pečulić, Miroslav 1967, 'Kritika teorijske misli o strukturi socijalističog drušva', *Socijalizam*, X, 11: 1384–1408.

*Pellicani, Luciano 1977, 'Sul Collettivismo Burocratico', in Bruno Rizzi, *Il Collettivismo Burocratico*, Milan: Sugarco edizione.

*Peralta [Benjamin Péret] 1946, *Le 'Manifeste' des exégètes*, Mexico: Editorial 'Revolución'.

Peregalli, Arturo and Sandro Saggioro 1995, *Amadeo Bordiga (1889–1970): bibliografia*, Paderno Dugnano: Colibri.

Peregalli, Arturo and Sandro Saggioro 1998, *Amadeo Bordiga: la sconfitta e gli anni oscuri (1926–1945)*, Milan: Colibri.

*Persson, Anita 1975, 'Klasstriderna i Soviet. Charles Bettelheim och övergångssamhället"', *Häften för kritiska studier*, VIII, 4: 45–53.

Piccard, E. 1960, *Simone Weil. Essai biographique et critique suivi d'une anthologie raisonnée des oeuvres de Simone Weil*, Paris: Presses Universitaires de France.

*Plogstedt, Sybille 1979, 'Bahro', *Courage*, January.

Polanyi, Karl 1957, *The Great Transformation*, Boston: Beacon Press.

Pollock, Friedrich 1929, *Die planwirtschaftlichen Versuche in der Sowjetunion*, Leipzig: Schriften des Instituts für Sozialforschung an der Universität Frankfurt am Main.

Pollock, Friedrich 1932, 'Die gegenwärtige Lage des Kapitalismus und die Aussichten einer planwirtschaftlichen Neuordnung', *Zeitschrift für Sozialforschung*, I: 8–27.

*Pollock, Friedrich 1941, 'State Capitalism: Its Possibilities and Limitations', *Studies in Philosophy and Social Science*, IX: 200–25.

*Pommier, André 1974, 'Sur la restauration du capitalisme en URSS', *Communisme*, 12 (September–October): 55–79.

*Pouillon, Jean 1954, 'Staline: Catoblépas ou Phénix', *Les Temps Modernes*, IX, 2: 2233–47.

Prager, Rodolphe (ed.) 1978, *Les Congrès de la IVᵉ Internationale, vol. 1: Naissance de la IVe Internationale*, Paris: Ed. La Brèche.

Prat, Michel 1984, 'L'échec d'une opposition internationale de gauche dans le Komintern, 1926', *Communisme. Revue d'Etudes Pluridisciplinaires*, 5: 61–75.

Preobrazhenskii, E.A. 1926, *Novaia ekonomika. Opyt teoreticheskogo analiza sovetskogo khoziaistva*, Moscow: Kommunisticheskaia Akademiia. Sektsiia Ekonomiki. [*The New Economics*, Oxford: Clarendon Press, 1965.]

*Purdy, David 1976, *The Soviet Union: State-Capitalist or Socialist. A Marxist Critique of the International Socialists*, London: Communist Party.

*Rabassière, Henri [Heinz Pächter] 1954, 'And Can There Be Peace?', *Dissent*, I, 3 (Summer): 242–7.

Rabehl, Bernd 1973, 'Die marxistische Theorie der Transformationsgesellschaft am Beispiel der Entwicklung der russischen Revolution', in *Gesellschaftsstrukturen*, edited by Oskar Negt and Klaus Meschkat, Frankfurt am Main: Suhrkamp.

*Rabehl, Bernd 1975, 'Der "neue" Staat und die Keimformen einer "neuen" Klasse in der Sowjetunion', in Dutschke and Wilke (eds.) 1975.

Rabehl, Bernd 1977, 'Die Stalinismusdiskussion des internationalen Kommunismus nach dem XX. Parteitag der KPdSU', in *Entstalinisierung. Der XX. Parteitag der KPdSU und seine Folgen*, edited by Manfred Crusius and Manfred Wilke, Frankfurt am Main: Suhrkamp.

*Rabinovitch, Sonia 1935, 'L'Etat Soviétique est-il oui ou non un Etat prolétarien?', *L'Etudiant Socialiste*, November: 6–7.

Radziejowski, Janusz 1978, 'Roman Rosdolsky: Man, Activist, and Scholar', *Science and Society*, 42: 198–210.

Raina, Peter 1978, *Political Opposition in Poland 1954–1977*, London: Poets and Painters.

*Rakovski, Marc [György Bence and Janos Kis] 1974, 'Le marxisme devant les sociétés soviétiques', *Les Temps Modernes*, 341 (December): 553–84. ['Marxism and the Analysis of Soviet Societies', *Capital and Class*, 1 (Spring 1977): 83–105.]

Rakovski, Marc [György Bence and Janos Kis] 1976, 'L'Union du Capital et de la Science passé et present', *Les Temps Modernes*, 355 (January): 1241–70.

*Rakovski, Marc [György Bence and Janos Kis] 1978, *Towards an East European Marxism*, London: Allison & Busby.

*Rakovsky, Christian 1929, 'Pismo Kh.G. Rakovskogo o prichinakh pererozhdeniia o gosudarstvennogo apparata', *Biulleten' Oppozitsii*, 6: 14–20. ['The "Professional Dangers" of Power', in *Selected Writings on Opposition in the USSR, 1923–30*, edited and introduced by Gus Fagan, London: Allison & Busby, 1980.]

*Redaktionskollektiv 1976, 'Zur Entwicklung der Neuen Linken in Ungarn', *Politikon*, 50 (February): 2–9.

Rees, Richard 1966, *Simone Weil – A Sketch for a Portrait*, London: Oxford University Press.

*Reichman, Henry 2004, [Review of Resnick and Wolff 2002, and Haynes 2002], H-Russia, November (H-RUSSIA@H-NET.MSU.EDU).

Reinhartz, Dennis 1981, *Milovan Djilas: A Revolutionary as a Writer*, New York: Columbia University Press.

*Reinstein, Boris 1974, 'Der "Sozialimperialismus" als höchstes Stadium des Schematismus', *Die Internationale*, 3 (March): 44–75.

*Renner, Karl 1917, *Marxismus, Krieg und Internationale. Kritische Studien über offene Probleme des wissenschaftlichen und des praktischen Sozialismus in und nach dem Weltkrieg*, Stuttgart: J.H.W. Dietz Nachf.

Resnick, Stephen A. and Richard D. Wolff 1987, *Knowle©e and Class. A Marxian Critique of Political Economy*, Chicago: The University of Chicago Press.

*Resnick, Stephen A. and Richard D. Wolff 1993, 'State Capitalism in the USSR: A High-Stakes Debate', *Rethinking Marxism*, 6–2 (Summer): 46–67.

*Resnick, Stephen A. and Richard D. Wolff 1994a, 'Between State and Private Capitalism: What Was Soviet "Socialism"?', *Rethinking Marxism*, 7–1 (Spring): 9–30.

*Resnick, Stephen A. and Richard D. Wolff 1994b, 'Capitalisms, Socialisms, Communisms', *Current Perspectives in Social Theory*, 14: 135–50.

*Resnick, Stephen A. and Richard D. Wolff 1994c, 'The End of the USSR: A Marxian Class Analysis', in *Marxism in the Postmodern Age*, edited by Antonio Callari, Stephen Cullenberg and Carole Biewener, New York: Guilford Press.

*Resnick, Stephen A. and Richard D. Wolff 1994d, 'Lessons from the USSR: Taking Marxian Theory to the Next Stop', in *Whither Marxism*, edited by Bernd Magnus and Stephen Cullenberg, London: Routledge.

*Resnick, Stephen A. and Richard D. Wolff 2002, *Class Theory and History. Capitalism and Communism in the USSR*, London: Routledge.

*Revolutionary Union 1974, *How Capitalism Has Been Restored in the Soviet Union and What This Means for the World Struggle*, Chicago: Revolutionary Union.

*Riasanovsky, Nicholas V. 1963, '"Oriental Despotism" and Russia', *Slavic Review*, 22: 644–9.

*Richards, Frank [Frank Füredi] 1987, 'The Myth of State Capitalism', *Confrontation*, 2: 87–113.

*Richards, Frank [Frank Füredi] 1989a, 'The Myths of Gorbymania', *Living Marxism*, 8 (June): 18–23.

*Richards, Frank [Frank Füredi] 1989b, 'Theses on Stalinism in the Gorbatchev Era', *Confrontation*, 5 (Summer), 101–10.

*Richardson, Al 1991 [Review of Daum 1990], *Revolutionary History*, 3, 4 (Autumn): 34–6.

Richardson, Al 1996, 'Michel Pablo (1911–1996)', *Revolutionary History*, 6, 2–3 (Summer), 255–6.

*Ridley, F.A. 1947, 'Comment', *Left*, 128 (June): 139–40.

*Riechers, Christian 1977, 'Die Ergebnisse der Revolution "Stalins" in Russland', *Jahrbuch Arbeiterbewegung*, V: 139–68.

Rieland, Wolfgang 1977, *Organisation und Autonomie. Die Erneuerung der italienischen Arbeiterbewegung*, Frankfurt: Neue Kritik.

Rigby T.R. 1977, 'Stalinism and Mono-Organizational Society', in *Stalinism. Essays in Historical Interpretation*, edited by Robert C. Tucker, New York: Norton.

*Rigby, Tom 1998, 'Stalin's Russia: Capitalism Without Capitalists?', *Workers' Liberty*, 45 (March): 43–8.

*Rilling, Rainer 1978, 'Zur Geschichte der Sozialismusanalyse in der intellektuellen Linken der BRD seit Mitte der 60er Jahre', in *Beiträge zur Sozialismusanalyse*, I, edited by Peter Brokmeier and Rainer Rilling, Cologne: Pahl-Rugenstein.

*Rimbert, Pierre 1948, 'Révolution directorale et socialisme', *La Revue Socialiste*, New Series, 20 (April): 353–70 and 21 (May): 542–53.

*Rimbert, Pierre 1958, 'Djilas prisonnier de la nouvelle classe', *La Revue Socialiste*, New Series, 115 (March): 296–307; 116 (April): 424–35; 117 (May): 535–43 and 118 (June): 656–66.

Rivière, François 1974, 'Pour l'Ecole de Budapest', *Les Temps Modernes*, 337–8 (August-September): 2736–47.

*Rizzi, Bruno 1937, *Dove va l'URSS?*, Milan: La Prora.

*R[izzi], Bruno 1939, *La bureaucratisation du monde*, Paris: Imprimerie Les Presses Modernes. [An English translation of pp. 11–99 in Rizzi, *The Bureaucratization of the World*, trans. Adam Westoby, London: Tavistock, 1985.]

*Rizzi, Bruno 1962, *La lezione dello stalinismo. Socialismo e collettivismo burocratico*, Rome: Opere Nueve.

*Rizzi, Bruno 1967, *Il Collettivismo burocratico*, Imola: Galeati.

*Rizzi, Bruno 1970, 'Quale socialismo?', *Terzo Mondo*, 9: 81–5.

*Rizzi, Bruno 1971, 'Sulla natura dell'URSS: replicando a *Giovane Critica*', *Giovane Critica*, 28: 51–63.

*Rizzi, Bruno 1972, 'Società asiatica e collettivismo burocratico. Osservazioni a Melotti e a Carlo', *Terzo Mondo*, 18: 75–94.

Rizzi, Bruno 1983, 'Lettere a Trockij '38–'39', *Belfagor*, 38, 6 (30 November): 683–98.

Robinson, Cedric J. 1983, *Black Marxism. The Making of the Black Radical Tradition*, London: Zed Books.

Röder, Werner and Herbert A. Strauss (eds.) 1980, *Biographisches Handbuch der deutsch-sprachigen Emigration nach 1933*, Vol. I: *Politik, Wirtschaft, Öffentliches Leben*, Munich [etc.]: K.G. Saur.

*Rogozinski, Jacob 1980, 'Alternative et dissidence: Remarques sur *L'Alternative* de Rudolf Bahro', *Les Temps Modernes*, 412 (November): 809–41.

*Rojas, Mauricio J. 1981, 'Den ursprungliga ackumulationen i det byråkratiska samhället av sovjetisk typ: en omvärdering av Sovjetunionens historia', *Häften för kritiska studier*, XIV, 3: 21–45.

Romano, Joseph 2003, 'James Burnham en France: l'import-export de la "révolution ·managériale" après 1945', *Revue Française de Science Politique*, 53: 257–75.

Romano, Paul [Phil Singer] and Ria Stone [Grace Lee] 1946, *The American Worker*, Detroit: Facing Reality Publishing Committee.

*Rosdolsky, Roman 1959, 'Zur Analyse der russischen Revolution', in *Die Sozialismusdebatte. Historische und aktuelle Fragen des Sozialismus*, edited by Ulf Wolter, West Berlin: Olle & Wolter, 1978.

Rosdolsky, Roman 1964, 'Friedrich Engels und das Problem der "geschichtslosen" Völker', *Archiv für Sozialgeschichte*, IV: 87–202. ['Engels and the "Nonhistoric" Peoples. The National Question in the Revolution of 1848', *Critique*, 18–19 (1987).]

Rosdolsky, Roman 1968, *Zur Entstehungsgeschichte des Marxschen Kapital*, 3 vols., Frankfurt am Main: EVA. [*The Making of Marx's 'Capital'*, 2 vols., London: Pluto Press, 1989.]

*Rossanda, Rossana 1972, 'Die sozialistischen Lander: Ein Dilemma der westeuropäischen Linken', *Kursbuch*, 30: 1–34.

*Rotermundt, Rainer 1977, 'Oktoberrevolution und Sozialismus. Zur Bedeutung des Massenbewusstseins für die Herausbildung nichtkapitalistischer Produktionsverhältnisse', *Prokla*, 27: 77–102.

*Rotermundt, Rainer, Ursula Schmiederer and Helmut Becker-Panitz 1977, '"Realer Sozialismus" und realer Sozialismus. Bedingungen und Chancen einer sozialistischen Entwicklung in Gesellschaften sowjetischen Typs', *Jahrbuch Arbeiterbewegung*, 5: 9–37.

*Rotermundt, Rainer, Ursula Schmiederer, and Helmut Becker-Panitz 1979, *Die Sowjetunion und Europa. Gesellschaftsform und Aussenpolitik der USSR*, Frankfurt am Main: Campus.

*Rubel, Maximilien 1951, 'Réflexions sur la société directorale', *La Revue Socialiste*, New Series, 44 (February): 181–94.

Rubel, Maximilien 1960, *Karl Marx devant le bonapartisme*, The Hague: Mouton.

*Ruch, Ursula 1975, 'Die antikommunistische Verfälschung des realen Sozialismus durch den Trotzkismus', *Wissenschaftliche Zeitschrift der Martin-Luther-Universität Halle-Wittenberg. Gesellschafts- und sprachwissenschaftliche Reihe*, 24: 5–15.

*Rüdiger, Mogens and Vibeke Sørensen 1979, 'Teorier om Sovjetunionen sam overgangssamfund', *Historievidenskab*, 17: 65–114.

*Rühle, Otto 1920a, 'Moskau und wir', *Die Aktion*, X, 37–38 (18 September).

*Rühle, Otto 1920b, 'Bericht über Moskau', *Die Aktion*, X, 39–40 (2 October).

*Rühle, Otto 1924, *Von der bürgerlichen zur proletarischen Revolution*, Dresden: Am Anderen Ufer.

*[Rühle, Otto] 1939, 'The Struggle Against Fascism Begins With The Struggle Against Bolshevism', *Living Marxism*, IV, 8 (September): 245–55.

Rupnik, Jacques D. 1976, 'Conflicts au sein du movement communiste en Tchécoslovaquie au début des années trente: l'affaire Guttmann', *Revue Française de Science Politique*, 26: 770–99.

*Salvadori, Massimo L. 1973, 'La concezione del processo rivoluzionario in Kautsky (1891–1922)', *Annali Istituto Giangiacomo Feltrinelli*: 26–80.

*Salvadori, Massimo L. 1978a, 'Realtà sovietica e ideologia marxista', *MondOperaio*, 31, 1: 89–98.

Salvadori, Massimo L. 1978b, *Karl Kautsky and the Socialist Revolution, 1880–1938*, London: New Left Books.

*Sandberg, Mikæl 1981, 'Sovjet: ägande och makt', *Häften för kritiska studier*, XIV, 3: 4–20.

*Sandemose, Jørgen 1976, 'Kapitalismens utvikling i USSR – en litteraturstudie', *Røde Fane*, 2–3: 26–75.

*Sandemose, Jørgen 2002, 'Tilbake til USSR', in *Stat, religion, økonomie: Karl Marx om kapitalismens former*, Oslo: Aschehoug & Co.

*Santamaria, Ulysses and Alain Manville 1976, 'Lenin and the Problem of Transition', *Telos*, 27 (Spring): 79–96.

Sapir, Boris 1947, 'Is War with Russia Inevitable? An Examination of Burnham's New Thesis', *Modern Review*, I: 360–6.

Sapir, Boris 1979, 'Boris Ivanovitsj Nikolaevskij', in *Over Buonarroti, internationale avantgardes, Max Nettlau en het verzamelen van boeken, anarchistische ministers, de algebra van de revolutie, schilders en schrijvers*, edited by Maria Hunink et al., Baarn: Het Wereldvenster.

Sapir, Jacques 1980, *Pays de l'Est: vers la crise généralisée?*, Paris: Federop.

Sapir, Jacques 1989, *Les fluctuations économiques en URSS 1941–1985*, Paris: Editions de l'EHESS.

*Sapir, Jacques 1990, *L'économie mobilisée. Essai sur les économies de type soviétique*, Paris: La Découverte.

*Sapir, Jacques 1993, 'Régulation et transition', *Critique communiste*, 128–9 (February): 49–54.

*Sapir, Jacques 1997, 'Le débat sur la nature de l'URSS', in *URSS et Russie. Rupture historique et continuité économique*, edited by Rotame Motamed-Nejad, Paris: Presses Universitaires de France-Actuel Marx.

*Sara, Henry 1940, 'Not State Capitalism', *Left*, 40: 20–4.

Sarney, Ygal 2000, 'A Revolutionary Life', *International Socialism*, II, 87 (Summer): 137–49.

*Sawer, Marian 1978–9, 'The Politics of Historiography. Russian Socialism and the Question of the Asiatic Mode of Production, 1906–1931', *Critique*, 10–11: 15–35.

*Sawer, Marian (ed.) 1978, *Socialism and the New Class. Towards the Analysis of Structural Inequality Within 'Socialist' Societies*, [Australian Political Studies Association Monograph 19], Adelaide.

*Schäfer, Gert 1978, 'Was heisst bürokratischer Sozialismus? Versuch einer Würdigung von Rudolf Bahros "Anatomie des real existierenden Sozialismus"', *Prokla*, 31: 33–55.

*Schaff, Adam 1982, 'Les pays socialistes sont-ils socialistes?', *L'Homme et la Société*, 65–6: 3–21.

*Scharrer, Manfred 1976, 'Gefahren der Dialektik. Zur neueren Diskussion der Sowjetgesellschaft', *Der lange Marsch*, 23 (September): 10–11.

*Schlögel, Karl 1975, 'Bettelheim: Klassenkämpfe in der UdSSR', *Theorie und Praxis des Marxismus-Leninismus*, 1: 25–48.

*Schmidt, Wolf-Dietrich 1975, 'Dutschkes Leninismus-Kritik', *Das Argument*, 94: 991–8.

*Schmiederer, Ursula 1973, 'Zur Analyse von Übergangsgesellschaften. Kritik zu Johann Eggert "Die Sowjetgesellschaft"', *Links*, 49 (November): 15–18.

*Schmiederer, Ursula 1977, 'Der "reale Sozialismus", die Opposition und wir', *Links*, 86 (March): 17–18.

*Schmiederer, Ursula 1980a, *Die Aussenpolitik der Sowjetunion*, Stuttgart: Kohlhammer.

*Schmiederer, Ursula 1980b, 'Zum Problem von Bürokratie und Herrschaft im "realen Sozialismus"', *Soziologische Revue*, 3: 403–11.

*Schöler, Uli 1985, 'Otto Bauers Auseinandersetzung mit der Oktoberrevolution und dem sowjetischen Modell', in *Otto Bauer: Theorie und Politik*, edited by Detlev Albers, Horst Heimann and Richard Saage, West Berlin: Das Argument.

*Schöler, Uli 1987, *Otto Bauer und Sowjetrussland*, West Berlin: DVK–Verlag.

*Schöler, Uli 1991, *'Despotischer Sozialismus' oder 'Staatssklaverei'? Die theoretische Verarbeitung der sowjetrussischen Entwicklung in der Sozialdemokratie Deutschlands und Österreichs (1917–1929)*, 2 vols, Hamburg und Münster: Lit.

Schöler, Uli 1999, *Ein Gespenst verschwand in Europa. Über Marx und die sozialistische Idee nach dem Scheitern des sowjetischen Staatssozialismus*, Bonn: Dietz.

Scholer, Robert and Robert Kellogg 1966, *The Nature of Narrative*, Oxford: Oxford University Press.

Schoolman, Morton 1980, *The Imaginary Witness. The Critical Theory of Herbert Marcuse*, New York: The Free Press.
*Schulze, Peter W. (ed.) 1974, *Übergangsgesellschaft. Herrschaftsform und Praxis am Beispiel der Sowjetunion*, Frankfurt am Main: Fischer Taschenbuch.
*Schulze, Peter W. 1977, *Herrschaft und Klassen in der Sowjetgesellschaft. Die historischen Bedingungen des Stalinismus*, Frankfurt am Main: Campus
*Schuman, Frederick L. 1976, 'More on the Nature of Soviet Society', *Monthly Review*, 27, 10 (March): 1–4.
*Schuman, Frederick L. 1980, 'Born-Again Capitalism', *Monthly Review*, 32, 6 (November): 48–51.
Schwarz, Solomon M. 1951, *Labor in the Soviet Union*, New York: Praeger.
*[Sedova, Natalia] 1951, 'Text of Letter to SWP from Natalia Trotsky', *The Militant*, 4 June.
*Senghaas, Dieter 1980a, 'Sozialismus – Eine entwicklungsgeschichtliche und entwicklungstheoretische Betrachtung', *Leviathan*, VIII: 10–40.
*Senghaas, Dieter 1980b, 'Wittfogel Redivivus', *Leviathan*, VIII: 133–41.
*Serge, Victor 1947, 'L'URSS a-t-elle un régime socialiste?', *Masses – Socialisme et Liberté*, 9–10 (June–July): 21–4.
Seton-Watson, Hugh 1956, *The East European Revolution*, New York: Praeger.
Shachtman, Max 1940a, 'The Crisis in the American Party. An Open Letter in Reply to Comrade Leon Trotsky', *New International*, VI: 43–51.
*Shachtman, Max 1940b, 'Is Russia a Workers' State?', *New International*, VI: 195–205.
Shachtman, Max 1951a, 'Comrade Natalia's Indictment', *Labor Action*, 11 June.
*Shachtman, Max 1951b, 'The 4th International's Capitulation to Stalinism', *Labor Action*, 25 June.
*Shachtman, Max 1962, *The Bureaucratic Revolution. The Rise of the Stalinist State*, New York: The Donald Press.
*Shachtman, Max and Earl Browder 1950, 'Is Russia a Socialist Community?', *New International* (May–June): 145–76.
Shortall, Felton C. 1994, *The Incomplete Marx*, Aldershot: Avebury.
*Silver, Geoffrey and Gregory Tarpinian 1981, 'Marxism and Socialism: A Response to Paul Sweezy and Ernest Mandel', *Review of Radical Political Economics*, XIII, 1 (Spring): 11–21.
Sinclair, Louis [no date], *The IS-Papers*, II, Typescript, Amsterdam: International Institute of Social History.
*Sinigaglia, Roberto 1973, *Mjasnikov e la rivoluzione russa*, Milan: Jaca.
Skrzypczak Henryk 1980, 'Rudolf Bahro oder die Wiedergeburt des Marxismus aus dem Geiste der Religion', *Internationale wissenschaftliche Korrespondenz zur Geschichte der deutschen Arbeiterbewegung*, 16: 125–91.
*Smith, H. 1937, 'Trotsky and Proletarian Dictatorship', *International Council Correspondence*, III, 4 (April): 27–32.
*Socialist Party of Great Britain 1948, *Russia since 1917: Socialist Views of Bolshevik Policy*, London: SPGB.
Söllner, Alfons 1987–8, 'Marcuse's Political Theory in the 1940s and 1950s', *Telos*, 74 (Winter): 65–78.
Sohn-Rethel, Alfred 1971, *Warenform und Denkform. Aufsätze*, Frankfurt am Main: EVA.
Sohn-Rethel, Alfred 1972, *Geistige una Körperliche Arbeit. Zur Theorie der gesellschaftlichen Synthesis. Erweiterte und ergänzte Ausgabe*, Frankfurt am Main: Suhrkamp. [*Intellectual and Manual Labour. A Critique of Epistemology*, London: Macmillan, 1976.]
Soltysiak, Grzegorz 1992, 'Grupa Hassa', *Karta*, 7: 57–77.
*Soviet Studies Project 1981, 'The Concept of State Capitalism', *Progressive Labor Magazine*, XIV–1 (Spring): 8–19.
*Spencer, William 1939, 'Is Russia a Workers' State?', *Revolt*, II–8: 4–9.
Spohn, Wilfried 1975, 'Die technologische Abhängigkeit der Sowjetunion vom Weltmarkt', *Prokla*, 19–20–21: 225–59.

*Spohn, Wilfried 1978, 'Geschichte und Emanzipation. Bahros Beitrag zur Sozialismus-Diskussion', *Prokla* 31: 5–31.

*Sprenger, Rudolf [Helmut Wagner] 1933–4, 'Das gesellschaftliche Gesicht des Bolschewismus', *Rote Revue*, XIII: 314–20.

*Sprenger, Rudolf [Helmut Wagner] 1940, *Bolshevism: Its Roots, Role, Class View and Methods*, trans. Integer [Herman Jenson], New York: International Review.

Sprenger, Rodolfo [Helmut Wagner] 1947, *El Bolchevismo. Su papel. Sus metodos. Su filiación. Sus objetivos*, Santiago-Chili: Imprinta Nueva.

*Spurkeland, Trond 1974, 'Stalinismens fallit', *Vardøger*, 6: 159–94.

*Stahl, Peter 1949–50, 'Der Schicksalsweg der bolschewistischen Jakobiner', *pro und contra*, 2 (December 1949): 11–27; 3 (January 1950): 23–28 and 4 (February 1950): 7–8.

*Stark, David 1981, 'Consciousness in Command', *Socialist Review*, 57 (May-June): 128–49.

Steenson, Gary P. 1978, *Karl Kautsky 1854–1938. Marxism in the Classical Years*, Pittsburgh: University of Pittsburgh Press.

Stehr, Uwe 1973, *Vom Kapitalismus zum Kommunismus. Bucharins Beitrag zur Entstehung einer sozialistischen Theorie und Gesellschaft*, Düsseldorf: Bertelsmann.

Steiner, Helmut 1990, 'Der aufrechte Gang eines DDR-Ökonomen: Fritz Behrens (1909–1980)', *Utopie kreativ*, 2 (October): 80–4.

Steiner, Helmut 1992, 'Fritz Behrens. Lebensbilanz eines sozialistischen Wissenschaftlers', *Deutschland-Archiv*, 25: 1160–8.

*Steiner, Herbert 1967, 'Am Beispiel Otto Bauers – die Oktoberrevolution und der Austromarxismus', *Weg und Ziel. Monatsschrift für Fragen des wissenschaftlichen Sozialismus*, Special issue, July: 3–21.

*Steinhauer, Erwin 1978, 'Europa, Weltrevolution und "nichtkapitalistischer Weg"', *Theorie und Praxis des Marxismus-Leninismus*, 3: 50–64.

Stephan, Cora 1974, 'Geld- und Staatstheorie in Hilferdings *Finanzkapital*', *Gesellschaft. Beiträge zur Marxschen Theorie*, 2: 111–54.

*Sternberg, Fritz 1951, *Kapitalismus und Sozialismus vor dem Weltgericht*, Hamburg: Rowohlt. [*Capitalism and Socialism on Trial*, trans. Edward Fitzgerald, New York: Greenwood Press, 1968.]

*Sternberg, Fritz 1952, *So endete es … Von der Oktoberrevolution zum reaktionärsten Staat der Welt*, Cologne: Bund Verlag.

*Sternberg, Fritz 1955a, 'Ein Beitrag zur Charakterisierung des russischen Staates', *Gewerkschaftliche Monatshefte*, 3: 169–72.

*Sternberg, Fritz 1955b, 'Der soziale Gehalt der russischen Diktatur', *Gewerkschaftliche Monatshefte*, 6: 374–8.

Sternberg, Fritz 1963, 'Conversations with Trotsky', *Survey. A Journal of Soviet and East European Studies*, 47: 146–59. [An expanded and revised version was published as: 'Gespräche mit Trotzki. Ergänzte und überarbeitete Fassung des 1963 in "Survey" erschienenen Essays', in Grebing 1981.]

*Steuermann, Carl [Otto Rühle] 1931, *Weltkrise – Weltwende. Kurs auf Staatskapitalismus*, Berlin S. Fischer.

*Stone, George 1947, 'Where Is Russia Going?', *Left*, 134 (December): 277–81.

*Stone, George 1948, 'The Failure of the Apologists', *Left*, 137 (March): 55–60.

*Stojanović, Svetozar 1967, 'The Statist Myth of Socialism', *Praxis*, 3, 2: 176–87.

Stojanović, Svetozar 1968, 'Još jedanput o etatističkom mitu socijalizma. Odgovor Miroslavu Pečujliču', *Socijalizam*, XI, 1–2: 191–8.

*Stojanović, Svetozar 1973, *Between Ideals and Reality. A Critique of Socialism and Its Future*, trans. Gerson S. Sher, Oxford: Oxford University Press. [Originally: *Izme^au Ideala i Stvarnosti*. Belgrade: Prosveta, 1969.]

Strachey, John 1933, *The Coming Struggle for Power*, New York: Covici, Friede.

*Stuart, J.B. 1965, 'Deutschers Meinung über die Trotzkisten', *Die Internationale*, 10: 51–63.

Stutje, Jan Willem 2004, 'Ernest Mandel in Resistance: Revolutionary Socialists in Belgium, 1940–1945', *Left History*, 10, 1 (Fall-Winter): 125–52.

*Stuurman, Siep 1974, 'Stalinisme en anti-communisme', *Amsterdams Sociologisch Tijdschrift*, 1, 4: 113–41.

*Stuurman, Siep 1979, *Het reëel bestaande en het noodzakelijke socialisme*, Amsterdam: Van Gennep.

*Stuurman, Siep 1980, 'State Property and the Nature of the Soviet Ruling Class', *Monthly Review*, 31, 11 (April): 51–6.

*Süss, Walter 1979, 'Bürokratische Rationalität und gesellschaftliche Synthesis in der Konstitutionsphase des sowjetischen Systems', *Prokla*, 35: 133–70.

Sweezy, Paul M. 1942, *The Theory of Capitalist Development. Principles of Marxian Political Economy*, Oxford: Oxford University Press.

*Sweezy, Paul M. 1947, 'Les illusions de la révolution directorale', *La Revue Internationale*, 19 (November–December): 179–82.

*Sweezy, Paul M. 1968, 'The Invasion of Czechoslovakia: Czechoslovakia, Capitalism and Socialism', *Monthly Review*, 20, 5 (October): 5–16.

*Sweezy, Paul M. 1969, 'Reply', *Monthly Review*, 20, 10 (March): 10–19.

*Sweezy, Paul M. 1970, 'Reply', *Monthly Review*, 22, 7 (December): 14–21.

*Sweezy, Paul M. 1974, 'The Nature of Soviet Society', *Monthly Review*, 26, 6 (November): 1–16.

*Sweezy, Paul M. 1975, 'The Nature of Soviet Society II', *Monthly Review*, 26, 8 (January): 1–15.

*Sweezy, Paul M. 1976a, 'Transition au socialisme ou transition socialiste?', *Les Temps Modernes*, 355 (January): 1296–8.

*Sweezy, Paul M. 1976b, 'Paul Sweezy Replies', *Monthly Review*, 27, 10 (March): 11–14.

*Sweezy, Paul M. 1977a, 'Réponse à Bernard Chavance', *Les Temps Modernes*, 375 (October): 527–33.

*Sweezy, Paul M. 1977b, 'Bettelheim on Revolution from Above: The USSR in the 1920's', *Monthly Review*, 29, 5 (October): 1–18.

*Sweezy, Paul M. 1977c, 'Paul Sweezy Replies', *Monthly Review*, 29, 1 (May): 13–19.

*Sweezy, Paul M. 1978, 'Is There a Ruling Class in the USSR?', *Monthly Review*, 30, 5 (October): 1–17.

*Sweezy, Paul M. 1979, 'Paul Sweezy Replies to Ernest Mandel', *Monthly Review*, 31, 3 (July–August): 76–86.

*Sweezy, Paul M. 1980, 'Post-Revolutionary Society', *Monthly Review*, 32, 6 (November): 1–13.

*Sweezy, Paul M. 1981, 'Paul Sweezy Replies', *Monthly Review*, 33, 1 (May): 55–6.

*Sweezy, Paul M. 1985a, 'After Capitalism – What?', *Monthly Review*, 37, 3 (July–August): 98–111.

*Sweezy, Paul M. 1985b, 'Rejoinder', *Monthly Review*, 37, 4 (September): 56–61.

*Sweezy, Paul M. 1986, 'A Final Word', *Monthly Review*, 38, 7 (December): 38–41.

*Sweezy, Paul M. and Charles Bettelheim 1971, *On the Transition to Socialism*, New York: Monthly Review Press.

Sweezy, Paul M. and Leo Huberman 1964, 'Peaceful Transition from Socialism to Capitalism?'. *Monthly Review*, 15, 11 (March): 569–90.

*Symposium 1938: 'Was the Bolshevik Revolution a Failure? A Symposium', *Modern Quarterly*, 11, 1 (Autumn): 8–28.

Syré, Ludger 1984, *Isaac Deutscher, Marxist, Publizist, Historiker. Sein Leben und Werk 1907–1967*, Hamburg: Junius.

*S.Z. Tübingen 1977, 'Bürokratische Herrschaft und Arbeitsteilung. Kritik der Sowjetgesellschaft', *Links*, 88: 13–15.

Szelényi, Ivan 1977, 'Notes on the "Budapest School"', *Critique*, 8 (Summer): 61–7.

*Szelényi, Ivan 1978–9, 'The Position of the Intelligentsia in the Class Structure of State Socialist Societies', *Critique*, 10–11: 51–76.

*Szelényi, Ivan 1980, 'Whose Alternative?', *New German Critique*, 20 (Spring-Summer): 117–34.

*Szymanski, Albert 1979, *Is the Red Flag Flying? The Political Economy of the Soviet Union Today*, London: Zed Press.

*Tacchinardi, Riccardo and Arturo Peregalli 1990, *L'URSS e i teorici del capitalismo di stato*, Rome: Lacaita.
*Tarbuck, Ken 1969–70, 'The Theory of State Capitalism: A Clock without a Spring', *Marxist Studies*, II, 1: 7–25.
*Tautin, Pierre 1947, 'Le centralisme bureaucratique', *La Revue Internationale*, 17 (Summer): 31–3.
*Ter-Grigorjan, G.G. 1978, 'Karl Kautsky und die Theoretiker des Austromarxismus über die Probleme der sozialistischen Revolution und des Sozialismus', in *Bürgerliche und kleinbürgerliche ökonomische Theorien über den Sozialismus (1917–1945)*, edited by Werner Krause, Berlin [GDR]: Akademie-Verlag.
*Texte zur Stalinfrage 1979, Hamburg: Reents.
*Thomas, Martin 1997, 'Stalinism and State Capitalism', *Workers' Liberty*, 43 (November): 41–6.
*Thomas, Martin 1999–2000, 'The USSR and Non-Linear Capitalism', *Workers' Liberty*, 59–60 (December–January): 55–6.
Thompson, E.P. 1978, *The Poverty of Theory and Other Essays*, London: Merlin Press.
*Thompson, Paul 1980, 'The Origins and Basis of State-Collectivism', in *The Nature of So-Called Socialist Societies*, London: Big Flame International Committee.
*Thompson, Paul and Guy Lewis 1977, *The Revolution Unfinished? A Critique of Trotskyism*, Liverpool: Big Flame.
*Tibert, G. 1972, 'A propos de la nature de l'URSS', *Critiques de l'économie politique*, 7–8: 47–56.
*Ticktin, Hillel 1973, 'Towards a Political Economy of the USSR', *Critique*, 1: 20–41.
*Ticktin, Hillel 1974a, 'Political Economy of the Soviet Intellectual', *Critique*, 2: 5–21.
*Ticktin, Hillel 1974b, 'Socialism, the Market and the State', *Critique*, 3: 65–72.
*Ticktin, Hillel 1975, 'The Capitalist Crisis and Current Trends in the USSR', *Critique*, 4: 101–9.
*Ticktin, Hillel 1976, 'The Contradictions of Soviet Society and Professor Bettelheim', *Critique*, 6: 17–44.
*Ticktin, Hillel 1976–77, 'The USSR: The Beginning of the End?', *Critique*, 7: 88–93.
*Ticktin, Hillel 1978a, 'The Class Structure of the USSR and the Elite', *Critique*, 9: 37–61.
Ticktin, Hillel 1978b, 'Detente and Soviet Economic Reforms', in *Soviet Foreign Policy – Its Social and Economic Conditions*, edited by Egbert Jahn, London: Allison & Busby.
*Ticktin, Hillel 1978–9, 'Rudolf Bahro: A Socialist without a Working Class', *Critique*, 10–11: 133–9.
*Ticktin, Hillel 1979–80a, 'The Afghan War and the Crisis in the USSR', *Critique*, 12: 13–25.
*Ticktin, Hillel 1979–80b, 'The Ambiguities of Ernest Mandel', *Critique*, 12: 127–37.
*Ticktin, Hillel 1982, 'Trockij and the Social Forces Leading to Bureaucracy', in *Pensiero e azione politica di Lev Trockij*, edited by Francesca Gori, Milan: Leo S. Olschki, II.
*Ticktin, Hillel 1986, 'The Year after the Three General Secretaries: Change Without Change', *Critique*, 17: 113–185.
*Ticktin, Hillel 1987, 'The Political Economy of Class in the Transitional Epoch', *Critique*, 20–1: 7–25.
*Ticktin, Hillel 1988, 'The Contradictions of Gorbachev', *Journal of Communist Studies*, 4, 4 (December): 83–99.
*Ticktin, Hillel 1990, 'The Nature of the Disintegration of the Stalinist System of the USSR', *Research in Political Economy*, 12: 209–52.
*Ticktin, Hillel 1991, 'The International Road to Chaos', *Critique*, 23: 9–32.
*Ticktin, Hillel 1992a, *Origins of the Crisis in the USSR. Essays on the Political Economy of a Disintegrating System*, Armonk: Sharpe.
*Ticktin, Hillel 1992b, 'Permanent Chaos Without a Market: The Non-Latinamericanization of the USSR', *Studies in Comparative Communism*, 25, 3 (September): 242–56.
*Ticktin, Hillel 1993, 'The Growth of an Impossible Capitalism', *Critique*, 25: 119–132.

*Ticktin, Hillel 1995a, 'Leon Trotsky and the "Russian Mode of Production"', in *The Ideas of Leon Trotsky*, edited by Hillel Ticktin and Michael Cox, London: Porcupine Press.

*Ticktin, Hillel 1995b, 'Leon Trotsky's Political Economic Analysis of the USSR', in *The Ideas of Leon Trotsky*, edited by Hillel Ticktin and Michael Cox, London: Porcupine Press.

Ticktin, Hillel 2000, 'Why the Transition Failed: Towards a Political Economy of the Post-Soviet Period in Russia', *Critique*, 32–33: 13–41.

*Ticktin, Hillel and Wlodzimierz Brus 1981, 'Is Market-Socialism Possible or Necessary?', *Critique*, 14: 13–39.

*Tökei, Ferencz 1977, *Zur Dialektik des Sozialismus*, Budapest: Akademiai Kiadó. [Originally: *A szocializmus dialektikajahoz*, Budapest: Kossuth Konyvkiado, 1974.]

*Tomlinson, J. 1977, 'Hillel Ticktin and Professor Bettelheim – A Reply', *Critique*, 8: 53–9.

*Tresse, Pierre 1954, 'Russia: Method of Analysis', *Dissent*, I, 4 (Autumn): 399–405.

*Trotsky, L. 1920, *Terrorismus und Kommunismus. Anti-Kautsky*, Hamburg: West-Europäisches Sekretariat der Kommunistischen Internationale. [*Terrorism and Communism. A Reply to Karl Kautsky*, Ann Arbor: University of Michigan Press, 1961.]

Trotsky, Leon 1925, 'Erklarung des Genossen Trotzki gegen die Zeitschrift "La Revolution Prolétarienne"', in *Die Linke Opposition in der Sowjetunion*, II, edited by Ulf Wolter, West Berlin: Olle & Wolter,1975.

Trotsky, Leon 1929, 'Interview by the *Osaka Mainichi*' (April 24, 1929), in *Writings of Leon Trotsky [1929]*, New York: Pathfinder 1975.

*Trotsky, Leon 1931, 'Problemi razvitiia SSSR', *Biulleten' Oppozitsii*, 20 (April): 1–15. ['Problems of the Development of the USSR – Draft Theses of the International Left Opposition on the Russian Question', in *Writings of Leon Trotsky [1930–31]*, New York: Pathfinder, 1973.]

*Trotsky, Leon 1933a, 'Klassovaia priroda sovetskogo gosudarstva', *Biulleten' Oppozitsii*, 36–37 (October): 1–12. ['The Class Nature of the Soviet State', in *Writings of Leon Trotsky [1933–34]*, New York: Pathfinder, 1975.]

*Trotsky, Leon 1933b, 'The Degeneration of Theory and the Theory of Degeneration', in *Writings of Leon Trotsky [1932–33]*, New York: Pathfinder, 1972.

*Trotsky, Leon 1937a, 'Chetvertyi Internatsional i SSSR', *Biulleten' Oppozitsii*, 54–55 (March): 49–52. ['The Fourth International and the Soviet Union', in *Writings of Leon Trotsky [1935–36]*, New York: Pathfinder, 1970.]

*Trotsky, Leon 1937b, *The Revolution Betrayed. What is the Soviet Union and Where Is It Going*, London: Faber & Faber.

*Trotsky, Leon 1938a, 'Nerabochee i neburzhuaznoe gosudarstvo?', *Bjulleten' Oppozitsii*, 62–63 (February): 15–9. ['Not a Workers' and Not a Bourgeois State?', in *Writings of Leon Trotsky [1937–38]*, New York: Pathfinder, 1976.]

*Trotsky, Leon 1938b, 'Discussion with Trotsky III: The Russian Question', in *Writings of Leon Trotsky [1937–38]*, New York: Pathfinder, 1976.

*[Trotsky, Leon] 1938c, 'Agoniia kapitalizma i zadachi Chetvertogo Internationala', *Biulleten' Oppozitsii*, 66–67 (May–June): 1–18. ['The Death Agony of Capitalism and the Tasks of the Fourth International', in Leon Trotsky, *The Transitional Program for Socialist Revolution*, New York: Pathfinder, 1977.]

*Trotsky, Leon 1938d, 'Prodolzhaet li eshche sovetskoe pravitel'stvo sledovat' printsipam, usvoennym 20 let tomu nazad?', *Biulleten' Oppozitsii*, 66–67 (May–June): 19–21. ['Does the Soviet Government Still Follow the Principles Adopted Twenty Years Ago?', in *Writings of Leon Trotsky [1937–38]*, New York: Pathfinder, 1976.]

*Trotsky, Leon 1939, 'SSSR v voine', *Biulleten' Oppozitsii*, 79–80 (August–October): 1–9. ['The USSR in War', in Leon Trotsky, *In Defense of Marxism*, New York: Pathfinder, 1973.]

Trotsky, Leon 1940a, 'Dvoinaia zvezda: Gitler-Stalin', *Biulleten' Oppozitsii*, 81 (January): 1–7. ['The Twin-Stars: Hitler-Stalin', in *Writings of Leon Trotsky [1939–40]*, New York: Pathfinder, 1973.]

Trotsky, Leon 1940b, 'Manifesto of the Fourth International on the Imperialist War and the Proletarian World Revolution', in *Writings of Leon Trotsky [1939–40]*, New York: Pathfinder.

Trotsky, Leon 1973, *In Defence of Marxism*, New York: Pathfinder Press.

Trotzki, Leo 1988, *Schriften 1: Sowjetgesellschaft und stalinistische Diktatur*, 1.2 (1936–1940), Hamburg: Rasch und Rohring.

Ulmen, G.L. 1978, *The Science of Society. Toward an Understanding of the Life and Work of Karl August Wittfogel*, The Hague: Mouton.

Ulmen, G.L. 1981, 'Über Wittfogels Weg zur Marxschen Auffassung Russlands'. Foreword in Karl Marx, *Enthüllungen zur Geschichte der Diplomatie im 18. Jahrhundert*, edited by Karl August Wittfogel, Frankfurt am Main: Suhrkamp.

*Unger, F. 1969, 'Zum Problem des Revisionismus in der Übergangsgesellschaft', *Sozialistische Politik*, I, 4 (December): 104–13.

Uoroll, R.L. [R.L. Worral] 1940, 'Iavljaetsia-li SSSR proletarskim ili kapitalisticheskim gosudarstvom?', *Sotsialisticheskii Vestnik*, 7 (459).

*[Urbahns, Hugo] 1929a, 'Über den Konflikt Russland-China', *Fahne des Kommunismus*, 3, 31 (23 August) and 32 (30 August).

*[Urbahns, Hugo] 1929b, 'Einige theoretische Hinweise', *Fahne des Kommunismus*, 3, 33 (6 September), 34 (13 September), 39 (25 October) and 40 (8 November).

*Valić, Dominique 1975, 'Kritik der Dutschke'schen Leninkritik', *Die Internationale*, 6: 62–93.

Vance, T.N. [Ed Sard] 1950, 'After Korea What? An Economic Interpretation of U.S. Perspectives', *New International*, 145 (November–December): 323–33.

Vance, T.N. [Ed Sard] 1951, 'The Permanent Arms Economy', *New International*, 146 (January–February): 29–45; 147 (March–April): 67–92; 148 (May–June): 131–59; 149 (July–August): 232–48; 150 (September–October): 251–66; 151 (November–December): 333–59.

*Varga, Eugen 1970, 'Die Nomenklatur: wie sowjetisch ist die Sowjetunion?', *Wiener Tagebuch*, 3 (March): 4–7.

*Varlet, Claude 1978, *Critique de Bettelheim*, I, *La révolution d'octobre et les luttes de classes en URSS*, Paris: Nouveau Bureau d'Edition.

Vega, Alberto [R. Maille] 1952, 'La crise du bordiguisme italien', *Socialisme ou Barbarie*, 11 (November-December): 26–46.

*Vidal Villa, J.M. 1977, 'La URSS: Una nueva sociedad de clase', *El Viejo Topo*, 5 (February): 19–22.

*Vidal Villa, J.M. 1978, 'Eurocomunismo y nueva sociedad de clase', *El Viejo Topo*, 11 (August): 17–21.

*Vincent, Jean-Marie 1982, 'Trotsky et l'analyse de l'URSS', in *L'URSS vue de gauche*, edited by Lilly Marcou, Paris: Presses Universitaires de France.

*Vogt-Downey, Marilyn (ed.) 1993, *The USSR 1987–1991: Marxist Perspectives*, Atlantic Highlands: Humanity Books.

Voinea, Şerban [Gaston Boeuve] 1955, *La Morale et le socialisme*, Ghent: La Flamme.

*Voinea, Şerban [Gaston Boeuve] 1965a, 'L'Union Soviétique est-elle une société socialiste?', *La Revue Socialiste*, New Series, 179 (January): 40–53.

*Voinea, Şerban [Gaston Boeuve] 1965b, 'L'Union Soviétique est-elle un "capitalisme d'état"?', *La Revue Socialiste*, New Series, 187 (November): 394–416.

*Voslenskij, Michael S. 1980, *Nomenklatura. Die herrschende Klasse der Sowjetunion*, Vienna: Molden.

*[Wagner, Helmut] 1934, 'Thesen über den Bolschewismus', *Rätekorrespondenz*, 3 (August): 1–22. ['Theses on Bolshevism', *International Council Correspondence*, 1, 3 (December 1934): 1–18.]

Wagner, Helmut 1968, 'Mit den Waffen von Karl Marx. Junge Polen wider den Monopolsozialismus', *Osteuropa*, XVIII: 628–43.

*Wajda, Mihaly 1985, 'A quoi le "socialisme réel" répond-il?', *Les Temps Modernes*, 468–9 (July–August): 88–102.

Waldschmidt, Hans-Jürgen 1966, *Lenin und Kautsky – Verschiedene Wege der Weiterentwicklung des Marxismus*, Würzburg: Inaugural Dissertation.

*Warski, Adolf [Warszawski] 1922, *Rosa Luxemburgs Stellung zu den taktischen Problemen der Revolution*, Hamburg: Verlag der Kommunistischen Internationale.

*Weber, Henri 1982, 'La Russie soviétique et le "pape du marxisme" Karl Kautsky', in *L'URSS vue de gauche*, edited by Lilly Marcou, Paris: Presses Universitaires de France.

*Weber, Hermann 1971, 'Zwischen kritischem und bürokratischem Kommunismus. Unbekannte Briefe van Clara Zetkin', *Archiv für Sozialgeschichte*, XI: 417–48.

Weber, Hermann 1984, 'Susanne Leonhard gestorben', *Internationale wissenschaftliche Korrespondenz zur Geschichte der deutschen Arbeiterbewegung*, 20: 155–6.

Weber, Max 1972, *Wirtschaft und Gesellschaft. Vollständiger Nachdruck der Erstausgabe von 1922*, Tübingen: (J.C.B. Mohr/Paul Siebeck). [English edition of Part I: *The Theory of Social and Economic Organization*, trans. A.R. Henderson and Talcott Parsons, London: William Hodge and Co., 1947.]

*Weil, Felix 1928, 'Rosa Luxemburg über die russische Revolution', *Archiv für die Geschichte des Sozialismus und der Arbeiterbewegung (Grünberg-Archiv)*, XIII: 285–98.

*Weil, Simone 1933, 'Allons-nous vers la révolution prolétarienne?', *La Révolution Prolétarienne*, 158: 311–19.

*Weinberg, G. 1952, 'Kann Staatskapitalismus ein Schritt zum Sozialismus sein?', *Funken*, II, 9 (February): 10–13.

*Weinberg, G. 1953, 'Gefährliche Illusionen', *Funken*, III, 12 (May): 14–16.

West, John [James Burnham] 1935a, 'Roosevelt and the New Congress', *New International*, II, 1 (January): 1–3.

West, John [James Burnham] 1935b, 'The Roosevelt "Security" Programme', *New International*, II, 2 (March): 40–3.

West, John [James Burnham] 1935c, 'The Wagner Bill and the Working Class', *New International*, II, 6 (October): 184–9.

West, John [James Burnham] 1936, 'Will Roosevelt Be Re-Elected ?', *New International*, III, 2 (April): 33–6.

Westoby, Adam 1981, *Communism since World War II*, Brighton: Harvester Press.

*Westoby, Adam 1985, 'Introduction', in Bruno Rizzi, *The Bureaucratization of the World*, London: Tavistock.

*Westoby, Adam and Tim Wohlforth 1978, *'Communists' Against Revolution. The Theory of Structural Assimilation*, London: Folrose Books.

Wiggershaus, Rolf 1994, *The Frankfurt School: Its History, Theories and Political Significance*, Cambridge: Polity.

*Wildt, Andreas 1979, 'Totalitarian State Capitalism: On the Structure and Historical Function of Soviet-Type Societies', *Telos*, 41 (Autumn): 33–57.

*Willen, Paul 1955, 'What Manner of Change in Russia?', *Dissent*, II, 1 (Winter): 71–5.

*Wittfogel, Karl A. 1950, 'Russia and Asia', *World Politics*, II, 4 (June): 445–62.

*Wittfogel, Karl A. 1953, 'Ruling Bureaucracy of Oriental Despotism: A Phenomenon that Paralyzed Marx', *Review of Politics*, XV: 350–9.

*Wittfogel, Karl A. 1957, *Oriental Despotism. A Comparative Study of Total Power*, New Haven: Yale University Press.

*Wittfogel, Karl A. 1960, 'The Marxist View of Russian Society and Revolution', *World Politics*, XII: 487–508.

*Wittfogel, Karl A. 1963b, 'Reply', *Slavic Review*, XXII: 656–62.

*Wittfogel, Karl A. 1963a, 'Russia and the East – A Comparison and Contrast', *Slavic Review*, XXII: 627–43.

Wolfe, Bertram D. 1948, *Three Who Made the Revolution – A Biographical History*, New York: Dial Press.

*Wolin, Simon 1974, 'Socialism and Stalinism', in *The Mensheviks from the Revolution of 1917 to the Second World War*, edited by Leopold H. Haimson, Chicago: University of Chicago Press.

*Wolter, Ulf 1975, *Grundlagen des Stalinismus*, West Berlin: Rotbuch.

*Wolter, Ulf (ed.) 1978, *Antworten auf Bahros Herausforderung des 'realen Sozialismus'*, West Berlin: Olle & Wolter. [*Rudolf Bahro. Critical Responses*, edited by Ulf Wolter, White Plains: M.E. Sharpe, 1980.]

Worcester, Kent 1995, *C.L.R. James. A Political Biography*, Albany: State University of New York Press.

*Worrall, R.L. 1939, 'U.S.S.R: Proletarian or State Capitalist?', *Modern Quarterly*, XI, 2 (Winter): 5–19; also in *Left*, 39 (1939): 319–24 and 40 (1940): 19–20.

Worrall Tribute 1996, 'A Tribute to Ryan Worrall (1903–1995)', *Revolutionary History*, 6, 2–3 (Summer): 249–51.

Wright, Steve 2002, *Storming Heaven. Class Composition and Struggle in Italian Autonomist Marxism*, London: Pluto Press.

*Yvon, M. [1936], *Ce qu'est devenue la Révolution russe*, Préface de Pierre Pascal, Paris: La Révolution Prolétarienne.

*Yvon, M. 1938, *L'URSS telle qu'elle est*, Préface d'André Gide, Paris: Gallimard.

*Zaremba, Zygmunt 1957, 'Groupe, couche ou classe dirigeante?', *La Revue Socialiste*, New Series, 111 (November): 418–27.

*Zarembka, Paul 1992, 'The Development of State Capitalism in the Soviet System', *Research in Political Economy*, 13: 123–61.

*Zaslavsky, Victor 1978, 'Regime e classe operaia in URSS', *MondOperaio*, XXXI, 6: 74–83. [Viktor Zaslavsky, 'The Regime and the Working Class.in the USSR', *Telos*, 43 (1979–80).]

*Zaslavsky, Victor 1979, 'La struttura di classe della società sovietica', *MondOperaio*, XXXII, 5: 107–16.

*Zaslavsky, Victor 1982, *The Neo-Stalinist State: Class, Ethnicity and Consensus in Soviet Society*, New York: M.E. Sharpe.

*Zaslavsky, Victor 1984–5, 'Soviet Society and the World Systems Analysis', *Telos*, 62 (Winter): 155–67.

*Zetkin, Clara 1922, *Um Rosa Luxemburgs Stellung zur russischen Revolution*, Hamburg: Verlag der Kommunistischen Internationale.

*Zimin, Alexander 1977, 'On the Question of the Place in History of the Social Structure of the Soviet Union', in *The Samizdat Register*, I, edited by Roy Medvedev, New York: W.W. Norton.

*Zimine, Alexandre 1982, *Le stalinisme et son 'socialisme réel'*, Paris: Ed. La Brèche.

Zimin, Aleksandr Aleksandrovich 1984, *U istokov stalinizma: 1918–1923*, Paris: Izd-vo Slovo, 1984.

Zimmermann, Rüdiger 1978, *Der Leninbund. Linke Kommunisten in der Weimarer Republik*, Düsseldorf: Droste.

Znaniecki, Florian 1919, 'Methodological Note', in Florian Znaniecki, *On Humanistic Sociology*. Chicago: University of Chicago Press, 1969.

Index